W9-AWB-352

Scratch off to
reveal passcode

IMPORTANT

HERE IS YOUR REGISTRATION CODE TO ACCESS MCGRAW-HILL
PREMIUM CONTENT AND MCGRAW-HILL ONLINE RESOURCES

For key premium online resources you need THIS CODE to
gain access. Once the code is entered, you will be able to
use the web resources for the length of your course.

Access is provided only if you have purchased a new book.

If the registration code is missing from this book, the registration
screen on our website, and within your WebCT or Blackboard course
will tell you how to obtain your new code. Your registration code can
be used only once to establish access. It is not transferable.

To gain access to these online resources

1. USE your web browser to go to: **www.mhhe.com/lenkeit3**

2. CLICK on "First Time User"

3. ENTER the Registration Code printed on the tear-off bookmark on the right

4. After you have entered your registration code, click on "Register"

5. FOLLOW the instructions to setup your personal UserID and Password

6. WRITE your UserID and Password down for future reference. Keep it in a safe place.

If your course is using WebCT or Blackboard, you'll be able to use this code to
access the McGraw-Hill content within your instructor's online course.

To gain access to the McGraw-Hill content in your instructor's WebCT or
Blackboard course simply log into the course with the user ID and Password
provided by your instructor. Enter the registration code exactly as it appears to
the right when prompted by the system. You will only need to use this code the
first time you click on McGraw-Hill content.

These instructions are specifically for student access. Instructors are not
required to register via the above instructions.

The McGraw-Hill Companies

Higher Education

Thank you, and welcome to your
McGraw-Hill Online Resources.

ISBN-13: 978-0-07-310776-9
ISBN-10: 0-07-310776-X
T/A LENKEIT: INTRODUCING CULTURAL ANTHROPOLOGY, 3/E

REGISTRATION CODE

The McGraw-Hill Companies

Mc
Graw
Hill **Higher Education**

Laura Zaffos

INTRODUCING
CULTURAL
ANTHROPOLOGY

CURRENT WORLD POLITICAL REGIONS

ABBREVIATIONS

ALB.	ALBANIA
AUST.	AUSTRIA
BELG.	BELGIUM
BOS.	BOSNIA AND HERZEGOVINA
BULG.	BULGARIA
DEN.	DENMARK
DOM. REP.	DOMINICAN REPUBLIC
CRO.	CROATIA
CZECH.	CZECH REPUBLIC
EST.	ESTONIA
GER.	GERMANY
HUNG.	HUNGARY
LAT.	LATVIA
LITH.	LITHUANIA
LUX.	LUXEMBURG
MAC.	MACEDONIA
NETH.	NETHERLANDS
ROM.	ROMANIA
RUSS.	RUSSIA
SER.	SERBIA and MONTENEGRO
SLOVK.	SLOVAKIA
SLOVN.	SLOVENIA
SWITZ.	SWITZERLAND
U.A.E.	UNITED ARAB EMIRATES

ARCTIC OCEAN

GREENLAND

CANADA

UNITED STATES

ATLANTIC

BERMUDA

OCEAN

THE BAHAMAS

MEXICO

CUBA
DOM. REP.
PUERTO RICO
ST. KITTS AND NEVIS
ANTIGUA AND BARBUDA
JAMAICA
DOMINICA
BELIZE
HAITI
BARBADOS
HONDURAS
ST. LUCIA
GUATEMALA
NICARAGUA
GRENADA
ST. VINCENT AND
EL SALVADOR
PANAMA
THE GRENADINES
COSTA RICA
TRINIDAD AND TOBAGO
VENEZUELA
SURINAME
FRENCH GUIANA
COLOMBIA
GUYANA

PACIFIC

ECUADOR

PERU

BRAZIL

OCEAN

BOLIVIA

PARAGUAY

CHILE

ARGENTINA

URUGUAY

150°W

120°W

90°W

60°W

FALKLAND ISLANDS

SOUTH GEORGIA ISLAND

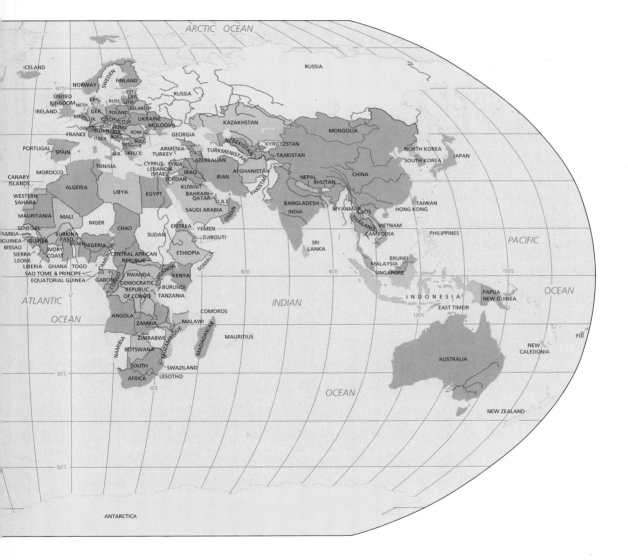

INTRODUCING CULTURAL ANTHROPOLOGY

Third Edition

Roberta Edwards Lenkeit
Modesto Junior College

Boston   Burr Ridge, IL   Dubuque, IA   Madison, WI   New York
San Francisco   St. Louis   Bangkok   Bogotá   Caracas   Kuala Lumpur
Lisbon   London   Madrid   Mexico City   Milan   Montreal   New Delhi
Santiago   Seoul   Singapore   Sydney   Taipei   Toronto

Higher Education

Published by McGraw-Hill, an imprint of The McGraw-Hill Companies, Inc. 1221 Avenue of the Americas, New York, NY 10020. Copyright © 2007, by the McGraw-Hill Companies, Inc. All rights reserved. Previous edition © 2001 by Mayfield Publishing Company. No part of this publication may be reproduced or distributed in any form or by any means, or stored in a database or retrieval system, without the prior written permission of The McGraw-Hill Companies, Inc., including but not limited to, in any network or other electronic storage or transmission, or broadcast for distance learning. Some ancillaries, including electronic and print components, may not be available to customers outside the United States.

This book is printed on acid-free paper.

1 2 3 4 5 6 7 8 9 0 VNH / VNH 0 9 8 7 6

ISBN-13: 978-0-07-310773-8
ISBN-10: 0-07-310773-5

Publisher: *Phillip A. Butcher*
Sponsoring editor: *Kevin Witt*
Development editor: *Thom Holmes*
Marketing manager: *Dan Loch*
Production editor: *Anne Fuzellier*
Production supervisor: *Rich DeVitto*
Design manager: *Cassandra Chu*
Cover design: *William Stanton*
Interior design: *Linda Roberston and Glenda King*
Art editor: *Robin Mouat*
Manager, photo research: *Brian Pecko*
PowerPoints: *Mark Stephens*
Compositor: *Thompson Type*
Text and paper: *Printed in 10/12 Janson on 50# Publishers Matte*
Printer: *Von Hoffman Press*
Cover image: Eagle Hunters of Mongolia, © Hamid Sardar/Corbis

Library of Congress Cataloging In-Publication Data
Lenkeit, Roberta Edwards.
    Introducing cultural anthropology / Roberta Edwards Lenkeit.—3rd ed.
      p. cm.
    Includes bibliographical references and index.
    ISBN-13: 978-0-07-310773-8 (alk. paper)
    ISBN-10: 0-07-310773-5 (alk. paper)
      1. Ethnology. I. Title.

GN316.L46 2006
306—dc22

                          2006040988

www.mhhe.com

To Don and Allison
for all of the 3PRIM8 memories

BRIEF CONTENTS

CONTENTS

10 Political Order, Disorder, and Social Control: Who Decides?   214

11 Belief Systems: How Do We Explain the Unexplainable?   238

ANTHROPOLOGY AROUND
US BOXES

TO THE INSTRUCTOR

◎ THE STORY OF THE BOOK

I decided to write this text when driving across the country during a sabbatical leave. My husband (also an anthropologist) and I were discussing the selection of a text for the following semester — again. This quest repeated itself every year. Our approaches and styles of teaching the introductory cultural anthropology course are different, but we share common goals: to assure that students learn the basic concepts and approaches of anthropology; to focus on the usefulness of the anthropological approach to their lives; to introduce the field and its holistic nature; and to highlight the scientific nature of anthropology. We have each used nearly every text on the market at one time. And we were frustrated. We were frustrated by encyclopedic texts, by texts that emphasized theory and were written in styles that were too formal, by shorter texts that lacked visual interest and targeted upper division students, and by texts that seemed to ignore the other fields of anthropology. We discovered that many colleagues shared our frustration.

At the time I belonged to (and still do) a unique, semiformal group of anthropologists in northern California who taught introductory level anthropology courses at different types of colleges, both two and four year. The focus of our get-togethers was pedagogy. We shared what works. Listening to concerns of colleagues in this forum contributed to my desire to write a text that was relatively short, more informal, and built around pedagogy that incorporated the holistic nature of anthropology and emphasized the scientific approach.

◎ THE APPROACH OF THE TEXT

The last twenty-five years have seen a dramatic increase in both the data of anthropology and in theoretical issues within the discipline. It is impossible to fit everything into an introductory course, and it is my view that it is also pedagogically unsound. Less can be more. I have come to the conclusion, based on teaching introductory anthropology courses for more than thirty years, that my main task as a teacher is to excite students about the *possibilities* of anthropology and to teach them the core perspectives, concepts, and methods of anthropology.

I have also endeavored to write an approachable text. I tried to write as though I am talking directly to the student while maintaining an appropriate scholarly tone. In many places throughout the text, I have included examples and stories to which students can relate so that they can see how anthropology is part of our everyday lives.

Pedagogy has also been an important part of my overall design. As I wrote, I kept in mind the importance of signposting important concepts and presenting a reasonable number of detailed examples to illustrate points. Concepts are also presented visually wherever possible. Students are asked to apply concepts they have learned throughout the book.

Ideas are also reinforced throughout the text — the holistic, comparative, scientific, and humanistic perspectives of the discipline. The occasional relevant issue from archaeology and biological anthropology is woven into the text to emphasize the holistic view. Students are asked in the Try This feature to make hypotheses and devise ways to test them. Contributions of the humanistic perspective are also noted.

The text is designed as an anchor text so that ethnographies, topical books, and collections of readings can be part of the course's assigned readings. I believe that including such books gives students in-depth insights into one culture and a holistic perspective on topics. I believe strongly that students need an anchor text that presents basic concepts in the field and provides a framework around which the ethnographies, other readings, and lectures can build.

I've used an eclectic approach to theoretical issues throughout, and I've used ones that are practical as part of my "less-is-more" philosophy and pedagogical approach. When students have a firm understanding of a few paradigms, they have a foundation on which to examine others — and think critically about all.

◎ HALLMARK FEATURES

- A manageable number of brief chapters, which can easily be covered in a semester, offer a brief introduction to the field.
- An emphasis throughout on how anthropology is relevant to students can be found in many examples and stories. In addition, the final two chapters demonstrate the relevance of anthropology to students' future lives — in their work and in their community.

- A pedagogy that asks students to think critically. The Try This activity prompts are integrated throughout the text and ask students to ponder, compare, analyze, hypothesize, and apply the concepts they have just read about. These are purposefully written at a variety of levels. A few are simple and don't require much analytical thought (for example, those labeled Ponder or Consider). Others require more engagement by asking students to discuss issues. Those with prompts such as Compare, Contrast, Analyze, Apply, and Hypothesize are intended to stimulate students' integrative thought process by helping them apply concepts, perspectives, and methods.

- Learning objectives, chapter summaries, study questions, and suggested readings at the end of chapters offer learning support.

- A strong visual appeal achieved through a wealth of concept illustrations and color photos. This provides pedagogical support for students.

- Two chapters unique to briefer texts: a chapter on fieldwork that offers firsthand accounts of the challenges of acquiring data, and a chapter that looks at sexuality across cultures. Both of these are topics that beginning students are curious about, and both topics stimulate lively debate.

- Organization by standard topics to fit the teaching styles of most professors, while at the same time reflecting my pedagogical focus for students by clustering chapters into three sections: basic concepts and methods, cross-cultural adaptive patterns, and applying the anthropological perspective.

- A personal writing style applauded by reviewers.

◎ WHAT'S NEW TO THIS EDITION

- New section in Chapter 13 on **Anthropology and Globalization** includes material on **colonialism** and **hegemony** with focus on **tourism** studies and **ethical dilemmas,** plus technology and mass communication. Another new section **Culture Change: A Brief Historical Overview** has material on theory. Substantially revised sections include How Cultures Change and How Change Is Studied.

- New Chapters 5 and 6 expand previous coverage of subsistence strategies and resource allocations, as follow:

  - Chapter 5, **Subsistence Strategies and Resource Allocation I: What Challenges Face Foragers,** contains more background on models of cultural evolution and cultural ecology and updates on foragers today.

- Chapter 6, **Subsistence Strategies and Resource Allocation II: How Did Food Production Transform Culture?,** contains expanded material on agriculture and features associated with intensive agricultural lifeways, including more material on stratification in chiefdoms and states, and new materials on market exchange and currency use.
- **New and Updated Anthropology Around Us boxes.** These boxes focus on current and timely issues that illustrate how the perspectives, topics, and concepts of anthropology are part of our everyday lives. Changes include
  - Chapter 6, "Is Slow Food Making a Fast Comeback?"
  - Chapter 9, "Does Gender Affect Attitudes About Circumcision?"
  - Substantial update of Chapter 7 box, "Outdated Traditions?"
  - Other **boxes are updated throughout.**
- Expanded **glossary** and expanded **marginal running glossary** help students to focus on important terms as they are introduced.
- Several new and updated **chapter openers** provide vignettes that relate to the chapter's contents. Well received in the book's second edition, these are designed to draw the student into the chapter and show the relevance of the topics to their lives.
- Chapter 3, **Fieldwork,** includes new ethnographic-based material on life shock.
- Chapter 7, **Marriage, Family, and Residence,** has an expanded section on sister exchange marriage and an expanded Anthropology Around Us box that includes marriage finance.
- Chapter 8, **Kinship and Descent,** is updated with a revised section on kindred groups within bilateral descent systems and a new section on **Voluntary Association Groups.**
- Chapter 10, **Political Order, Disorder, and Social Control,** includes more text discussion on homicide in foraging societies and updated statistics in Table 10.1 on **Murder Rates.**

◎ SUPPLEMENTS

As a full-service publisher of quality educational products, McGraw-Hill does much more than just sell textbooks. They create and publish an extensive array of print, video, and digital supplements for students and instructors. *Introducing Cultural Anthropology* boasts a comprehensive supplement package. Orders of new (versus used) textbooks help to defray the cost of developing such supplements, which is substantial. Please consult your local McGraw-Hill representative for more information on any of the supplements.

For the Student

The Student's Online Learning Center   This free, Web-based, partially password protected, student supplement features a large number of helpful tools, activities, links, and useful information at *www.mhhe.com/lenkeit3*. To access the password-protected areas of the site, students must purchase a new copy of the text. Designed specifically to complement the individual chapters of the text, students access material by text chapter. Exciting activities and resources include

- Try This Internet exercises that offer chapter-related links to Web sites and activities for students to complete based on those sites.
- Chapter objectives, outlines, and overviews that are designed to give students signposts for understanding and recognizing key chapter content.
- PowerPoint lecture notes that offer point-by-point notes of chapter sections.
- Multiple choice and true/false questions that give students the opportunity to quiz themselves on chapter content.
- Essay questions that allow students to explore key chapter concepts through their own writing.
- A glossary that illustrates key terms.
- An audio glossary that helps students with difficult-to-pronounce words through audio pronunciation help.
- Vocabulary flashcards that allow students to test their mastery of key vocabulary terms.
- General Web links that offer chapter-by-chapter links for further research.
- Links to *New York Times* articles where students have immediate access to articles on chapter-related content.
- Links to useful information on careers in anthropology.

PowerWeb   This feature is offered free with the purchase of a new copy of the text and is available via a link on the Student's Online Learning Center. PowerWeb helps students with online research by providing access to high-quality academic sources. PowerWeb is a password-protected site that provides students with the full text of course-specific, peer-reviewed articles from the scholarly and popular press, as well as Web links, student study tools, weekly updates, and additional resources. For further information about PowerWeb, visit *www.dushkin.com/powerweb/pwwt1.mhtml*.

For the Instructor

The Instructor's Resource CD-ROM   This easy-to-use disk provides

- PowerPoint lecture slides that give professors ready-made chapter-by-chapter presentation notes.

- A computerized test bank offering numerous multiple choice, short answer, and essay questions in an easy-to-use program. McGraw-Hill's EZ Test is a flexible and easy-to-use electronic testing program. The program allows instructors to create tests from book-specific items. It accommodates a wide range of question types, and instructors may add their own questions. Multiple versions of the test can be created, and any test can be exported for use with course management systems such as WebCT, BlackBoard or PageOut. EZ Test Online is a new service and gives you a place to easily administer your EZ Test-created exams and quizzes online. The program is available for Windows and Macintosh environments.

- A complete Instructor's Manual offering helpful teaching tips along with chapter-by-chapter overviews, learning objectives, outlines, key terms, and suggested class activities.

The Instructor's Online Learning Center   This password-protected site offers access to all of the student online materials plus important instructor support materials and downloadable supplements such as

- An image library that offers professors the opportunity to create custom-made, professional looking presentations and handouts by providing electronic versions of many of the maps, charts, line art, and photos in the text along with additional relevant images not included in the text. All images are ready to be used in any applicable teaching tools including the professor's own lecture materials or McGraw-Hill provided PowerPoint lecture slides.

- A complete Instructor's Manual offers helpful teaching tips along with chapter-by-chapter overviews, learning objectives, outlines, key terms, and suggested class activities.

- PowerPoint lecture slides give professors ready made chapter-by-chapter presentation notes.

- Links to professional resources provide useful links to professional anthropological sites on the Internet.

PowerWeb   This resource is available via a link on the Instructor's Online Learning Center. PowerWeb helps with online research by providing access to high-quality academic sources. PowerWeb is a password-protected site that provides instructors with the full text of course-specific, peer-reviewed articles from the scholarly and popular press, as well as Web links, weekly updates, and additional resources. For further information about PowerWeb, visit *www.dushkin.com/powerweb/pwwt1.mhtml.*

PageOut: The Course Web Site Development Center   All online content for the text is supported by WebCT, Blackboard, eCollege.com, and other course management systems. Additionally, McGraw-Hill's PageOut service is available to get professors and their courses up and running on-line in a matter of hours, at no cost. PageOut was designed for instructors just beginning to explore Web options. Even a novice computer user can create a course Web Site with a template provided by McGraw-Hill (no programming knowledge necessary). To learn more about PageOut, visit *www.mhhe.com/pageout.*

Videotapes   A wide variety of full-length videotapes from the *Films for the Humanities and Sciences* series is available to adopters of the text.

◎ ACKNOWLEDGMENTS

Special acknowledgment, love, and gratitude to my husband, best friend, and colleague, Don A. Lenkeit. In this, as in previous editions, his eagle eye, in-house editing, and generous gift of assistance (plus an uncanny ability to provide sustenance just when I needed it on those long writing days) kept the project going. He also again co-authored the Instructor's Manual and Online Learning Center. Thanks to our daughter and colleague K. Allison Lenkeit Meezan. She even took time from tending baby Katherine to read sections and make suggestions. To the resident felines — Mr. Darwin for monitoring the printer, and Mrs. Hobbes for paperweight duty — your attentiveness to this edition was appreciated.

I am grateful to colleague and friend Debra Bolter for being an astute sounding board for revision ideas and for reading and commenting on various sections. To Bill Fairbanks for your many insightful suggestions, thank you. To Rob Edwards and the members of the California Community College Anthropology Teacher's group (formerly the A 2-4-6 group), thanks for all of the years of stimulating meetings on the teaching of anthropology. To Jan Beatty who supported this project in the first place, you will always be a part of it, as will all of the wonderful folks at Mayfield. The reviewers of previous editions whose suggestions are reflected here still, I acknowledge and thank you again.

Special appreciation to Kevin Witt, senior editor Anthropology/ Criminal Justice, who continues to believe in this project, and to senior development editor Thom Holmes for his guidance with this edition. I am indebted to Brian Pecko, photo research manager, who is a pleasure to work with and excels at locating the perfect image. Thanks also to editorial coordinator Teresa Treacy, for attending to myriad details; production editor Anne Fuzellier, for making the process go smoothly; design manager Cassandra Chu and art editor Robin Mouat, for the appealing design and visuals; copyeditor Joan Pendleton, for her eagle eye; sales manager Dan Loch and his team, for all of their marketing acumen; and production supervisor Randy Hurst, for bringing the various pieces together.

The reviewers of this edition are owed my special thanks for all of their insightful comments and many helpful suggestions. They are

Marc A. Rees, University of Louisiana at Lafayette

Lynne Miller, Mira Costa College

Katherine C. Donohue, Plymouth State University

Art Barbeau, West Liberty State College

Christina Beard-Moose, Suffolk County Community College

Jon A. Schlenker, University of Maine at Augusta

Mary Kay Gilliland, Pima Community College

Margaret S. Bruchez, Blinn College

Carl Hefner, University of Hawaii–Kapiolani Community College

Jennifer Molina-Stidger, Sierra College

Amy J. Hirshman, University of Michigan–Flint

Shepherd M. Jenks Jr., Albuquerque TVI Community College

 # TO THE STUDENT

Anthropology often conjures up exotic visions of distant peoples, places, and customs. But this is only part of what cultural anthropology is about. It is about examining humanity from every angle and looking at how all aspects interrelate — what we call the holistic approach. It is about the common denominators of the human experience, as well as the differences. What constitutes the exotic is usually no more than those customs different from our own. I've written this text as a brief introduction to the core concepts in cultural anthropology. It is a summary of what we have learned from our quest to understand the adaptive patterns of human cultures.

My philosophy of teaching is that less can be more. If you can digest a concept and a solid example, I believe that you will remember it. Too many examples when you are first learning about a subject can muddy everything. If you engage with this text, you will have a strong foundation to do further work in anthropology. Even if you don't plan to go on in anthropology, the perspectives of anthropology will provide you with much that is useful. Cultural anthropology is applicable to many fields — health care, law enforcement, education, retail business, and any other field that requires working with people. Anthropology is inherently fascinating. We discover things about ourselves as we examine other cultures, and I hope that you will enjoy this process of discovery.

◎ HOW TO USE THIS BOOK

You'll find many learning tools both within the text and at the text's Online Learning Center:

- Objectives at the beginning of each chapter state the aims of the chapter and are signposts to what you will learn. If you carefully read these and the chapter summary first, you will have an excellent framework to help you focus as you read. Additionally, chapter objectives, chapter outlines, chapter overviews, and PowerPoint lecture notes are available at the Student's Online Learning Center. This free Web-based, partially password-protected, supplement can be found at *www.mhhe.com/lenkeit3*.

- Important anthropological concepts and terms are set in bold type throughout the text and are clearly explained. The running glossary placed in the margins helps you to focus on these important terms, and the glossary at the back of the book provides an alphabetical list of all these terms along with their definitions. Go to the Online Learning Center to test your mastery of key vocabulary by using the vocabulary flashcards. The audio glossary at this site helps you with difficult-to-pronounce words.

- Study questions appear at the end of each chapter so that you can test yourself on chapter content. Multiple choice and true/false questions posted at the Online Learning Center give you the opportunity to quiz yourself on chapter content and receive immediate feedback. Essay questions allow you to explore key chapter concepts through your own writing.

- The Try This prompts in the text were written to actively engage you with the material you've just read. Some of them are rather simple, and you can respond by just thinking about them. Others require you to be analytical and ask you to demonstrate your creativity and critical thinking skills. Recent research in the field of cognitive science reinforces that learning is tied to active involvement with a subject. Bottom line — if you engage with the Try This exercises, you will learn more about anthropology. Additionally, Try This Internet exercises at the Online Learning Center offer chapter-related links to Web sites and activities for you to complete based on these sites.

- References within the text are placed in parentheses and the full reference can be found in the bibliography. You'll also find suggested readings that will direct you to sources for further study. The Web site addresses I've provided were current at the time the book went to press.

- More activities and links are available at the Online Learning Center, such as additional Web links, links to *New York Times* related articles, and links to information on careers in anthropology, plus PowerWeb — an online research tool that provides you access to full text articles from high-quality academic sources and more.

◎ NEW TO THIS EDITION

The text has been **updated throughout.** There are now **two new chapters** on subsistence strategies and resource allocation — one focuses on foraging societies and the other on societies that produce food. This provides chapters of more manageable length. The important topic of globalization is now included with examples drawn from tourism and mass media.

WALKTHROUGH

A Brief Text ▶

With its manageable number of brief chapters, *Introducing Cultural Anthropology* offers a concise introduction to the field, which can easily be covered in a semester and be supplemented by ethnographies, topical books, and collections of readings.

◀ ## Unique Applications

Students are asked to think critically and apply concepts they have learned throughout the book in unique Try This activities.

A Lively Writing Style ▶

Spiced with humor, anecdotes, and an overall conversational tone, *Introducing Cultural Anthropology* reflects the author's thirty years of award-winning teaching and her understanding of how to reach beginning students.

Anthropology Around Us

This stimulating boxed feature focuses on current and timely issues that illustrate how the perspectives, topics, and concepts of anthropology are part of our everyday lives.

Enticing Chapter Openers ▶

New and updated chapter openers provide vignettes that are designed to draw the student into the chapter content and show how anthropology is relevant.

Two New Chapters Expand Coverage

Two chapters on subsistence and resource allocation provide more coverage than the previous one chapter in the last edition.

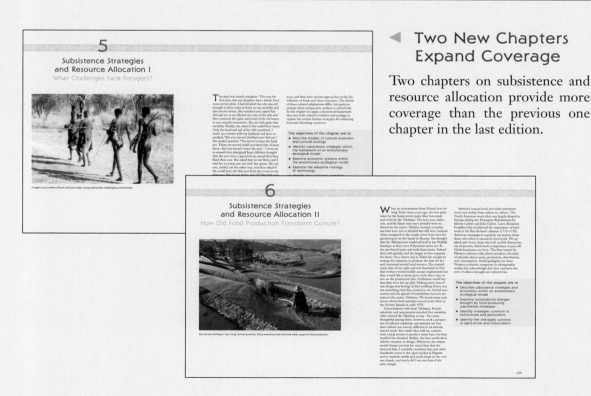

An Outstanding Visual Program ▶

A strong visual appeal, achieved through a wealth of unique concept illustrations and color photos, provides pedagogical support for students.

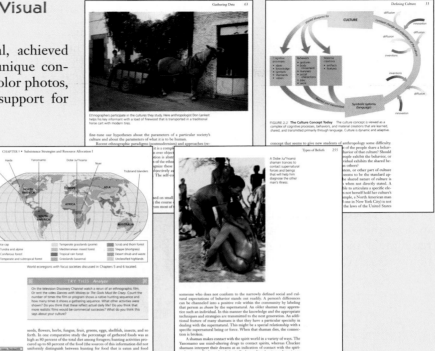

◀ Extensive Supporting Pedagogy

Learning objectives, chapter summaries, study questions, suggested readings, and Web sites offer learning support in every chapter.

Helpful Marginal Support ▶

The marginal thumbnail maps highlight the appropriate area under discussion while a new marginal running glossary helps students focus on terms as they are introduced.

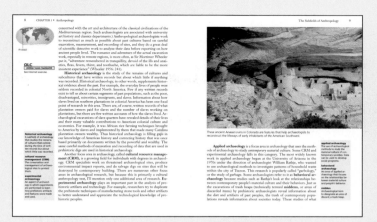

◀ ## Help on Reading Ethnographies

The appendix "How Do You Read an Ethnography?" gives students practical steps that they can take to get the most out of reading ethnographies and comparing ethnographies to one another.

Updated Online Learning Center Web Site ▶

This free Web-based supplement offers students a large number of helpful tools, activities, links, and useful information while offering professors an Image Bank and other valuable resources. In-text icons clearly guide students to information on a particular topic that is available on the Online Learning Center.

PART ONE

BASIC CONCEPTS AND METHODS IN ANTHROPOLOGY

T HIS PART OF THE TEXT ADDRESSES THE CORE CONCEPTS AND METHODS OF cultural anthropology. Chapter 1 describes the various subfields of anthropology together with the uniqueness of the anthropological approach to the study of humans. Central to our field's perspective is the concept of culture, which is explored in Chapter 2 by considering various definitions and delineating the unique features of culture. A discussion of recent critiques of the culture concept is also included. In addition, the text examines the anthropological perspective on culture, ethnicity, and race in light of the data from biological anthropology. Next, given that anthropologists gather most of their primary data from field situations, the methods and challenges of ethnographic fieldwork are described in Chapter 3 using examples from my personal experiences. Finally, Chapter 4 turns to language, the symbolic system on which culture depends, and outlines the essential approaches of linguistic anthropology.

The chapters included in Part I are those that provide the foundation concepts and approaches of cultural anthropology. These are the platforms on which the remainder of the topics and chapters will build. The primary goal of the chapters in this part of the book is to provide you with the background for further analysis of cultural similarities and differences presented in Parts II and III. Practical applications of anthropology to your life will become evident as you follow the suggestions given in the Try This boxes in each chapter.

◀ A woman navigates a traditional reed boat on Lake Titicaca in the Andes.

1

1

Anthropology
What Are Its Subfields and Perspectives?

Anthropologist Bruce Knauft shares field tabulations with a senior Gebusi man.

As we view ourselves through anthropological lenses, each day we can experience a world made more interesting and understandable. Today my morning began with some thoughts generated by archaeology, cultural anthropology, and biological anthropology. While sipping my first morning coffee, I glance at the kitchen floor. I make a mental note to sweep it because I spot a paper clip, two popcorn kernels, the top to a ballpoint pen, wisps of hair from the resident cat, and unidentifiable crumbs lying within three inches of the baseboard. The center of the floor is clean. I smile as I think about the implications of the *fringe effect*. This archaeological principle, which states that objects are more likely to accumulate next to walls than in traffic areas, helps to explain the distribution of artifacts in the archaeological record.

Issues and concepts of cultural anthropology flood my mind as I read a news headline that "honor killings" of Iraqi women are increasing. According to the article, a study by the Iraqi Ministry of Women's Affairs reports more than 400 rapes from 2003 to 2005, with more than half of the victims later being killed by members of their family. The so-called honor killings occur where traditional Islamic values hold that women embody the family honor. If a woman is raped, dishonor befalls the family; and some believe that only in killing her can the family honor be regained. The United Nations Commission on Human Rights lists more than fifteen countries where such killings have been recorded. Women's rights activists are working to bring world attention to this problem and other violent acts against women, such as the much-publicized dowry deaths in India — brides killed because they did not bring a large-enough dowry into the marriage — or female genital mutilation. Yet these acts reflect cultural values with long traditions in some cultures. Anthropology documents that our culture is powerful in shaping how we respond to such issues.

Another article is about gangs in my city. The racial overtones of conflicts between gangs are central to the article. I sigh and contemplate whether biological anthropologists will ever be able to effectively communicate that the biological data do *not* support the validity of the notion of biological races. If the media would stick with the term *ethnic group* (a cultural grouping) rather than *racial group*, much scientific misunderstanding could be avoided. Ethnic identity is learned. No ethnic behaviors are inborn.

I'm running late. I quickly finish my breakfast (what I eat and when I eat are culturally learned behaviors), I shower and dress (ideals of personal cleanliness and styles of appropriate dress are also culturally learned behaviors), and I leave for my first class.

This recounting of the start of my day should have you thinking that anthropology is a broad field of study. It is, and this chapter introduces you to its subfields and their relationships.

The objectives of this chapter are to

- Describe the goals of anthropology
- Introduce the scope and subfields of anthropology
- Delineate how anthropology is unique
- Explain how anthropology is a scientific discipline

Cultural anthropologists study the diversity of cultural adaptations, including shelter. There are similarities and differences between the structure of housing on this street in Tunisia and on the street where you live.

OLC
mhhe•com/lenkeit3

See chapter outline and chapter overview.

WHAT ANTHROPOLOGISTS STUDY

Anthropology provides a window to our past, a mirror for our present, and a lens through which we look to the future. Anthropologists research, observe, analyze, and apply what they learn toward an understanding of the many variations of the human condition. A grounding in past human adaptations, both biological and cultural, contributes to our understanding of adaptations today.

The goals for anthropological research include (1) describing, explaining, and analyzing human cultural similarities and differences, (2) describing and assessing the cultural development of our species as revealed in the archaeological record, (3) describing and analyzing the biological evolution of the human species as evidenced in the fossil record, and (4) describing and explaining human biological diversity today. In other words, anthropologists want to understand us: *Homo sapiens*. This is an enormous task.

THE SUBFIELDS OF ANTHROPOLOGY

The word ***anthropology*** comes from the Greek terms *anthropos*, meaning man, and *logia* or *logos*, meaning science or study of. In other words, anthropology literally means the science or study of man. *Man* in this context refers to the human species in its entirety. Anthropology, being the science of man, has put us in a bit of an awkward position with the present focus on politically correct terminology. The alternatives *humankind* and *mankind* still have *man* as a root, and *Homo sapiens* is too academic for every-

anthropology
The science or study of *Homo sapiens* using a holistic approach.

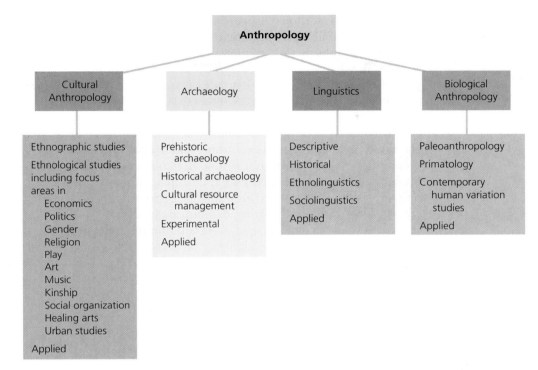

FIGURE 1.1 **The Four Fields of Anthropology**

day conversation. Most anthropologists settle for a potpourri of terms when referring to our species in the hope that they will not offend anyone and will manage to convey that their science includes all humans. The scope of our study of the human species includes all human groups, both cultural and biological, today and as they adapted and evolved in the past.

This text will follow the basic organization of the subfields of anthropology as recognized by the American Anthropological Association: cultural anthropology, archaeology, linguistics, and biological (also called physical) anthropology (Figure 1.1). Note that cultural anthropology, archaeology, and linguistics are all concerned with aspects of human culture. Many anthropologists add applied anthropology to this list as a fifth field of study, whereas others incorporate applied anthropology into each of anthropology's subfields.

Cultural Anthropology

Cultural anthropology is the description and comparison of the adaptations made by human groups to the diverse ecosystems of the earth. We call these adaptations *culture* (see Chapter 2 for an in-depth discussion of

cultural anthropology
A subfield of anthropology that focuses on human sociocultural adaptations.

this concept). Traditional areas of focus within cultural anthropology include ethnographic and ethnological research.

Ethnography is the descriptive study of one culture, subculture, or microculture based on fieldwork. The *field* situations can be quite diverse—in your own city or on the other side of the world; a whole community, a neighborhood, or a workplace. An ethnographer usually spends a minimum of one year in the field in order to record a complete yearly cycle of the culture. Most ethnographers realize, though, that one year is not nearly enough time to understand everything about a culture, so they commonly spend many years, off and on, with a particular culture or subculture, recording their way of life and how it changes. Other ethnographers focus on one aspect of the culture for a shorter period of time. For example, an anthropologist who is studying decision making within a large business corporation may spend a period of several months collecting data, reporting, and making recommendations. Often several anthropologists will study one culture together. Such ethnographic teams have been very successful because members can explore different questions and integrate their data into a more complete picture. These approaches are covered more fully in Chapter 3. Ethnographic works provide the specific data on which comparative ethnological studies are based.

Ethnology, the comparative study of cultures, presents analytical generalizations about human culture. The process leading to these generalizations involves explaining the similarities and differences in cultures. The subject of the comparison may be entire cultures or a particular aspect of culture such as gender, economics, violence, or shamanism. For example, a book titled *Tribal Economics* would be a comparative work that assesses how tribal cultures acquire food and other resources and how these resources are distributed. Such a work would be based on data about specific cultures that have been gathered in ethnographic fieldwork.

In its *Anthropology News* the American Anthropological Association publishes information from the four subfields, plus research interest groups (or sections) within the basic four subfields. To get an idea of the diverse interest areas in cultural anthropology, see Box 1.1.

Archaeology

Archaeology is the systematic study of the remains of previous cultures as a means of reconstructing the lifeways of people who lived in the past. To put it another way, archaeologists focus on culture, the culture of people we cannot interview or observe. We have only whatever remains in the sites they once occupied, which archaeologists use to study how these peoples adapted to their natural and sociocultural environments and how culture spread and changed through time. The goals of archaeological research are

ethnography
A written description of a culture based on data gathered from fieldwork.

ethnology
The comparative study of cultures with the aim of presenting analytical generalizations about human culture.

archaeology
The systematic study of the artifacts and ecofacts from past cultures as a means of reconstructing past lifeways.

BOX 1.1

The following is a sample of the American Anthropological Association sections that relate to cultural anthropology:

American Ethnological Society
Anthropology and Environment Section
Anthropology of Religion Section
Association for Africanist Anthropology
Association for Feminist Anthropology
Association for Political and Legal Anthropology
Council on Anthropology and Education
Council for Museum Anthropology
Council for Nutritional Anthropology
Culture and Agriculture Section
National Association for the Practice of Anthropology
Society for the Anthropology of Consciousness
Society for the Anthropology of Work
Society for Cultural Anthropology
Society for Humanistic Anthropology
Society for Medical Anthropology
Society for Psychological Anthropology
Society for Urban, National, Transnational/Global Anthropology
Society for Visual Anthropology

Professionals doing research in these areas use ethnographic and ethnological methods in their studies.

prehistoric archaeology
The analysis of the material remains of cultures that existed before the time of written records.

artifacts
Objects made by humans.

features
Nonportable evidence of technology at archaeological sites, such as roadways and fire hearths.

ecofacts
The remains of plants, animals, or naturally occurring nonorganic substances.

site
The location of archaeological remains such as artifacts and features.

(1) to establish time lines for past cultures, (2) to describe past lifeways, and (3) to understand the process of adaptation and change in prehistory.

There are a number of areas of focus in archaeology. **Prehistoric archaeology** is the study of the remains of cultures that existed before the time of written records. Prehistoric archaeologists analyze the **artifacts** (objects made or altered by humans, such as spear points, baskets, or computers), **features** (nonportable evidence of technology such as roadways, building foundations, and fire hearths), and **ecofacts** (natural materials such as plant or animal remains—fossils, pollen, and soils) that are found in archaeological **sites** (locations where evidence of human activity is found). This is one of the fields of anthropology that has most captured the imagination of the public. The Indiana Jones movies make archaeology appear romantic and adventuresome. It is, but not in the way portrayed in the films. (Indy, by the way, wasn't really an anthropological archaeologist. He was a classical archaeologist. Classical archaeology is primarily

Anasazi

OLC
mhhe•com/lenkeit3

See Internet exercise.

historical archaeology
A subfield of archaeology that studies the remains of cultures that existed during the time of written records but about which little was recorded.

cultural resource management (CRM)
The conservation and management of archaeological sites to protect them.

experimental archaeology
An aspect of archaeology in which experiments are performed to learn how prehistoric artifacts and features were made and used.

concerned with the art and architecture of the classical civilizations of the Mediterranean region. Such archaeologists are associated with university art history and classics departments.) Anthropological archaeologists work to reconstruct as much as possible about past cultures based on careful excavation, measurement, and recording of sites, and they do a great deal of scientific detective work to analyze their data before reporting on how ancient people lived. The romance and adventure of the actual excavation work, especially in remote regions, is more often, as Sir Mortimer Wheeler put it, "adventure remembered in tranquillity, devoid of the ills and anxieties, fleas, fevers, thirst, and toothache, which are liable to be the more insistent experience" (Wheeler 1956: 241).

Historical archaeology is the study of the remains of cultures and subcultures that have written records but about which little if anything was recorded. Historical archaeology, in other words, supplements historical evidence about the past. For example, the everyday lives of people were seldom recorded in colonial North America. Few if any written records exist to tell us about certain segments of past populations, such as the poor, disadvantaged, minorities, immigrants, and slaves. Information about how slaves lived on southern plantations in colonial America has been one focal point of research in this area. There are, of course, written records of what plantation owners paid for slaves and the number of slaves working on plantations, but there are few written accounts of how the slaves lived. Archaeological excavations of slave quarters have revealed details of their lives and their many valuable contributions to American colonial culture and economics. For example, it was African rice farming techniques brought to America by slaves and implemented by them that made many Carolina plantation owners wealthy. Thus historical archaeology is filling gaps in our knowledge of American history and correcting history that was once based primarily on documents written by the powerful and wealthy. The same careful methods of excavation and recording of data that are used in prehistoric digs are used in historical archaeology.

Another focus area in archaeology, called **cultural resource management (CRM),** is a growing field for individuals with degrees in archaeology. CRM specialists work on threatened archaeological sites, produce environmental impact reports, and do salvage digs on sites that will be destroyed by contemporary building. There are numerous other focus areas in archaeological research, but because this is primarily a cultural anthropology text, I'll mention only one additional area of research. **Experimental archaeology** plays an important part in the analysis of prehistoric artifacts and technology. For example, researchers try to duplicate the prehistoric techniques of manufacturing stone tools and other artifacts to better understand and appreciate the technological knowledge of prehistoric peoples.

These ancient Anasazi ruins in Colorado are features that help archaeologists to reconstruct the lifeways of early inhabitants of the American Southwest.

Applied archaeology is a focus area in archaeology that uses the methods of archaeology to study *contemporary* material culture. Some CRM and experimental archaeology falls in this category. The most widely known work in applied archaeology began at the University of Arizona in the 1970s under the direction of archaeologist William Rathje, who wanted to use archaeological methods to investigate patterns of household waste within the city of Tucson. This research is popularly called "garbology," or the study of garbage. Some archaeologists refer to it as **behavioral archaeology** because studies such as Rathje's look at the relationships between contemporary people's material culture and their behaviors. Just as the excavations of trash heaps (technically termed **middens,** or areas of discarded items) by prehistoric archaeologists reveal information about the diet and artifacts of past peoples, the trash of contemporary populations reveals information about societies today. These studies of what

applied archaeology
The use of archaeological methods to study the material culture of contemporary societies. Data can be used to develop social programs.

behavioral archaeology
An area of applied archaeology that focuses on the relationships between material culture and people's behavior.

midden
Archaeological term to designate an area of discard; a trash heap.

people discard can give us information that helps direct social programs and better understand waste disposal processes. In Rathje's Garbage Project, front-door interviewers found that 15 percent of respondents admitted to consuming beer. The trash discard data from this same area showed that over 80 percent of households consumed beer and 54 percent discarded over eight cans per week. Many other discrepancies were found between what householders told interviewers about their food and drink consumption and what they actually ate and drank. Data from the Garbage Project were so useful that this research expanded to include projects in other cities and an ongoing study of contemporary landfills.

Linguistics

Linguistics is the study of language. Anthropological linguists do not necessarily speak several languages (such a person is called a polyglot). Rather, linguists study language—how language is formed and how it works, the history and development of language, and its relationship to other aspects of culture. Linguistics became a part of anthropology for two reasons. First, language is the cornerstone of culture (more about culture in Chapter 2). Second, to do ethnographic fieldwork, anthropologists often had to begin by writing their own dictionaries and grammars of a native language. Today linguistics encompasses a number of research areas, including descriptive linguistics, historical linguistics, ethnolinguistics, and sociolinguistics.

Descriptive linguistics focuses on the mechanics of language. The linguist must first describe the sounds used in the language under study (called *phonology*). Sounds can be described according to the anatomical parts that are used to create them, such as the teeth, tongue, lips, voice, or lack of voice. Morphology and syntax, other aspects of describing a language, involve the identification of the smallest units of meaning in a language (morphemes) and the rules for combining words into sentences, what would popularly be called grammar (more about this in Chapter 4).

Historical linguistics works to reconstruct the history of languages, including their development and relationship to other languages. There are some limitations to historical linguistic research because not all contemporary languages have written forms, and many languages of past peoples did not have written records. Linguists can describe the comparative structure of contemporary related languages, however, and then use these comparisons to reconstruct some aspects of earlier forms of the root language.

Other categories of study in linguistic anthropology include ethnolinguistics and sociolinguistics. **Ethnolinguistics** is a specialized field that analyzes the relationship between a language and culture. It investigates questions such as Does your language create your reality? **Sociolinguistics** evaluates the relationship between language and culture with a focus on

linguistics
A subfield of anthropology that includes the study of the structure, history, and social aspects of human language.

descriptive linguistics
The part of anthropological linguistics that focuses on the mechanics of language.

historical linguistics
The study of the history of languages, including their development and relationship to other languages.

ethnolinguistics
A field of study in linguistics that analyzes the relationship between a language and culture.

sociolinguistics
A subfield of linguistics that analyzes the relationship between language and culture with a focus on how people speak in social contexts.

TRY THIS *Compare*

Select another of your introductory-level college courses—history, zoology, psychology, English, geography—and list three specific ways that the subject matter of anthropology is different from these disciplines and one way it is the same. Compare and discuss your list with that of a classmate.

how people speak in social contexts such as in the workplace or at home. (see Chapter 4 for details).

Biological Anthropology

Biological anthropology (also called **physical anthropology**) studies *Homo sapiens* as biological beings both in the present and in the past. Scientists working in this subfield seek to describe and explain the biological evolution of and variations in our species. To this end they also study the closely related primates (prosimians, monkeys, and apes) because their evolutionary history is similar to and related to ours. Three major areas of focus in biological anthropology include paleoanthropology, primatology, and contemporary human variation studies.

Paleoanthropology (the root word *paleo* means ancient) is the study of human biological evolution through an examination of the fossils of our ancient ancestors and relatives. Paleoanthropology relies heavily on comparative anatomy and evolutionary biology. For example, the researcher must know comparative details of the structure of leg bones between animals who walk on four legs (**quadrupeds**) and those who walk on two (**bipeds**) to determine whether an ancient femur (upper leg bone) belonged to an individual who walked bipedally. Some clues to bipedalism are found in the angle of the neck of the femur and in the distribution of weight, when standing, based on this angle.

The understanding and interpretation of the past requires an integration of information from many areas. Paleoanthropologists share information and interact with archaeologists as well as specialists from other fields such as geology and chemistry. For example, to understand the environment occupied by a fossil ancestor who lived fifty thousand years ago, the paleoanthropologist must collaborate with geologists who specialize in reconstructing paleoclimates and archaeologists who can reconstruct how this fossil ancestor made the stone tools found in the site.

Primatology is the study of our nearest animal relatives—the **primates.** This area of biological anthropology includes an investigation of the anatomy, physiology, genetics, and behaviors of apes, monkeys, and prosimians. We share many biological features with this group of animals, and data about their adaptations aid us in understanding *Homo sapiens.*

biological anthropology
A subfield of anthropology that studies humans as a biological species. Also called physical anthropology.

physical anthropology
See *biological anthropology.*

paleoanthropology
The study of human biological evolution.

quadruped
An animal that walks on four limbs.

biped
An animal that walks on two legs.

primatology
The study of nonhuman primates.

primates
Animals in the order Primates; includes humans, apes, monkeys, and prosimians.

Homo sapiens
The taxonomic designation for humans.

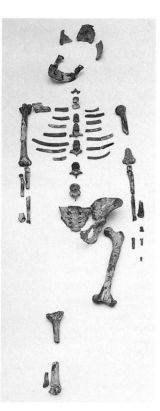

The Lucy fossils from the Hadar region of Ethiopia are examples of evidence that can be used by paleoanthropologists to reconstruct our early ancestors. Note the complete upper leg bone (femur). The angle of the head of the femur, plus the features of the pelvis, indicate that Lucy walked bipedally.

See Internet exercise.

A common misunderstanding about primate research regards our relationship to chimpanzees. They are clearly our closest relative in the animal world, but they do not represent our ancestor. Rather, chimps and humans diverged from a common ancestor about 8 to 10 million years ago, and since then each species has evolved separately.

Contemporary human variation studies, another area of research in biological anthropology, focus on living humans and how our anatomy and physiology vary. Genetics, including DNA research, contributes greatly to such studies, the long-range goal of which is to account for and offer explanations for the variation among humans, as well as to demonstrate our many similarities and shared biological adaptations. For example, if a difference in the frequency of a genetic disease is established for one particular population compared to others, research is undertaken to explain the frequency from an evolutionary viewpoint. Anthropologists working in this area often collaborate with geneticists and medical scientists.

Specialists known as **forensic anthropologists** apply their knowledge to legal issues. They are usually trained in biological anthropology, although they work closely with archaeologists who recover human remains. Forensic studies on human skeletal material can reveal such information as the sex of the individual, cause of death, diseases suffered, and nutritional deficiencies. This information can be useful in helping to identify human remains in natural disasters as well as to identify cause of death in homicide cases.

◎ HOW ANTHROPOLOGY IS UNIQUE

Several key features of how anthropologists view *Homo sapiens* make our perspective unique: holism, fieldwork, the comparative method, and the perspective of cultural relativism. Other academic disciplines also use some of these features—biologists, for example, do fieldwork. Anthropology, however, is the only science that pulls all of these aspects together to study humanity.

Anthropology Is Holistic

Anthropology is a **holistic** science, which means that anthropologists view *Homo sapiens*, and the evolutionary ancestors of modern humans, in the broadest context possible—as both biological beings and cultural beings through a time span of approximately 5 million years (Figure 1.2). In other words, we study everything about people for as long as humans and their immediate humanlike precursors have existed as a species. We keep this broad, integrated perspective no matter what specific detail of human life we might be investigating. For example, a paleoanthropologist will con-

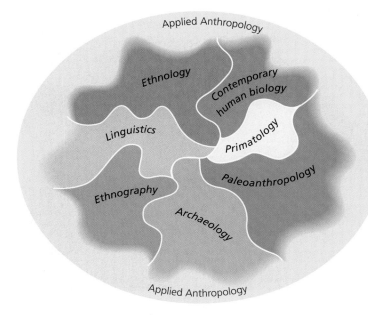

FIGURE 1.2
Anthropology is a holistic study of all cultural and biological aspects of the human species. Cultural anthropology includes ethnographic and ethnological studies as well as linguistics and archaeology. Biological anthropology includes paleoanthropology, primatology, and studies in contemporary human biology. Applied research encompasses all of anthropology.

sider the cultural adaptations (including tool use and possible social behavior) of the biological ancestors of modern humans. The broad time frame covered by anthropology is significant because anthropologists believe that any insights about contemporary human adaptations, either biological or cultural, should be made with an eye to past adaptations.

Anthropologists Do Fieldwork

Specialists in the various subfields of anthropology work to maintain their holistic vision. An extension of holism is to collect primary data in natural field settings. In the following paragraphs I discuss the types of data gathered in the field by the different kinds of anthropologists.

Cultural Anthropology in the Field   Cultural anthropologists gather their primary data in the field. Insights about peoples and their lifeways take on a whole new dimension when one experiences their culture firsthand. Anthropologists reason that to describe and explain the cultural adaptations and worldview of a tribe in Brazil, an urban gang in the United States, or cannery workers in Japan one must participate in the culture. We believe that to really know another culture, subculture, or microculture one must commit to spending extensive time in that cultural environment. Ethnographic data, as noted earlier in this chapter, are the raw materials with which comparative analysis is done. Chapter 3 gives an in-depth discussion of the methods of ethnographic fieldwork.

contemporary human variation studies
The study of the biological variation in living humans.

forensic anthropologist
An applied biological anthropologist concerned with legal issues. Frequently focuses on the identification of skeletal material and the cause of death.

holistic
An integrated perspective that assumes interrelationships among the parts of a subject. Anthropology studies humans from a holistic perspective, including both biological and cultural aspects.

ANTHROPOLOGY AROUND US

Forensic Anthropology in the News

Forensics is a hot topic in the media. Forensic anthropologists identify the bones and teeth of missing persons, use skull comparisons to determine the sons of an Egyptian pharaoh, and run DNA analysis to determine if bones buried in a Spanish cathedral are those of Christopher Columbus. They determine the age and sex of skeletal remains and analyze impact wounds on bones to determine what implement made the wound. All of these topics of investigation have made headlines in recent years. The methods and data of forensic anthropologists are exhibited weekly on television dramas and in news articles, though these sources often do not distinguish between forensic anthropologists, forensic pathologists (medical doctors), odontologists (dentists), and police homicide investigators. The American Board of Forensic Anthropologists provides a rigorous program of certification in forensic anthropology that is similar to board certifications in medical specialty areas.

Forensic anthropology illustrates the holistic nature of anthropology. Human cultural behaviors in the way people use their bodies have an effect on bone development and the development of diseases such as osteoarthritis. A recent book, *Atlas of Occupational Markers on Human Remains* by Luigi Capasso, Kenneth A. R. Kennedy, and Cynthia A. Wilczak (Teramo, Italy: edigrafital SpA-S. Atto, 1999), describes nearly 150 conditions that reflect specific behaviors. Some of these conditions have nontech-

nical names such as Pipe Smoker's Teeth (mechanical marks on upper and lower incisor teeth caused by pipe smoking and regularly holding other hard objects in the teeth, such as a police officer's whistle) and Floorwalker's Foot (bony spurs and bursitis evidenced in several locations and caused by walking on hard pavement). The presence of such conditions helps forensic experts identify aspects of the lifestyle or work habits of the person whose skeleton is under investigation.

◎ Can you suggest the type of bone damage evidence that results from travel over rough terrain, such as on a snowmobile? Go to http://www.news.cornell.edu/releases/april99/occu_markers.hrs.html to find out if you are correct.

Anthropologists collect data primarily in field settings. Nadine R. Peacock is shown interacting with Efe individuals in the Ituri rain forest of the Congo.

Archaeology in the Field   Archaeologists must dig and recover artifacts and ecofacts before they can begin the technical analysis of these materials in the lab. Fieldwork is the first step of data acquisition. Each archaeological site is mapped and recorded before digging begins. Excavation and measurement are done with care so that the exact location of each artifact, ecofact, and feature is recorded before any items are removed from the ground. Such detail is important for revealing patterns of artifact distribution. For example, the location of food preparation tools may always be inside of the house wall features for one prehistoric culture and outside of the walls for another.

Linguistics in the Field   Primary data are also gathered in the field for most aspects of linguistics. Descriptive linguistics depends on interactions with native speakers. Although this can take place in a laboratory setting, the majority of the initial work of describing the structure and other aspects of languages has been done in field settings. This fieldwork may be important to later understandings of how the language is used by individuals, and it may reveal features such as special language forms used when in the presence of elders.

Biological Anthropology in the Field   Paleoanthropologists who analyze and explain human evolution must have fossils to evaluate; to gather fossils they go into the field. The idea of human fossil hunters searching the

Gombe

barren, exposed early Pleistocene layers of Africa's Olduvai Gorge tickles the soul of adventure in all of us. The field studies of primatologists Jane Goodall, who studies chimpanzees at the Gombe Preserve in Tanzania, and Dian Fossey, who observed gorillas in Rwanda, made world headlines and offered new perspectives on the behavior of these animals in their natural habitats. We now have over thirty years of field studies focusing on the Gombe chimpanzees and decades with another group of chimps on the Ivory Coast. The insights that we have gained about their behaviors are surprising and humbling. Observations of the Tai population of chimpanzees on the Ivory Coast of Africa, for example, show mother chimps *demonstrating* tool use to their offspring in the form of using rocks for cracking nuts.

The investigation of contemporary primate anatomy combines field observations with laboratory work. Research on chimpanzee locomotor anatomy involves describing the locomotor behavior of chimps in their natural habitat plus measuring, dissecting, and describing muscles and bones of deceased chimpanzees in the laboratory.

Biological anthropologists who study the variations in contemporary humans also gather data in the field—blood samples, specimens for DNA testing, morphological measurements—as they endeavor to explain human biological diversity. Of course, the follow-up analysis of much of this data is accomplished using computer and lab facilities.

Anthropologists Focus on the Comparative Method

Anthropologists gather and compare as much data as possible before making generalizations. We do not rely on data from just one study to make interpretative or analytical statements about the human condition. To examine the structure of human families, for example, a cultural anthropologist would look at data in the Human Relations Area Files that have been gathered from field studies in hundreds of different cultures. Features of family structure would be compared, and the similarities and differences would be described, numerically tabulated, and statistically analyzed. These data would be used to generate hypotheses to explain the variations noted, which in turn would necessitate formulating ways to test the hypotheses.

The **comparative method** is also used in archaeology, linguistics, and biological anthropology. Paleoanthropologists use the comparative method when a new fossil skull is discovered. Comparative anatomical studies are carried out on many specimens before tentative assessments and interpretations are given. The interpretation is tentative because we continue to compare each new fossil as it is discovered; with more comparative data, the earlier interpretations may need adjustments. As you might imagine, the comparative approach makes for some lively discussions among anthropologists, because the data aren't always as clear as we would wish. The comparative method as described here is part of scientifically oriented an-

comparative method
The methodological approach of comparing data. Anthropologists use the comparative method.

Members of cultures that do not eat protein-rich insects often react ethnocentrically when they see this behavior in other cultures. Here a Thai girl is enjoying a snack of fried grasshopper.

thropology. **Humanistic anthropology** focuses on the uniqueness of every individual and every culture and would not use the comparative method.

Anthropologists Use the Perspective of Cultural Relativism

One additional perspective of anthropology adds to its uniqueness. Anthropologists approach the study of other cultures using a perspective known as cultural relativism. **Cultural relativism** is the idea that any aspect of a culture must be viewed and evaluated within the context of that culture. The job of the anthropologist who is applying this perspective is to describe a cultural trait, custom, belief, activity, or any part of a culture and to show how it fits into the values and traditions of that cultural system. In other words, the anthropologist objectively describes a custom and then discusses how it is viewed within that culture. **Ethnocentrism,** the opposite of cultural relativism, makes value judgments when describing aspects of another culture. The value judgment is based on comparing elements of one's own culture with that of another culture; the other culture is "wrong," "weird," "strange," "unethical," or "backward." Any value-laden statement that uses one's own culture as the basis for the comparison reflects cultural ethnocentrism.

Consider this statement uttered by a non-Inuit: "The Inuit eat raw seal liver and they relish this traditional food." This statement is made from a relativistic perspective. It describes what the Inuit do and how they feel

humanistic anthropology
A label for research that focuses on individuals and their creative responses to cultural and historical forces.

cultural relativism
The perspective that any aspect of a culture must be viewed and evaluated within the context of that culture.

ethnocentrism
Making value judgments based on one's own culture when describing aspects of another culture.

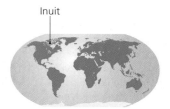

Inuit

about it. Now, consider a person who is not an Inuit making this statement: "The Inuit have the repulsive custom of eating raw seal liver." This is an ethnocentric statement because the term *repulsive* evaluates the eating of raw liver from the cultural viewpoint of the speaker.

Ethnocentrism is a part of everyone and of every culture. We all judge other cultures' customs and behaviors based on our own customs and behaviors. It is socially transmitted. One rarely speaks of it, and even your best friend will only rarely tell you that it is showing. Its symptoms can appear at any time, but they are most apparent when traveling in another country or watching a television program concerning other cultures. A trip to your local shopping center may also trigger ethnocentrism if you encounter people of other cultures and subcultures who dress, speak, and act differently than you do. It is important to recognize that cultural ethnocentrism is different from egocentrism, where one makes negative value judgments that are based on personal belief or behavior. Ethnocentrism is based on the culture of a social group.

Ethnocentrism can lead to conflict and misunderstanding. It can be considered to have adaptive value, however, because it may create social cohesion and help to hold a group together. The approach of cultural relativism, by contrast, can lead to an appreciation for, and understanding of, other cultures. In the previous example, a person with a relativistic approach to world cultures would acknowledge that raw seal liver is different from the food she eats. Further, she would acknowledge that if she grew up in a culture where parents and siblings all ate raw liver she would probably enjoy eating it too.

Taking a perspective of cultural relativism does not mean that you should start eating raw meat. It means that you understand that behavioral differences, and the values behind them, are learned and are simply different. Such an approach can contribute to greater awareness, tolerance, and acceptance of people with different cultural backgrounds. Throughout the history of cultural anthropology as an academic discipline, the perspective of cultural relativism has guided research efforts. Figure 1.3 shows that a reliance on fieldwork, the comparative method, and a holistic perspective, together with cultural relativism, combine to make anthropology a unique academic discipline.

Should There Be Any Universal Values?

It seems reasonable to be relativistic about food preferences and modes of food consumption. But how can an American be culturally relativistic about practices such as female circumcision? Most Americans and peoples of many other cultures would say unequivocally that this practice is wrong, bad, evil. Why? If we are being completely candid, we would have to admit that it is wrong mainly because we don't do it. We would cite health, safety,

❈ TRY THIS ❈
Consider

Could you eat raw liver for your next meal? Is it possible for anyone to set aside all of their ethnocentric attitudes? Discuss this with a classmate.

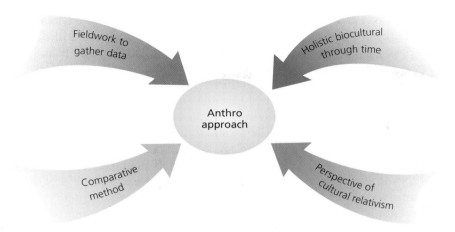

FIGURE 1.3
These four approaches, when used in concert with one another, give anthropology its unique perspective.

and feminist issues and universal human rights to justify our objections to the practice. For the record, not all anthropologists agree about the degree to which we should apply cultural relativism or whether there is or should be a universal set of values for evaluating human rights.

◎ THE SCIENTIFIC APPROACH IN ANTHROPOLOGY

To explain humanity, anthropologists apply a scientific approach. One of my favorite statements about science was made by Eugenie C. Scott of the National Center for Science Education. Scott states, "The goal of science is to explain how the natural world works. As humans are part of the natural world, they can be studied scientifically" (Scott 1996: 52). In his book *Reclaiming a Scientific Anthropology* (1997), Lawrence Kuznar recaps the history of anthropological science and delineates its current position, goals, and methodological principles. The goals include "knowing the empirical world, being able to explain and predict phenomena in the world, and generating progressively more accurate knowledge by proposing theories that can be scrutinized and refined through time" (Kuznar 1997: 30). Anthropologists strive to reach these goals by using the scientific method.

A key feature of the scientific method is the formulation of hypotheses to explain relationships among data. A hypothesis is an educated guess that explains a given phenomenon. Criteria used to judge the worth of a hypothesis include whether it is relevant, testable, and compatible with previous well-established hypotheses. Other important characteristics of a hypothesis include its power to explain or predict and its simplicity. A hypothesis, then, is not just a guess but a reasonable explanation that is formulated after a problem area is identified and background investigation

TRY THIS
Hypothesize

Formulate a hypothesis that could account for the different treatment of time in Brazilian culture as compared to North American culture. Offer two ways to test your hypothesis.

has been completed. Anthropologists use the scientific method when they include the formulation and testing of hypotheses with a careful definition of terms, quantification, and application of mathematical principles such as statistical methods.

You and I make hypotheses all the time. If students are fifteen minutes late to class, I might hypothesize that they ignored their alarm clock this morning and slept in. Or I might hypothesize that if the fog was thick in the rural areas this morning, then students might have had to drive more slowly, thus making them late to class. Both of these hypotheses are relevant, simple, and compatible with previous well-established hypotheses, and they explain the tardiness of the students. There are simple and obvious ways to test both of the hypotheses.

If I am late to class, you might make the same two hypotheses. These are two very probable and compatible reasons for lateness to class in our North American culture. If I were a visiting professor in a Brazilian university, I would need to formulate my hypotheses in ways that are relevant to Brazilian culture. Being fifteen minutes tardy in Brazil is culturally equal to being about one to two minutes late in North American culture and therefore is of no importance. No explanation for the lateness is needed. By using a scientific approach, one can decrease the likelihood of ethnocentric bias affecting the explanations given as one researches behavior in other cultures.

If the scientific method is used in trying to explain a phenomenon, then science is being done. Since anthropologists use the scientific method as they work to explain human biological evolution and variation and human cultural behavior, anthropology is a science. The social (or behavioral) sciences, where cultural anthropology is placed, have not been particularly effective in communicating that we use scientific methods.

There are a number of significant difficulties in consistently using the scientific method when investigating and explaining human cultural behavior. First, anthropologists are concerned with a very complex subject—human beings. No two humans have been raised in exactly the same way, nor have any two people had exactly the same life experiences. Second, anthropologists are often unable to isolate variables or perform experiments to test aspects of *Homo sapiens* in the same manner that other scientists carry out tests, in part because much of our research is based on observation in natural field settings where variables cannot be as easily controlled as they are in a laboratory setting. Another reason is that human behavioral researchers have ethical limitations, which does not mean that other sciences don't have ethical standards, but rather that additional standards are applied when we are dealing with human subjects. Finally, the explanations offered by anthropologists are often based on context. The context in which a behavior takes place must be considered. Therefore, an explanation may not have wide application. In ideal scientific explanations, place should not affect the veracity of the explanation.

For example, if we strive to explain why polyandry (marriage of one woman to two or more men at the same time) is practiced in a culture, we begin with a thorough, objective description of all aspects of the culture we are studying. A hypothesis is formulated that takes into account what we know about this particular culture and what we know about other cultures where polyandry is practiced (the comparative method discussed earlier in this chapter). Then the hypothesis is tested. If the hypothesis holds true for the tests and data from other cultures show the same consistent correlations as the original society, we may be able to make a generalization about why polyandry is practiced. The formulation of such generalizations is one of the goals of cultural anthropology.

The desire to maintain large landholdings was cited as a reason for the practice of polyandry by Tibetans living in northern Nepal in the 1987 study by Melvyn C. Goldstein. In this particular case, brothers share a wife, thus keeping the male-owned lands from being split up as property is passed from one generation to the next. Prior to Goldstein's work, one explanation for the practice of polyandry was that there was a shortage of women as a result of the practice of female infanticide. Goldstein's research revealed that there had never been institutionalized female infanticide in Tibet. Another early explanation for the practice of polyandry suggested that poor soil fertility and crop yields required brothers to share a wife in order to avoid starvation. Although ecological factors do play a role in the practice of polyandry in Tibet, Goldstein did not find polyandry to be a means of preventing starvation.

Of course, you might read this and think, Well, why not just *ask* members of the culture why they practice polyandry? Good question. Although every culture has members who are quite analytical and very helpful to the anthropologist, most people in a culture don't know why particular customs are followed.

> ### ✤ TRY THIS ✤
> #### Explain
> You are a member of a culture where the primary marriage practice is monogamy. Explain why we have only one spouse at a time.

Tibetans

◎ POSTMODERNISM IN ANTHROPOLOGY

Postmodernists place the discipline of anthropology in the humanities rather than in the sciences. A humanistic view focuses on the uniqueness of each individual and on individual creativity within the confines of society and culture. This means that ethnographers must look to individual informants and record their voices and perspectives. It also means that the postmodern approach downplays the comparative method and quantitative analysis.

Postmodernism is considered a theoretical perspective with different meanings to different people (see Marcus and Fischer 1986; Fischer 1997; and Kuper 1999). Basically anthropologists with this theoretical perspective question the use of the scientific method in anthropology. They view culture as an abstraction. Further, they argue that it is impossible to

postmodernist
One who uses the paradigm of postmodernism.

postmodernism
A complex theoretical perspective that applies a humanistic approach to ethnography with a focus on individuals and their voices.

be objective when studying other cultures. They focus on the premise that ethnographer objectivity is not possible because observers are always influenced by their own culture and social position, as well as by their feelings about what they observe. Therefore postmodernists claim that most theoretical constructs are not valid.

Although the postmodern movement is controversial, it has influenced anthropologists to be sensitive to issues such as power (as in when the ethnographer comes from a powerful culture and the native person being interviewed does not). It has also contributed to advocacy for a more vigorous representation of the native viewpoint. Many ethnographers, both those who use a scientific approach and those who use a postmodernist approach, now request that natives read and comment on their ethnographic data before they are published.

SUMMARY

Anthropology is the study of humans throughout the world spanning approximately the last 5 million years. It is a holistic discipline, meaning that it views humans in the broadest possible context as both biological and cultural entities. This perspective is maintained regardless of the specific research undertaken. The four subfields of anthropology as recognized by the American Anthropological Association are cultural anthropology, archaeology, linguistics, and biological (or physical) anthropology. The holistic perspective, the use of the comparative method, fieldwork as a primary means of data acquisition, the perspective of cultural relativism, and avoidance of ethnocentrism make anthropology a unique discipline. Anthropologists seek to explain human cultural behavior using the scientific method. At the same time, anthropology includes a humanistic perspective.

Study Questions

OLC
/ mhhe•com/lenkeit3
See Self Quiz.

1. What do anthropologists study? What are the four subfields of anthropology, and what do anthropologists working within each subfield study?
2. How is anthropology unique as a discipline?
3. Contrast the perspectives of ethnocentrism and cultural relativism.
4. Anthropologists use the scientific method to investigate and explain human cultural behavior. Why is it sometimes difficult to apply the scientific method in studies of other cultures?

Suggested Readings

Barfield, Thomas, ed. 1997. *The Dictionary of Anthropology.* Malden, Mass.: Blackwell. A basic reference for serious anthropology students. Contains more than

500 entries—short definitions and articles that expand on theoretical concepts and approaches. Contributions are by leading anthropologists.

Endicott, K. M., and R. Welsch. 2005. *Taking Sides: Clashing Views on Controversial Issues in Anthropology*, 3rd ed. Guilford, Conn.: McGraw-Hill/Dushkin. Opposing viewpoints regarding various issues in anthropology, including ethical dilemmas.

Feder, Kenneth L. 2007. *Frauds, Myths, and Mysteries: Science and Pseudoscience in Archaeology*, 5th ed. New York: McGraw-Hill. A must-read for anyone interested in archaeology. This book gives insight on how to approach and evaluate claims about prehistory that appear in the popular media.

Park, Michael Alan. 2005. *Biological Anthropology*, 4th ed. New York: McGraw-Hill. An excellent introduction to the field of biological anthropology.

Podolefsky, A., and P. J. Brown, eds. 2001. *Applying Anthropology: An Introductory Reader*, 6th ed. Mountain View, Calif.: Mayfield. Essays on the usefulness and relevance of anthropology addressing human social problems.

Rathje, William, and Cullen Murphy. 2001. *Rubbish! The Archaeology of Garbage*. Tucson: University of Arizona Press. An entertaining and provocative book about Rathje's Garbage Project. Demonstrates the application of archaeological methods to contemporary issues.

Suggested Web Sites

http://www.aaanet.org/resinet.htm
This excellent collection of links is organized and maintained by the American Anthropological Association and includes links to all aspects of anthropology resources on the Internet. It also has information about careers in anthropology.

http://archaeology.la.asu.edu
Maintained by the Archaeological Research Institute (Arizona State University), this site is an indispensable resource on all aspects of archaeology. Individual links are to specific subject areas in archaeology such as mapping, faunal and flora analysis, ceramics, and so on.

http://www.news.cornell.edu/releases/april99/occu_markers.hrs.html
This site describes examples of forensic anthropological information regarding evidence on human skeletal remains from many occupations.

http://www.forensicanthro.com/
This easily navigated site links to all aspects of forensic anthropology.

http://www.indiana.edu/~wanthro/theory.htm
Prepared by Indiana University anthropology students. The site presents an overview of major anthropological associations and subdisciplines, plus "hot topics" from the 1970s through the late 1990s.

http://www.mnsu.edu/emuseum/information/biography/index.shtml
Short biographical sketches of over 800 anthropologists created by students at Minnesota State University, Mankato.

OLC
mhhe·com/lenkeit3
See Web links.

2

Culture

What Makes Us Strangers When We Are Away from Home?

I had just cut a piece of chicken on the plate in front of me. I placed the knife on the upper right rim of the plate and transferred my fork from my left hand to my right hand and raised the tines of the fork bearing the chicken to my mouth. As I listened to a remark made by the man sitting on my right, I glanced down the length of the banquet table. There were twenty-five college professors, high-ranking government officials, and individuals representing various private organizations sitting at my table. I suddenly realized that I was the *only* person with a fork grasped in my right hand. Everyone else retained the fork in their left hand as they ate their meat, as is the Canadian custom. I *knew* that Canadians used table utensils in the European manner, but my behavior with utensils was learned in my culture of birth, American. I felt that everyone at the banquet table was looking at me and that I might as well be wearing a sign that said, "I Am an American." I quickly shifted my technique with the fork and pondered how cultural behaviors such as this were indeed what make us strangers when we are away from our own culture.

I spent two years living and teaching in Canada. The experience related above is an example of the many mistakes I made when trying to fit in with my surroundings. I knew that Canadian culture and its regional and ethnic variations were different from American culture and its many regional and ethnic variations. I tried very hard to view experiences through an anthropological lens, to note cultural similarities as well as differences. Yet I was and remained in most ways a stranger in this setting, because of my cultural upbringing.

Culture is an abstract concept. You can't touch it or see most of it, and much of it can't be measured. But it has molded each of us into who and what we are: the way we dress, what we eat for dinner *and how we eat it*, how we speak, what color we paint our houses, *and* what we think about these things. It makes us strangers when we are away from home because sights, smells, sounds, values, traditions, behaviors, objects, and the way other people think are not what we expect.

Culture is also what makes others view us as different from them. Understanding the role of culture in shaping us can provide an intellectual tool for better understanding who we are and why other individuals or groups of people are similar to or different from us. At the most fundamental level, anthropologists believe that if we examine other cultures we can come to better understand our own. As I tell my students, "How can you know Modesto [my city] if you only know Modesto?" This chapter explores the concept of culture.

OLC
mhhe•com/lenkeit3

See chapter outline and chapter overview.

The objectives of this chapter are to
◆ Explain how anthropologists define culture
◆ Delineate important aspects of culture
◆ Discuss subcultures, ethnic groups, and race
◆ Describe culture in the subfields of anthropology
◆ Critique the concept of culture

◀ The culture of Spain is reflected in this street scene from Santander, Cantabria, Spain.

Culture is what makes us strangers when we are away from home. Picture yourself in each of these settings and consider how different each is from your own cultural setting. Mealtime differs in the Arctic (*upper left*), in New Guinea (*right*), and in the Kalahari Desert of Africa (*bottom left*), where these people are preparing an ostrich egg omelet.

culture
The sum total of the knowledge, ideas, behaviors, and material creations that are learned, shared, and transmitted primarily through the symbolic system of language. These components create a pattern that changes over time and serve as guides and standards of behavior for members of the society. The term *culture* is used in the abstract as well as to refer to a specific culture.

◎ DEFINING CULTURE

What exactly is **culture?** Abstract concepts such as culture are difficult to define. Other abstract concepts that are well known are love, justice, and equality. Not everyone, including experts in these areas, will agree on the precise definition of any of these concepts. Definitions are about using words to say what a word means. There are nuances of meaning between words, which is why it is difficult to obtain a consensus about the phrasing of a definition. This is particularly true of abstract concepts like love and culture. A writer's theoretical orientation or research focus may affect the words chosen to use in a definition. A poet uses different words than an attorney does when explaining what love is. The words an ecolog-

A communal bath house in Japan. Not all Japanese people use traditional bath houses today, yet they would recognize this as a part of Japanese culture.

ically minded anthropologist uses to describe culture are different from those chosen by a postmodernist-oriented anthropologist. This does not mean that we are speaking of something different when we use the term *culture*. We just place different emphasis and use different words to explain the concept.

The culture concept is also a generalization. Even when speaking about a specific culture, we are making a generalization. No two Japanese people, for example, know or practice all aspects of Japanese culture. So when we speak of Japanese culture, we are citing a generalized version of the Japanese culture. A Japanese individual may think and act based on her traditional Japanese cultural roots sometimes and not at other times, even in similar situations. Ask anyone born and raised in England or Spain or Iran or the United States who visits Japan on a holiday, and they will indicate that the Japanese culture is different from their own culture.

Culture is a word that is used daily by many people all over the world. Most of these people do not mean precisely the same thing when they use the word. But as I read and listen to the usage of the word *culture*, I believe that most people know that it is an abstract idea. And I think that most people *get* the notion that this thing called culture makes people think and act in particular ways and that it is learned. Dissecting the idea of culture has been a hot topic in academic circles in the past, and it still is today.

Exactly what is culture? Does it really exist? How can we convey what it is? One way to examine what culture means to anthropologists is to look at definitions of culture and statements about culture. The definitions in Boxes 2.1, 2.2, and 2.3 are arranged in chronological order and represent a sampling only.

◈◈◈   BOX 2.1   *Definitions of Culture: Group A*   ◈◈◈

Culture . . . is that complex whole which includes knowledge, belief, art, law, morals, customs, and any other capabilities and habits acquired by man as a member of society. (E. B. Tylor 1958: 1; originally published in 1871)

Culture means the whole complex of traditional behavior which has been developed by the human race and is successively learned by each generation. (Mead 1937: 17; quoted in Kroeber and Kluckhohn 1952: 90)

Culture may be defined as the totality of mental and physical reactions and activities that characterize the behavior of the individuals composing a social group. (Boas 1938: 159; quoted in White and Dillingham 1973: 32)

Culture is . . . that complex whole which includes all the habits acquired by man as a member of society. (Benedict 1929: 806)

By culture we mean all those historically created designs for living, explicit and implicit, rational, irrational, and non-rational, which exist at any given time as potential guides for the behavior of men. (Kluckhohn and Kelly 1945: 97)

Components of Culture

The definitions in group A (Box 2.1) are primarily lists of the various components of culture. Different words are used, but the definitions communicate essentially the same ideas. Culture consists of x, y, and z. In fact, if you were listening today to a group of anthropologists discussing culture, various specific components of culture would be mentioned. These components may be arranged in several categories (see Figure 2.1): (1) cognitive (processes of learning, knowing, and perceiving): ideas, knowledge, symbols, standards, values; (2) behavior (how we act or conduct ourselves): gestures, manners of eating, marriage ceremonies, dancing, social interactions; and (3) artifacts (human material creations): tools, pottery, clothing, architectural features, machines. In other words, within this group of definitions, culture consists of what people process cognitively and how the cognitive processes are reflected in human behaviors and in the artifacts, or objects, that humans create.

Cognitive Processes   What people think, how they think, what they believe, and what they value are a part of culture. Cognitive processes are not themselves directly observable, but they provide the framework of people's choices. All of the knowledge and perspective an individual acquires while growing up within a particular social group, including both formal and informal learning, is included in this component of culture. We cannot view the cognitive processes that create a value system within an individual's

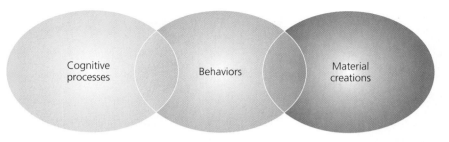

mind, but we can view the *outcome* of those processes. If honesty is a value held by a culture (or subculture or microculture), we should be able to observe members of this culture carrying out behaviors that reflect this value.

Behaviors   Human behavior can be observed and described and includes all of the things we do—ways we use our bodies, all social interactions, and all creative expressions, such as playing a musical instrument or dancing. Cultural anthropologists spend much of their time in the field observing, describing, and recording behavior. Such descriptions include daily activities as well as ceremonial events that may occur only once a year or at periodic intervals. Descriptions of behavior in a natural setting include similar execution of behaviors as well as the many individual variations that occur. Ethnographers are trained to collect and record these data using a variety of techniques. The field methods ethnographers use are discussed in Chapter 3.

Material Creations   What people create, from artifacts to features, are products of human cultural activities. Ethnographers record and describe the artifacts and features of living cultural groups, whereas archaeologists describe artifacts and features made by peoples of past cultures. Artifacts and features provide a window into the minds and cultures of the people who make them. The examination of an 18,000-year-old cave painting, a contemporary artist's sculpture, an 11,000-year-old Clovis projectile point, the intricacies of a computer chip, and the latest engineered automobile design all tell us something about the individuals and cultures that produced them.

The objects we make reflect what and how we think. We can consider an artifact, whether a current or ancient one, as a fossilized idea (Deetz 1967). For example, a Yurok basket maker has an idea conceptualized in her brain of the basket she wants to make. She proceeds to make it, drawing on all of her knowledge and experience of where and how to gather raw materials plus the procedures for manufacturing the basket. Because her knowledge and experience have been shaped by her culture, the artifact she creates will reflect that culture. She will choose raw materials and

TRY THIS
Ponder

Try to recount everything you have done today. Was it exciting? Or is most of your day made up of mundane tasks and behaviors? Focus on one specific behavior such as brushing your hair or teeth. Can you remember how you learned to do it? Did imitation play a role in your learning? Or did one person or many people teach you how to do it? Did trial and error play a role in your learning? Observe other family members doing this same behavior. Do they do it the same way you do?

Pomo   Apache

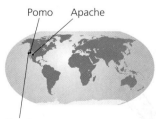

Yurok

How many attribute differences can you identify between the Apache basket (*left*) and the Pomo baskets (*right*)?

process them according to the traditions of her people, perhaps with an occasional innovation. Such traditions dictate the attributes of the finished basket. An **attribute** is a discrete feature, such as the shape of the lip of the basket, a particular design element, or the location of that design element on the basket. Clusters of attributes combine to make an artifact. Hence the idea and the culture behind it are, in effect, producing a fossilized idea.

Cultural Processes

Each definition of culture in group B (Box 2.2) includes something about the process of how culture is acquired, shared, and transmitted—in other words, how we learn it. These definitions began to appear in the 1930s and 1940s as anthropologists became increasingly interested in the *processes* of culture. Leslie White, an anthropologist who wrote extensively on this aspect of culture, pointed out that culture is learned, shared, and transmitted to future generations primarily by *symbolic systems.*

The most obvious symbolic system humans use is language—both spoken and written. It is primarily through language that we humans learn the cultural complexity that allows us to survive. Other ways of learning include observation and imitation of others, and trial and error.

White's definition also emphasizes that humans do not inherit culture genetically. This is what he meant by the phrase "extrasomatic context" in his definition. The word *soma* is derived from the Greek word that means pertaining to the body, and *extra* in this case means outside. So culture is outside of the physical body; it is not genetically inherited, though one could argue that it is dependent on having a physical body, including a complex brain. One is not born with a preference for eating peanut butter or a

attribute
A discrete characteristic of an artifact. Attributes include shape, size, design elements and their placement, and techniques of manufacture.

> ◇◇◇ **BOX 2.2** *Definitions of Culture: Group B* ◇◇◇
>
> *We define culture as that class of things and events dependent upon symboling, products of symboling, considered in an extrasomatic context.* (White 1959: 234; White and Dillingham 1973: 29)
>
> *Culture consists of patterns, explicit and implicit, of and for behavior acquired and transmitted by symbols, constituting the distinctive achievement of human groups, including their embodiment in artifacts; [historically derived and selected] ideas and especially their attached values.* (Kroeber and Kluckhohn 1952: 181)
>
> *The culture of any society consists of the sum total of the ideas, conditioned emotional responses, and patterns of habitual behavior which the members of that society have acquired through instruction or imitation and which they share to a greater or less degree.* (Linton 1936: 288)

belief in a particular deity. You learn what foods to eat because they are the foods that are traditional and available in the environment of your culture. You learn about your god from your parents and other adults in your social group. You are taught how many husbands or wives you should have at one time.

A recent student of mine was born in Korea, of Korean parents, and adopted as an infant by an American couple of European ancestry. She grew up speaking English and behaving and thinking as an American person, including all her gestures, facial expressions, prejudices, and values. Anthropologists use the term **enculturation** to describe the process of learning one's culture while growing up in it. To become enculturated is to become a member of your culture in all respects.

When an entire society consists of sixty individuals, about the size of many foraging band societies, most individuals do in fact share most values and exhibit most shared behaviors. This is because members of the culture interact with one another on a daily basis and thus reinforce values and behaviors. Individuals who deviate from the usual, shared way of doing things suffer ridicule and humiliation. Such sanctions are effective in returning the offender to the acceptable pattern of behavior. Small cultural groups such as this are called **homogeneous cultures** because most ideas, values, knowledge, behavior, and artifacts are shared by most individuals. In larger cultures, often referred to as **heterogeneous cultures,** there are fewer shared components. In a large, complex heterogeneous culture like the United States, shared components might be citizenship, liberty to pursue the American dream, and sharing the same governmental system.

> ❋ TRY THIS ❋
> *Consider*
>
> What is one behavior or value that is part of your culture? Do you personally behave in this way or live by this value? Can you think of a behavior or value that is part of your culture that you personally do not conform to?

enculturation
The process of learning one's culture while growing up in it.

homogeneous culture
Cultural group that shares most ideas, values, knowledge, behaviors, and artifacts. Typical of small cultural groups such as foragers.

heterogeneous culture
Cultural group that shares only a few components. Typical of large societies such as states, where there are many subcultures such as ethnic groups.

> ◈◈ **BOX 2.3** *Definitions of Culture: Group C* ◈◈
>
> *Culture is best seen not as complexes of concrete behavior patterns—customs, usages, traditions, habit clusters—as has, by and large, been the case up to now, but as a set of control mechanisms—plans, recipes, rules, instructions (what computer engineers call "programs")—for the governing of behavior.* (Geertz 1973: 44)
>
> *The culture concept . . . denotes an historically transmitted pattern of meanings embodied in symbols, a system of inherited conceptions expressed in symbolic forms by means of which men communicate, perpetuate, and develop their knowledge about and attitudes toward life.* (Geertz 1973: 89)
>
> *A system of shared beliefs, values, customs, behaviors, and artifacts that the members of a society use to cope with one another and with their world and that are transmitted from generation to generation through learning.* (Bates and Plog 1990: 466)
>
> *Culture: the ideals, values, and beliefs members of a society share to interpret experience and generate behavior and that are reflected by their behavior.* (Haviland 1999: 36)

Blueprints

More recently, definitions of culture have focused on how it supplies a blueprint for behavior and the values that shape behavior (see Box 2.3). Culture supplies meanings, understandings, and ideas and is transmitted symbolically. Clifford Geertz, using a computer analogy, says that culture supplies *programs* for guiding people's behavior (1973). Ward Goodenough has written that "culture, then, consists of standards for deciding what is, standards for what can be, standards for deciding how one feels about it, standards for deciding what to do about it, and standards for deciding how to go about doing it" (Goodenough 1963: 258–59). Decades of ethnographic work have shown that there is enormous variation within any culture, and yet the blueprints, or programs, for behaviors are enculturated within a particular social group so that adult members share the same basic standards. Figure 2.2 shows how all the different definitions of culture work together to describe this complex concept.

Additional Features of Culture

Culture Is Shared   A social group shares *among* its members most of what constitutes its culture. This is a point that would stimulate lively discussion among a group of anthropologists. The notion of culture being shared is often a difficult property to articulate and is also an aspect of the

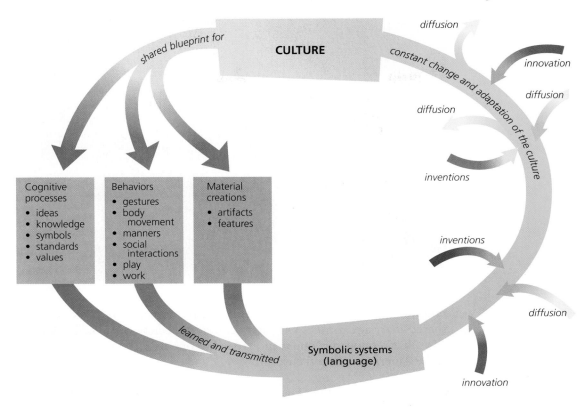

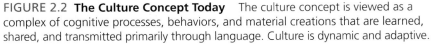

FIGURE 2.2 **The Culture Concept Today**   The culture concept is viewed as a complex of cognitive processes, behaviors, and material creations that are learned, shared, and transmitted primarily through language. Culture is dynamic and adaptive.

concept that seems to give new students of anthropology some difficulty. How much of culture is shared? If 51 percent of the people share a behavior, is this enough for it to be considered a behavior of that culture? Should the requirement be that 65 percent of the people exhibit the behavior, or should it be 95 percent? And what if an individual exhibits the shared behavior or value on some occasions and not on others?

That the knowledge, behavior, value system, or other part of culture is shared by *most* individuals in the culture seems to be the standard applied by the majority of anthropologists. The shared nature of culture is implied in most definitions of culture, even when not directly stated. A member of a culture will recognize and be able to articulate a specific element of her culture *even if* that individual does not herself hold her culture's attitude or exhibit a specific behavior. For example, a North American man who has two wives (one in San Francisco and one in New York City) is not practicing the form of marriage dictated by the laws of the United States

Examine this California house. What features does it share with houses in your North American neighborhood?

nor the religious standards of Christianity. If this man were asked what the shared marriage form is in North American society, he would acknowledge that monogamy, one man married to one woman at any given time, is the American cultural custom.

Culture Is Cumulative, Dynamic, Adaptive, and Diverse   Anthropologists' observation that culture is cumulative is amply supported by the data of the archaeological and historical records. Discoveries—be they technological or ideological—are stored by language so that a culture builds through time. A culture adapts in response to its environment. The changing environment may be the result of alterations in the weather, such as a drought. Or it may be a change involving territorial infringement by a neighboring cultural group. To survive, the culture must respond by adapting to the change, accommodating it in some manner. Sometimes these changes are slow and go almost unnoticed; at other times the changes are quick and dramatic.

Culture is constantly changing. It changes internally through the fickleness of popular fads—the latest music, foods, slang, clothing fashions. It changes internally through **innovations** and **inventions**—new ideas and combinations of old ideas to create new things. Culture changes because of external influences through a process of **diffusion,** or the voluntary borrowing of items and ideas from other cultures. Most aspects of any contemporary culture have diffused from other cultures.

Consider what you know about how adaptive and diverse culture is. People eat everything from fungus to flowers to fowl to fettuccine. Make your own list of foods based on what you have read and seen in films or on

innovation
Something totally new.

invention
Something new that is created based on items or ideas that already exist.

diffusion
The borrowing and exchange of items or ideas between cultures.

These Spanish children participate in a traditional village Saints' Day festival. Everyone in the village shares the knowledge of this festival even if they do not participate in it.

the Internet. Inuit peoples of northern Canada learned to hunt seals through the ice and ate the raw meat, blubber, organs, and blood. Many Americans, especially those in California, have learned to eat the immature flower of the artichoke plant. Human cultures have adapted to a vast number of environmental conditions.

As noted previously, no culture or subculture is a tidy package in which everyone shares all knowledge, behaviors, or artifacts. Within a specific culture or subculture there is variation. During the time I lived in Spain, I became aware of the many differences among the various geographic regions of the country. Yet all who lived in those regions considered themselves Spaniards. My Guatemalan students from the cities consider themselves quite separate from rural Guatemalans. Rural farming communities in the United States are made up of people who share clusters of behaviors, values, knowledge, artifacts, and cognitive rules that govern their behaviors and values. These are different from the clusters of these features found in an inner city. Even within both the farm community and the inner city, there are many variations and many subcultural clusters along with the shared features.

TRY THIS
Analyze

Select three aspects of your culture: one tool that you use, one belief that you hold, and one behavior that you demonstrate. Research the origin of the tool, belief, and behavior to see if you can determine where they originated.

Compare your list with that of a classmate. Hint: a dictionary or encyclopedia or the World Wide Web are good starting points for your research.

Culture Is Integrated All of the parts of a culture are intermingled. This integrated nature of culture creates a pattern, and it is this pattern that an anthropologist endeavors to describe and explain. Cultural patterns typically reflect ecological and other adaptations that have occurred over time. Sea goddesses are worshipped by people who live near the sea, and the technology of such a society reflects knowledge of the sea and its resources. A society of desert dwellers has a different pattern of integrated parts—economic systems, technological systems, ideological systems, kinship

A recent Hmong New Year's celebration in Fresno, California. Members of this ethnic group will recognize the features of the traditional clothing worn by these girls.

TRY THIS
Discuss

Discuss the value of honesty with a classmate. Identify three specific ways that Americans (who share the cultural value of being honest) actually behave dishonestly.

ideal culture
What people believe they should do.

real culture
What people can be observed to do.

systems, political systems—each of which contributes to the cultural whole. This model has justifiably come under criticism. A culture isn't a tidy integrated whole. If it were, then it would be static. But cultures, in fact, are constantly changing. There are, however, clusters and patterns that at any given time uniquely identify a specific culture.

◎ IDEAL CULTURE AND REAL CULTURE

Anthropologists think in terms of **ideal culture** and **real culture.** Ideal culture consists of what people believe they *should do,* such as brushing their teeth after every meal or being honest, whereas real (or actual) culture is what people can be observed doing. In the case of brushing teeth, as you know, most of us are doing well if we brush twice a day. Here, there is a gap between ideal and real behavior. Brushing your teeth is also an example of an explicit cultural behavior, related to body hygiene, that can be directly observed. Honesty is a cultural value that can also be used to illustrate the dichotomy between the ideal and the actual. An objective

ANTHROPOLOGY AROUND US

Cute Protein

It is easy to identify ethnocentrism when it comes to food preferences. On moral grounds we consider what *we* eat to be correct food to eat. We base this not on nutritional evidence but on cultural custom. Most North Americans don't eat what a recent news article called *cute* protein—puppies, cats, bunny rabbits, and monkey. We don't eat certain protein on moral grounds—horse, whale, and porpoise. In the 1998 General Election, California passed a state law forbidding the sale of horsemeat as food for humans. The city of San Francisco recently passed an ordinance against the selling of dogs for consumption. Never mind that some recent immigrant populations include dog or horse on their traditional menus. Legislation is pending before the 109th Congress (2005–2006) on a bill that will effectively bar the sale of horsemeat overseas for human consumption.

Marvin Harris disagrees with the arguments explaining what we eat on its appearance or on moral issues. He notes that chicken, pigs, and cows

are *efficient* sources of protein production compared to cats and dogs. This, in his view, is the reason to eliminate cats and dogs from our diet, not because they are cute pets (Harris 1998: 198).

◎ **What do you think? Is the eating of certain animals and not others a practical or moral issue? Why?**

anthropologist would find that Americans value honesty but do not always practice it. In a fieldwork situation, the anthropologist attempts to balance what people say with what they can be observed doing. So this distinction—ideal versus real—is very useful.

◎ SUBCULTURES AND ETHNIC GROUPS

Subcultures

Smaller groups within a larger cultural complex are called **subcultures.** These groups share behaviors, values, attitudes, and artifacts among their members. For example, college students constitute a subculture. The term **microculture** is sometimes used to denote even smaller groups in which values, behaviors, attitudes, and artifacts are shared. International students on a college campus would constitute a microculture. The terms *subculture* and *microculture* are often imprecise and are sometimes used interchangeably. The only real agreement seems to be that these are units that share

subculture
Smaller group within a large cultural complex. Behaviors, values, attitudes, and artifacts are shared by group members.

microculture
The smallest subgroup within a culture that shares specific cultural features such as values or behaviors.

TRY THIS ✿
Analyze

You are enrolled in an anthropology class and are therefore a member of the student subculture. Quickly list the artifacts, values, and behaviors that you share with other members of this subculture and that, taken together, are not part of the larger North American culture. Compare your list with that of a classmate.

certain aspects and that they are part of a larger cultural group. Figure 2.3 is one representation of the interrelationships of culture, subcultures, and microcultures. The abstract idea of culture is often referred to as culture with a capital letter *C*. A specific culture, subculture, or microculture is referred to with a lowercase *c*.

Ethnic Groups

People who live in large heterogeneous cultures usually belong to several subcultures. Some of these subcultures share common languages or linguistic features not shared by all members of the larger culture. Members of subcultures may also share behaviors, beliefs, values, attitudes, and artifacts that are not shared by the rest of the population of the larger culture. One type of subculture is popularly called an ethnic group. **Ethnic groups** are subcultures that are characterized by members sharing a particular culture of origin, often one from another country. The language of the country of origin, rather than the official language of the adopted country, is often the primary language spoken in the homes of these subcultural groups. Ethnic group subcultures are often confused with race because popular perceptions are that an ethnic group consists of people of the same skin color and thus represents a biological group.

◎ RACE

OLC
mhhe•com/lenkeit3

See Internet exercises.

ethnic group
A type of subculture characterized by members sharing a culture of origin, often one originating in another country.

race
Biologically: a group within a species that shares a cluster of genetically determined traits. No such trait clusters occur among *Homo sapiens*. Culturally: a social construct based on perceived cultural differences.

Humans have spent an extraordinary amount of energy, ink, and paper on the issues associated with human race. Exactly what is a human race? Do human races really exist, and, if so, how many races are there? Or is race, as one biological anthropologist puts it, "at best . . . just another four-letter word, empty of any biological significance" (Brace 2000b: 321)? A biological **race** is a segment of a species that is distinguishable from other segments based on a cluster of distinct biological traits. The view of the majority of biological anthropologists today is that human biological races do not exist and that this term should be abandoned. Yet the term *race* persists, and many people believe that races are real, definable biological entities. After all, people do look different, don't they? And aren't physical features determined by genetics? On one level, the answer to these questions is yes, but these two issues are typically oversimplified.

Anthropology is in a unique position to shed light on issues of race because of the holistic nature of the discipline. Recall the earlier statement that the culture concept is important in studies of biological anthropology because culture is the primary adaptive mechanism of our species. Conversely, biology has influence on human culture. Both biology and culture influence the physical appearance of human bodies; and the more sophisticated that science becomes, the more we understand the interrelationship.

Prior to the compilation of an extensive database in comparative anatomy, physiology, and genetics, anthropologists tried to classify varieties of people. A race was viewed as a subspecies, and human races were based on physical features, geographic areas, and other criteria, even perceived personality traits. As data accumulated during the twentieth century, it became clear that there is only one species of *Homo sapiens* and no living subspecies. No group of humans has a *cluster* of genetic traits that separates it from other groups.

The scientific reality of human diversity is complex. To prepare the proper mind-set for considering this issue, think about the following two historical examples as analogous to the way that most people view race today. The history of science records a time when people believed that the world was flat because it *looked* flat when one stood and looked out at the horizon. And before Copernicus provided both the hypothesis and the data to prove that the earth revolved around the sun, people believed the opposite, that the sun rose in the east, moved overhead, set in the west, circled behind the earth, and rose again the next morning in the east. We can *see* the sun progress across the sky from dawn to dusk. It appears each morning on the horizon opposite the one where it set. Therefore, it must circle behind the earth during the night. Races, it is argued, must exist because people look different from other groups. Or is it that we *perceive* differences, and are these perceptions enculturated and reinforced by our social group?

Human Biological Variation: Clines and Plasticity

Three features of the evolution of *Homo sapiens* point to humans belonging to one species with no biological subspecies or races. First, clinal variations in many traits have been documented. Biologists use the term **cline** to describe the variation of a particular trait along a geographic continuum. These are results of natural selection that fine-tuned and adapted human biological features to a variety of microenvironments. Second, the malleability of many traits has been demonstrated. The term **plasticity** is used in biological anthropology to describe biological traits being malleable, or pliable. Genes code for the potential of trait development, but the environment in which growth occurs affects the manifestation of this genetic potential. In other words, the traits show plasticity. Third, culture created circumstances that altered human evolution in many ways over the course of human development: Clothing and fire replaced fur for warmth, and tools took the place of teeth in food procurement and defense. Because this is an introductory cultural anthropology text, the following discussion only touches on the vast body of data that relate to the topic of human variation and support the idea that biological races do not exist in our species. This discussion gives you a sample of the data to support the statement that there are no biological human races. I am going to get a bit technical

cline
The variation of a biological trait along a geographic continuum. Human skin pigments show distribution along a cline from the equator north and south.

plasticity
The pliability or malleability of a biological feature. An individual's genetic growth potential is malleable depending on nutrition, maternal health, and exposure to sunlight.

here because I want you to see the type of data that biological anthropologists have researched.

Skin Color Clines   Human skin color is an example of a cline — it shows gradual change over large geographical areas. Most peoples do not have personal experiences that allow them to see the realities of world cline variations. North Americans, for example, had limited contact with diverse world populations until recently. A person with dark skin pigmentation was identified as African because North Americans had seen only West African peoples (the sources of the slave trade of the eighteenth and nineteenth centuries), whose skins were dark. But the African continent consisted, during aboriginal times as it does today, of tremendous diversity in skin pigmentation, ranging from people with lighter skin in the northeast to very dark skin in Central Africa and lighter pigmented skin again in the south. Most North Americans were simply ignorant of this variation as well as the existence of the very dark skinned peoples in India, New Guinea, western Australia, and Melanesia.

Skin color depends on the amount of **melanin** (a pigment) distributed in our skin. The amount of melanin depends on the rate at which it is synthesized in specialized cells located in the lowest level of our skin (Molnar 2002: 222–23). Complex processes are involved in the synthesis of this pigment. Melanin blocks the penetration of **UVB** light (B-range **ultraviolet radiation**) to the bottom layers of skin cells. UVB damage at the underlying cell layers leads to skin cancers on the surface of the skin. Skin with little melanin allows the penetration of UVB. Dark natural pigment or well-tanned skin blocks up to 95 percent of UVB (Brace 2000b: 297). Several hypotheses can explain how natural selection may have worked to produce variation in the rate of melanin synthesis. I'll discuss only two of these hypotheses but encourage you to read further on this entire subject. The suggested readings at the end of the chapter will give you a good place to begin.

The vitamin D hypothesis. The exposure of human skin to ultraviolet radiation from the sun is important for healthy bone development. The outer layers of skin synthesize vitamin D_3. Studies have demonstrated that vitamin D_3 formed by direct skin exposure to ultraviolet radiation is the most important form of the vitamin and that the dietary form of the vitamin (D_2) does not precisely duplicate it (Bogin 1988: 141). Vitamin D aids the intestines in the absorption of calcium and in other physiological reactions associated with healthy bone development (Bogin 1988, Brace 2000b). Vitamin D is essential to growth and development, but too much of this vitamin can be toxic (Molnar 2002: 234). Dark skin guards against too much ultraviolet radiation reaching the lower layers of the skin, thus protecting peoples near the equator from vitamin D toxicity by reducing the skin's synthesis of vitamin D, while at the same time producing enough of the vitamin for health. Near the equator then, natural selection favored

melanin
A pigment in the outer layer of the skin. It is responsible for skin color and blocks UVB from damaging lower layers of the skin.

UVB
Ultraviolet radiation from the sun in the B wavelength.

ultraviolet radiation
A part of the electromagnetic energy from the sun that is not visible to the human eye.

individuals with dark skin; they lived longer and produced more children than individuals with pale skin.

The vitamin D hypothesis also explains the distribution of populations with less skin pigment. Peoples with the lightest skin pigments are found in northern and southern latitudes far away from the equator. In human evolutionary history, as populations moved farther away from equatorial zones, natural selection favored individuals with less skin melanin. They survived longer and produced more offspring than did individuals with more pigment because light skin is more efficient than darkly pigmented skin in synthesizing vitamin D. This ultimately resulted in some populations with almost no melanin, such as those in Norway and Finland.

Culture allowed humans to survive in latitudes to which they were not biologically adapted. People created clothing, built shelters, and made fires to keep warm. Clothing covered most of our skin surface, thus limiting the amount of ultraviolet radiation hitting the skin. In northern latitudes, individuals who had dark skin and who wore clothing were at risk of not getting enough vitamin D to ensure the healthy growth and development of the skeleton. Diets rich in fish oils, and the cultural practice of putting bundled up infants out in a sheltered spot in the sun (where faces were exposed to ultraviolet radiation), appear to be cultural adaptations that contributed to healthy bone development in these northern populations. Even though such populations did not know about the importance of vitamin D, people made some cause-and-effect connections between health and survival of infants who received such treatment. Such behaviors then became part of the folk traditions of these peoples.

The folate hypothesis. This hypothesis suggests that the evolution of dark skin in equatorial regions was related to the metabolite folate. **Folate** is essential for the production of healthy sperm and the development of the neural tube in embryos. UVB can destroy folate. Dark pigmentation, it is argued in this hypothesis, was selected for in individuals because it protects against the UVB destruction of folate. Thus individuals with more darkly pigmented skin produced healthy offspring (Jablonski and Chaplin 1999).

Studies since the 1950s confirm that skin colors are adaptive, though we can't prove precisely which hypothesis is the correct explanation for this evolutionary adaptation. It may be that elements of each of these and other hypotheses are responsible for the distribution of human skin color. To further complicate matters, what seem to be anomalies exist in skin color distribution. The native peoples of Alaska and Canada, for example, don't seem to "fit" with the explanation of selection for lighter skin as populations moved away from the equator. For help in explaining these apparent discrepancies, we can turn to the archaeological record and historical linguistics—the holistic approach again. Data from these anthropological subfields demonstrate that populations such as the native populations of

folate
A metabolite essential for sperm and embryonic neural tube development that is destroyed by UVB.

Alaska moved *recently* to these latitudes—recent in terms of earth history, about twelve thousand years ago. They have not been in the extreme northern latitudes long enough for natural selection to show a decrease in pigmentation (Brace 2000b: 301). The ancestors of peoples in the Nordic countries of Finland and Norway, by comparison, have lived there for at least six hundred thousand years, and perhaps longer.

Stature and Plasticity   Biological plasticity means that traits determined by genes (in other words, coded by DNA) are influenced in the way they develop and grow. The degree to which a human grows to his or her full genetically coded height depends on factors such as nutrition during early years of life and the mother's health history. Poor nourishment or disease during the mother's growing years results in her having smaller stature, body size, and a smaller reproductive system. To state it another way, her body's ability to pass nutrients on to her fetus is compromised. A mother with this history gives birth to a baby of low birth weight, and data show that this child tends to grow slowly, reaching a shorter adult height than a well-nourished child of a healthy, well-nourished mother (Bogin 1998). Thus the child's adult height is not a direct reflection of his or her full genetic potential.

Developmental research comparing the skeletal growth of wild and captive chimps documents a slower pattern of growth in the wild populations. This suggests that nutrition affects the plasticity of skeletal development in our close primate relative as well (Zihlman, Bolter, and Boesch 2004).

Human growth rates are affected by exposure to light as well as nutrition. Research in Guatemala and Africa demonstrated that the growth rate of healthy children was more rapid during the months of the year when there was the most direct exposure to sunshine (i.e., with no clouds or haze blocking the sun) (Bogin 1988: 141).

People from populations with low socioeconomic resources and poor nutrition show height increases when they emigrate to more affluent countries, find work, and provide better lives for their children. Cultural assistance programs such as school breakfast and lunch programs, and prenatal care, plus the consumption of treated drinking water result in better health. Data on Mayan refugees from Guatemala, now living in Los Angeles, California, show an average height increase of 2.2 inches in one generation (Bogin 1998).

The demonstration of the adaptation and plasticity of human traits requires us to acknowledge that using any *biological traits* as a basis for classifying human groups is useless. Biological adaptation is a process that has been ongoing since the emergence of our first ancestors millions of years ago. It continues today. A comprehensive look at the DNA of modern humans shows that greater variation exists *within geographic areas and ethnic groups than between such groups.*

Race as a Social Construct

Culture, not biology, is the primary adaptive mechanism of humans, and it has been for a very long time. We were, and are, able to alter our environments and to create artifacts and behaviors that allow us to survive in new and different places. People moved about, married, had children, moved again, and their children did the same. This resulted in the reshuffling of genetic material and changes in material culture, behaviors, values, and beliefs through diffusion. Shifts in cultural identity and appearance occurred over and over again.

We compare others to ourselves. The process of distinguishing between *us* and *them* leads to classifying *others* into groups. These groups are based on differences we perceive or myths we have heard. Our perceptions are based primarily on the cultural traditions of others—their behaviors, religion, values, dress, hairstyles, as well as their geographic origin (or the geographic origin of their ancestors). We create categories of people based on all of these traditions. But these are *not* categories with a biological basis. Rather they represent customs and behaviors of others. Such categories are more correctly identified as *social constructs*. They are culturally based classifications.

OLC
mhhe•com/lenkeit3
See Internet exercises.

◎ CULTURE IN THE SUBFIELDS OF ANTHROPOLOGY

Since one of the hallmarks of anthropology is that it is holistic (discussed in Chapter 1), this is an appropriate place to show how the subfields of anthropology use the culture concept. Even when anthropologists are carrying out specialized research, the culture concept helps us to retain the holistic perspective (Figure 2.3).

Cultural anthropologists study the various dimensions of culture by describing and analyzing living cultures, subcultures, and microcultures. The dimensions of culture studied include, but are not limited to, language, family, kinship, gender, social organization, technology, economics, political structure, law, treatment of disease, play, myth, religion, body decorations, art, and music. Think about your own life and experiences. Every segment of your life has been influenced by the culture of your birth.

Archaeologists also study culture. The primary goals of archaeology are to reconstruct the lifeways of peoples of the past and to understand as much as possible about how their cultures interacted with the natural environment and other cultures. An understanding of the processes of living cultures is critical to archaeologists as they go about interpreting the human cultural past. Analogy with the present is a primary tool used by archaeologists to reconstruct how peoples lived in the prehistoric past. For example, an arrowhead from a prehistoric site is interpreted as an arrowhead in

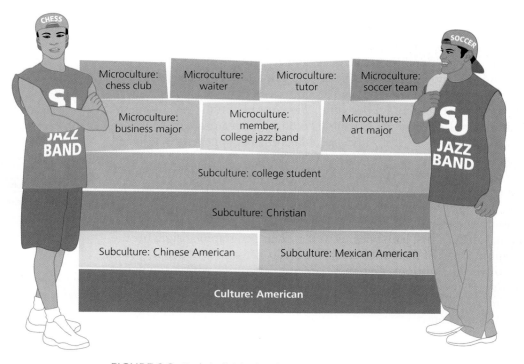

FIGURE 2.3 Each individual within large heterogeneous cultures may also belong to numerous subcultures and microcultures. Each subculture and microculture is shared with others. What artifacts, values, and behaviors would these two individuals share with each other?

large part because living people use them in this way. Although most archaeologists point out that caution must be exercised when using analogous arguments, they also acknowledge that the use of cultural analogies is an important tool for reconstructing the past.

Linguistic anthropologists study the unique symbolic communicative process of *Homo sapiens*, language. Culture depends upon language. We share and transmit the components of culture by using language. Linguistic variations occur within cultures and subcultures and between people of different status and gender. Linguistic anthropologists investigate and describe these variations in language and language usage.

Biological anthropologists recognize that culture has been a primary adaptive mechanism for humans in the past. It was not how fast our ancestors ran or how big their teeth were that determined their survival. Rather, it was their flexibility in adapting behaviorally to their environment and their ability to transmit the skills they learned to future generations that made them successful. We humans can adjust to our environments and change our environments by using our cultural heritage. We can build shelters, make fires, and put on clothing in cold environments to which we are not biologically suited; we can transform deserts by importing water, and we can survive droughts by building dams and reservoirs.

Biological anthropologists must keep human cultural adaptation in mind as they study the fossil remains of our ancestors, genetic variation in contemporary human populations, and contemporary diseases. Human biology has been influenced by culture. Early in human evolution, natural selection favored people with large incisor teeth. Incisor teeth were used as tools, and the members of society that had big incisors survived longer and thus were able to reproduce more and pass along the genes for big teeth. The fossil record shows a reduction in incisors beginning around one hundred thousand years ago (Brace 1995: 215). This reduction corresponds with the appearance of many types of sharp-edged tools in the archaeological record. In terms of natural selection we would hypothesize that with a reduction in selective pressures for big incisors, more people with smaller incisors survived and thus reproduced as often as did individuals with big teeth. This led after a time to a population with smaller incisors than in the past.

◎ CHALLENGES TO THE CULTURE CONCEPT

For some time now, a faction within cultural anthropology has been challenging the concept of culture. Advocates of this view believe that the concept is oversimplified and is too rigid. Moreover, they contend that it is a concept that does not reflect reality. These critics point out that culture is not homogeneous and uniformly shared, nor is it static and unchanging, nor is it a neatly packaged and integrated whole. It is my view that such criticisms are not new and that they focus on issues that most anthropologists have, in practice, acknowledged for decades. It has also been my experience that students recognize that all behaviors, thoughts, and material objects are not uniformly shared by everyone within a social group, that there is much variation, and that cultural change is continuous. I have reflected this position in my discussion of the concept.

Variations in culture—both through time and at a single point in time—cause complexity for those who try to describe the concept of culture. Christoph Brumann sifts through insights about the culture concept in his 1999 article "Writing for Culture," which appeared in the journal *Current Anthropology*. Several of his points need to be emphasized. First, culture is transmitted over time. This should be viewed as a complex process that is not exact. Many factors affect enculturation, and the transmission of a culture may be altered accordingly. Second, there are many variants within each culture, subculture, or microculture. An individual member of a culture may at any time make different choices from those made at another time. Third, the larger the group encompassed by the application of the term *culture*, the fewer the shared cluster of elements. These may be trivial things such as knowing of and consuming a particular soft drink or admiring and recognizing a particular musical artist (Brumann 1999).

Even with this complexity, Brumann argues that culture is a useful concept that we should keep, in part because "there is no denying that many ordinary people have grasped at least part of anthropology's message: culture is there, it is learned, it permeates all of everyday life, it is important, and it is far more responsible for differences among human groups than genes" (Brumann 1999: 12). To reiterate the theme of this chapter, your culture is what makes you a stranger when you are away from home. Everyone who has experienced living in another cultural environment will recognize that this is true. Finally, culture is a valid, if complex, concept.

SUMMARY

Culture is a concept that is used in each of the four fields of anthropology. Culture is an abstraction, a concept that refers to the sum total of the learned and shared knowledge, ideas, values, behaviors, and material items of a group of humans. It is learned largely through the symbolic system of language. A culture varies internally and is in a continual state of change. It is acquired through a process called enculturation and includes ideal and real elements. Ethnic groups and other subcultures make up the large complex heterogeneous cultures of much of the modern world. The members of a large heterogeneous culture share with one another fewer aspects of their culture than is the case in small homogeneous cultures, where everyone shares many more elements.

Ethnic groups and other subcultures are often confused with race. Biological anthropology demonstrates that our species cannot be divided into biological races because there is too much variation in traits. Additionally, culture influences human biology. Race is a social construct.

Study Questions

OLC
mhhe•com/lenkeit3

See Self Quiz.

1. Explain the anthropological concept of culture. Support your discussion with examples from your own experiences.

2. Discuss how an understanding of the concept of culture can be useful when one is engaged in international business or travel. Cite specific examples from other assigned course readings.

3. "Your culture is what makes you a stranger when you are away from home." Discuss this statement with reference to an assigned reading or your own personal experience. Select two specific components of the culture concept and relate them to this statement and the other reading or your experience.

4. Why do anthropologists argue that race is a social construct and that there are no biological races in the human species?

Suggested Readings

Brace, C. Loring. 2005. *"Race" Is a Four-Letter Word: The Genesis of the Concept.* New York: Oxford University Press. Exceptional historical overviews of the concept with emphasis on cultural and historical events of the past five hundred years that shape the scientific analysis of the concept.

Brumann, Cristoph. 1999. Writing for Culture. *Current Anthropology* 40 suppl. (February). A good overview of the history and current attitudes about the culture concept.

Gould, Stephen J. 1996. *The Mismeasure of Man.* New York: Norton. A very accessible account of how nineteenth- and twentieth-century biological research on human variability was influenced by prevailing social attitudes.

Kroeber, A. L., and C. Kluckhohn. 1963. *Culture: A Critical Review of Concepts and Definitions.* New York: Vintage. A review of over one hundred definitions of culture. Reissued 2001 by Greenwood Press, Westport, Conn.

Kuper, Adam. 1999. *Culture: The Anthropologists' Account.* Cambridge: Harvard University Press. A history and critique of the concept of culture in American anthropology.

Molnar, Stephen. 2002. *Human Variation: Races, Types, and Ethnic Groups,* 5th ed. Upper Saddle River, N.J.: Prentice-Hall. Very readable, clear, and succinct presentation of data on human biological diversity. Demonstrates the fallacy of the race concept.

Suggested Web Sites

http://www.indiana.edu/~wanthro/theory.htm
This easy-to-navigate site emerged out of a graduate anthropology seminar at Indiana University that summarizes the theoretical changes in specific facets of anthropology since the 1970s.

OLC
mhhe•com/lenkeit3
See Web links.

http://www.mnsu.edu/emuseum/information/biography/index.shtml
This site provides biographical information on over five hundred prominent anthropologists (and scientists from other disciplines) who have influenced the growth of anthropology since the nineteenth century. It was created and is maintained by the anthropology students at Minnesota State University (Mankato).

http://www.wsu.edu/gened/learn-modules/top_culture
Created by Eric Miraglia (Washington State University, Pullman) several years ago, this site offers an excellent overview of the culture concept, from basic to more theoretical perspectives offered by historical and contemporary scholars.

http://anthropology.tamu.edu/news.htm
This is the best single source for anthropological topics in the mass media. Maintained by the anthropology department at Texas A&M University, the site has weekly updates.

3

Fieldwork
How Are Data Gathered?

On our first evening in the small community in Spain, my family made our first contact with the locals by using string figures, a very old form of entertainment. One needs only a bit of string and a good story to tell, so it is a perfect game for travelers with limited luggage. At the end of a *paseo* (stroll) we sat on a bench in the plaza and did the string figures with our daughter, Karen, age nine. We have been enjoying the art of string figure making for many years, and our daughter always had string with her. Soon several community children joined us. They casually corrected our Spanish accents as we chatted and taught them several figures. The next evening these children brought friends. One young boy, Pablo, age nine, was accompanied by his grandfather. The grandfather taught us a figure he had learned as a boy. Soon more of the children were joining in our evening string figure sessions. Pablo is now a university student. He and his family became some of our best sources of information during our stay. They have also become special friends over the years. Karen and Pablo now correspond on the Internet, which shows how good global relationships may be built with a little string and cross-cultural openness and understanding.

Fieldwork. The very idea creates images of romantic adventure in exotic places. Reality is often another experience altogether. Homesickness and physical ills such as dysentery may be the more persistent experiences at first. Still, learning about another culture by participating in the society for extended periods of time yields a quality of information and perspective not available by other means. The difficulties and challenges encountered in the field usually dissipate with time as one acquires a working knowledge and understanding of the society's culture.

The society whose culture is under study may consist of workers on a shop floor assembly line in a North American manufacturing company, the people of a tribal village in Indonesia, or an urban neighborhood in Johannesburg, South Africa. In other words, anthropological fieldwork can involve the study of the microcultures or subcultures of contemporary urban societies as well as the cultures of traditional folk societies.

You will recall from Chapter 1 that the gathering of data in a natural, or "field," setting is also carried out by researchers in the other disciplines of anthropology. All anthropologists who gather their data in the field, whether they are sociocultural anthropologists, archaeologists, linguists, or biological anthropologists, usually participate in a cultural setting distinct from their own; each will encounter some of the same issues and difficulties associated with ethnographic data gathering, and all are schooled in the basics of its techniques (as a part of their holistic training in anthropology). A colleague who is a biological anthropologist emphasized this point as she recounted her fieldwork experiences in Bolivia. Her work involved gathering spit (saliva) for DNA studies of lactation. She found that time spent in establishing rapport with the local women resulted in high levels of cooperation in the study.

Fieldwork is exciting and challenging. My family still talks about how much fun it was to share string figures that first evening in Spain. Of course successful fieldwork involves much more than having fun. This chapter explores the processes and issues involved in doing ethnography.

The objectives of this chapter are to

- ◆ Explain the background preparations for doing ethnographic fieldwork
- ◆ Describe the ethical standards that govern the fieldworker
- ◆ Describe the methods employed by fieldworkers and the problems associated with each method
- ◆ Discuss some of the challenges associated with fieldwork

◀ Anthropologist Robert Bailey is interacting with a member of the Ngali Ngali of the Ituri forest in Africa.

◎ PREPARING FOR THE FIELD

OLC
mhhe•com/lenkeit3

See chapter outline and chapter overview.

The anthropologist setting off into a field situation carries a virtual tool box containing such basic methodological implements as cultural relativism, the culture concept, the holistic perspective, and the comparative method. The researcher will have honed these concepts and approaches while earning an undergraduate degree and completing two to four years of graduate work prior to undertaking major ethnographic research. During this time she will have studied, discussed, and debated these ideas along with the theories, data, and fieldwork of other anthropologists. She will also have thoroughly examined the ethical standards set by the discipline of anthropology.

Ethics

Anthropologists are very concerned with ethical issues associated with fieldwork. Researchers and teachers belong to many different cultures, subcultures, and microcultures, and within each of these groups we have moral and ethical obligations. We also have ethical obligations to our communities and society at large as well as to the discipline of anthropology. Most of all we have responsibilities to the peoples whose lives we study. The American Anthropological Association (AAA or "triple A" as the members usually call it) represents all subfields of the discipline and developed its code of ethics with the purpose of providing "guidelines for making ethical choices" to those doing fieldwork in anthropology: "Because anthropologists can find themselves in complex situations and subject to more than one code of ethics, the AAA Code of Ethics provides a framework, not an ironclad formula, for making decisions" (from the Code of Ethics of the AAA, approved June 1998).

OLC
mhhe•com/lenkeit3

See Internet exercises.

The primary ethical responsibility for cultural anthropologists is toward the people with whom they work. The code of ethics requires that researchers must always be open about the purpose of their projects; they must never misrepresent themselves to their informants. They must fully inform everyone involved about the potential impact of their projects and do everything possible to ensure that no one is harmed physically or psychologically in any way. They must be open about the sources of funding and support for the project.

The full text of the code of ethics is available at the AAA Web site (see Suggested Web Sites at the end of the chapter). Also at this site are excerpts from the *Handbook on Ethical Issues in Anthropology*, special publication number 23 of the AAA, which contains sections on specific ethical cases and their solutions, such as "Robbers, Rogues, or Revolutionaries: Handling Armed Intimidation," "Hiding a Suspect," or "The Case of the

Falsified Data." Ethical considerations have the highest priority among anthropologists and are a major part of training prior to field research.

Theoretical Models

Each anthropologist has likely found a particular theoretical platform from which to launch her or his field effort. A theoretical position serves as a framework to generate working hypotheses that will explain various aspects of the culture being studied—cognitive issues, behaviors, or material elements of culture. Remember that one of the most important foundations of the scientific method is its ability to correct itself. Over time, scientists fine-tune our understanding of humanity when more data are gathered and existing hypotheses are modified, accepted, or rejected.

I am partial to a theoretical perspective known as cultural ecology. This model has been popular since the 1970s and holds that cultural systems should be viewed as adaptive interactive systems between people and their environments (including both the natural environment and the environment provided by other societies). I also find a functionalist model useful. This theoretical model, made famous in the early 1900s by British social anthropologists Bronislaw Malinowski and A. R. Radcliffe-Brown, holds in part that a culture works, or functions, by virtue of all of its segments (economics, politics, kinship, etc.) working together. Further, a particular custom may be viewed as functioning to individually or collectively fulfill the needs of the members of a society (e.g., the need for food, shelter, social interaction, beliefs).

It should be obvious that these theoretical models are more complex than what I have presented here. Entire books and courses at the upper-division university level are devoted to the comprehension and assessment of theoretical models. Evaluating and debating the merits of such models can be stimulating for professional anthropologists as they strive for better ways to understand the human condition. Beginners in the field of anthropology are less well equipped with background data to undertake an in-depth critique of the various paradigms (models). What beginners should remember, though, is that models are devices for explaining and understanding; they are vehicles with which to formulate hypotheses. A great deal of testing is required before we can tentatively accept a model's explanation of human behavior. Later chapters will draw from several theoretical models, including those briefly mentioned here. In this way you can begin to see how theoretical models are used to explain data.

Approaches to Ethnography

The early years of anthropology were marked by what are now termed classic ethnographies. These accounts were holistic, objective descriptions of

TRY THIS
Analyze

Contemplate the functions of the American Fourth of July holiday. Can you think of three ways that this celebration meets the needs of the members of our society individually and collectively? Compare your list with that of a classmate.

a society's way of life. Although these ethnographies contain much data, critics claim that they described cultures in somewhat idealized, romanticized terms. Societies were described with little, if any, reference to internal strife, culture change, or interaction of the group with other societies. Additionally, the roles or perspectives of the individual native members of the society were seldom included.

Today many ethnographers take an approach called **reflexive ethnography.** This broad category refers to accounts that include the personal perspectives and reactions of the fieldworker while immersed in the field situation. Data are often presented as if a dialogue is taking place between one or more native informants and the ethnographer, thus resembling a literary writing rather than a scientific description. Such ethnographies typically do not include comparative data or the quantification of data. They reflect a humanistic and postmodernist view.

Still other ethnographers blend approaches. These ethnographers demonstrate commitment to the scientific method with emphasis on objective observation, comparative method, and quantification of data (review the discussion of the scientific approach in Chapter 1). At the same time, they include some reflexive elements, such as comments on their feelings while gathering data, and perspectives and voices of the native members of the society.

Research Proposals, Funding, and Budgets

Before undertaking field research, it is necessary to obtain funding for the project. Many public and private foundations are dedicated to the support of scientific research. Such institutions require detailed proposals to be submitted before they will grant financial support. The proposal process typically includes a statement of purpose, details of the methods that will be employed to gather data, proposed time parameters, potential applications for the results of the research, and a detailed budget. Often it is also required that the study be published in an appropriate professional journal within a specific period of time after the research is completed. Many universities and corporations employ professional experts to help with the preparation of grant proposals, particularly the budget portions.

Budget preparation is often complex and can be a particularly thorny issue for the anthropologist who is going to another country, especially because fluctuating monetary exchange rates and different cultural expectations regarding money usage are not always predictable. What most Americans would consider bribes, for example, may be a normal part of certain transactions in other cultures. An additional consideration in budgeting is the financial responsibility one has at home, such as making mortgage payments, renewing insurance policies, and paying local, state, and federal taxes.

reflexive ethnography
An approach to fieldwork that focuses on the personal experiences and perspectives of the ethnographer, as well as the voices of the native members of a culture.

ANTHROPOLOGY AROUND US

Ethnography in the Workplace

Native peoples of distant lands are only part of the anthropological agenda today. All around us ethnographers are quietly contributing to the solution of workplace issues. Today's native populations include workers, managers, and clients. In one project, reported in *U. S. News & World Report* (August 10, 1998), anthropologist Ken Erickson worked for months as a butcher learning to slice and cut meat in a slaughterhouse. He was investigating why there had been a wildcat strike. Managers thought the problems were due to language barriers. By being a participant observer and becoming a part of this microculture both during and after work, Erickson showed that the real issue was the attitude of managers. Managers treated the workers as though they were stupid, and the workers resented this. They wanted respect for their skills. This project resulted in new training programs.

Another company hired an anthropologist to solve a problem with its service repair program. The anthropologist became a participant observer and was trained as a repairman. After several months he reported that the training program didn't teach workers an important part of service repair—showing clients how to fix minor problems themselves. Repair call-backs dropped dramatically when the new training in how to teach clients basic repairs was implemented. More than two thousand anthropologists in the United States are practicing outside of academia. About 40 percent work as

business consultants, and the rest do applied work in forensic anthropology, medical anthropology, archaeology, and other areas.

◎ What is one problem area on your campus or in your workplace that might be solved if someone actually got to know the job through doing the job?

◎ ENTERING THE NATIVE COMMUNITY AND ADAPTING

Because every field situation is unique, there are few guidelines for how an ethnographer should enter another society. However, since the 1960s, anthropologists have been writing about various issues they have encountered while doing fieldwork, including initial contact with the subject culture.

Common situations have emerged from such accounts. These accounts, plus networking with veteran ethnographers, serve to prepare the novice ethnographer for possible difficulties. There are two basic approaches for initial entry to the field environment: (1) have someone experienced in the society introduce you, and (2) enter by yourself. If you elect to have someone familiar with the community introduce you, there is a potential snag if the "natives" bear any animosity toward that person. Indeed, this has happened to ethnographers on numerous occasions, particularly when government officials are involved. What about the alternative of simply arriving by yourself? This is the approach that my husband and I took when we lived in northern Spain in a community with a population of fifteen hundred. It worked in our situation, in part because luck entered the picture in the form of our landlord.

Northern Spain

There were no rental offices, no local papers with classified ads, and no apartment buildings in this village or the surrounding area. When we arrived, we simply looked for signs in windows that advertised rooms to rent. We found two such signs, but the rooms proved unsatisfactory for a family. We then began asking shopkeepers if they knew of any flats to rent. One particularly friendly man directed my husband to ask at a local bar for Javier, who might know someone with a flat to rent. Javier, the bar owner, indicated that he did know someone who might rent a part of his home, and he said he would be glad to make introductions when Enrique arrived. Enrique, to our relief, had a furnished flat to rent that served our needs and was within our budget. As the weeks passed, we found Enrique to be a veritable encyclopedia of knowledge—from local and national history to contemporary issues. He knew everyone and could always be counted on when we needed information. It was only months later that we discovered he had served on the governing body of the village for many years and was held in high esteem. Serendipitous luck for us!

Adapting Physically and Psychologically

The first month or two in a field setting is a time of adaptation. Issues of where and how to obtain food and shelter, adjustment to temperature and humidity, and staying healthy seem to take a disproportionately large amount of time when you are in a new setting. Mundane issues such as learning the schedule for the local bus and discovering the normal rhythms of your new environment take time—more time or less time depending on how different the setting is from what you are accustomed to.

After making the essential adaptations such as finding a steady source of food and acceptable shelter, many fieldworkers experience a "honeymoon" phase. Everything is new. You are *in the field* gathering data. The fieldworker recognizes that these moments are the realization of a goal pursued for several years. These first weeks are often very exciting.

These are traditional homes in northern Spain. In the past, animals were kept on the ground floor, and the family lived above. Note the Roman castle ruins on the far hill.

Once the initial honeymoon period is over, problems may surface. Most of us have experienced a new situation—new job, new school, new neighborhood. Everything seems positive. Coworkers go out of their way to be nice, or the neighbors bring a plate of cookies to welcome you. After a time, you begin to be less pleased as problems surface at work and at home.

Culture Shock   The label **culture shock** is used to denote all of the resultant feelings and emotions people have when prolonged exposure to another society's culture makes them feel helpless, homesick, disoriented, angry, depressed, frustrated, or all of the above. (These are the most typical symptoms.) Actually, it is a large stew pot of emotions, and it is brought on because you are a stranger. You do not understand much of what is happening around you. You are embarrassed by your lack of ability to do things that any five-year-old member of this society can do. You are aware that you'll be in this setting for an extended period of time. As all of these

culture shock
A label for the resultant feelings of homesickness, disorientation, helplessness, and frustration that occur after prolonged exposure to an unfamiliar culture.

> ### TRY THIS *Discuss*
>
> Discuss with a classmate the pros and cons of the following approaches to entering the field in London's gay district of Soho.
>
> 1. Go to the area and rent a room; then hang out at a local pub.
> 2. Get acquainted with the local bobbies (police), and have them introduce you to people in the neighborhood.
> 3. Join the local gay and lesbian rights group.
> 4. Suggest another approach.

feelings simmer, a voice inside cries, "What am I doing here? I'll never use the different verb tenses correctly or understand the significance of various forms of social address" or ". . . I just want to go home." It is not easy to admit to yourself that you are experiencing these things, let alone to admit it to others. As R. Lincoln Keiser recounted in his discussion of his fieldwork with the Vice Lords, a Chicago street gang, "On the streets of the ghetto I was functionally an infant, and like all infants, had to be taken care of. I did not understand the significance of most actions and many words. . . . When you are an infant in age, it is one thing to be help-less, but when you are twenty-nine years old, it is quite something else. This feeling of helplessness was very difficult for me to handle. In the early part of my research it often made me feel so nervous and anxious that the events occurring around me seemed to merge in a blur of meaningless action" (Keiser 1979: 94–95). (Figure 3.1)

Virtually every ethnographer, whether working in a distant, exotic set-ting in another country or studying, for example, political processes in the capital city of his or her own country, has experienced culture shock to a greater or lesser degree. Many tourists have experienced culture shock even with fairly limited exposure to another cultural setting. Culture shock can happen at home too. I have had reentry students at my college confide in me that they experienced culture shock when they first returned to college. During the first two weeks they often felt disoriented and frustrated and wondered why they ever thought that they could return to school. They went home every day with a headache. But as they began to understand the academic culture and how to function within it, these symptoms subsided. It is the same way in long-term fieldwork situations.

Tourists often escape feelings of culture shock because they insulate themselves from a variety of experiences in other cultures. These are often the very situations that would give them a better understanding of what life is like in another society and culture. The choice of traveling with an or-ganized group from one's own society, often composed of people from the same cultural or subcultural background, provides a highly choreographed

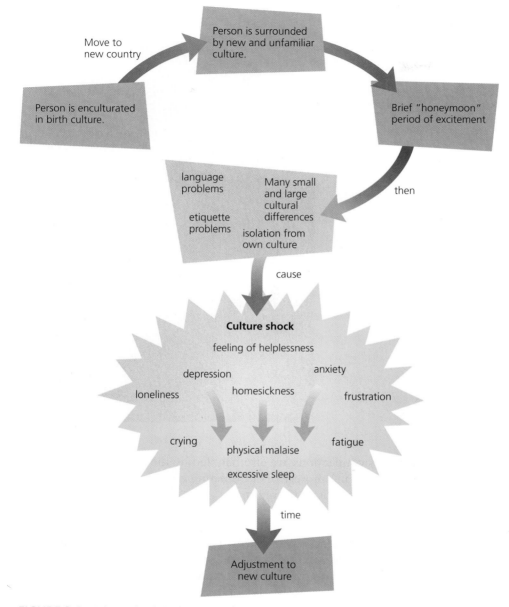

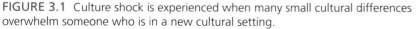

FIGURE 3.1 Culture shock is experienced when many small cultural differences overwhelm someone who is in a new cultural setting.

experience. In such situations one has some exposure to the local culture—local cuisine, museums, architecture, dress, and plumbing. People speak a different language. There is usually a guide to handle major decisions like where to eat, sleep, or even shop for souvenirs. It is not unusual to have the guide be responsible for menu selections and room assignments. Airline,

Energy is expensive in Spain, so most people dry their wash on lines that run outside of their windows.

train, and bus connections are also handled by the guide, who is familiar with the local area. A protective or insulating group of fellow travelers usually keeps culture shock to a minimum.

My own symptoms of culture shock were brought on mostly because of difficulties with the language. It seemed that my several semesters of university-level Spanish courses and brief conversations with Spanish-speaking students had not prepared me to actually use the language. I was often corrected by Enrique for an incorrect usage of, for example, the subjunctive verb tense. At one level I knew that he was trying to be helpful, yet he never corrected my husband, who made many more mistakes than I did. I *knew* that this was a culture-specific gender issue (men did not correct other men, particularly in front of women), but it still created tremendous frustration at times during our first month in the community. Many other small issues contributed to culture shock. There was a lack of sufficient warm water for a shower. Our *cama de matrimonio* (double bed) did not adequately accommodate our tall frames. There were also time-consuming domestic chores, such as having to hang all of our wash on clotheslines outside our back window and then being on constant alert to quickly retrieve it when the frequent rain squalls began. We had to shop for meal preparation items each day because we had a very small refrigerator. Obtaining additional contact lens solution required an extended bus trip and consumed an entire day.

Happily, culture shock passes as one begins to adjust to the new culture. I recall the first time I was able to make a little joke in Spanish to Enrique and was rewarded with a hardy laugh and his congratulations on the subtlety of my remark. And both my husband and I came to relish the daily trips to the bakery, the small market, and the fresh fish store where our preferences became known and we were always greeted with smiles. *"Señora, buenos días. Cuantos kilos de sardinas hoy?"* ("Good day! How many kilos of sardines today?") My family loved the small fresh sardines that were a local favorite.

Life Shock   Another experience that may confront an ethnographer is **life shock.** Life shock refers to a single sudden experience that is so unexpected that one does not have any time to deal with it psychologically. The result is that the person vomits, faints, or becomes hysterical. While in your own society, you function with an arsenal of psychological barriers that accumulated as you matured. We have become insulated to many unpleasant occurrences because we have seen actual events on the nightly news, on the streets where we live, or reenacted in the movies.

A former professor of mine described his experience of life shock while conducting his third field season in Southeast Asia. He was sitting just inside a thatched hut interviewing a woman he knew well about details of kinship organization. She was nursing her child. In an instant he smelled, heard, and saw that the baby had defecated in its mother's lap (babies wore no diapers); the mother continued talking about kinship, but gave a quick whistle, and a mongrel dog appeared and licked her lap and the baby's bottom clean. The fieldworker stumbled out the hut's door and vomited. While in the process, he reported that he actually thought "So this is life shock."

It is possible to experience life shock in familiar surroundings, though it is more common when the subject is surrounded with the unfamiliar. A student recently recounted to me an episode that brought about a life shock reaction for him. He was in military boot camp, and it was the end of a long, tiring day of physical activity. He and his fellow recruits were standing at attention in their barracks in two lines facing each other, when, without any warning, the fatigued soldier next to my student fell forward crashing to the floor. His face hit the cement and, accompanied by a hollow crunching sound, blood and teeth splattered the surrounding area (the young soldier needed numerous reconstructive surgeries to repair the damage).

❋ TRY THIS ❋
Hypothesize

Review several films or television dramas you have seen recently, and consider the number of ways violence has been portrayed. Write a hypothesis regarding the relationship between this part of your enculturation and the likelihood of you experiencing life shock. Compare your hypothesis with that of a classmate. How might you test your hypothesis?

---

life shock
A sudden unexpected experience that causes one to faint, become hysterical, or vomit. More likely to occur when immersed in an unfamiliar setting.

A man standing opposite the fallen recruit promptly vomited, and my student said his stomach turned over and he felt the vomit rising in his own throat. Others in the immediate vicinity to this event were disturbed but did not have any reactive physical symptoms—no life shock experience. The student told me that he was relieved to discover that there was a label for this reaction, and it somewhat eased his long-standing embarrassment over his behavior. Ethnographers and travelers have had similar experiences. It is somewhat reassuring to be able to identify your reaction and understand the reason behind it.

Establishing Rapport

Establishing **rapport** (a harmonious relationship) is an important ingredient for successful fieldwork. Techniques that have proven successful in accomplishing this include speaking the local language, respecting confidences, being generous with your time, and being forthright about your intentions and research. Most Americans have personally experienced being in a new school, new neighborhood, or new job. You have acquired some skills at meeting new people and trying to connect with them in a manner that will result in a positive working relationship. The same techniques generally work in other societies, although the ethnographer must carefully observe and ask for advice whenever possible.

Sometimes behaving in the manner of one's hosts will move relationships in the direction of good rapport, but one must proceed with caution. Napoleon Chagnon finally stumbled on this approach when first living among the Yanomamo peoples of Venezuela. He had worked hard to cut a palm tree and make some boards to place on the bottom of his canoe in order to keep his gear dry. He discovered later that day that several Yanomamo had made paddles for their own canoes by chopping up these new floor boards. Frustrated and angry he shouted at them, explained all of the work he had done to make the boards, and generally showed how he had suffered. As he tells the story, "Then, with exaggerated drama and finality, I withdrew my hunting knife as their grins disappeared and cut each one of their canoes loose and set it into the strong current of the Orinoco River where it was immediately swept up and carried downstream. I left without looking back and huffed over to the other side of the river to resume my work" (Chagnon 1997: 18). He was later told by the village headman, "with an approving chuckle" (Chagnon 1997: 18), that he had done the right thing. He goes on to discuss how his relationship with the Yanomamo improved whenever he stood up for himself and didn't let them bully him.

One technique for getting acquainted and initiating rapport that my family successfully used in Spain involved sharing **string figures,** as discussed in the vignette at the beginning of the chapter. We have used string figures in a number of different settings and in different countries, and they

rapport
A harmonious relationship.

string figures
A type of entertainment in which designs, or figures, are created by weaving string on the fingers. Patterns, tricks, and catches are performed and are often accompanied by stories.

Ojibwa person making a string figure.

have always worked to create relaxed and enjoyable interactions. People also seem quite interested in the historical and cross-cultural perspectives about string figures and often ask where they can learn more. A short course of instruction on the topic is included in Appendix B (How Do You Make String Figures?), along with references and Web sites for you to visit and learn more. Enjoy!

◎ GATHERING DATA

A comparison of the ethnographic literature reveals that there are a number of successful activities with which to begin gathering data. These activities are intermingled with adapting, getting settled, and gaining rapport.

Getting the lay of the land, both figuratively and literally, is basic. Making a detailed map of the area and doing a census are often the first activities employed to gather data because in most societies they are neutral and nonthreatening. Spending time with people and talking with them, as well as offering to pitch in and help with chores, can give you time and opportunity to observe activities. Moreover, it gives the locals time to size you up and sort out their feelings about your presence. Of course, people

❈ TRY THIS ❈
Analyze

Look in your assigned ethnographies and readings for examples of how anthropologists have established rapport. Authors seldom label activities that they employ to establish rapport as such, but now that you are alert to the importance of rapport in getting started in the field, you should be able to offer an analysis of how they achieved it based on the ethnographer's discussion. For example, Chagnon's act of cutting loose the Yanomamo canoes helped to establish rapport.

will be curious about the ethnographer. The journal I kept of my time in northern Spain contains one such example. On the first day of our third week living in the area, I was paying for my daily purchase at the small local market, and the owner, a friendly man, questioned me as to how my husband and I were able to enjoy such a long holiday. I responded by telling him about our projects and how we came to this village and said that we would be there for several months. I was queried again in the bread store and later at the fish market. Locals were accustomed to visitors coming to the area for a week or ten days on holiday from the hot, central part of the country, but we had exceeded that time frame and they were interested to know why. That evening my landlord's wife, who owned the hair salon, told me that two of her clients that afternoon had recounted my conversation with the market owner!

Role of the Fieldworker

The anthropologist in the field situation strives to achieve the role of **participant observer.** The ideal role is to participate in the society and learn about the culture and concurrently maintain the eye of an objective observer. One tries to see and experience the world as the native member of the culture does and record it. This insider's perspective is called the **emic** view. At the same time, the ethnographer aspires to present the analytical view of an objective observer. The outsider's view is labeled the **etic** view.

Participant observation has been at the heart of cultural anthropology since the early 1900s. Contemporary cultural anthropologists still rely on participant observation to give the uniquely anthropological perspective of a culture, subculture, or microculture. At the same time, we have incorporated sampling techniques developed by mathematicians and sociologists into our process of analysis, and these are used to gather data from large populations and to perform the statistical analysis of those data.

The ideal of participant observation is not without difficulty. The gender of the fieldworker, for example, may determine how he or she will be received in the field setting. One's gender may limit access to persons or events. Difficulties may arise for the participant observer that involve ethical issues. This is one reason the AAA has adopted a code of ethical standards. Another potential problem involves objectivity. Something of the personality and cultural background of the individual ethnographer does show in ethnographic accounts. No matter how hard one tries, it is impossible to be totally removed and objective. Nevertheless, the unique views that ethnographers can gain by actually living and interacting on a daily basis with people is unparalleled in its potential. Although each culture and each ethnographer are unique, cultural patterns emerge from careful ethnographic studies. Restudies and comparisons can help us to

participant observer
The role of an anthropologist doing ethnographic fieldwork.

emic
An insider's view of a culture. This perspective in ethnography uses the categories and ideas that are relevant and meaningful to the culture under study.

etic
An outsider's view of a culture. This perspective in ethnography uses the categories of the anthropologist's culture to describe the culture under study.

participant observation
The process of an anthropologist doing ethnographic fieldwork.

Ethnographers participate in the cultures they study. Here anthropologist Don Lenkeit helps his key informant with a load of firewood that is transported in a traditional horse cart with modern tires.

fine-tune our hypotheses about the parameters of a particular society's culture and about the parameters of what it is to be human.

Recent ethnographic paradigms (postmodernism) and approaches (reflexive ethnography) acknowledge that it is a complex process. Some individuals would reject the idea that we can ever objectively describe another culture. They suggest that any description is abstract and incomplete at best, or that it contains the personal bias of the ethnographer at worst. Scientifically oriented ethnographers recognize these complexities and continue to do what science does—to as objectively as possible describe and offer explanations for human behavior. The self-correcting nature of science will continue.

Sampling Methods

Historically, anthropologists have focused on small societies or small segments of larger societies, where during the course of their fieldwork they come in contact with and gather data from most of the inhabitants. When

TRY THIS
Analyze

Think of two reasons it might be necessary to select people to interview using a judgment sample. Do you think this form of bias is acceptable? Why or why not?

studying larger communities or societies, the anthropologist may become intimately involved as participant observer with a particular neighborhood and its people while gathering data from other segments of the population by employing sampling methods. A **random sample** aims at eliminating bias by giving everyone an equal chance of being interviewed or observed. This method in its most basic form involves placing each person's name on a slip of paper, placing the slips into a container, and then, without looking, reaching into the container, mixing the slips, and withdrawing a predetermined number. The names selected would constitute the sample; the sample's size would depend on the percentage of the population the researcher has decided to use as a database.

Households could be randomly selected by giving each house in the community a sequential number and then, using a mathematical table of random numbers, identifying the sample households from the compiled list. Random sampling can also be stratified (called a **stratified random sample**) by dividing the society's members into categories such as age, gender, wealth, and so on. A number of individuals are then selected from each category.

When the anthropologist selects informants based on her own evaluation of their knowledge, skills, or insights that may contribute to the depth or breadth of the study, the sample is called a **judgment sample.** The nature of participant observation is such that most ethnographers use data gathered from native members of the culture who have been selected using a judgment sample.

random sample
A sample method in which all members of a population have a statistically equal chance of being chosen.

stratified random sample
A random sample with divisions into categories such as by age or socioeconomic level.

judgment sample
A sample that is chosen based on the judgment of the ethnographer.

informants
Native members of a society who give information about their culture to an ethnographer.

Problems with Sampling

The use of judgment sampling leaves anthropologists vulnerable to criticism because opinion and potential bias are involved. This is one reason that ethnographic research is said to be both a science and an art. Random sampling methods can also be criticized. Although in this case everyone has an equal chance of being selected in a random sample, such a sample may not yield the full range of knowledge, behaviors, and cultural values that are in fact part of the culture under study. This is particularly true if the sample size is small.

Use of Informants

Informants, members of the society under study who are interviewed about the various aspects of the culture, may be selected by random sample as noted above. Some prefer to use the terms *collaborator, teacher,* or *friend* rather than the term *informant.* Informants act as teachers and guides for anthropologists as they seek to understand various aspects of the culture

Bronislaw Malinowski with some of his Trobriand informants. He was a participant observer among the Trobrianders for several years (1914–1918) and wrote several ethnographies about their society.

of the society from the insider's perspective (emic view). Anthropologists select **key informants** using a judgment sample. A key informant is a member of the native culture who works closely with the fieldworker. Ethnographers are usually indebted to their key informants. Enrique, one of my key informants in the village in Spain, often anticipated my queries and wanted to make certain that I correctly represented his life, his community, and his country to all of my North American students. I was grateful for his sharp intellect, his political acumen in the community, and his friendship. Indeed, my daughter came to call Enrique and his wife, Teresa, *abuelo* and *abuela* (grandfather and grandmother), and she remembers fondly learning to prepare Spanish treats like *chocolate* (a hot chocolate made with whole milk that has special bar chocolate melted in it) and *churros* (a deep-fried pastry something like a doughnut) in Teresa's kitchen.

Problems with using informants include the possibility of informants being untruthful or giving "ideal" rather than "actual" cultural information. Such problems can usually be corrected with more time in the field,

key informant
An ethnographic interview subject who has been selected by judgment sample; a knowledgeable native who plays a major role in teaching the ethnographer about the informant's culture.

along with interviews and conversations with additional informants. Several ethnographers have had to discard months of data when inconsistencies and even coordinated group lying were uncovered by the fieldworker.

Interview Methods

Approaches to interviewing include **formal interviews** (also called **structured interviews**) and **informal interviews** (also called **unstructured interviews**). Formal interviews involve asking specific, scripted questions in the same sequence each time. Every interview is conducted in the same manner and, if possible, in the same setting. The attempt is made to eliminate as many distracting variables as possible. Any follow-up questions are also scripted. The goal of this approach is to solicit data that can be compared and validated.

Informal interviews are almost like a conversation—very open ended—and they are allowed to wander where the informant takes them. The ethnographer may ask something like "tell me about courtship customs," or "how does a person become a leader in your community?"

Formal Interviews   One advantage of formal interviews is the reduction of situational bias, because all respondents are asked the same questions in the same sequence and under the same conditions where possible. Another advantage is that comparable data are gathered. The ease of quantifying results is also an advantage. On the other hand, forcing the anthropologist to solicit responses that focus on the specific questions prepared by the fieldworker may be a disadvantage. The questions may not have centered on issues that are perceived to be important to the native. In short, the *wrong* questions may be asked and important questions may be missed. The time spent in this endeavor may inhibit or prevent the raising of additional issues that the interviewer deems important.

Informal Interviews   In an informal interview informants tell the ethnographer what is important to their culture. The interview can take place whenever an opportunity is present. Informants are more likely to reveal *actual* culture rather than *ideal* culture in a more relaxed setting. The primary disadvantage of informal interviewing is the difficulty encountered in quantifying information. In short, the fieldworker is less able to control the specific variables of the working hypotheses.

Problems with interviewing, whether formal or informal, often center on methods of recording the data. With informal interviews, the ethnographer may not be able to write down enough details of what the informant is saying, or an informant may carefully edit what he or she says if a tape recorder is being used or the ethnographer is observed writing down every word. This is where good rapport and honesty about your research is important in creating a comfortable interview situation.

One solution is to use only informal interviews during the initial part of data gathering and then, with the aid of key informants, to prepare a more formal set of interview questions or interview code sheets, which are forms with questions and common responses that can quickly be checked off during an interview.

Genealogical Method

When anthropologists began doing field ethnography, they often focused on small hunter-gatherer or horticultural societies. They found that everything revolved around kin relationships, and as a result much time was spent on gathering data about kinship relationships. The collection of such kinship information is called the **genealogical method.** Numerous patterns of such relationships emerged as this early field data began to be compared by ethnologists. Details of the types of categories that such data disclosed are delineated and discussed in Chapter 7.

Life Histories

Another method of gathering data in the field is to record **life histories** of individual members of the society. This involves extensive interviews and conversations with individual informants. Most ethnographers incorporate life histories with other data-gathering techniques because they are particularly useful in reconstructing something of events prior to the ethnographer's visit. The life history approach has also been the focus of research that resulted in the portrait of Nisa, a member of the African !Kung San peoples of the Kalahari Desert. *Nisa: The Life and Words of a !Kung Woman*, written by Marjorie Shostak in 1981, is a provocative look at the changes in San culture that Nisa experienced.

By comparing the life histories of a number of individuals within a culture, anthropologists find that patterns begin to emerge, which in turn provide a window to the changes that have affected a culture. This essential point reinforces the premise that culture is dynamic and continually in the process of change and adaptation. Of course, one must be cautious using information gained in a life history. Individuals often selectively remember events of the past and may even alter them in subtle ways.

Photography

Visual anthropologist John Collier states that "the nonverbal language of photo realism is the language that is most understood interculturally and cross-culturally" (Collier 1967: 4). The still photographs that accompanied

TRY THIS
Interview

Develop a set of questions, both formal and informal, and then interview an elder member of your culture. This can be an interesting and rewarding experience in its own right, but it will also give you some insight into the interview process and life history data.

OLC
mhhe•com/lenkeit3

See Internet exercises.

genealogical method
The ethnographic method of recording information about kinship relationships using symbols and diagrams.

life history
The ethnographic method of gathering data based on extensive interviews with individuals about their memories of their culture from childhood through adulthood.

Life history interviews can offer a window to how a culture has changed. Marjorie Shostak used this technique among the !Kung San (Ju/'hoansi) of the Kalahari Desert, Africa (shown here). Images such as this one can also be compared over time.

ethnography in the 1940s were soon accompanied by film, later by video records, and now by digital images. Photographs are a unique frozen image of an event or aspect of behavior and can be used as an analytical tool. In the investigation of proxemics (the space between people) or marriage ceremonies or the production of material culture, photographs have been especially important. The possibilities are endless. Some ethnographers take their own images and later ask informants about aspects of the image and what is happening in it. Others take film crews of photographic specialists to the field with them. The results give both anthropologists and the public unique insights into other cultures. Of course, there can be problems with taking photographs in the field situation. You may be viewed as a spy or be faulted for invading people's privacy. Consider, for example, how you might react if someone pulled out a video camera and recorded an argument you were having with your significant other. Sensitivity and ethical considerations must be maintained when using such techniques. During my stay in Spain, there were many times I would have liked to have recorded a particular image, but it was clearly inappropriate to do so.

Anthropologist Bruce Knauft uses a laptop computer to record data among the Gebusi in Papua New Guinea. His field data were later analyzed and reported in numerous publications.

◎ ANALYZING DATA AND PREPARING A REPORT

The analysis of data begins in the field, but the majority of such work is done after the ethnographer returns from the field. Data are quantified and statistical analysis is completed. The development of computers has been a boon to comparative analysis of ethnographic field data. The quantitative data on food sources or data on residence patterns can be quickly assembled and analyzed.

The reporting of data gathered during ethnographic fieldwork may be in the form of an ethnographic monograph (a book about a single culture based on fieldwork). Articles based on fieldwork data are also reported in professional journals, such as *Current Anthropology* or *American Anthropologist*. Such articles are directed at research academicians and use a technical, formal style. Ethnographic data are also reported in the form of papers that are read at professional conferences. Short nontechnical articles are often written for publications such as *Natural History* (the magazine of the American Museum of Natural History) or *Smithsonian* (published by the Smithsonian Institution).

✖ TRY THIS ✖
Ponder

Identify a travel or tourist experience you have undertaken with friends or family. Were there situations or places where the taking of photographs might have been inappropriate?

Assume that a group of foreign tourists has arrived in your community. Describe three places or situations where you would be uncomfortable having your photograph taken.

SUMMARY

Data gathered in a field setting are a hallmark of anthropological research and provide a unique perspective on other cultures. Ethnographers prepare for this experience by drafting a proposal and budget for the research and seeking funding. They draw on all of their background in anthropology when they enter the native community, whether it is a community in an urban setting, a business corporation, or a remote tribal village. The AAA Code of Ethics provides guidance to the ethnographer.

The adaptation phase of fieldwork includes arranging for shelter and food and coping with culture shock and sometimes life shock. The fieldworker must establish rapport with members of the culture while gathering initial data such as mapping and census taking. The active phase of fieldwork involves being a participant observer—literally observing behavior as objectively as possible and analyzing it (the etic view) while participating to the extent allowed by the local people. Random and judgment samples are used to select informants who will provide information about their culture. Key informants provide an insider's perspective (the emic view) and act as teachers and guides. Both formal and informal interview methods are used to gather information; each approach complements the other. Additional ethnographic methods commonly employed include the genealogical method, collecting life histories, and photography.

Study Questions

OLC
mhhe•com/lenkeit3
See Self Quiz.

1. Discuss the field methods employed by anthropologists and the problems associated with each. Cite specific examples from ethnographic accounts that are part of your additional assigned reading.

2. Discuss both the importance and the limitations of participant observation in fieldwork.

3. Evaluate the use of formal and informal interviewing techniques, and suggest ways to determine the validity of the data gathered by each method.

4. Review your own work, school, and life experiences, and discuss a specific conflict situation in which the use of participant observation to gather data would have provided unique insights. Identify the sides in the conflict. Where did the "data" or information used by each side in the situation originate? How, specifically, might the data gathered by a trained anthropologist, who adheres to the anthropological code of ethics, help each side understand the other?

5. What are the primary ethical responsibilities of ethnographic fieldworkers?

Suggested Readings

Bohannan, Paul, and Dirk Van der Elst. 1998. *Asking and Listening: Ethnography as Personal Adaptation.* Prospect Heights, Ill.: Waveland Press. A short, clearly written account of how anthropology developed the approach of ethnography and how it has changed from the 1880s to the present. Focuses on how everyone can use the ethnographic approach in their lives.

Devita, P. R., and J. D. Armstrong, eds. 2001. *Distant Mirrors: American as a Foreign Culture,* 3rd ed. Belmont, Calif.: Wadsworth. Anthropologists from other cultures share their observations and experiences of working in the United States. In the perspective of the book, North Americans are the "other."

Kutsche, Paul. 1998. *Field Ethnography: A Manual for Doing Cultural Anthropology.* Upper Saddle River, N.J.: Prentice-Hall. A series of five small field assignments aimed at giving students a taste of doing fieldwork and learning about the ethnographic experience, both traditional and reflexive.

Spradley, James P. 1997. *Participant Observation.* New York: Holt, Rinehart and Winston. A step-by-step guide for conducting ethnographic research.

Suggested Web Sites

http://www.indiana.edu/~wanthro/theory.htm

This easy-to-navigate site emerged out of a graduate anthropology seminar at Indiana University that summarizes the theoretical changes in specific facets of anthropology since the 1970s.

OLC
mhhe•com/lenkeit3

See Web links.

http://www.anthro.mankato.msus.edu/information/biography/index.pl

This site provides biographical information on over five hundred prominent anthropologists (and scientists from other disciplines) who have influenced the growth of anthropology since the nineteenth century. It was created and is maintained by the anthropology students at Minnesota State University (Mankato).

http://www.tamu.edu/anthropology/news.html

This site is the best single source for anthropological topics in the mass media. Maintained by the anthropology department at Texas A&M University, the site has weekly updates.

http://www.aaanet.org/committees/ethics/ethcode.htm

This site presents the Code of Ethics of the American Anthropological Association.

http://www.aaanet.org/committees/ethics/ch3.htm

Twelve case studies are presented at this site. These are drawn from the AAA *Handbook on Ethical Issues in Anthropology* <http://www.aaanet.org/committees/ethics/toc.htm>.

4

Language
Is This What Makes Us Human?

Symbols, such as gestures, are a part of a culture's shared communication system. What is this baseball official communicating?

"*¿Cerveza?*" asked the woman behind the produce and meat counter at the small market. *Cerveza* means beer in Spanish. My husband repeated his request for "*un media kilo de cerezas, por favor*" [a half kilo of cherries, please]. This request was accompanied by exaggerated body language as he tilted his head, raised his eyebrows, and looked at the display of cherries in the box to his right. With a puzzled expression on her face that suddenly transformed into a smile, she said, "*¡Claro! ¿Queres cerezas, verdad?*" [Of course, you want cherries, correct?] "*Si, si,*" responded my spouse. The Castilian Spanish pronunciation was difficult for my husband. Learning a new language, one that has sounds that are not produced in one's native tongue, is difficult for most adults. The more different the sounds and the anatomy used to produce those sounds—teeth, tongue placement, and lips—the harder it seems to be. Children are more flexible. Our daughter speaks Spanish with barely a perceptible American English accent because she was immersed in Spanish as a child.

The study of language has a long history in anthropology, partly because of the preoccupation of early anthropologists with the study of aboriginal cultures. In order to conduct fieldwork in these cultures the ethnographers needed to speak the local language. These efforts led to studies of the structure of the language and to the writing of grammars and dictionaries. This work in turn led to investigations into differences in language usage within a culture, by age, class, and gender. Of course symbolic verbal communication may be combined with nonverbal symbolic communication. My husband often used this technique, as in the situation at the market. Because we were in a cultural setting where nonverbal cues were similar to those of our own culture, this strategy worked. Awareness of acceptable verbal and nonverbal symbols is important to avoid misunderstandings when one is in a different culture.

Symbolic communication is the foundation on which culture is built. Nearly all of what constitutes culture—cognitive processes, behaviors, and material creations—depends on some form of symbolizing. We use many forms of symbolic communication—spoken and written language, visual images, sounds, and fragrances—virtually anything that we can detect with our senses has been used as a symbol by humans. Our ability to symbolize is a unique human feature as far as we know right now. Language is our most important and most highly developed symbolic system. Some anthropologists have hypothesized that language actually shapes human perceptions.

The objectives of this chapter are to

- Describe how anthropologists study language
- Discuss the relationship between language and culture
- Distinguish between human and nonhuman systems of communication
- Describe how nonverbal communication supplements verbal communication

Anthropologist Gillian Gillison records an interview with performers from a New Guinea ritual theater. Tape recordings are valuable to the study of language.

◎ THE STUDY OF LANGUAGE

OLC
mhhe•com/lenkeit3
See chapter outline and chapter overview.

OLC
mhhe•com/lenkeit3
See Internet exercises.

Linguistics is the study of language. Language is a symbolic system consisting of sounds that are used to communicate thoughts and emotions. Linguists study language—how language is patterned and how it works, the history and development of language, and its relationship to other aspects of culture. To do ethnographic fieldwork, anthropologists have often had to begin by compiling their own dictionaries and grammars of the languages of the cultures they study because there are no formal language texts available similar to what we now associate with university-level language programs. Today, linguistics encompasses a number of research areas, including historical and descriptive linguistics. The relationship between language and culture is the focus of ethnolinguistics and sociolinguistics.

Descriptive Linguistics

The part of linguistics that focuses on the mechanics and patterning of language is called **descriptive linguistics.** To describe a language, a linguist must first describe the sounds used in the language under study.

descriptive linguistics
The part of anthropological linguistics that focuses on the mechanics of language.

phonology
The general study of the sounds used in human speech.

Phonology   The general study of the sounds used in speech is called **phonology;** phonetics includes the methods for describing the details of speech sounds. All of the sounds of human speech can be identified and described using the methods of phonetic analysis. Linguists use an internationally recognized system of symbols to represent the various sounds

> ## TRY THIS *Listen*
>
> This is a sample of the letter *a* in English, the dictionary symbols used to represent it, and key words for practicing the sound. Can you hear the differences in sounds? Much skill and practice are needed to accurately record the sounds used in a particular language.
>
> | Symbol in English Dictionary | Key Words |
> |:---:|:---|
> | ă | fat, cat |
> | ā | mate, ape |
> | â | care, share |
> | ä | car, are |

of speech. Check out the key to pronunciation at the front of any dictionary for a sample of this symbolic system.

Regional dialects often result in different vowel phonemes being used for a word. In the United States, for example, the word *car* is pronounced differently in New Jersey than in Arizona.

Different languages use some of the same sounds and many that differ from the ones you use. Sounds can be described according to the anatomical parts that are used to create them, such as the vocal cords, tongue, teeth, and lips. For example, a labiodental fricative is a sound made using lips and teeth with friction created by passing the teeth over the lip. The English letters *v* and *f* are formed in this manner. Because we learn the sounds of our own language from birth, the sounds of other languages seem strange to us and are often difficult to copy. You have experienced different sounds, as well as the frustration of trying to create those sounds, if you have studied a second language. This is especially true if the language you are learning is quite different from your native language. George Lucas, writer and director of the *Star Wars* series of films, created distinctly different sounds and sound combinations as distinguishing features of the different galactic cultural groups represented in the films. Lucas acknowledges that he is a student of anthropology and that he uses insights gained from anthropological data when he creates his fantasy worlds.

Minimum units of sound are the building blocks of a language. English, for example, has forty-six minimum units of sound—many letters in the English alphabet have more than one pronunciation. The **phoneme** is the smallest unit of sound that will indicate a difference in meaning. Hence, in English, *p* (as in *pit*) is a phoneme. Another phoneme is *b* (as in *bit*). Each of these minimum units of sound when combined with the phonemes in the word *it* (which contains two phonemes) changes the meaning of the words—*pit* and *bit*. It is important to note that the *p* and *b* do not carry any meaning by themselves. Linguists use the International Phonetic Alphabet

phoneme
The smallest unit of sound in speech that will indicate a difference in meaning.

FIGURE 4.1
Phonemes combine to
form morphemes.

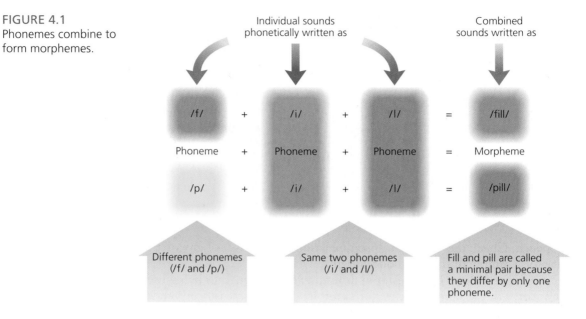

(IPA) of symbols to denote all of the various sounds made in human speech. When IPA symbols are used to transcribe speech in a specific language, anyone familiar with the IPA will be able to correctly pronounce those words. (Figure 4.1)

Morphology and Syntax   The other units of descriptive linguistics are morphology and syntax. The **morpheme** is the smallest combination of sounds that carry a meaning (e.g., *pit*). Each language has rules that govern how words are formed. In English, verbs must have a tense indicating when the action is occurring: past, present, or future. Often the tense is indicated by the addition of a morpheme to a root word—wash, wash*ed*, wash*ing*. The sentence *Dan wash Mary car* does not sound correct to a native English speaker, though it is in correct form for the sentence itself. That is to say, the subject, verb, and object are in the correct order. If the sentence is altered to read *Dan washed Mary's car*, it makes sense. English rules also dictate that the relationship between Mary and the car be included. Each language has such morphological rules about words that are often hard for nonnative speakers to learn. This is true because most languages have exceptions to their usual morphological rules.

   Syntax is the manner in which minimum units of meaning (morphemes) are put together into phrases and sentences. In other words, syntax is what we English speakers would call grammar. Sentence structure in some languages will place verbs after nouns; in other languages the verb is placed first. Still others place the verb at the very end of a sentence. Differences in syntax present us with an interesting cross-cultural problem.

TRY THIS
Compare

Can you think of any phonemes in the English language that can stand alone and carry meaning? What about in Spanish, German, Tagalog, or Mandarin? Ask your friends who speak other languages.

morpheme
The smallest combination of sounds in human speech that carry a meaning.

syntax
The manner in which minimum units of meaning (morphemes) are combined.

How do we explain these differences? Why have humans created so many ways to organize their grammars? And do these differences result in differences in our perceptions of the world around us? Linguists involved in the subfields of ethnolinguistics and sociolinguistics investigate these issues.

Historical Linguistics

Historical linguistics studies the relationships of languages to one another and reconstructs how languages change over time, though no general theory about the causes of change has been developed. One way to study language change takes the form of looking at how the phonology of a language changes over time. Shifts in vowel pronunciation, for example, have been studied. Linguists have established that all English long vowels underwent phonetic change during the fifteenth and sixteenth centuries that involved the raising of the tongue height toward the palate during pronunciation.

Social prestige seems to be a factor in which variations of pronunciation are adopted over time, as in the case of the word *meat* becoming pronounced like *meet*. Immediately after the vowel pronunciation shift noted above, the words *meet*, *meat*, and *mate* were pronounced differently. Then for a time *meat* and *mate* were both pronounced about like *mate* is pronounced today. Later *meat* changed to be pronounced like *meet*, the way the word is pronounced in standard language today (Comrie 1997: 236, Weinreich et al. 1968: 95–188).

Language and Culture

Ethnolinguistics is a specialized field that analyzes the relationship between a language and culture. It seems clear that culture influences language, certainly in the way that vocabulary is elaborated. There are many ethnographic examples of vocabularies that reflect adaptive features of a culture. I remember my fascination when first reading Evans-Pritchard's ethnography of the Nuer (1940), an East African pastoral society in the southern Sudan. I could scarcely believe that one could have so many words to describe a cow. There are hundreds of Nuer words used to describe cows—their color, color pattern combinations, and configurations of horns. Cattle are a central aspect of Nuer life. They provide food in the form of blood, milk, and occasionally meat. They are the primary currency in bride price. Men can recite generations of genealogies of each of their cattle. Cattle serve as links with dead ancestors. Evans-Pritchard wrote that a knowledge of the rich vocabulary relating to cattle was central to working with and describing Nuer culture. I think of the Nuer each time I drive by cattle ranches and look at grazing cattle. My family has tried to delineate our own working vocabularies for describing cattle, and our vocabulary list is short indeed.

historical linguistics
The study of the history of languages, including their development and relationship to other languages.

ethnolinguistics
A field of study in linguistics that analyzes the relationship between a language and culture.

The Nuer of Sudan, Africa, use a rich vocabulary to describe their cattle. Young boys tend the cattle and often recite poems to their favorite animals.

Nuer

Sapir-Whorf hypothesis
A hypothesis about the relationship between language and culture that states that language constructs perceptions.

Even within microcultures the influence of culture on vocabulary is apparent. My daughter brought this to my attention when she was about three years old. We were standing with a neighbor in the back garden when suddenly my daughter said, "Look, Mom! There's a white-crowned sparrow together with the house finches at the bird feeder." My neighbor looked puzzled and said, "Do you mean one of those little brown birds?" My daughter's vocabulary for naming and classifying birds is a result of being in a family and social group that talks about birds a great deal.

The debate surrounding the influences of language on culture—or of culture on language—has been going on for decades. It is also a topic that has interested beginning students of anthropology because of its far-reaching implications. After studying the language of the Hopi and other cultures, Benjamin L. Whorf developed the idea that a language forces the native speaker of that language to perceive the world differently. Whorf worked closely with anthropologist and linguist Edward Sapir on issues relating to language and culture. The **Sapir-Whorf hypothesis** states that language constructs our perception of reality. The English philosopher Ludwig Wittgenstein phrased the notion a bit differently when he suggested that the limits of language define the limits of one's world.

Early in the debate about the validity of this hypothesis, cultural vocabularies were often cited as examples of culture constructing realities. With this argument, the Nuer would "see" cattle differently from the way a North American (even a rancher) does because of the extensive vocabulary Nuer children acquired. Another argument put forth to support the hypothesis involves vocabularies to describe colors. Speakers of English usually name seven colors when viewing a rainbow—red, orange, yellow, green, blue, indigo, and violet. Shona speakers have only three names for the colors of the rainbow—orange, red, and purple are grouped under one word. Blue and green-blue are described by one term, and yellow and yellow-green colors are described with one word (Thompson 1975). Does this mean that Shona speakers see only three colors, or does it mean that they need or use only three terms in their daily life? Studies have clearly shown that all peoples can physiologically distinguish between small color variations. When two colors or two color hues are shown to individuals in various cultures and they are asked whether color A is the same as color B, everyone says that they are different. But when asked to name each color, they often will give one term for closely associated colors, as do the Shona speakers.

Data and testing have shown that the richness of vocabulary seems merely to give a more detailed map to one's world, not, as Sapir-Whorf suggest, a different reality. Typically, expanded and rich vocabularies correspond to items that are important to the culture. Perhaps you noticed this when you listed the specialized vocabulary of a specific sport or job in the Try This box.

Where the Sapir-Whorf hypothesis may have validity is in the area of verb usage and grammatical structure. Benjamin Whorf argued that the Hopi saw the world differently because they expressed verbs differently. Speakers of English have past, present, and future tenses, and thus they see the world as a linear sequence of events. Hopi, according to Whorf's analysis, have no past or future tense. Rather, they view things in one of two ways: things that are in existence *now*, and things that are in the process of *becoming*. Hence, according to Whorf, the past for the Hopi is viewed as events that accumulated in preparation for the present, rather than as a series of events that happened sequentially and are now over, which is how an English speaker would view the past. Whorf said that the things that Hopi do now are part of preparing for things that will come. He believed that many of the activities of Hopi life were tied to these ideas of preparing, such as preparing the earth to plant and the many festivals and rituals associated with these preparations. According to Whorf, the Hopi perception of the world is different because of their language structure.

Others have contended that what Whorf saw was distorted. They argue that, because no one ever knows a second language and culture like a native, it is impossible to know exactly how people of another language and culture perceive the world.

�֍ TRY THIS ✗
Analyze

How is the vocabulary of a subculture or microculture to which you belong influenced by areas of importance for that subculture? Make a list of terms you use that describe something that is part of your microculture. Do friends who are not a part of the same subculture understand that vocabulary or the nuance of differences in attributes that the different symbols (words) represent?

Suggestion: Consider what specialized vocabulary is associated with a specific sport or job.

Hopi

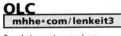

OLC
mhhe•com/lenkeit3

See Internet exercises.

This North American Hopi may see the world differently than an English speaker due to the structure of his native Hopi language.

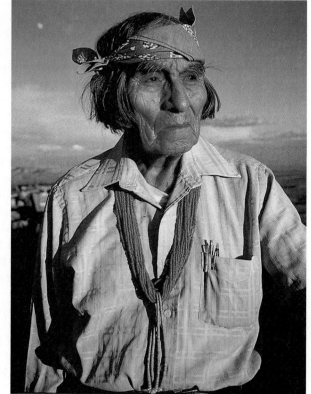

The evaluation of the relationship between language and culture is the primary task of **sociolinguistics**. Issues considered in this area of focus include different language usage among socioeconomic classes and among various groups and in various social situations or contexts. We all subconsciously switch between the content and structure of the language we use in different situations. When talking to a grandparent, you don't speak in the same way you do when enjoying an evening out with peers or at a job interview. Much can be learned about social relationships and status by paying attention to the way people talk.

Language is a marker of social class and stratification. This was demonstrated by a study in England by Trudgill (1974), who showed how parallel patterns of speech are used by different classes. In this study, class membership was based on criteria such as occupation, father's occupation, education, and income. Higher-class speakers used standard forms of pronunciation whereas lower classes used nonstandard forms. For example, upper-class speakers used *ing* (written phonetically as /ng/) in words such as runn*ing*; by contrast, lower-class speakers used *n* (written /-n/ phoneti-

sociolinguistics
A subfield of linguistics that analyzes the relationship between language and culture with a focus on how people speak in social context.

cally) to pronounce the word as runn*in* (Bonvillain 2000: 142). Other parallel patterns also clustered within class groupings.

Ethnicity also has an impact on language usage. In the United States the subsystem of English known as African American Vernacular English (AAVE) has been studied extensively in both its social and linguistic components. The origins of AAVE appear to come from two sources, although this is debated in linguistics. AAVE has features of phonology and morphology that seem to derive from white southerners (whose speech reflects their Scots-Irish ancestors). It also contains rules of syntax that derive from Creole. Like other languages AAVE has rich variations that adapt to situational contexts such as social factors (formal or informal situation), topics of conversation, and status relationships between individuals participating in the conversation. It is often used to show solidarity between a speaker and someone she or he is talking to. Many members of the African American community—working- and middle-class African American adults, African American students on college campuses, and rap and hip-hop artists—use AAVE to symbolize community membership, regardless of whether they were enculturated in the use of AAVE (Bonvillain 2000; Morgan 2001).

> **TRY THIS**
> *Consider*
>
> Does your language have a word for the back of the knee or the place in the arm that is at the front of the elbow?

The Complexity of Languages

All human languages are complex. None is more difficult than another. It is our ethnocentrism—based on our own phonemes, morphemes, and syntax—that makes other languages seem more difficult or complex than ours. Of course, the more similar a language is to one's own, the easier it seems to be to learn. If one were to argue for one language being more complex than another, one would have to delineate criteria and then, depending on those criteria, measure the complexity of the languages in question. But what is the point of such an exercise?

All languages have different ways to categorize observable variations in the natural world. We, in a sense, create word maps of our world. Every language's mapping technique is different. The symbols used to denote locations on the map (phonemes and morphemes) vary, as do routes for getting from one place to another (syntax). These different maps will result in difficulties when translating from one language to another. If we compare the anatomical vocabulary of English with that of other languages, for example, some insight can be gained. Picture a human arm and add labels for its parts. For example, in English we have the words *arm*, *hand*, and *fingers*. The Arawak of South America distinguish between *daduna*, the upper arm and shoulder, and *dakabo*, the hand and lower arm. How would an Arawak who has learned English translate a speech in which the English word *hand* is used? She would likely use the term *dakabo* (Hickerson 1980: 107). Those of you who have learned another language know of many instances in which there is no English equivalent to the concept in Spanish, Chinese, Japanese, German, or French.

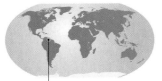

Arawak

ANTHROPOLOGY AROUND US

Language and Gender

The ethnographic literature is resplendent with examples of gender differences in language usage. Closer to home each of us confronts such differences daily. Gender-neutral terms such as *chairperson* and *mail carrier* have replaced gender-specific terms *chairman* and *mailman* in most areas of North American life. Less obvious gender distinctions have been brought to our attention but are changing slowly, if at all.

Deborah Tannen tells us that men hear and speak a language of status and independence. Women, by contrast, hear and speak a language of intimacy and connections. She argues that we are enculturated this way. Boys learn their approach to language as they play sports, where the group is structured and status is earned and negotiated. Boys show off, boast, and compete to win. Girls play most often in pairs or small groups; intimacy is important in these settings; and peer pressure causes even bright, talented girls to be humble. Tannen also argues that boys learn to be direct with their speech whereas girls learn to be indirect. A female boss asks her secretary to *please* type a letter and to *do her a favor* and hold any calls while she is in a meeting. A male boss is usually more direct, simply telling the secretary to type the letter and hold the calls. These differences in approach are learned and gender specific. A man may view a woman boss who asks someone to please do something as a favor to her to be showing self-deprecation and weakness (Tannen 1990, 1994).

◎ Have you been in a boss-employer situation in which gender differences, as mentioned here, were obvious? Did you consider this to be gender-specific language behavior, or did you interpret it another way?

◎ HUMAN VERSUS NONHUMAN SYSTEMS OF COMMUNICATION

How does human language differ from the communication system of other animals? Several aspects of language that have been identified as being unique include production and displacement. As far as we are currently able to determine, these aspects of language are found only in human language.

Symbols can and do change. Humans create new symbols as a need arises. The word *Internet* was created in the 1990s to describe a new communication system using computer technology. Additionally, we adjust or reassign meaning to already existing symbols when need or whim dictates. The word *mouse* acquired a new meaning when used to describe a mechanical object with a wire attached that is used to move a cursor on a computer screen. Reassigned meanings are found in the sentence "Allison is surfing the Web." A generation ago these symbols referred exclusively to riding ocean waves and to something spun by a spider.

The creative flexibility of the human symbolic system enables communication about time and place—this is called **displacement.** We can think about or discuss events in the past or the future, or events that are not within immediate proximity to our senses. Human communication is called an open system because it has both of these features: the creation, combination, or alteration of symbols and displacement. Scientific studies of the communication systems of other animals show limited and unchanging numbers of vocal signals. Moreover, the call sounds that are used always communicate about objects and happenings within the immediate experience of the animal, such as finding food or encountering danger. Calls are specific and discrete and cannot be combined. Such communication systems are referred to as closed systems. The longitudinal research study of communication among the Gombe population of chimpanzees in Africa provides no evidence of new sounds being created nor any evidence of these animals being able to displace with vocalization. Young chimpanzees learn their behaviors from their social groups through imitation combined with trial and error. Young humans use these forms of learning as well, but the overwhelming amount of what we humans learn is acquired through the symbolic process of language.

Some other animal species, notably various primate species, have been taught human symbolic communication in laboratory settings. American Sign Language (ASL) has been taught to chimpanzees and gorillas, for example. These animals are able to learn some of the ASL symbols created by humans, and once they have learned them (and presumably the concept behind them), they have, in fact, both created and displaced using ASL. These animals, however, do not create or displace using the call systems of their species as far as science is currently able to determine. The chimpanzee Kanzi clearly uses symbols and has acquired a vocabulary of over 150 lexigrams. He and other apes were taught using geometric figure symbols called **lexigrams** rather than with ASL. They too can displace. Controversy exists, however, over whether Kanzi and the others make and use syntax. They do place symbols in order, but this is limited to compositions that equal those of human children of about two years of age (Foley 1997: 77).

Noam Chomsky (1988) argues that humans are born with innate attributes for acquiring language. He argues that the role of the culture that we grow up in is of secondary importance in language acquisition. The data

displacement
The ability of humans to communicate symbolically about distant time and space.

lexigrams
Geometric figure symbols used to teach apes symbolic communication.

This primatologist is interacting with a chimpanzee using American Sign Language (ASL). Female chimps who have learned ASL have been observed using signs with their offspring.

from the various ape studies suggest that the chimps, with whom we share a recent biological past, may have some innate attributes for acquiring and using a symbolic system. Does this support Chomsky's view regarding human language?

Nonhuman primates also use some forms of nonverbal communication within their social groups—postures, gestures, facial expressions. Research on chimpanzees in the wild, for example, shows that there are traditions of nonverbal communication and these vary between populations. These communications are learned through direct observation and imitation; they are not genetically based (instinctual). Among human primates, nonverbal communications are important forms of symbolic communication that often combine with spoken language.

◎ SILENT LANGUAGE AS PART OF SYMBOLIC COMMUNICATION

Emblazoned on the cover of *Newsweek* magazine on February 5, 1973, was a photograph of a U.S. serviceman smiling at the camera and holding up his right hand with his index and middle fingers extended and separated forming a V. His ring finger and pinkie were bent and held against his palm with his thumb, and the back of his hand faced toward the camera. The word *peace* was boldly printed just below the *Newsweek* logo. Many Americans probably didn't give this a second glance, assuming that the GI was flashing the gesture for peace. Some Europeans recognize this silent language sym-

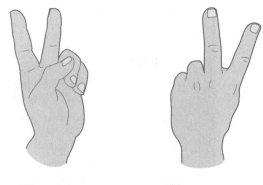

This gesture
means peace

This gesture
is obscene

bol as an obscene gesture. It conveys the same message as the extended middle finger to an American. It is possible that this GI was making an obscene gesture to communicate his views at that point in history. Given a second, closer look at the photo, one notices that the serviceman's smile looks odd. It's not a broad, tooth-showing grin Americans would associate with great joy, but one of wry cynicism.

Examples of this gesture appearing in the press abound. During a trip to Poland, then-president Ronald Reagan was photographed with arm outstretched giving the V sign of index and middle fingers extended, thumb holding the other two fingers pressed against his palm with his palm toward him. In the foreground of the photo, Mrs. Reagan was also giving the V sign, but with her palm turned away from her. One wonders what the crowds were thinking. Surely advisors ought to be advising presidents about gestures that may cause cross-cultural misunderstandings.

Nonverbal communication was labeled silent language by Edward Hall. **Silent language** refers to the myriad nonverbal ways that we communicate within a culture. Such communication may take the form of (1) kinesics (the use of the body), (2) proxemics (the use of space), (3) cultural time (the use and treatment of time), (4) words, (5) silence, and (6) material culture. Silent language symbols are learned, as are all aspects of culture, through the enculturation process. Silent language can be one of the most difficult aspects of another culture to learn because it is not formally taught. It can be misinterpreted by people with different cultural or subcultural backgrounds. Lack of awareness of another culture's silent language can lead to embarrassment and misunderstandings. Because it easily generates frustration, it can feed one's ethnocentrism. Lack of awareness of silent language may even be dangerous, as in the case of inadvertently wearing a gang's colors or using a gesture that carries a confrontational message. Silent language is a powerful form of communication.

silent language
All of a culture's nonverbal symbolic systems of communication, including kinesics and proxemics.

This North American A-OK sign has a very different meaning in some other cultures.

Kinesics

The opening paragraph of this section describes an example of kinesics. **Kinesics** is the study of the use of the body in communication. Specific kinesic studies analyze cultural gestures, facial expressions, and body positions. Common gestures such as the North American A-OK sign, made by placing the forefinger and thumb in a circle, can create misunderstandings outside of the United States. In some countries this gesture refers to a part of the anatomy and is used as a grave insult. In Japan it means money, and in France it means that you think someone is a zero. In Malta and parts of Italy at one time it was a male homosexual gesture soliciting sex.

The familiar North American "come here" gesture of motioning with the palm held up, fingers folded into palm, and the index finger alternately extended and crooked toward the body can also be insulting when viewed through the lens of another culture. A student of mine from the Philippines recounted that an older relative of his, a recent immigrant to the United States, quit a job as a busboy in a restaurant because he constantly felt insulted when people would use this gesture toward him. In the Philippines this gesture is used to call animals, and the older relative felt that he was being treated like a dog. Because he was enculturated to interpret the gesture in a different way, even when the North American meaning was explained to him, the gesture made him very uncomfortable.

Remember that gestures are symbolic and the meaning assigned to them may change from time to time even within one culture. For this reason, I

kinesics
The use of the body to communicate—gestures, posture, and facial expression.

believe that it is more important to be alert to silent language issues rather than simply to memorize the meaning of gestures for various cultures.

We are all familiar with facial expressions, and most of us do a good job of reading them within our own culture. We've all had friends ask us if something is wrong when we thought that we were hiding our sadness or pain. Something about our facial expressions or the way we were holding our bodies communicated our true emotion. A student who was enculturated in Cambodia remarked that in his culture it was considered an insult and very bad manners to look at a teacher when she was talking to you. He was confused when he first entered an American classroom. He said that even after seven years in the American school system it was hard for him to look instructors in the eye when they spoke. In traditional American culture, people who don't look at you when you speak are considered inattentive and shifty, or even dishonest.

Body positions, such as arms tightly folded across the chest, also communicate. Actors are particularly good at studying and using body position as a means of communicating an attitude or emotion. The next time you watch a movie, try to articulate what it is about the body position and movement used by a particular actor that is communicating to you. The process of interpretation or reading of silent language cues happens almost instantly, and researchers are currently attempting to understand this complex process (Archer 1980).

Proxemics

Another area of silent language is called **proxemics,** the study of how people of different cultures and subcultures perceive and use space. Touch, spacing, and territorial distance between bodies are all aspects of proxemics.

According to Edward T. Hall (1959), the use of space within middle-class American culture is broken into four main distances in social relations and business: intimate, personal, social, and public. Those who have been enculturated into the middle-class American subculture understand these proxemic categories very well, though they were never formally taught about them. When sharing intimate information with a friend, middle-class Americans move in close, usually about six to eighteen inches. We lower the volume of our voices to a whisper or near whisper and share the bit of gossip or personal thought. As we grew up, we also learned about how far away to stand in ordinary conversation, and we learned to use the appropriate voice level. We become aware of these cultural spatial distances when someone violates them.

A visitor from a Latin American country, for example, often stands in our *intimate* space while using a voice level that we would use in personal or social distance. The middle-class American's reaction is to back away, trying to get comfortable with the distance. The Latin American visitor is

proxemics
The study of the use of space in communication.

suddenly uncomfortable and tries to move closer. The ethnocentric voice in the American's head is beginning to register: pushy, pushy Latin. The Latin's ethnocentric inner voice is beginning to say cold, stand-offish North American. Unless one or both are culturally aware, unpleasant feelings will likely arise about the other person. If this happens to take place within the context of a business meeting, it does not bode well for the outcome of negotiations. It must be noted that this is an example only. Within Latin America, there are variations in the details of proxemics, just as there are proxemic variations within most societies.

At a state dinner in Korea, then-president Bill Clinton made a proto-col flub involving spacial expectations. When Clinton stepped to the micro-phone for his after-dinner speech, he invited a translator to stand between himself and Korean president Kim Young Sam, who was seated. It is an in-sult in Korea for anyone to stand between two heads of state. The breech of protocol was reported by the world press.

Cultural Time

Time is another aspect of silent language. For the American business exec-utive in an Arab country, frustrations about time can be particularly annoy-ing. Five minutes in American time is about fifteen minutes in Arab time. To an American executive, a fifteen-minute wait in an outer office requires an apology. To an Arab, the equivalent cultural time would be forty-five minutes. The American feels that the Arab is rude indeed for being so late. The Arab feels right on time or even a bit early for the appointment and perceives that the American has been pushy and uptight. Looking anthro-pologically at the situation, we see that the Arab has only made the Amer-ican wait the equivalent of about three minutes, U.S. time. The two simply operate on different value systems of expectation regarding time. We are enculturated to function with one particular concept of time. Awareness and understanding of different silent language systems is clearly important for international understanding in business and politics. The challenge is for us to acknowledge and learn to respect cultural differences at all levels.

Words

Words may have meanings other than the formal, generally recognized ones. Alternative meanings of common words are usually understood by members of a culture. Such silent language can, however, be quite confus-ing to members of other cultures. The phrase "see you later" caused many problems for foreign students at my college. In many cultures, customs of hospitality dictate that "see you later" means, literally, that the person ex-pects to *see you later*. Foreign students report feelings of frustration when expecting to see a new friend stop by their apartments and the person never comes. Or the foreign student drops in on the new friend and is received

Material objects and artifacts often communicate socioeconomic information to members of a society. Compare these two North American family residences.

with an uncomfortable coolness. Such experiences result in the new student viewing American students as unfriendly. Eventually they come to realize that "see you later" is merely a ritualized phrase of departure.

One immigrant from Thailand has recounted her experience and the disappointment she felt because of misunderstanding the silent language of words when she arrived in the United States. In Thailand the greeting "how are you?" is understood as genuine interest in one's welfare and requires polite reciprocal discussion in detail of one's current condition. When new American acquaintances acted bored or amused over her response to this common greeting, she was hurt and confused. She of course

TRY THIS
Consider

List four words or phrases you commonly use that carry meanings other than the literal, dictionary meanings and could cause problems for a newly arrived foreign student on your campus. Compare your list with that of another student.

TRY THIS
Analyze

Identify one meaning of silence in student subculture and note a specific example of it. Discuss this with several classmates. Do you share understanding of the meaning of this nonverbal communication?

TRY THIS
Ponder

Think of two specific artifacts in your subculture and what they communicate. Jot down your artifacts and their message and discuss them with a friend.

ultimately understood that in the United States "how are you?" is a ritual greeting and nothing more. The correct American response is "I'm fine" or "OK, how are you?" (Natadecha-Sponsel, in DeVita and Armstrong 1998: 68–69).

Silence

Silence is also a form of nonverbal communication. Its use is situationally dependent, and there is much variation in its use within a culture. In American culture, and most other cultures where this has been studied, status and social hierarchies are revealed in studies of silence. When two individuals of unequal social standing interact, high-ranking individuals talk more and low-status individuals are silent more (Bonvillain 2000: 44).

Material Culture

Artifacts and features are also part of silent language communication. Members of a particular culture share an understanding of the symbolic meaning of their material culture, and someone from another culture does not. Artifacts such as clothing, jewelry, home furnishings, and make of vehicle can silently communicate about issues such as socioeconomic status, ethnic group membership, and job status. On our campus, wearing Wrangler jeans and a leather belt with a silver buckle communicates that this student is an aggie (agricultural major). Features, such as backyard swimming pools or the number of household bathrooms, also communicate socioeconomic status.

SUMMARY

Language is a symbolic means of communication. Because it is the primary means by which humans acquire culture, its structure has been studied by anthropologists. The phonology, morphology, and syntax of language involves detailed analysis. Human language differs from the communication systems of other animals because we have *open* systems in which new symbols are produced and displacement is a feature. The call systems of other animals are *closed* systems of communication because the features of openness and displacement have not been demonstrated to be present. All human languages are equally complex.

The nonverbal symbolic communication systems of silent language are important aspects of culture—kinesics, proxemics, time, words, silence, and artifacts with alternate meanings. They are examples of cultural behaviors that we gain through enculturation and rarely think about, though they are powerful agents of communication. A lack of awareness of differences in silent language can lead to embarrassment and misunderstanding that can significantly undermine cross-cultural communication.

Study Questions

1. What are the types of studies that are undertaken by anthropological linguists?

2. What is silent language? Discuss how a knowledge of silent language is important if one is engaged in international travel or business. Cite examples from readings, the Internet, or print media to illustrate your discussion.

3. Describe three aspects of silent language that are discussed in one of your assigned ethnographies and cite specific examples.

4. Discuss how human language is different from the communication system of wild chimpanzees.

OLC
mhhe•com/lenkeit3
See Self Quiz.

Suggested Readings

Hall, Edward. 1949. *The Silent Language.* Berkeley: University of California Press. This remains one of the most readable and concise introductions to the cross-cultural impact of nonverbal symbolic systems.

Bonvillain, Nancy. 2003. *Language, Culture and Communication: The Meaning of the Messages,* 3rd ed. Upper Saddle River, N.Y.: Prentice-Hall. An introduction to the many meanings of language and how these meanings are used. Demonstrates the similarities and differences in human language.

Duranti, Alessandro, ed. 2001. *Linguistic Anthropology: A Reader.* Malden, Mass.: Blackwell. A sophisticated mix of classic articles and new research in anthropological linguistics.

Foley, W. A. 1997. *Anthropological Linguistics: An Introduction.* Cambridge, Mass.: Blackwell. Wide-ranging coverage of anthropological linguistics. If you have only one book on the subject, this is the one to have.

Tannen, D. 1990. *You Just Don't Understand: Women and Men in Coversation.* New York: Ballantine. A popular treatment on gender differences in conversation styles.

Suggested Web Sites

http://www.sil.org/linguistics
This site has an emphasis on the researching of undocumented indigenous languages around the world. It provides significant resources to assist fieldworkers and researchers.

http://www.ethnologue.com/web.asp
Affiliated with SIL International (formerly known as the Summer Institute of Linguistics, Dallas, Texas), this site enables easy access to information on more than seven thousand languages spoken in 231 countries. Regular updates are posted to the site.

http://anthro.palomar.edu/language/default.htm
This site provides an overview of language and anthropological linguistics. It addresses all aspects of human communication.

OLC
mhhe•com/lenkeit3
See Web links.

PART TWO

CROSS-CULTURAL ADAPTIVE PATTERNS

FOR AT LEAST 2 MILLION YEARS MEMBERS OF OUR GENUS (*HOMO*) HAVE HAD to cope with the same basic issues that all people on earth encounter today. We all have to eat. We require protection from natural elements. We must cope with other inhabitants of our territories—from viruses and varmints, flora and fauna, bacteria and beasts to family, friends, and foe. We have to manage interpersonal relationships, including group decision making and conflict. We need to express ourselves and consider issues such as why we are here, why things happen, and what happens after we die. These issues are interwoven, and each culture has evolved ways to address them. Many choices have been made along the way.

Part II of this text gives a summary of what we know, or believe we know, from over one hundred years of cultural anthropology. My goal is to present the results of widespread comparisons of ethnographic data—in other words, the results of ethnological analysis. I will organize this information within a loosely structured evolutionary-ecological framework. A uniform perspective is achieved when materials are organized in this manner, and it makes for a good starting point. Using this format also encourages critique and debate, and you'll find that there is quite a bit of this in the literature—and rightly so, because lively debate is what pushes science forward and ultimately leads to understanding.

The chapters in Part II are grouped together because they represent topics and issues common to people everywhere. Anthropologists have studied these topics for generations. The adaptive strategies discussed are diverse in detail, but many similar *patterns* emerge when ethnological analysis is employed. These patterns are emphasized in each chapter.

◀ Crickets are being harvested in China to supplement the local diet.

5

Subsistence Strategies
and Resource Allocation I
What Challenges Face Foragers?

Foragers such as these African Ju/'hoansi often occupy particularly challenging environments.

The meal was nearly complete. This was the first time that my daughter had a whole fried trout on her plate. I had decided that she was old enough at three years to learn to eat carefully and spit out the bones. She watched and copied her dad and me as we filleted one side of the fish and then removed the spine and most of the rib bones in one smooth movement. She ate with gusto but carefully. Finally, she asked if she could have more. Only the head and tail of her fish remained. I made eye contact with my husband and then remarked, "But you haven't finished your fish yet." She looked puzzled. "You haven't eaten the head yet. There are several small succulent bits of meat there. And you haven't eaten the eyes." I went on to remark that aboriginal Inuit children thought that the eyes were a special treat, except that they liked them raw. She asked how to eat them, and I told her to scoop one out with her spoon. She ate one, smiled, ate the other one, and then asked if she could have the fish eyes from the trout on my plate too. She is now thirty and still likes fish eyes.

What we consider acceptable to eat, what we consider nutritious, what we consider delicious, is learned. We all have to eat. People make choices about what to eat, they acquire food in different ways, and they have various approaches to the distribution of foods and other resources. The details of these cultural adaptations differ, but patterns emerge when comparative analysis is carried out. In this chapter we apply a theoretical framework that uses both cultural evolution and ecology to explain the various human strategies for obtaining food and allocating resources.

The objectives of this chapter are to
- Describe models of cultural evolution and cultural ecology
- Identify subsistence strategies within the framework of an evolutionary-ecological model
- Examine economic systems within the evolutionary-ecological model
- Examine the adaptive strategy of technology
- Identify the strategies common to foraging

◎ AN EVOLUTIONARY-ECOLOGICAL PARADIGM

OLC
mhhe•com/lenkeit3

See chapter outline and
chapter overview.

We all have to eat. Because food is essential for survival, this is where we will begin our look at human adaptations and the data compiled by anthropologists. This chapter and the next are concerned with how human groups acquire and use their resources to obtain or produce food and how food and resources are distributed and consumed. To make the material more manageable for you, I have divided it into two chapters. The first focuses on models used for analysis and the adaptations of foraging societies. The second focuses on societies that produce their food. The data will be presented primarily within the framework of two theories—cultural evolution and cultural ecology. To state this another way, the framework around which the chapter is constructed is an eclectic one that draws mainly on these two theoretical approaches. When I was a beginning college student I found the study of theoretical models a nuisance. After a time, I realized that such models, with their hypotheses to explain vast amounts of data, are quite useful. To begin we will consider models and model building. This will give you an idea of the process that goes into developing a theoretical model (a representation of something).

Models assist one to approach material in an organized manner, and they provide a foundation for the comparison of cultural data. The evolutionary-ecological model used here provides an introductory perspective on the study of subsistence and economics.

The Evolutionary Model

Cultural evolution models delineate a sequence of culture change over time and the processes at work in this change. The first such models suggested that culture change moved in a direction from simple to complex. These were presented in the 1860s, having been stimulated by Charles Darwin's book *On the Origin of Species* (1859), which discussed the mechanism for biological evolution. These early attempts to explain cultural evolution were later labeled **unilineal evolution** because they laid out a sequence of cultural stages rather like rungs of a ladder. All cultures had mounted each rung, or were in the process of doing so, to reach the top rung of civilization (see Chapter 13 for a description of one such model by L. H. Morgan). By the early 1900s archaeological and ethnographic field data demonstrated that the early unilineal evolutionists were mistaken, and other theories developed to explain cultural similarities and differences.

Cultural evolution became a hot topic again in the 1940s, 50s, and 60s. Models were again influenced by biological evolution, but anthropologists were careful to point out that while analogies could be made to biological evolution, cultural evolution was different. After all, societies did

cultural evolution
A model for the development of society that delineates a sequence of cultural change over time.

unilineal evolution
Early theoretical school that postulated that all cultures proceeded through a series of successive stages.

not reproduce genetically, and cultural adaptations were transmitted from one generation to the next using symbols. V. Gordon Child, Leslie White, Julian Steward, Elman R. Service, Marshall D. Sahlins, and others developed the most popular models. Each attempted to explain human cultural diversity, understand the varieties of human adaptations—ranging from small-scale societies based on foraging to large-scale industrialized societies based on intensive agriculture—and delineate patterns of human sociocultural development over time. I like aspects of many of the models. I like the idea of cultural evolution, perhaps because the holistic approach was emphasized in my education, and these models drew data from archaeology, biological anthropology, ethnography, and ethnology. Following is a quick summary of several of the later evolutionary models. Elements of these contribute to the evolutionary sequence presented as an organizing framework in this chapter, although I've drawn most heavily from Sahlins and Service.

V. Gordon Child, an archaeologist, viewed a series of major technological developments as responsible for cultural growth and believed that environmental factors stimulated adaptations as well as impeded cultures from growing. Leslie White outlined a model of cultural evolution that he called **neoevolution.** White proposed to assess a culture's level of evolutionary development by measuring its output of energy per person per year to procure and maintain people's basic needs, such as food and water. This idea, presented in his book *The Evolution of Culture* (1959), was exciting to read about. But it became clear that it would be impossible to actually apply his mathematical formulas to real cultures because, for example, there were too many variables, such as differences in soil fertility, which resulted in different calorie contents for foods grown in different regions. Julian Steward rejected White's approach of trying to apply a formula to all cultures. Rather, Steward gathered both historical and archaeological data on a number of societies occupying a similar habitat and was able to document a similar *pattern* of how the cultures changed over time (how they evolved). Steward's model became known as the model of **multilinear evolution** because he hypothesized that the evolutionary pattern would differ for different habitats. For example, one pattern would be exhibited by groups living near the mouth of river-valley systems and a different evolutionary pattern by societies in a desert, tropical rain forest, or other habitat—hence, the name multilinear evolution.

Marshall D. Sahlins and Elman R. Service (1960) built their model as stages of general evolution. "General cultural evolution is the successive emergence of *new levels of all-round development*" (emphasis mine) (Sahlins and Service 1960: 28). They based their stages of cultural development on broad sociocultural adaptations. These adaptations were in the areas of social organization, including kinship types and political organization, and systems of distribution. Service focused on social organization in his writing

neoevolution
A model of cultural evolution based on types of technology and food-procurement strategies, and the sociocultural adaptations that resulted from them.

multilinear evolution
An evolutionary model of culture emphasizing different development patterns for societies in different habitats.

(1962); Sahlins developed categories of economic redistribution (Sahlins 1968; 1972). They analyzed how new sociocultural adaptations resulted from changes that began with technology and food-getting strategies. They identified the stages of hunting-gathering bands, horticultural and pastoral tribes, agricultural chiefdoms, and finally state societies based on intensive agriculture. The next sections provide some of the evidence from archaeology and ethnography that contribute to this model.

Building the Model: Archaeological Evidence   It is useful to dig into the archaeological record (okay, pun intended) for evidence to support an evolutionary model of human cultural adaptations. Humanity began several million years ago in Africa, when recognizable hominid (humanlike) ancestors first emerged. They had cranial capacities about one-third the size of modern *Homo sapiens'*, and they walked bipedally. At least three genuses and several species of early hominids have been found that exhibit these basic features, and there is lively discussion as to which were our direct ancestors. The evidence demonstrates that at least one of these species made stone cutting tools, known as **Oldowan tools** (after the site at Olduvai Gorge in Africa where they were first discovered). Oldowan tools date to about 2 million years ago and are found in numerous sites of comparable dates throughout south and east Africa. Earlier tools, with a date of about 2.5 million years ago, have been identified at the site of Gona, Ethiopia, but as of yet widespread evidence of these tools has not been established. Fossil bones of various species of savanna animals have been found at the same sites as the Oldowan tools. Such bones appear to have been scavenged from the carcasses of animals after they were killed by large predators. Studies have been made of these fossil animal bones using scanning electron micrography, and numerous bones have marks that show specific characteristics that could have been made only by stone tools. Moreover, these cut markings often overlie the chew marks made by the teeth of the carnivores, indicating that the hominids scavenged from carnivore kills (Shipman 1984). This and other evidence point to a scavenging and foraging lifestyle for our early ancestors.

The Oldowan tools provide us with the first substantial material evidence of human culture. By a million years ago, our ancestors were making improved tools, including **Acheulean hand axes.** The hand ax attests to the increased technological abilities of their makers, including a consistent shape. Skills that were passed on to each new generation became incorporated into the knowledge base of the group. The archaeological record tells us that humans were foraging for a wide array of plant and animal foods for hundreds of thousands of years before they discovered how to domesticate plants and animals. The transition to fully sedentary lives based on the cultivation of plants was slow, and it took many more years before technological innovations and concentrations of population led to

These Oldowan tools were made by striking several flakes off of the core rock. The flakes had sharp edges and were probably also used for cutting.

Oldowan tools
A very early African tool-making tradition associated with the first members of *Homo*.

Acheulean hand axes
Part of an African and European tool tradition associated with *Homo erectus* and *Homo ergaster*. The tradition also includes cleavers and some flake tools.

the development of agriculturally based city-states and finally nation-states. This prehistoric chronology provides the structure for an evolutionary model of cultural development. Of course, many aspects of human behavior and thought do not leave direct archaeological evidence, but the *sequence* of the appearance of the food-procurement strategies is clear.

It must be emphasized that the unfolding of cultural adaptations through time was not linear. Ideas diffused between groups, just as they do today. There were periods of quick change and other periods of gradual change. Viewed as a whole, we can see a sequence that supports a model of cultural evolution.

Building the Model: Ethnographic Data   The next part in the development of the evolutionary-ecological model came from ethnography and ethnology. Data from societies with similar means of acquiring food were grouped together. In the case of hunter-gatherer-foragers the best-described societies (more than fifteen from five continents) were used as a database by Service (Service 1979). When compared, these cultures from diverse environments, but with similar food-procurement strategies, turned out to have other sociocultural adaptive strategies in common, such as the organization of kinship, type of leadership, or system of distribution. This became the basis of Service's and Sahlins' stages of cultural evolution. They hypothesized that over time, as new adaptations in food procurement developed, new adaptive sociocultural features also emerged.

Tools such as this Acheulean hand ax were an improvement over the Oldowan tools. They are worked on both sides and have straighter, sharper edges.

The Ecological Model

The **ecological model** of cultural development grew out of extensive research in anthropology (and the biological sciences) during the 1970s and 1980s and continues today. This perspective views a culture as part of a larger global ecological system with each aspect of the system interacting with all the other parts. Julian Steward wrote that "**cultural ecology** is the study of the processes by which a society adapts to its environment. Its principle problem is to determine whether these adaptations initiate internal social transformations of evolutionary change" (Steward 1968: 337). The relationship of an organism to its habitat (where it lives) is its adaptation. Human adaptations are the processes used by groups of people to alter their relationship to a habitat over time (Cohen 1968: 3). Human adaptations are cultural, not biological.

What circumstances must humans adapt to? Natural resources are finite in any environment, and each society develops within a specific physical environment that includes soils, elevation, water, minerals, wind, humidity, number of hours of sunlight, temperature (and seasonal variations), and the fauna and flora. Also, each society and its culture develops within a sociocultural environment that involves contact and interaction

ecological model
A model that views a culture as part of a larger global ecological system with each aspect of the system interacting with all of the other parts.

cultural ecology
The study of the processes by which a society adapts to its environment.

TRY THIS
Hypothesize

Jot down another possible hypothesis for adaptive strategies for foragers in desert environments. How might you test your hypothesis?

with other humans and their cultures. The dynamic, complex system that results is the focus of the ecological model.

Various specific models have been offered by ecologically oriented theorists as they examine what influences foraging behaviors. For example, paradigms known as **optimal-foraging models** have been developed, and these models aim at understanding how foragers optimize the gathering of food with the least expenditure of time, calories, or other factors. The choices available to the forager are considered, as are issues such as preparation time necessary to make the food edible. This model and others apply the scientific method and are useful for generating hypotheses for the study of past and present human adaptations.

For example, in researching the adaptive strategies of foragers living in a desert environment, one might make this hypothesis: If water sources are limited in a desert environment, then movements of foraging camps correspond to availability of water sources. Such a hypothesis can then be evaluated against the data available on foragers living in desert environments. The anthropologist might also consider how foragers in this particular environment optimize their gathering strategies.

The Evolutionary-Ecological Model

The bringing together of the models of cultural evolution and cultural ecology allow the anthropologist to take both a micro view and a macro view of cultural processes. This is the **evolutionary-ecological model.** When ethnographic fieldwork focuses on the micro adaptations (up close and in detail) of a particular society within its environment, the ethnographer is at the same time adding to our general knowledge of how human cultures adapt—the macro view. This macro view requires an alliance between ethnography, ethnology, and archaeology as data are compared between prehistoric and contemporary cultural adaptations. Such comparisons add to our understanding of both the past and the present.

optimal-foraging model
A model that aims at understanding how foragers optimize the gathering of food.

evolutionary-ecological model
A paradigm of human culture that combines both the neoevolutionary and ecological perspectives.

Economics and the Model

Economics is the study of how society acquires and uses resources to produce food and goods and how these are distributed and consumed. To study the production of food and goods, economic anthropologists must look at the natural resources and the technology used to acquire and process raw products and foods. They examine the units of production (individuals, households, private companies) and the division of labor and labor specialization (by gender and age), plus the means by which food, goods, and services are distributed and how they are consumed. Attitudes, traditions, and motivations about work and the acquisition of material possessions may also be studied. To present a more holistic perspective,

I have integrated these topics into the presentation of types of subsistence within the evolutionary-ecological model.

◎ TECHNOLOGY AS AN ELEMENT IN PRODUCTION STRATEGIES

Stone tools represent a large portion of the artifacts recovered in archaeological excavations (because they do not decompose as natural fibers do). It follows that the study of a prehistoric culture's adaptations often begins with stone tool technology. Technology is also a starting point for examining the economic adaptations of contemporary cultures, because technology is used in obtaining, producing, and distributing food and goods.

Anthropologists define **technology** as consisting of three components—knowledge, skills, and tools. These are used by humans when they manipulate and interact with their environment. Did your definition have all of these elements? Nearly all of my students over the years have focused on tools or machines when I asked them to define technology. Certainly this is one aspect of technology, but it is a narrow perspective. The knowledge that you carry around in your brain is a tool kit. This knowledge tool kit consists of a catalog of information that you have acquired, numerous manuals with procedures for problem solving, a list of social rules for successful collaboration with others, a checklist with procedures for evaluating risk, and a book of past successes and failures. Because environments have finite resources, the knowledge of how to use those resources to obtain food is critical. Many aspects of the analysis of technology relate to the optimal-foraging models mentioned previously.

The skills component of technology consists of the behaviors people have learned to use to manipulate their environment. The tools component of technology consists of all of the objects that are used to perform various tasks. Knowledge, of course, plays a role in deciding which skills to use. Tools are created through a combination of (1) knowledge of available raw materials, (2) knowledge and skills to obtain the raw materials, and (3) knowledge and skills to manipulate the raw materials to make the desired object. For example, you may know that obsidian (volcanic glass) rock when broken is sharp. To create a projectile point for the tip of an arrow, you must know where and how to obtain obsidian, you must have the understanding and skills to precisely control the breaking process to remove flakes, and you must know how to create a finished projectile point that can be attached to the shaft of the arrow.

The element of choice is a part of all cultural behavior, and a culture's technology reflects its choices. A society may know of numerous available protein sources but choose to use just a few of them. Why, for example, do North Americans include cows and not horses as part of their diet?

TRY THIS
Define

Quickly, define technology. What is it? Give two examples.

TRY THIS
Ponder

Check through your knowledge tool kit and consider how you would decide whether to eat a bag of wild mushrooms that have been collected by a friend. Check your catalog of information, your manual for problem solving, your list of social rules, your checklist for evaluating risk, and your book of past successes and failures. Process all of this knowledge and decide.

---

technology
The knowledge, tools, and skills used by humans to manipulate their environments.

TRY THIS *Compare*

Compare and contrast the natural environmental elements that humans would have to cope with in each of these photos. Discuss these elements with a classmate and together consider how contact and interaction with neighboring cultures might alter how these groups choose to modify the environment or the way they use it.

Great Basin landscape

Amazon rain forest landscape

TRY THIS   *Analyze*

Select a section from an assigned ethnography or other reading that focuses on a society's food-procurement strategies. Analyze the information available and sort the technological strategies into the categories of knowledge, skills, and tools. Naturally these are tightly intertwined aspects of technology, but new insights can be gained by trying to separate them. Compare how you sorted the information with how a classmate sorted it. What might account for the differences in your lists?

Why do most people in Thailand include insects such as praying mantises as part of their diet, whereas North Americans ignore insects as a protein source? Choices were made generations ago by our ancestors, and each of us has been enculturated into a society where the acceptable choices are in place.

The skills used in obtaining and processing food may also reflect cultural choices. For example, someone who wants fish for dinner could use fly-fishing skills to catch fish or use a fish trap or distribute a poison in the water that will stun or kill the fish. This person might even make different choices on different occasions. Choices are also made when making a tool—which material to use in making the object, which manufacturing technique to use, which design elements to include. When particular choices are made consistently within a society, regardless of the reasons for those choices, we speak of them as **traditions.** For example, the choice to make a pot from red clay rather than gray clay may simply reflect a cultural choice (provided that several colors of clay are available and the clays' qualities are otherwise equal). Or, if the red clay produces a stronger, less-fragile finished pot, we could say that the choice is based on a functional assessment of this attribute that is valued by the users of such pots. Often we do not know why a choice was made. Ethnographers have learned that people may make a choice simply because it is tradition in their culture; no one living knows why that choice was made originally.

My preference in the study of technology is to observe and describe what the technology *does* for the people it serves—a functional and ecological approach. How does the technology function within the adaptive strategies of the society? According to this perspective, technology's most important function is to aid the procurement of food and water and help to maintain body temperature. Technology also helps an individual or group maintain contact with other people through communication and travel. Finally, many tasks are made easier through technology. As you read the following pages, keep the definitions and functions of technology in mind.

traditions
Cultural choices consistently made by a society and practiced generation to generation.

ANTHROPOLOGY AROUND US

Edible Insects

In the summer of 2004, more than 12 million acres of northern Nevada were crawling with *Anabrus simplex Haldeman* (commonly called Mormon crickets)—two- to three-inch long relatives of grasshoppers. The insects eat nearly every plant in their path as they move, covering about a half mile per day. This was the worst infestation of the insects in fifty years. At the same time, the U.S. Department of Agriculture reported in 1998 that nearly 10 million people in the United States, one-third of them children, live in households in which some members experience hunger.

People around the world capitalized on the ebb and flow of insect populations by routinely incorporating insects into their diets. Insects are nutritious. According to the Entomology Society of America, various insects—termites, locusts, houseflies, spiders, and ants, for example—contain more protein (24 to 64 percent protein) than do chicken, beef, pork, or lamb (17 to 23 percent protein). Additionally these insects are low in fat and cholesterol.

In the region that is now California and Nevada, native peoples consumed wasp larva, bees, ants, and Mormon crickets. The Tatuya people of the Amazon basin near the border of Brazil and Colombia ate approximately twenty different species of insects. Chinese peasants ate large quantities of insects, especially silkworm pupae, whereas the upper classes partook of exotic dishes of silkworm pupae plus numerous other insects such as cicadas and giant water beetles (Harris 1998: 156–61). Preparation of such food includes roasting and drying. The taste of pupae and grubs is reported to be like lobster.

Even modern North Americans, who generally consider such fare repulsive, eat insects in a variety of foods. For example, peanut butter is allowed by U.S. government food regulations to have sixty in-sect fragments per hundred grams, while tomato paste, pizza, and other sauces may contain up to thirty insect eggs or two maggots per hundred grams.

◎ It has been suggested that the commercial raising of insect pupae would supply a cheap and environmentally friendly form of protein. What do you think of such a proposal? Are you able to see this issue through an objective lens?

◎ FORAGING AS A SUBSISTENCE STRATEGY

Foraging is food procurement that involves collecting wild plant and animal foods and was the earliest adaptive strategy used by humans. The archaeological record shows that people were foragers for hundreds of thousands of years before the domestication of plants and animals. In the 1960s the label "hunting and gathering" was used to designate peoples who obtained food in this fashion, and the emphasis was placed on men being responsible for providing most of the group's food through hunting. Foods gathered by women were considered supplemental. This interpretation was both biased and oversimplified. In the following decades, ethnographers began to actually weigh and measure foods, evaluate the nutritional content of foods, and assess the contributions of both women and men to food procurement. The result was a much more complex picture of food procurement, and the term *foraging* better represents this human activity.

Media images of foraging peoples can be biased, resulting in misleading stereotypes. Early televised films of foraging societies like the Dobe Ju/'hoansi (pronounced "doebay zhutwasi" according to Lee 1993) and the Mbuti pygmies were and are often misleading in their portrayals of food procurement by foraging peoples. Hunting activities are emphasized in these films because they involve stalking strategies and show dramatic action. Hunting can also be dangerous, as in the case of pygmies, armed only with spears, hunting elephants. Such scenes can be used to create drama in a film sequence, whereas berry picking and mushroom gathering don't provide much excitement, drama, or danger. Film producers aim for commercial success more than scholarly accuracy (which makes sense from a business standpoint), but such film footage led (and still leads) to stereotypes. One such stereotype is that native peoples who hunt and gather are primitive, simple, and backward. Another is that the natives are "noble savages"—idealized, romanticized peoples living in harmony with nature. Both perceptions are inaccurate. Be alert to question what you see on television or at the theater.

It is also important to continually remind ourselves that all subsistence patterns change and adapt over time. Foragers are not like fossils representing preserved remnants of the past. The same applies to horticultural and pastoral peoples (described in Chapter 6).

The Foraging Spectrum

Foraging represents a spectrum of food-getting activities. The sample tabulation in Table 5.1 gives a sense of the combination of enterprises that contribute to the diets of foragers. Foods gathered include berries, nuts,

foraging
A food-procurement strategy that involves collecting wild plant and animal foods.

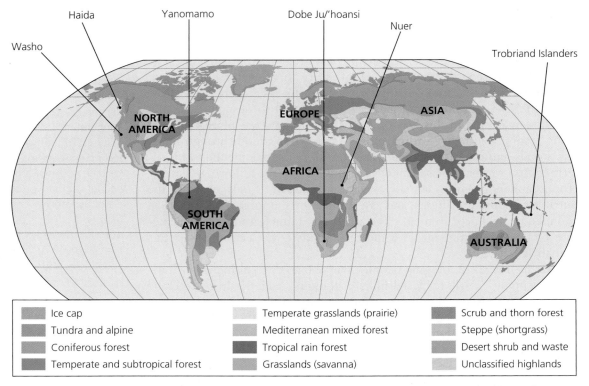

World ecoregions with focus societies discussed in Chapters 5 and 6 located.

TRY THIS *Analyze*

On the television Discovery Channel watch a rerun of an ethnographic film. Or rent the video *Dances with Wolves* or *The Gods Must Be Crazy*. Count the number of times the film or program shows a native hunting sequence and how many times it shows a gathering sequence. What other activities were shown? Do you think that these reflect actual daily life? Do you think that more realistic films would be commercial successes? What do you think this says about your culture?

OLC
mhhe•com/lenkeit3

See Internet exercises.

seeds, flowers, herbs, fungus, fruit, greens, eggs, shellfish, insects, and so forth. In one comparative study the percentage of gathered foods was as high as 80 percent of the total diet among foragers; hunting activities procured up to 60 percent of the food (the sources of this information did not uniformly distinguish between hunting for food that is eaten and food that is traded to nearby groups for horticultural produce) (Kelly 1995).

TABLE 5.1	Diet Sources of a Sample of Foraging Cultures			
Population Density (persons per 100 km²)	Group	Gathering %	Hunting %	Fishing %
0.02	Caribou Inuit, North America	10	50	40
62–96	Haida, North America	20	20	60
1.9	Plains Cree, North America	20	60	20
103	Maidu, North America	50	30	20
10–16	Dobe Ju/'hoansi, Africa	80	20	0
17	Mbuti, Africa	30	60	10
86	Andamese, Andaman Islands	40	20	40

Source: Based on data in Kelly 1995. Gathering includes plant materials, insects, small game, and sometimes shellfish. Fishing includes sea mammals and shellfish.

Features Associated with Foraging Lifeways

The general features associated with foraging lifeways that have been revealed by ethnological analysis are consistent, even though many details differ. These general features are sometimes called correlates to the foraging lifeway.

Production Based on Technological Mastery   Foragers have impressive technological mastery of their environment. It is not unusual to find foragers who are knowledgeable about more than a hundred edible plant species. They have the knowledge, skills, and tools to obtain these foods and prepare them for consumption. For example, the aboriginal Washo peoples of the Great Basin region of western North America drew upon a vast knowledge of food sources as they moved from the desert floor on the eastern side of the Sierra Nevada mountains and the foothills on the western slopes to the shores of Lake Tahoe at an elevation of 6,000–10,000 feet. They had to know about soils and microclimates as they searched for edible plants. Wild lettuces, for example, might be available in one spot whereas conditions nearby might be such that the lettuce had not yet emerged. Chokecherries may ripen in one region weeks before they ripen in another.

Washo

Hunters must know the habits and behaviors of the animals they hunt. Pronghorn antelope, known by the Washo and other Native Americans

Ju/'hoansi hunters snare hares in underground burrows. One listens to activity on the end of his snare, while the other probes a burrow. Extensive Knowledge of the environment is a survival feature of foragers.

for their curiosity, could be lured within range of a bow. Mule deer required a different strategy. One strategy employed by Washo deer hunters was to stalk their prey while wearing a disguise—a stuffed deer head with body skin attached and draped over the hunter's shoulders. Experienced hunters were known to be able to move extremely close to herds of deer while wearing such disguises.

The Washo and other native populations of California relied on acorns as a primary food source. Acorns have high concentrations of tannic acid, are bitter to the taste, and if consumed are poisonous. Therefore, before they could be eaten, a laborious process had to be carried out. First, the acorns were gathered and shelled, which involved knowing the location of and ripening time for acorn-bearing oak trees. After shelling, the acorns were toasted and ground by hand using either a portable flat *mano* with a *metate* for grinding or a bedrock mortar and pestle. The resulting product had to be as fine as flour; otherwise it could not be properly leached of the tannic acid. I have ground acorns in this way and can

Acorn meal, once it is processed, provides more than 90 percent of the protein, fats, and carbohydrates found in wheat. This woman is leaching acorn flour in a cloth-lined sand pit (Carson Valley, Nevada, 1966).

attest that it takes quite a bit of time to grind the acorn meal to the proper consistency. Moreover, pestles commonly weigh from two to five pounds, so one gets a real upper-body workout from the process. Finally, the acorn flour was placed in a sandy depression near a creek, and water was repeatedly poured over the flour to leach out the poisonous tannic acid. An alternative method involved placing the flour in a tightly woven basket and pouring water over the flour. Only then could this nutritious food be cooked and eaten.

Nomadic Lifestyle   Most foragers are nomadic. They must move with the availability of food and water. As an adaptive strategy, foraging must be fine-tuned to a particular environment. The frequency of movement is orchestrated to coincide with the availability of specific plants, animals, and water. The Washo were on the move from early spring, as soon as the Sierra snows began to melt, until the beginning of winter. Though they had many sources of food available to them, these were often widely dispersed, necessitating almost continual movement.

❀ TRY THIS ❀
Compare

Compare the technology (knowledge, skills, and tools) involved in the preparation of acorn meal with the technology you personally must use to eat a bowl of oatmeal (or your favorite cereal). What technology must be used by others before you are able to purchase your oatmeal or cereal?

Haida

TRY THIS
Hypothesize

Why did some human groups stay on land with a very low carrying capacity? Write a hypothesis about the relationship between environments with low carrying capacities and human groups remaining for generations in such environments. How could you test or evaluate your hypothesis?

carrying capacity
The maximum population that a habitat can sustain.

bands
A type of society common in foraging groups and marked by egalitarian social structure and lack of specialization.

family band
A type of band organization consisting of nuclear family units that move independently within an area. Joins others when resources are plentiful; travels alone at other times.

Foragers must also cope with risky situations. Unpredictable variation in weather or other ecological variables require flexible solutions, such as more frequent movement of camps when foods are scarce or maintaining camps by a year-round water hole during a drought. In the latter case, individuals would in essence be tethered to the water hole and would have to travel longer distances to forage.

Interestingly, there are foraging societies that did not move, such as the Haida of the North Pacific coast. The abundant salmon, other fish species, shellfish, and deer in their territory assured the Haida, and other societies along the northwest coast, a plentiful food supply. This in turn allowed for a large population concentration. Groups such as the Haida make the creation of evolutionary models difficult, because such groups do not meet all the criteria of the model.

Biologists developed the concept of **carrying capacity**—the maximum population that a habitat can sustain, or carry. It is determined by the availability of food, water, and shelter and by the existence of predators and disease. The previous statement implies that the calculation of a region's carrying capacity is a simple matter. It is really quite complex because issues such as the nutritional quality of food—vitamins, minerals, and protein—are part of the equation, not merely how much food is available. Because foragers are not food producers, they must be regarded as just another species, and their population size is limited by the carrying capacity of their environment. Humans, of course, have culture as their primary adaptive mechanism and this can affect carrying capacity. A foraging group's accumulated knowledge of food resources, their ability to plan ahead and predict when a source will be available, and their ability to alter their behaviors accordingly may be factors in maximizing the carrying capacity potential for foragers in a particular region.

Organization of Groups   Foragers are organized into groups that anthropologists label **bands.** At the time of early contact and study by anthropologists (1900–1950), foragers commonly lived in groups based on two types of kinship. One type is a **family band,** which consists of a number of nuclear families (parents and their offspring) living within an area. These individual families come together to form a larger group when resources are abundant and split up again when resources are scarce or widely dispersed. This coming together and breaking apart characterizes many foraging societies. Sometimes, too, foragers move from one location to another simply to be nearer to a particular relative. In other words, choice of where to live and when to move may be motivated by issues other than resource availability. The Washo exemplify this pattern with wide dispersal of families and individuals during most of the year. Patterns of movement for the Washo were quite fluid, with each family or individual making independent decisions about when and where to go. During the

A Ju/'hoansi woman foraging. She can identify more than 100 edible plant species.

fall piñon nut harvests and early spring fish-spawning runs, numerous families came together. Winter camps, too, consisted of clusters of families.

The second type of foraging group is a **patrilocal band,** which numbers about fifty people and is made up of several nuclear families who are related through their male members—for example, a man and his wife, their three sons, and their wives and children. This is called residing in a patrilocal residence group (see Chapters 7 and 8 for details of kinship, and see Chapter 10 for a discussion of political structure). The goal or ideal in such foraging groups is patrilocal residence (that is, living near the husband's family), but people often live according to other arrangements at any given point in time. Among the Dobe Ju/'hoansi, for example, a girl is often married when quite young (eight or nine years old). In such cases, she and her husband typically live for years near her mother and father, moving to be with her husband's group only when she is older. Patrilocal bands live on land with more concentrated resources than the environments occupied by family bands. In other words, their environment's carrying capacity is greater and can support a larger group. In fact, fishing-based foragers

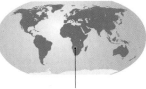

Dobe Ju/'hoansi

patrilocal band
A type of band consisting of related males and their wives and children who stay together and forage as a group.

usually have much higher population concentrations because of dependable and abundant food, as is true for the Northwest Coast societies, like the Haida, that depend on abundant salmon. Bands based on matrilocal residence (that is, living near the wife's family) are much less common and therefore are not listed as a *common* correlate to foraging.

Property and Ownership   Foragers have few material possessions. When everything one owns has to be carried from place to place on one's back, items are kept to a minimum. While the land and its resources are generally considered to belong to the whole group, particular resources may belong to a family and a tool might be personal property. For example, an Inuit woman's knife, or *ulu*, belongs to her, and among the Yurok of northern California, families owned acorn-bearing trees. Sharing, giving, receiving, and no one keeping track of what is given or received is the custom—a custom that is enculturated from infancy. Nonforagers, from tribal peoples to those who dwell in state-organized societies, have difficulty understanding this issue. Most access to tools occurs by sharing and borrowing rather than everyone having one of his or her own (living in close proximity facilitates sharing). Items given or received as personal gifts are often passed to the first person to admire them. Thus objects are constantly circulating within the group. Everyone always has something; everyone is equal. Many foraging societies have changed considerably since they began interacting more with contemporary industrialized societies. Some have begun to borrow ideas such as personal ownership.

Distribution of Resources   Foraging societies are marked by the economic distribution system known as reciprocity. **Reciprocity** is the enculturated pattern in which people give and receive items of value in predictable ways. The giving of food, a tool, or an item of personal adornment are examples of such value items. The giving of one's time in the form of helping to build a hut or watching someone's child also illustrates something of value. This giving of items of value is part of the fabric of band societies.

Marshall D. Sahlins (1968) identified the following three categories of economic reciprocity: (1) **Generalized reciprocity** is when everyone gives of time, food, and artifacts and no one keeps track of what is given or received. It commonly occurs between kin who are perceived as being close, such as parents, siblings, and spouses. These are people whom one interacts with regularly, and these individuals have an equal ability to give. (2) **Balanced reciprocity** involves the exchange of favors (such as helping with a task) or items while keeping mental records in the expectation that something of equal value will be returned within a reasonable period of time. This form of reciprocity usually takes place between those perceived as more distant relatives as well as those who are not related. Individuals

TRY THIS
Hypothesize

Develop two hypotheses that might explain communal ownership of land and its resources among foragers. Offer two specific ways to test your hypotheses.

reciprocity
A form of exchange that involves the mutual giving and receiving of food and other items between people who are socially equal.

generalized reciprocity
Institutionalized gift giving and exchange between close kin; accounts are not kept, and there is no expectation of immediate return.

balanced reciprocity
Exchange and gift giving with the expectation of a return of equal value within a reasonable period of time.

participating in this form of reciprocity also have an equal ability to give. Both giver and receiver have equal access to items that are given; neither is significantly wealthier than the other. (3) **Negative reciprocity** occurs when one tries to get more than is given often through haggling or even theft. Because it can create ill will, this giving typically takes place between unrelated individuals.

Among foragers, generalized reciprocity is dominant. It takes place, often on a daily basis, between persons who are close kin, which is everyone in the foraging band. Foragers are considered **egalitarian;** that is, members of the society have equal access to status, power, and wealth *within* the *same* category such as age or gender. For example, all male elders have equal access to status, power, and wealth. Everyone has an equal potential to give, and does. While thoughtful members of foraging bands have no doubt considered that it is in their own best interest to give goods and services, it is wrong to believe that members of such groups give only for selfish reasons. Enculturation results in this behavior being expected; most participants do not analyze it. Outsiders, such as anthropologists, are the ones to offer the analytical (or etic) view that this is how everyone survives.

Balanced reciprocity does not appear as a significant economic element within foraging societies. Rather, it surfaces when foragers interact with other societies. This is also the case with negative reciprocity—it is not usually undertaken with any person on whom you must depend or with whom you must maintain good relationships.

Nutritionally Balanced Diet   Foragers generally eat nutritionally balanced diets. The omnivorous nature of the diet of such peoples means that they use all possible food sources, though some choices are based on tradition. The foraging diet contains more variety than the diets of societies that produce their own foods and that specialize in two or three crops. The Washo used about 170 plant species and more than 30 animal species in their diet (D'Azevedo 1986; Downs 1966). Examine Table 5.2, and compare the diversity of the Washo diet to your own. For the Washo, none of these foods was in plentiful enough supply to support the population over an entire yearly cycle. However, at different times of the year specific foods were often plentiful. At Lake Tahoe, spawning runs of fish (trout in May and June, suckers in late June, and Lahoptan tui chub in July and August) provided large amounts of food. The various tributaries and rivers emptying into Lake Tahoe and other lakes within the Washo territory provided fish throughout the year. Fish were taken with spears, nets, hooks and lines, traps, and weirs and included ice fishing in winter. In the fall, harvests of piñon nuts could yield huge stores of rich nuts. A man and wife were said to be able to collect the equivalent of two gunny sacks full of nuts in a single day. Because of this diversity, foraging diets are generally more nutritious than the diets of food producers.

TRY THIS
Analyze

Where is generalized reciprocity used in modern American culture? Why? Where do we employ balanced reciprocity? Why? Discuss with a classmate. Is either form necessary for our survival? Why or why not?

negative reciprocity
An economic exchange aimed at receiving more than is given.

egalitarian
Refers to members of a society having equal access to status, power, and wealth.

TABLE 5.2 Most Important Foods Used by the Washo Peoples of Western North America			
Plants: 170 edible species, including		Animals: More than 30 edible species, including	
piñon nuts	Sierra plums	trout	ground squirrel
acorns	Sierra gooseberries	sucker fish	fox
chokecherries	manzanita berries	chub fish	badger
elderberries	watercress	rabbit	porcupine
serviceberries	wild rhubarb	mule deer	locusts
buckberries	mushrooms	pronghorn antelope	grasshoppers
currants	miners lettuce	bighorn sheep	bee larvae
wild lettuce	bitterroot	quail	fly grubs
sunflower seeds	sego lilies	sage grouse	caterpillars
wild mustard seeds	wild onions	prairie chicken	lizard
pigweed seeds	tule and cattail	waterfowl	bird eggs

Source: Based on data from D'Azevedo 1986 and Downs 1966.

An adaptive advantage to the foraging lifestyle is that the groups have the ability to shift to alternative food resources if a specific resource is unavailable because of weather, pests, or disease. Of course, starvation is a real possibility for foragers if weather conditions alter the usual levels of plant productivity, which in turn affects animal populations in the environment. Ecosystems are also disrupted by outside influences such as war, imperialism, revolution, and even tourism.

Low Energy Budgets   Foragers exist on **low energy budgets.** They generally have more leisure time than peoples with other types of food-procurement strategies. A low energy budget means that people expend a minimum of energy to acquire the basic needs for survival. A single woman walking to a nut tree and gathering the fallen nuts (rich in carbohydrates, protein, and fat) and cracking them to retrieve the meats inside, for example, has a lower yearly expenditure of calories than a woman growing a crop like corn or beans. Cultivating crops requires digging and preparing the soil, sowing seed, watering, weeding, and finally harvesting the crop before the food can be eaten.

low energy budget
The expenditure of minimum energy to acquire the basic needs for survival.

Economic Production Generalists   Foragers are generalists. Everyone knows just about everything associated with survival. Knowledge and skills are shared by all members of the group. No one specializes in just one activity to make a living. A woman knows how to hunt, though she may not do it often. A man knows how to cook and how to gather berries and nuts.

Kinship and Division of Labor   Foraging societies are kin based and have a flexible division of labor. All members of foraging groups are kin by blood or marriage or a fictive kin relationship. Fictive kin are people who are treated as though related by blood or marriage, such as a godparent. Each member knows her or his responsibilities and duties to each other member (see Chapter 8 for further discussion of the functions of kinship and Chapter 7 for consideration of other related issues). The division of labor, generally based on age and gender, may be flexible. Among the Washo, women generally gathered and prepared foods for drying and men hunted and fished. Ernestine Friedl (1978) and others have pointed out that the division of labor among foragers is usually more egalitarian than in agricultural and industrial societies. Friedl suggests that this is likely because both women and men contribute directly to the group's survival through food procurement.

Foraging Societies Today

Today there are few societies that live in the traditional foraging lifeways that were recorded from 1910 to 1960. It is fortunate that anthropologists were able to record the cultures of groups such as the Inuit, the Dobe Ju/'hoansi, the Mbuti, the Tiwi, and the Washo before the rapid changes that resulted from contact with industrialized societies. Of course, these societies also changed in the past. Few human groups were isolated and without contact with others, but contact was probably less frequent. Ethnographer Richard B. Lee noted that only one vehicle came to the Dobe area every four to six weeks during his 1963–64 fieldwork, whereas one every four to six hours was counted during 1986–87. Quick math will tell you that this is a change from about 12 per year in the early 1960s to between 1,400 and 2,200 in the late 1980s (Lee 1993: viii). During visits to Dobe in 1999–2001, Lee noted that road improvements reduced driving time into the area from 6–7 hours to only 2.5 hours, resulting in increased outside contact.

Health issues have emerged with dietary changes and more outside contact. The Dobe Ju/'hoansi in 1964 received 85 percent of their calories from foraging; in 1993 only about 30 percent of foods came from hunting and gathering, with the remainder consisting of meat and milk from domestic goats and cattle. Although they were once famous for having low blood pressure and cholesterol, restudies in the late 1980s of the same groups showed higher cholesterol and blood pressures in all ages (Lee 2002: 170). The Ju/'hoansi are now reporting cases of HIV-positive individuals, although the incidence is quite low, between 3 and 6 percent HIV-positive compared to national averages for Namibia of 22.5 percent and Botswana of 38 percent (Lee and Susser 2003).

Today the Dobe are subsisting primarily as farm laborers, though some hunt and gather part time. A new borehole (well) at Dobe now supports eight hamlets with 150 residents. There is a new preschool and a soccer field. Students attend a primary school 20 kilometers away (Lee 2002: 182). The people are taking an active role in the development of the region, including involvement in ecocultural tourism. The traditional values of egalitarianism and reciprocity are still held, and Lee believes that "Their commitment to egalitarian politics and reciprocity gives them a tremendous source of strength and persistence" (Lee 2002: 198).

Government officials, traders, tourists, medical personnel, and anthropologists all have an impact as locals see and interact with them. Anthropologists are interested in understanding human adaptations; this includes understanding the processes of how cultures change and adapt through time. Ongoing studies, such as Lee's with the Dobe Ju/'hoansi, provide us with vital information about the processes of cultural change.

SUMMARY

We all have to eat. The subsistence strategies of foraging, horticulture, pastoralism, and agriculture represent the major types of human food-procurement adaptations arranged in order of their emergence in the archaeological record. By viewing cultures within an evolutionary-ecological model, we are able to compare cultures with similar subsistence strategies. Overall patterns become apparent when it is established that each subsistence strategy results in a similar sociocultural adaptation. Foragers are bands of nomadic, kin-based, egalitarian societies without the ownership of property except for a few personal possessions or a particular resource. Generalized reciprocity is the dominant system of distribution found among these generalists; everyone shares in the technology, and the division of labor is flexible.

Foragers were not static in the past nor are they today. There was a time when forager bands were viewed as societies that were somehow, like fossils, preserved remnants of past ways of life. Some of these societies are being absorbed by industrialized neighbors; others have continued many aspects of traditional lifeways while selectively adopting aspects of their neighbor's adaptations.

Study Questions

OLC
mhhe•com/lenkeit3

See Self Quiz.

1. Describe foraging as a subsistence strategy, citing specific examples from the Washo and Dobe Ju/'hoansi.

2. Identify the adaptive features of technology and food procurement found in an ethnography assigned for class reading. How closely do these features match the general features of the adaptive strategy of foraging outlined in this chapter?

3. Compare and contrast generalized and balanced reciprocity. Cite a specific example of each from your own experience.

Suggested Readings

Bicchieri, M. G., ed. 1972. *Hunters and Gatherers Today*. Prospect Heights, Ill.: Waveland Press. Reissued 1988. Eleven chapters on hunter-gatherer societies from various parts of the world. Speaks to the diversity as well as the commonalities of the hunter-gathering adaptation.

Bohannan, Paul, and Mark Glazer. 1988. *High Points in Anthropology*, 2nd ed. New York: Knopf. Twenty-three cultural anthropologists responsible for seminal theoretical perspectives during the twentieth century are profiled. Of course, there will always be debate about who is included or excluded from the author's analyses of anthropology's "high points."

Harris, Marvin. 1998. *Good to Eat—Riddles of Food and Culture*. Prospect Heights, Ill.: Waveland Press. (Originally published 1985 as *The Sacred Cow and the Abominable Pig*.) Entertaining analysis of food preferences cross-culturally. Offers many insights into the dietary choices made by different cultures.

Knauft, Bruce. 2005. *The Gebusi: Lives Transformed in a Rainforest World*. New York: McGraw-Hill. As the title suggests, this ethnography describes the transformation of Gebusi life from the author's 1980 work to his return in 1998. Personal stories vividly transport the reader to the field.

Lee, Richard B. 2002. *The Dobe Ju/'hoansi*, 3rd ed. Belmont, Calif.: Wadsworth. This book covers decades of Lee's fieldwork among the Ju/'hoansi (formerly called the !Kung Bushmen) and is an excellent example of an ecologically focused ethnography. Lee offers insight into the diversity of adaptations made by foragers.

Plattner, Stuart, ed. 1989. *Economic Anthropology*. Stanford, Calif.: Stanford University Press. An indispensable resource covering the economic features of societies ranging from foraging to industrial.

Suggested Web Sites

http://anthro.palomar.edu/subsistence/default.htm

Effective overview of foraging, pastoralism, horticulture, and intensive agriculture supported with cross-cultural ethnographic information.

http://lucy.ukc.ac.uk/EthnoAtlas/societies.html

Organized by The British Academy, PORTAL is an online collection of resources dedicated to the humanities and social sciences. The "Ethnographic Atlas" offers a quick overview of selected cultures from Africa, the Middle East, North America, Asia, Oceania, Europe, and South America. Included is information about the culture's geography, environment, subsistence patterns, history (a brief overview), and other topics. Each analysis has a bibliography for additional research.

OLC
mhhe•com/lenkeit3

See Web links.

6

Subsistence Strategies and Resource Allocation II
How Did Food Production Transform Culture?

Rice terrace farming in Yuan Yang, Yunnan province, China maximizes both land and water usage for food production.

When an entrepreneur from Hawaii was visiting Tahiti many years ago, she was quite taken by the hand-woven palm fiber hats made and worn by the Tahitians. The hats were elaborate, and the finest ones were proudly worn to church by the native Tahitian women; everyday sun hats were not as detailed but still were unusual when compared to the simple straw hats worn for gardening or on the beach in Hawaii. She thought that the Tahitian hats would sell well in her Waikiki boutique as they were Polynesian native art. So she purchased some and took them home. Indeed they sold quickly, and she began to have requests for them. On a return trip to Tahiti she sought to arrange for someone to produce the hats for her and contacted several local weavers. She wanted many hats of one style and was frustrated to find that workers would readily accept employment but then would fail to show up to work after a day or two on the production line. Craftsmen would say that they were fed up (*fiu*). Making many hats of one design was boring. In fact working all day was not something that they wanted to do. Global economics and the spread of materialism had not yet seduced the native Tahitians. We heard many such stories about local attitudes toward work when in the Society Islands in early 1970.

Conversations with local Tahitians, French colonials, and missionaries revealed that outsiders often viewed the Tahitians as lazy. The more thoughtful among these, however, took a perspective of cultural relativism and pointed out that their culture was merely different in its attitude toward work. You could, they told us, contract with a local artisan to produce many hats, but they wouldn't be identical. Rather, the hats would show infinite variation in design. Moreover, the artisan would charge you less for varied hats than for identical hats. I carefully examined hats and other handmade items in the open market in Papeete and at roadside stands and small shops on the various islands, and rarely did I see any hats of the same design.

Attitudes toward work and what constitutes work vary widely from culture to culture. The North American work ethic was largely shaped in Europe during the Protestant Reformation by Martin Luther and John Calvin. Later, Benjamin Franklin fully secularized the importance of hard work in his *Poor Richard's Almanac* (1733–1758). American newspapers regularly run stories about those who achieve success by hard work. We applaud and revere those who toil and lift themselves out of poverty. Hard work is important; it pays off. Work dominates our lives. The first contact by Western cultures with others revealed a diversity of attitudes about work, production, distribution, and consumption. Anthropologists use these Western economic categories in ethnographic studies but acknowledge that they represent the view of others through our cultural lens.

The objectives of this chapter are to

- Describe subsistence strategies and economics within an evolutionary-ecological model
- Examine sociocultural changes brought by food-producing subsistence strategies
- Identify strategies common to horticulture and pastoralism
- Identify the strategies common to agriculture and industrialism

◎ THE EVOLUTIONARY-ECOLOGICAL MODEL CONTINUED

This chapter continues the discussion begun in Chapter 5. Here we consider how human groups acquire and use their resources to *produce* food and goods, how food and resources are distributed and consumed. Emphasis is on how subsistence strategies were changed by domestication and how socioeconomic adaptations occurred as a consequence. Again a holistic approach is maintained by interweaving discussion of subsistence strategies with economics, including production, division of labor and labor specialization, systems of distribution, and consumption. As with the discussion of foragers in the preceding chapter, sociocultural issues such as group organization and kinship are also touched on here because they too changed over time. Subsequent chapters cover kinship and political organization in more detail.

Some reminders: The evolutionary outline that is the framework of this presentation is the broad *sequential* one supported by archaeological and historical data; it does not mean that every culture progresses through exactly the same "stages" in development. The framework provides an organized way to introduce these topics. Every cultural group interacts in complex ways with its physical and social environment and has its own unique history of change over time. The theoretical perspective of cultural ecology also continues to be used insofar as societal adaptations are a focus.

◎ HORTICULTURE AS A SUBSISTENCE STRATEGY

Horticulture is a food-procurement strategy that is based on a simple level of crop production. Seeds or cuttings are planted without benefit of cultivation or preparation of the soil; no fertilizers are used, and no irrigation is undertaken. The data of archaeology have contributed to knowledge of when and where horticulture first emerged as a food-procurement strategy. Our assessment of this emergence is aided by recent technologies for the gathering of data from the past. For example, accelerator mass spectrometry (AMS) in conjunction with carbon-14 dating has made it possible to date a single seed about the size of a sesame seed. New flotation techniques allow for the recovery of tiny specimens such as seeds, seed coats, and insect wings. These techniques, in conjunction with the electron microscope (which enables us to measure the thickness of seed coats—an important determinant of domestication), have revealed much about early plant domestication.

Early archaeologists hypothesized that plant domestication originated in a few widely dispersed geographic locations—rice in southeast Asia, millet in Africa, wheat in Asia Minor, corn in Mexico. From these points of origin the crops were thought to have diffused to other regions. Recent

horticulture
A food-procurement strategy based on crop production without soil preparation, fertilizers, irrigation, or use of draft animals.

research, however, has revealed a much more complex and interesting process for this adaptation with many more centers of domestication and many more species of plants involved.

Bruce Smith has shown that *Chenopodium berlanderii* (a seed-bearing plant that yields tiny, highly nutritious seeds about the size of alfalfa seeds or poppy seeds) was domesticated east of the Mississippi River in North America about two thousand years before the arrival of *Zea mays* (corn), which diffused north from Mexico (Smith 1992). Further, Smith has demonstrated that other seed crops were domesticated in the same area and yielded nutrition-rich foods for prehistoric Native American populations as they learned to sow and harvest along the floodplains of river valleys. We should not be surprised to find that the shift from foraging ways of life to settled village life based on cultivating crops was a slow, gradual process rather than the revolution that was hypothesized earlier. It was most likely an adaptation to environmental and social stresses in particular habitats. Human culture is continually changing, some aspects slowly, others quickly, but even quick changes usually take close to a generation to be complete. Most horticulture developed in areas where there is sufficient rainfall to maintain crop growth or in floodplains where seasonal flooding provides moisture.

Features Associated with Horticultural Lifeways

Comparative analysis of societies with horticulture as the primary food-procurement strategy shows a number of sociocultural correlations with this type of food getting.

Production Based on Extensive Technology   Horticulturalists have extensive technology. The technology—knowledge, skills, and tools—used in simple cultivation is complex and requires understanding of plant cycles, seasonal weather conditions, soils, when and how to harvest, how to winnow hulls from seeds, and how to select and store seeds for the next season's planting. Horticulturalists need the knowledge and skills to manipulate nature rather than focusing on understanding their natural surroundings as foragers do. This attests to the cumulative nature of culture. Knowledge builds through time as new discoveries are made and passed on to each generation.

The Yanomamo of Venezuela and Brazil cultivate gardens that provide 80 to 90 percent of their food; the remainder comes from hunting and some gathering of wild plants and insects such as grubs. Plantains provide 80 percent of the calories that the Yanomamo consume, and most garden space is taken up by plantain trees. Each tree produces only one bunch of the banana-shaped fruit; then it is cut to the ground to make room for the young suckers that have been forming underground. Each sucker can grow into a new tree. Yanomamo gardeners must keep track of these planting and harvesting cycles to ensure continuous crops. Other

Yanomamo

cultivated plants include peach palm trees, sweet manioc (a starchy root), a type of taro, sweet potatoes, and sometimes avocados, papaya, and hot peppers. Inedible crops include cotton and tobacco (Chagnon 1997).

TRY THIS   *Compare*

Compare and contrast the technologies of horticulturists and your own society. Can we say that one is more complex than the other from the standpoint of an individual society member's knowledge?

Make an argument in support of the following statement: An individual forager has more complex knowledge than an individual member of North American society has.

Sedentary Lifestyle   Horticulturalists are sedentary. Unlike foragers, horticulturalists stay in one place for long periods of time—typically until the soil is exhausted. The most common type of horticulture is called **slash-and-burn** horticulture because ground cover is removed by cutting and burning. Large trees may be felled outright or girdled and allowed to die before they are burned. There are other local terms for this horticulture method (e.g., swidden), but the same process is used everywhere. You and I, as products of cultures with scientific technology, recognize that ashes contribute to the fertility of the soil, but slash-and-burn is primarily viewed by those who practice it as a means of clearing the land. When crop yield declines, new gardens are created by the same technique. Soils that have been exhausted in this way take many generations to recover sufficiently to support diverse plant life once more. At one time soil depletion was hypothesized as the only reason that horticulturalists moved. Today we know that declining soil fertility alone cannot account for village movements at least in the tropical forest of Amazonia. Napoleon Chagnon has reported that the Yanomamo created new gardens adjacent to maturing ones because it was more convenient to do so, and he documented cases of villages staying in the same area for sixty to eighty years. One reason to stay in the same area is that cuttings of large plantain suckers (which will yield a new crop of plantains sooner than a small sucker) sometimes weigh ten pounds or more, so moves of a few hundred yards are much easier than long-distance moves. Chagnon also reports that unpleasant, thorny vegetation that grows in maturing gardens is both tedious and painful to remove, and snakes become a problem in old gardens. These are logical reasons to make what he calls micro movements (Chagnon 1997: 71–72).

Larger Groups and Kinship Structures   Horticulture results in larger populations and kinship systems with more segments than those encoun-

slash-and-burn
The removal of plant materials by cutting and burning prepatory to planting.

This boy in Kenya is tending a rice field. The noise from banging on the can keeps the birds away.

tered among foragers. This is due to the increase in carrying capacity that results from food production. Having large numbers of people (from several hundred to tens of thousands) requires organization if the society is to work efficiently. Horticultural societies are kin based, meaning that kinship ties and the responsibilities that accompany them are what weave the fabric of such societies. Kin groups based on descent and residence are a consistent correlate to horticulturally based societies. The various types of descent and residence groups are discussed in Chapters 7 and 8, and political aspects of tribes are discussed in Chapter 10.

Property and Ownership   Unlike foragers, horticulturalists own property. Property ownership is by kin groups, and these groups—lineages and clans, for example—work the land and reap the benefits of their labors. Common patterns among horticulturalists include small settlements of several related kin groups that are surrounded by gardens and fields. Land rights belong to a family or lineage or larger kin group. This is not ownership in terms of legal deeds to the land, as recognized in state societies. Rather, members of the society recognize traditional land rights, and such lands are passed from generation to generation. For example, among the Trobriand Islanders (a Melanesian society off the east coast of New Guinea), gardens are owned by women and inherited through women. Horticulturalists also have more possessions than foragers. Extended living in one place, plus the need for tools to produce, harvest, store, and process the crops, results in more artifacts.

Poorer Nutrition   Horticulturalists have poorer overall nutrition than foragers. Vitamin and mineral intakes are reduced, or incomplete, because food is not as diverse. Both archaeological evidence from forensic analysis of the skeletons of prehistoric peoples and data from ethnography show that human nutrition and health declined with settled living and dietary reliance on one or a few grains. See Box 6.1 for an explanation of some of the negative consequences of diets based on the cultivation of domestic plants.

Higher Energy Budget   Horticulturalists have a higher energy budget than foragers. Many more calories are spent per person per week to procure basic survival needs. Clearing of land and planting of crops requires intense physical effort (horticulturalists do not use draft animals), but this is just the beginning of the planting cycle. Crops must be weeded, and birds and other animals must be deterred from eating the emerging seedlings. Harvest and preparation of foods for consumption as well as the maintenance of storage facilities must also be considered.

Economic Production Generalists   Horticulturalists, like foragers, are family-based generalists, not specialists. Each family must know how to carry out numerous tasks for survival; individuals do not support themselves singly by a specialized economic activity. Rather, all are involved in some aspect of tending the gardens.

Division of Labor   Horticulturalists have a well-defined division of labor. Men's work and women's work are clearly delineated and do not have the flexibility found among foragers. Some anthropologists have speculated that the more rigid division of labor that developed with horticultural economies may have been the beginning of important differences in the status of men and women. The issue of how rigid or flexible the division

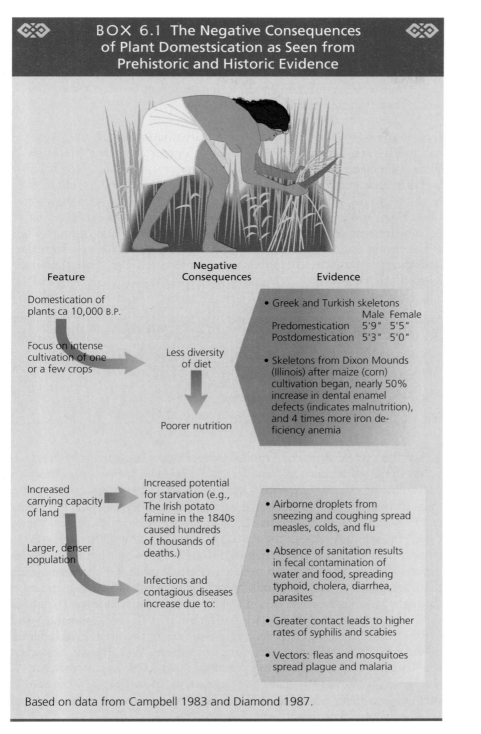

BOX 6.1 The Negative Consequences of Plant Domestsication as Seen from Prehistoric and Historic Evidence

Feature	Negative Consequences	Evidence
Domestication of plants ca 10,000 B.P.		• Greek and Turkish skeletons

Focus on intense cultivation of one or a few crops

Less diversity of diet

Poorer nutrition

	Male	Female
Predomestication	5'9"	5'5"
Postdomestication	5'3"	5'0"

• Skeletons from Dixon Mounds (Illinois) after maize (corn) cultivation began, nearly 50% increase in dental enamel defects (indicates malnutrition), and 4 times more iron deficiency anemia

Increased carrying capacity of land

Larger, denser population

Increased potential for starvation (e.g., The Irish potato famine in the 1840s caused hundreds of thousands of deaths.)

Infections and contagious diseases increase due to:

• Airborne droplets from sneezing and coughing spread measles, colds, and flu

• Absence of sanitation results in fecal contamination of water and food, spreading typhoid, cholera, diarrhea, parasites

• Greater contact leads to higher rates of syphilis and scabies

• Vectors: fleas and mosquitoes spread plague and malaria

Based on data from Campbell 1983 and Diamond 1987.

of labor is in societies with different systems of food procurement can be debated. This is one of the issues that is somewhat murky when viewed cross-culturally. For example, Annette Weiner reports that among the Trobriand Islanders growing yams is primarily men's work. She notes, however, that husbands and wives work together in the strenuous labor of soil preparation (Weiner 1988).

Distribution of Goods   The systems of distribution found among horticulturalists are similar to those among foragers, but the emphasis is shifted. Generalized reciprocity still dominates within the nuclear family and extends to some other close kin, such as lineage members, but outside of these groups balanced reciprocity is the norm. Gifts of food, possessions, time, and energy are calculated, and the expectation is that items of equal value will be reciprocated within a reasonable period of time. Thus alliances and interdependencies are formed outside of one's own lineage, and clan and status or reputation may be enhanced by participating in reciprocal exchanges.

TRY THIS   *Ponder*

Make a list of the ways you participate in balanced reciprocity with neighbors and business associates or classmates. How necessary are these reciprocal exchanges to your survival? What has taken the place of balanced reciprocity in our culture?

Trobriand
Islanders

In the case of the Trobriand exchange system known as the *kula*, ornately made white arm shells and red shell necklaces are at the center of an elaborate and complex balanced reciprocal exchange system. These items move between trade partners on a group of islands that form a rough circular ring, so the exchange has been called the kula ring. Men labor to match the size and value of these two types of shells. An individual receives an arm shell from one trade partner during a visit to another island and is expected to reciprocate with a necklace of equal value at a later time when the trade partner visits his island. Necklaces move in a clockwise direction through the islands, whereas arm shells move counterclockwise. Trade of foods and other items takes place peripherally to the kula exchange, and early analysis suggested that such trade was really the important function of the exchange. However, according to Annette Weiner, who restudied the Trobriands in the 1980s, men's status is tied to the kula exchanges. As she states, "Trobriand men create their own individual fame by circulating these objects that accumulate the histories of their travels and the names of those who have possessed them" (Weiner 1988: 9).

Trobriand kula objects have histories that accompany them on the traditional trade routes.

◎ PASTORALISM AS A SUBSISTENCE STRATEGY

The archaeological evidence shows that humans began domesticating animals and plants at about the same time—around ten thousand years ago. Horticultural economies, with supplementation from domesticated animals, thrived for some time before lifeways emerged that focused on herding. There were likely many different ecological conditions that fostered **pastoralism,** and many different animals have been the basis for a herding way of life—cattle, sheep, reindeer, goats, camels, horses, and llamas. Pastoralists learned to use many aspects of the animals they nurtured, maintaining the herds as a food bank reserve. Animals can eat natural plant materials that humans cannot consume directly, so animal husbandry may be viewed as an adaptive strategy that transforms energy sources into a form that humans can use. Milk, blood, hair, skin, bone, horn, antler, and hoof provide both sustenance and raw materials for making artifacts. Animals are rarely killed for food, usually only when associated with ceremonies

pastoralism
A food-producing strategy based on herding.

(which may occur throughout the year, thus providing consistent, if small, amounts of meat protein).

Similar to other adaptive strategies of the evolutionary-ecological model, variation is found in the specifics of each pastoral society, whereas some general correlates emerge cross-culturally. Elman Service noted many general sociocultural similarities between horticulturalists and pastoralists, aside from their food-procurement strategies. If one considers a continuum of adaptations from an evolutionary perspective, it would look like this: foraging, horticulturalism, horticulturalism with supplements of domestic animals, pastoralism.

Features Associated with Pastoral Lifeways

The following are the common features of the pastoralist adaptation as described in various ethnographies.

Nuer

Production Based on Sophisticated Technology   Pastoralists have sophisticated technologies. Knowledge of their environment must be extensive to know where and when to move their herds to fresh pastures. They have knowledge and skills to successfully breed and maintain their animals. The Nuer of the southern Sudan in Africa are a society that focuses on animal husbandry in the form of cattle herding. They also raise gardens of millet and beans, but herding is the focus of their food production. The environment they live in is essentially flat land with marshes and grassy plains where few trees grow. Rivers flow through the region and flood vast areas during the wet season, requiring the Nuer to move their herds to higher grounds until the water recedes. The sandy soils of these slightly elevated areas allow the growing of millet, but because they lack pasture and water, movement back to the grassy plains is necessary. Clay soils in the flats and marshy areas hold water, which in turn supports grasses during the dry season.

nomadic pastoralism
A herding adaptation that makes the most of available forage for animals by frequent habitat moves.

transhumance
A variety of pastoralism in which herds are moved seasonally.

Nomadic Lifestyle   Most pastoralists are nomadic. They must move frequently to fresh pastures. Ranching and dairy farming (which could be called sedentary pastoralism) are fairly recent occurrences in the history of human adaptations and are typically associated with industrialized societies. Two types of preindustrialized pastoral economies have been identified. **Nomadic pastoralism** is an adaptation that makes the most of available forage for the herd animals by frequent mobility. The entire group moves with their animals. **Transhumance** is a pastoral adaptation in which herds are moved seasonally such as up into mountains as spring and summer progress, or to rotating pasture areas. Only part of the group moves with the herds—men and boys, for example. Others stay in the home or village location. The Nuer, with their frequent moves because of the cycles of wet and dry, were labeled transhumant by E. E. Evans-Pritchard, who published accounts of their traditional life (Evans-Pritchard 1940).

A Nuer man and child attend cattle.

Large Populations   Pastoralism results in large populations and increases the carrying capacity of land that is relatively infertile. On land that can support only grass and scrub (and there is quite a bit of such land), pastoralism is an effective strategy that enables more people to live in an area than could live there by either foraging or horticulture. Pastoral people, who for obvious reasons are more widely dispersed across the landscape than horticultural groups, often consist of thousands of people. The Nuer numbered 200,000 when Evans-Pritchard worked among them in the 1940s.

Property Ownership   Pastoralists own property in the form of animals. The ownership of herd animals is at the core of the various groups who nurture and benefit from the animals. Because they are mobile, pastoralists have fewer material possessions than horticulturalists. There is much variation of detail regarding this feature of the pastoral lifeway because some pastoralists maintain semipermanent camps that they return to periodically and others use animals as beasts of burden to transport possessions.

Improved Nutrition   Pastoralists generally have better nutrition than horticulturalists, primarily because they have access to more complete protein in the form of milk, milk products, and blood. Pastoralists either maintain small kitchen gardens or trade with neighboring horticultural groups for grains and vegetables. The Nuer cattle supply milk, which is consumed fresh, sour, curdled, and as cheese. Blood let from veins in a cow's neck and collected in gourds is boiled and used as flavoring, or it is allowed to coagulate and is then roasted over hot coals before being eaten. Meat from cattle is eaten primarily at ceremonial occasions or if an animal dies. Millet is eaten as porridge and made into beer. Some beans and maize are also grown. A few wild dates can be found in Nuer territory, but there is little else in the way of wild fruits or vegetables.

High Energy Budget   The energy budget of pastoralists is higher than that of foragers. Husbanding herd animals requires constant vigilance to ensure that the pasture is adequate, water is available, and animals are protected from various natural hazards.

Kinship and Division of Labor   Pastoralists are kin-based groups in which the fabric of the society, as in the case of horticulturalists, is woven of various complex kinship ties and the responsibilities associated with them. Such large societies require organization if they are to function efficiently. Like large horticultural groups, societal organization and social interaction are based on kin descent and residence patterns. These large kin organizations are discussed in Chapters 7 and 8. Division of labor is by age and gender.

OLC
mhhe•com/lenkeit3
See Internet exercises.

Distribution of Goods   The systems of distribution found among pastoralists involve generalized reciprocity between nuclear family and lineage members and balanced reciprocity with most others who are more distantly related. Balanced reciprocity through barter and trade took place with adjacent societies in the past. Today pastoralists exist on the periphery of societies based on market exchange, and they participate to some extent in these systems. The Nuer today number over 1 million, and there have been many changes, including those caused by decades of civil war and unrest in the Sudan, yet emphasis on cattle remains central to their cultural values.

Horticulturalists and Pastoralists Today

Culture is dynamic. Restudies of tribal peoples illustrate this concept. Contact with other tribal peoples, missionaries, traders, colonial governments, soldiers, and tourists, as well as warfare, led to some acculturation and change for most tribal peoples. Two societies described in the previous sections, the Trobriand Islanders and the Nuer, experienced and are experiencing such changes. The Trobriand Islanders were first made famous by Malinowski's fieldwork that began in 1914. The Trobriands became part of the nation-state of Papua New Guinea in 1975. Participation in a cash economy, due in large part to tourism, has detracted from traditional social activities (Peters-Golden 2002). Annette Weiner reported in 1988 that Trobrianders resist change and despite much contact and a period of active tourism, they maintained important traditional beliefs. She attributes this to the role of women. Women traditionally controlled their own wealth by manufacturing items of economic value such as banana leaf fiber skirts and banana leaf bundles. The major use of these items is in the payments—from thirty to several hundred bundles—made to mourners after death (Weiner 1988: 30–49). When an important chief died, she reports, even university-educated Trobrianders living in the urban capital attended the traditional distribution ceremony that was held (Weiner 1988: 31). Trobrianders are increasingly involved with a global economy. In 2005 numerous Web sites promoted ecotourism in the Trobriand Islands.

The Nuer have experienced major upheavals since Evans-Pritchard recorded their way of life in the early 1930s. One civil war (1955–72) was fought to win autonomy for and unite the southern region. Then in the 1980s the national government proposed among other issues to divide the south into three regions (Hutchinson 1996: 3–4). Ethnographer Sharon Hutchinson was forced to leave her study area in Nuerland in 1983 due to the political unrest. She returned in 1990 and reports that the United Nations estimated that "more than 500,000 southern Sudanese had lost their lives as a direct consequence of war-provoked confrontations, famine, and disease" (Hutchinson 1996: 5–6). Additionally, thousands of Nuer were displaced from their homes and became refugees in camps in Ethiopia and Kenya. Programs were designed to help find permanent homes for them. This resulted in nearly four thousand Nuer emigrating to the United States by 1996 (Holtzman 2000). Survivors and refugees are adapting. Some in the Sudan are trying to recapture the old ways of life. Others, such as those living in Minnesota, are trying to adapt to new ways of life. Space does not allow further discussion here of either the complexities of the civil war or the current plight of the Nuer, but I encourage you to read more about updates on the Nuer, the Trobrianders, and other indigenous peoples (see the Suggested Readings section at the end of this chapter).

◎ AGRICULTURE AS A SUBSISTENCE STRATEGY

Agriculture is a subsistence-procurement strategy that is based on intensive, continuous use of land for the production of plant foods. One or more of these features is present: cultivation of soils, use of fertilizers, and irrigation. Soil cultivation is often elaborate and energy intensive. Draft animals or tractors are used to plow, to maintain cultivated land, and to harvest crops. Fertilizers are applied before planting and during plant growth, resulting in increased yields. Regular, planned irrigation ensures

agriculture
A subsistence strategy based on intensive, continuous use of land for the production of plant foods. It typically includes one or more of the following: cultivation of soils, use of fertilizers, and irrigation.

plant survival and optimum growth. As with the other systems of food production that have been discussed, there is a continuum of agricultural production. The range is from small single-family farm holdings to modern farming corporations. Small farms may use flood irrigation from a nearby river and have a single draft horse or ox. Large multifamily cooperative farms have complex irrigation systems and several draft animals or the use of a tractor that has been cooperatively purchased. Modern farms owned by corporations have thousands of acres in production and make extensive use of the resources and support of state-owned-and-operated irrigation systems and utilize energy from sources such as fossil fuels.

The archaeological record is resplendent with data for the emergence of agriculture, because it often, though not always, coincides with the emergence of population centers, or cities. Emerging agricultural strategies tend to focus on production of one or a few crops, thus requiring networks of markets for acquiring other foodstuffs and necessities. Or, as in the case of chiefdoms, people acquire a variety of goods through redistribution. As noted earlier, any model contains categories and divisions that are somewhat arbitrary, and this is certainly the case with the distinctions between horticultural and agricultural adaptations. There is in reality a continuum from simple horticulture to intensive agricultural societies, with many permutations and combinations. Remember as a starting point for comparative analysis, models, such as the evolutionary-ecological model, are useful.

Features Associated with Intensive Agricultural Lifeways

The following are correlates to the agricultural lifeway.

Production Based on More Levels of Technology   Agriculturalists have more levels of technology than horticulturalists, and they must have additional knowledge of plant cycles and soils. Technology at this level also includes detailed knowledge of plant-specific irrigation requirements. Irrigation systems are often quite creative and include water reservoirs and a variety of ways to deliver water to the crops (ditches, canals, and aqueducts). Farmers must know how to tame, train, and care for plow animals, or how to maintain and repair mechanical equipment. There are, quite simply, more different types of knowledge, skills, and tools. However, each individual's knowledge may not encompass all accumulated knowledge of the culture. We therefore need to take care that we do not consider agriculturally based societies as more advanced or better or smarter than societies with different food-procurement strategies. Agriculture, as with other human endeavors, emerged from cumulative, creative efforts of many people over many generations.

Terracing on Peruvian hillsides and a patchwork of irrigated fields adjacent to the Colorado River near Blythe, California, are testaments to the technology of intensive agriculture.

Sedentary Lifestyle   Agriculturalists are sedentary. The use of fertilizers to replace depleted soil nutrients means that farmers can remain on the same land for generations once it has been cleared, resulting in continuous residence and the construction of permanent structures—including storage facilities.

Stratified Societies   The carrying capacity of intensively cultivated lands increased dramatically. The well-known ancient Mexican city of Teotihuacan, for example, was in a region well suited for agricultural development, and by 2000 B.P. more than 60,000 people were living there (Feder 1996: 425). Clearly, concentrated numbers of people must have some form of societal organization. At one end of the agricultural continuum are **chiefdom** societies where the chief (this is most often a hereditary

chiefdom
A type of society with an office of chief, most commonly hereditary, social ranking, and redistributive economy.

Factory workers in Sri Lanka manufacture clothing for export to world markets. In nation-states many work at enterprises other than food production.

office) and his family have power and wealth that the other society members do not. This can be viewed as the beginning of **stratified societies**—societies with unequal access to resources within groups of the same gender and status. At the other end of the continuum are nation-states with many levels of stratification. Between are states with fewer levels of stratification (see Chapter 10 for more detail on chiefdoms and stratified societies). Food producers, merchants, and various levels of government developed to organize the distribution of food and other materials.

Property Ownership   Agriculturalists own property. Ownership may be in the form of farmland, animals, a house, or a shop. They have material possessions that often extend beyond those that are necessary for mere survival. This is partly due to the sedentary nature of such societies where possessions can accumulate.

Poor-Quality Nutrition   Agriculturalists, like horticulturalists, often have poor overall nutrition, because food intake is not diverse. When one moves up the spectrum of agriculture into contemporary industrialized societies, the availability of diverse diets through the market increases, but whether people take advantage of this availability to maximize their nutritional intake depends on many factors—income, education, and cultural ideas about acceptable food choices.

stratified society
A society with unequal access to resources within groups of the same gender and status.

Markets, such as this floating market near Bangkok, Thailand, are important in societies that have specialized the process of production.

Lower Energy Budget   Agriculturalists have a lower energy budget than horticulturalists from an individual member's perspective. Fewer calories are spent per person per week in order to procure basic survival needs, because machines have taken over much labor-intensive work. For example, horse-drawn plows or tractors may have replaced hand tools used to till the soil. The overall energy consumption by the whole society, including that required to run machinery, may be high, but each individual is expending fewer calories to obtain food. The exceptions to this pattern are state societies with peripheral peasant cultures. The latter are farmers who produce food for their families rather than to sell for profit. The peasants have some dealings with the markets of the state society, but they are marginal.

Economic Production Specialists   Agriculture is based on economic specialization, and subsistence activities are no longer based solely on the efforts of the family. People make a living by specializing and selling their goods (foods, crafts, manufactured items, etc.), skills, or services in exchange for currency, which is then used to exchange for items that are not produced by the family, whereas among foragers, horticulturalists, and pastoralists, everything produced within the family was for exchange with other members through reciprocity.

Division of Labor   There are many combinations and permutations to the division of labor among agricultural societies. Roles are determined by the specific traditions of individual cultures. In pre-industrial societies, roles are most often assigned according to gender or age. Among industrialized societies the division of labor is more flexible.

Systems of Distribution   The systems of distribution in state-organized societies are redistribution and market exchange. **Redistribution** is a system of exchange in which material tribute or tax is paid to a central authority, which could be a chief, a large landowner if a sharecropping system is in place, or a central government if everyone owns property. The tribute gift or tax (which may be in the form of an actual portion of one's crop or a percentage of one's resources) is used to support the central authority, which could be an individual (such as a chief) or a governmental system. The surplus, beyond that used to maintain the authority itself, is redistributed to the population in the form of goods and services. In Polynesian chiefdoms, for example, surplus tribute that has been given to the chief is often redistributed as food and drink for ceremonial occasions.

Market exchange involves goods or services being traded or sold at a market. These are transactions in which supply and demand dictate the prices of the goods or services. Currency (we call this money) is often used in market exchange. The use of currency is more impersonal than face-to-face exchanges of reciprocity. Also, currency is portable—whether shells, beads, coins, or paper. You can easily carry it or save it, and it is permanent (i.e., it won't deteriorate). Currency is also divisible, and change can be readily made. This is not the case in direct barter exchanges, because one cannot easily divide a live pig if a transaction does not involve items of equal value. **Barter,** where goods and services are exchanged for other goods or services without the use of currency, was likely the first means of market exchange before the use of currency (Williams 1997).

Markets vary in the types of currency used. Objects such as shells, furs, gold, or silver that are used as the medium of exchange are technically termed **commodity money.** The exchange item itself is of value. Paper currency is a medium of exchange that is backed by gold or silver. Nation-states introduced paper currency because it was easier to store and transport than gold or silver coins and could not be melted down. Paper money as a medium of exchange today is called **fiat money** (also called credit money)—paper money backed by the legal power of a nation-state and its claim of the economic value of the money. This money can be used to purchase goods and services; but, as in the United States today, it cannot be redeemed for gold and silver (Robbins 2005: 10).

Cowrie shells (primarily *Cypraea moneta*) have a rich history of use as currency in parts of Africa. In the interior of the continent the shells crossed many cultural areas and coexisted as currency with gold, silver, brass, salt bars, beads, and cloth (Saul 2004: 73). Cowrie shell money in Ghana provides an interesting case of both commodity and fiat monies coexisting

redistribution
A system of exchange in which wealth is reallocated; found in chiefdom and state societies.

market exchange
The trading of goods and services through the use of currency.

barter
Exchange of products that does not involve currency.

commodity money
Currency in the form of valued objects such as shells or gold.

fiat money
Paper currency backed by a nation-state's claim of its value.

ANTHROPOLOGY AROUND US

Is Slow Food Making a Fast Comeback?

Large-scale corporate-owned farming has diffused globally in recent years. Such farming places emphasis on corporate earnings and on growing single crops bred for long shelf life and characteristics that make them easier to harvest and transport to market. Small farmers are displaced, rural communities decline, and many people end up living in urban poverty, particularly in Africa and India. Fast food chains diffused around the globe over the same time period and are now ubiquitous in urban settings.

Slow Food, an international movement that promotes food and wine culture, also advocates and defends traditional food-production methods based on organic techniques and plant biodiversity (Slow Food 2005). The opening of a McDonald's in Piazza Spagna in Rome in 1986 spurred Carlo Petrini to found Slow Food. He is passionate about rediscovering and promoting "authentic culinary tradition." The association opposes foods that all taste the same—the standardized taste of supermarket and fast foods. Slow Food also advocates the consumption of seasonal, locally grown foods of many varieties. The Slow Food Foundation for Biodiversity notes that 30,000 vegetable varieties have become extinct in the last century (Slow Food Foundation 2005). Slow Food advocates ask consumers to compare the taste of a supermarket apple or tomato, genetically engineered and waxed for long shelf life, to that of an heirloom variety organically grown and picked the same morning that it is bought at a farmers market.

The Slow Food movement currently has an active membership of 83,000 in Europe, the United States, and Japan; and mainstream agriculture is taking notice, reports *Successful Farming* (February 2005). A recent (2004) international convention, Terra Madre, held in Turin, Italy, was attended by 4,000 farmers from 130 nations who came to learn about building local markets. The U.N.'s Food and Agriculture Organization reports American specialty producers have taken note of how improved organic growing practices increased production in various regions of the globe, and many were in attendance (Dilly 2005: 49)

Slow Food is about better-flavored and more nutritious food, diversity of available foods, and what advocates label sustainable food production. And, as the name implies, it is about slowing down and enjoying food with family and friends.

◎What do you think? Is Slow Food likely to gain momentum? What do you see as positive outcomes of the movement globally? Do you perceive any potential negative outcomes of the Slow Food movement?

Cypraea moneta shells (money cowrie). These were used as currency in Africa and on many islands in the Pacific.

🏵 **TRY THIS** 🏵
Research

Using your favorite search engine, research *Cypraea moneta*. Name societies on three different continents where this cowrie was used as currency.

today. The shells were used as a medium of exchange before the introduction by colonial governments of the West African pound and later the fiat currency known as the cedi (the name is believed to be derived from the Ghanaian word *sede*, for cowrie). Among the Dagaaba of Northwestern Ghana they are still used for money alongside the cedi. Cowries are pierced and threaded on strings, or counted individually, and are used in a variety of transactions. The nonmonetary uses for cowries include use in religious rituals, for adornment and decoration, and as funeral displays and marriage transactions (Yiridoe 1995). Several analysts suggest that governmental instabilities in the past encourage the Dagaabe to save cowries, particularly if they do not have wage income. And because cowries are still accepted currency and may be exchanged for cedis, they may provide a savings hedge against uncertain economic times (Yiridoe 1995).

Many agriculturally based societies function by a combination of redistribution and market exchange. Reciprocity is still in use but is focused primarily within a circle of family and friends and is no longer necessary for survival—everything can be purchased in the marketplace or received from governmental agencies. Both redistribution and market economies are associated with stratified cultures. See Chapter 10 for more information on stratification.

SUMMARY

Food producers emerged after foragers in the history of human cultural development. This does not mean that they are more advanced. Rather, they adapted in new ways to environmental changes and challenges. While there is enormous diversity in the specific plants and animals that are raised for food, general patterns of sociocultural adaptations are apparent.

Horticulturalists and pastoralists are societies of both sedentary (horticulturalists) and nomadic (pastoralists) food producers; both are kin based, and property ownership, usually by a kin group, is at the core of the social complex. Agriculturally based societies are diverse in form—a continuum exists from those with the most basic features of agriculture carried out by extended families or villages to the intensive mechanized agriculture of industrialized societies. Agriculturalists own property individually, are stratified, have centralized authority, and are marked by systems of redistribution and market exchange, where currency is used.

Study Questions

1. Compare and contrast the foraging adaptation and the horticultural adaptation with respect to technology.

OLC
mhhe•com/lenkeit3

See Self Quiz.

2. Identify the adaptive features of technology and food procurement found in an assigned ethnography. How closely do these features match the general features of one of the subsistence strategies outlined in this chapter?

3. Compare and contrast reciprocity, redistribution, and market exchange.

4. Compare and contrast the subsistence strategies and distribution systems of horticultural and agricultural societies.

Suggested Readings

Evans-Pritchard, E. E. 1940. *The Nuer.* Oxford: Oxford University Press. The classic original ethnography on a tribal society.

Hutchinson, Sharon E. 1996. *Nuer Dilemmas.* Berkeley: University of California Press. A landmark and riveting account of the Nuer and what civil war and social unrest have done to these people.

Plattner, Stuart, ed. 1989. *Economic Anthropology.* Stanford, Calif.: Stanford University Press. An indispensable resource covering the economic features of societies ranging from foraging to industrial.

Weiner, Annette B. 1988. *The Trobrianders of Papua New Guinea.* New York: Holt, Rinehart and Winston. Weiner revisited the Trobriand Islanders made famous by Bronislaw Malinowski in his 1922 book *Argonauts of the Western Pacific.* Weiner provides a perspective on women's roles and work in this horticultural society that were lacking in Malinowski's treatment, as well as a view of how this culture has changed.

Suggested Web Sites

http://anthro.palomar.edu/subsistence/default.htm
This site provides an effective overview of foraging, pastoralism, horticulture, and intensive agriculture supported with cross-cultural ethnographic information.

OLC
mhhe•com/lenkeit3
See Web links.

http://lucy.ukc.ac.uk/EthnoAtlas/societies.html
Organized by the British Academy, PORTAL is an online collection of resources dedicated to the humanities and social sciences. The "Ethnographic Atlas" offers a quick overview of selected cultures from Africa, the Middle East, North America, Asia, Oceania, Europe, and South America. Included is information about the culture's geography, environment, subsistence patterns, history (a brief overview), and other topics. Each analysis has a bibliography for additional research.

http://lrs.ed.uiuc.edu/students/xiaoyu/atlases.html
Prepared by anthropology students at the University of Illinois, Urbana-Champaign, the site has links to a variety of ethnographic atlases from the United States and England.

7

Marriage, Family, and Residence
What Are the Possibilities?

Weddings in most societies contain specific traditions. This is a Parsi wedding in Mumbai, India.
The ceremony includes the ritual exchange of rings. The Parsi are an ethnic group that originated
in Persia (now Iran).

The last loop and button have been sewn, all thirty-two are in place marching majestically down the back of the white satin gown. I have labored for hours over this dress, alternating between being pleased that our daughter asked me to make her wedding dress and wondering what possessed me to agree to do this. As I worked I contemplated the human institution of marriage and the traditions and customs surrounding it. The tradition of a white bridal dress, worn by brides of European ancestry and the Judeo-Christian religion, symbolizes purity. Among many Hindus the bride wears a traditional sari of red and white, often embroidered with gold, the red symbolizing fertility and abundance and the white, purity. Red is also the traditional color of the bridal dress worn in China, where this color is considered lucky. In past times, as now, there is much variation in bridal attire both between and within cultures. Some traditions are associated with belief systems whereas others are secular. Diffusion of traditions is also apparent in ceremonies today when elements of cultures and subcultures join.

Our daughter's marriage is not an arranged marriage. It has no formal financial exchanges associated with it such as bride price (or bridewealth), which is common in tribal pastoral societies, or dowry (a European tradition). My husband and I will not be washing the couple's feet with water and milk to signify purification (a Hindu custom). We won't be setting off firecrackers to frighten away evil spirits (a Chinese custom). Nor will the bride and groom jump over a broom signifying their entrance into marriage (a practice in some sub-Saharan African cultures). But there is a white dress with a train, a veil, a tiered cake, attendants, something old, something new, something borrowed, and something blue (all European American customs).

With her marriage, our daughter will acquire a whole new set of kinsmen—in-laws, we call them in North America. This will not only expand her family but also bring new obligations to her life. Duties that are different from those in other cultures, and yet ones that are alike. The recognition of these obligations, and the actions based on them, are of course the *ideal* cultural traditions associated with in-laws in North American society. Reflecting another North American ideal, my daughter and her husband will set up their own independent household.

Marriage and the purpose it serves for individuals and for societies have been of interest to anthropology since the 1860s. Merchant seamen's stories of the "strange" marriage customs they encountered in other lands caught the attention of early anthropologists. Models of cultural evolution, developed by men such as Scottish lawyer John McLennan, built on these stories and stimulated much debate in academic circles. When subsequent anthropologists began formal ethnographic studies, the starting point was often to focus on marriage, family, and kinship customs. The myriad forms of these cultural institutions speak again to the adaptive nature of human culture.

This chapter presents cross-cultural data on marriage, families, and the issue of where people reside after marriage.

The objectives of this chapter are to
- Describe marriage rules found across cultures
- Describe marriage forms and their functions
- Examine mate choice and marriage finance
- Describe types of families and their functions
- Describe residence patterns and their functions

FIGURE 7.1
**Symbols Used in
Kinship Diagrams**

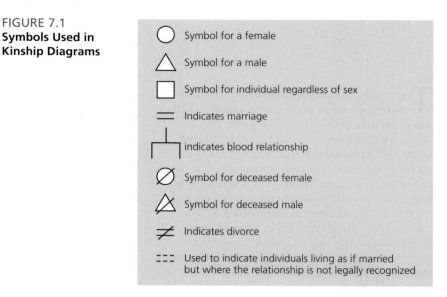

○ Symbol for a female

△ Symbol for a male

□ Symbol for individual regardless of sex

═ Indicates marriage

⊥ indicates blood relationship

⊘ Symbol for deceased female

◺ Symbol for deceased male

≠ Indicates divorce

⁼⁼⁼ Used to indicate individuals living as if married
but where the relationship is not legally recognized

◎ DIAGRAMMING KINSHIP

OLC
mhhe•com/lenkeit3

See chapter outline and
chapter overview.

Kinship diagrams are a shorthand method of representing and giving a
clear visual picture of kin relationships. The symbols used in anthropological kin diagrams are shown in Figure 7.1. It is worthwhile to learn
these symbols before you read about marriage, family, and residence in
this chapter and about kinship and descent in Chapter 8 because (1) linguistic confusion can result when terms are translated from native languages to English, and (2) it is easier to trace and understand complex
relationships with the use of these visual images.

A point of reference is always designated in a kin diagram by the designation *Ego*. When you interview someone, she or he is Ego in the diagram you draw. Knowing the person who is Ego is important because
information about kin relationships, obligations, and terminology will be
different when there is a change in the point of reference. Anthropologists also use a short method to *write* about kin relationships. There is no
standardization to these abbreviations, but a simple approach is to use the
first two letters of a kin term. For example, mother is written Mo, father
is Fa, daughter is Da, sister is Si, and wife is Wi. If one is speaking about
the blood kin relationship of one's mother's sister's daughter, it becomes
MoSiDa. Other terms and their short form are husband, Hu; child, Ch;
brother, Br; and son, So. Relationships by marriage (in-laws) are designated by the use of these terms as well. One way to write sister-in-law
is BrWi. Other ways to designate a sister-in-law are HuBrWi (if Ego is
a female) and WiBrWi (if Ego is a male).

Another method is to use the first letter of the kin relationship: mother (M), father (F), husband (H), wife (W), daughter (D), son (S), brother (B), and sister (Z). Because both son and sister begin with the same letter, Z is used for sister. According to this second shorthand method, mother's sister's daughter is MZD. When I was a beginning student I mixed up the Z and the S with this system, so I prefer to use the two-letter system.

TRY THIS *Consider*

You are Ego in the following diagrams. What terms would you use if you were telling me who each person was in relationship to you? Quickly copy these diagrams on a sheet of paper and write the terms that apply using one of the shorthand methods just discussed.

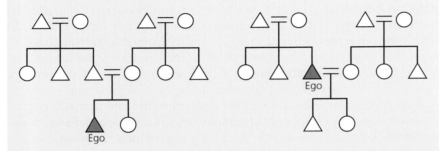

Now, look at the two diagrams. The designation of Ego is clearly important to the ethnographer gathering interview data because terms will change as Ego changes. This is an important point to remember when reading a complex kinship diagram.

◎ MARRIAGE RULES

Exogamy and Endogamy

All cultures have rules about whom it is appropriate to marry. Some are formal rules that are part of the society's legal system; others are informal. Two marriage rules found in most cultures are the rules of exogamy and endogamy. A rule of **exogamy** specifies that a person must marry outside of a designated group of people. The most common group specified by exogamy is the **nuclear family** (i.e., a married couple and their children). Exogamous rules in nearly all cultures also include kin other than the nuclear family. The exception is found where a leader, such as a chief in ancient Hawaiian culture, was to marry his sister in order to retain a concentration

exogamy
A cultural rule that dictates that one must marry outside of a designated group (e.g., outside of one's lineage, clan, or village).

nuclear family
A married couple and their children.

of special powers in his offspring. Great variety exists across cultures concerning which kin are part of the forbidden group. In some cultures you cannot marry cousins. In other cultures you can marry certain cousins but not others. Sometimes a whole village is included in an exogamous rule. The members of a culture do not usually analyze the purpose or function of rules such as exogamy. We all have grown up with such rules in place. It is just the way things are. Anthropologists, however, are interested in trying to explain why such rules exist.

One hypothesis offered to explain exogamous rules is that they prevent incest, which in turn prevents deformities in offspring. This is the explanation given most often in North American culture for the exogamous rules that prohibit marriage to close relatives. (Is this the hypothesis you jotted down in the Try This exercise?) Did exogamous rules originate to prevent incestuous relations within a society? This explanation seems unlikely as a universal reason for the origin of these rules because anthropologists have studied cultures in which conception was not believed to be connected to sexual intercourse and yet taboos against incest existed. In such societies it was believed that clan spirits entered a woman's body to produce a child. The past tense is used in the previous sentence because today most peoples understand the biological realities of conception. Many non-Western cultures, however, made the biological connection, so perhaps the hypothesis about incest and unhealthy children is a correct explanation for the origin of exogamous rules in some cases. Modern genetics teaches that mating within a small group of individuals with a similar genetic background may increase the chances of recessive bad genes combining. The *probability* increases, which is not the same as a definite statement that a deformity will result if these genes combine.

Other hypotheses to explain the origin of exogamous rules include the suggestion that exogamous rules help to extend territory, create political alliances, or stimulate trade. Still others have suggested that exogamous rules came about to reduce conflict within families, where sexual liaisons with kin would cause jealousy. Each of these hypotheses has some data to support it. Perhaps societies developed exogamous rules for different reasons or combinations of reasons.

Endogamy, or endogamous rules, specify the groups *within* which a person should or must marry. A rule whereby a person is told to marry someone from the same religion is an endogamous rule. Other endogamous rules found in different world cultures include rules to marry within the same race or ethnic group, within the same socioeconomic stratum, or occasionally within the same descent group such as a clan (clans and other descent groups are discussed in Chapter 8). So, one function of endogamy is to maintain cultural identity. If you marry someone with the same background and status, there is less chance that customs will change or that conflict will occur between extended family over important values and beliefs.

The Levirate and the Sororate

The levirate and the sororate are preferential marriage rules found in many cultures. Each specifies whom one should marry if one's spouse dies. Both rules serve the purpose of ensuring that everyone is economically protected in the case of a spouse's death. Such customs also ensure that the deceased person's children are raised by members of his or her group and that alliances remain between the families.

The **levirate** specifies that if a woman's husband dies, she should marry one of his brothers. Thus the levirate is often called brother-in-law marriage. The **sororate**, sister-in-law marriage, designates that a man should marry his wife's sister should his wife die. See Figure 7.2 for diagrams illustrating levirate and sororate marriage rules.

To anyone raised in contemporary North American cultures, levirate and sororate rules will likely generate ethnocentric reactions. We shudder at the thought of marriage to someone we don't love and may not even like. We have come to equate love with marriage. A bit of historical and cross-cultural research, however, reveals that throughout most of human history, in most places, marriages occurred for economic reasons. Romantic love was viewed as a poor basis for marriage and even as abnormal (Stephens 1963: 200–206). To be objective (and culturally relativistic) in considering the value of the levirate and the sororate, one must set aside the attitudes about romantic love that have been the basis of marriage in contemporary Western cultures only for the past century or so. Moreover, remember that we are examining *ideal* patterns of kinship within cultures—ethnographers have recorded data indicating that women do sometimes reject these rules even in societies where the custom is expected.

Those who read the Bible will recognize the custom of the levirate from the Old Testament (Deuteronomy 25: 5–10). These verses state that the marriage of the deceased man's brother to his widow should take place if there are no sons, a requirement that is not present in all instances of the levirate. The first son then born to the woman would be considered the son of the deceased brother. George Murdock in his sample of 250 societies reported that 127 cultures (51 percent) practiced the levirate and 100 (40 percent) practiced the sororate (Murdock 1949: 29). Certainly the

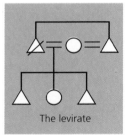

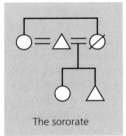

FIGURE 7.2
The Levirate and the Sororate

levirate
A marriage custom in which a widow marries her deceased husband's brother.

sororate
A marriage custom in which a widower marries a sister of his deceased wife.

ANTHROPOLOGY AROUND US

Outdated Traditions?

Why marry? A recent study at Rutgers University revealed that heterosexual men in today's North American society remain bachelors because it is easy to have sex outside of marriage, and they were fearful of the economic responsibilities of marriage, including having and rearing children. They wanted instead to find a soul mate— a woman who would hold the same view on most issues and would make no demands on them (The State of Our Unions, http://marriage.rutgers.edu). Recent census data indicate that more people than ever are living together (and presumably having sex) without marriage. According to the 1980 U.S. Census there were 1,589,000 unmarried couple households; in 1990 there were 2,856,000, and in 2000 there were 4,746,000.

If you do marry, who pays for it? Long-standing American traditions include a wedding, reception, and honeymoon. Traditionally the bride's family was responsible for financing the wedding and reception party, while the groom's family financed the honeymoon. Wedding guests brought gifts aimed at helping the couple set up their new home. Engaged couples today increasingly make requests for cash to help pay for the wedding, a home mortgage, or honeymoon expenses, according to a *New York Daily News* article in June 2005 by Michelle Megna ("Toasters are out! We want money!"). Etiquette experts call such requests crass and in poor taste. Advocates of the money-for-marriage movement claim that it is becoming a trend. One online money registry documents a fourfold increase in registered couples, from 254 in 2003 to about 1,000 in 2005. They also point to customs in other countries where the bride and groom are given money or even homes, although the latter usually come from family members. Another online registry for honeymoons claims 12,000 clients in 86 countries and calls the honeymoon money registry a twenty-first century tradition.

◎ Ask two of your unmarried male friends what they think of the Rutgers study results. Are they searching for a soul mate? Do they plan to marry? What do you think? Is money-for-marriage a twenty-first-century replacement for other cultures' traditions of dowry and bridewealth?

widespread practice of these customs attests to their important functions in many cultures.

◎ MARRIAGE FORMS AND FUNCTIONS

All societies studied by anthropologists have some form of marriage ceremony. Marriage is an event that marks an important change in both the **status** (a person's position in society) and **role** (the part a person plays in society) of individuals. In this case the change of status is from being single to being part of a couple with new responsibilities and rights. With marriage individuals take on new roles; now they are a wife or a husband and perhaps a step parent in addition to their roles as daughter or son.

Anthropologists have noted the following features about marriage in most societies: (1) Marriage includes an exclusive sexual relationship between the partners (remember we are talking about the *ideal* here), (2) marriage usually involves some degree of economic interdependency—including property and labor, and (3) marriage legitimizes the couple's offspring in the eyes of the group, and child-rearing responsibilities are expected from the couple. There are exceptions to one or more of these features in at least some societies. For example, many cultures accept extramarital sex (most often for males), and in some cultures, such as the Nayar, these three features of marriage were absent in historic times. Because the Nayar presented an interesting case to ethnologists, I will briefly describe it to you to illustrate the variations that marriage can take.

The Nayar are found in Malabar in southwest India. They are a society in which descent is traced through women. In the past the Nayar were a warrior caste, and men were full-time soldiers who spent most of their adult lives away from their homes either living in barracks or away at war. When they returned home, it was to the house where they were born, their mother's house. Young Nayar women were often household servants in Brahmin (upper caste) households and were often concubines to men of the household. Nayar marriage relationships were problematic to maintain under these circumstances, and an inventive system evolved.

Before puberty a Nayar woman was formally married to a man from a family with whom her family had a special relationship. The two were together for a few days, and then the marriage ended. The woman usually never saw this husband again, though she and her future children might mourn when this man died. After this marriage the woman was considered an adult and was free to take up to a dozen lovers. Each lover was part of a formal relationship approved by her family, and the man was required to give the woman gifts three times a year until the relationship ended. The "visiting husbands" as they were called, spent the night with a woman, leaving a shield or sword outside of her door so that other men

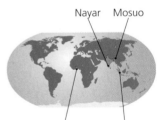

Nayar   Mosuo

Ashanti   Menangkabau

status
A person's position in society.

role
The culturally assigned behaviors and expectations for a person's social position.

with whom she had a similar relationship knew that another "husband" was visiting that night. The visiting husbands never resided with a woman, did not have any economic obligation to support her, and came and went as their military duties dictated. When a child was conceived, one of the visiting husbands established the child's legitimacy by claiming paternity and presenting gifts to the woman and to the midwife who delivered the child. He had no further economic responsibilities for this child, though he might take a social interest in it. The child lived with and was the economic responsibility of its mother's group. Although this custom is no longer practiced (it was outlawed by British colonial rule), it illustrates how cultures are flexible and develop many strategies to accommodate their survival. In this case men were away from home most of the time attending to their military duties. It made sense that the stable family unit centered on women. Men lived in their mother's and sister's household when they were at home.

The Nayar are not the only cultures whose customs do not align with the more common features of marriage described here. Space does not permit a discussion of additional examples, but you might want to research the Menangkabau of Malaysia, the Mosuo of China, and the Ashanti of Ghana, other societies that have developed creative solutions to complicated situations associated with marriage.

> **TRY THIS** *Consider*
>
> Quickly review what you believe to be the advantages of a monogamous marriage. Jot down these advantages, and keep them in mind as you read on.

Monogamy

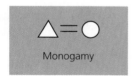

FIGURE 7.3
Monogamy

monogamy
A form of marriage in which one woman is married to one man.

polygamy
Multiple-spouse marriage.

Monogamy, the form of marriage in which one woman is married to one man (Figure 7.3), is the most common form of marriage around the world. It is not, however, the most preferred; monogamy is the ideal and preferred form of marriage in only eighty-one cultures out of a sample of four hundred cultures (20 percent), according to a 1967 survey based on the Human Relations Area Files data (Textor 1967: 124). As a result of divorce or death, many individuals in monogamous societies will be in a series of monogamous marriages over the course of their lives (this is sometimes referred to as serial monogamy).

Polygamy

Polygamy refers to marriage in which there is more than one spouse (*poly* means *many*, and *gamy* means *marriage*). It is a word that the media use, but it is a poor choice because it does not indicate whether there are many husbands or many wives (Figure 7.4).

Polygyny **Polygyny** is the specific case in which a man has more than one wife (an example diagram is shown in Figure 7.5). Cross-cultural research indicates that this is the preferred form of marriage in 314 cultures out of 400 (79 percent) (Textor 1967: 124). This research surveyed societies with populations numbering in the millions as well as those with populations of fewer than one hundred, so keep in mind that the percentage of cultures practicing a custom is not the same as the number of people worldwide who practice the custom. Furthermore, many societies have cultural rules that permit marrying multiple partners, which is what the society's members, both male and female, desire. Economic realities, however, often interfere with a man's ability to have multiple wives. As a result, most individuals participate in monogamous marriages.

The functions of polygyny include the opportunity for a man to gain status by having more than one wife and particularly by having many children. Polygyny is most common in preindustrial societies where horticulture or pastoralism is the basis of economic life. More wives means more workers. More wives means more children. More children also means more potential workers. Thus there is often an economic advantage to having more than one wife. Political status can also be gained by having more than one wife, as in the case of Melanesian Big Men, for whom fathering many children is also a way to gain prestige. Typically the wealthiest men are likely to have many wives because they can afford bridewealth payments. There is, of course, a negative side to polygyny. It can be expensive to maintain more than one household (if this is required within a particular culture), and jealousy (often over favoritism shown to one wife's children) can cause difficulties. Another drawback occurs when polygyny causes a shortage of wives for poor men.

FIGURE 7.4
Polygamy Polygamy means multiple spouses and does not distinguish between these two marriage types.

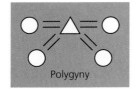

Polygyny

FIGURE 7.5
Polygyny

TRY THIS *Analyze*

If you are a woman, jot down two advantages of having co-wives. If you are a man, jot down two advantages of having more than one wife.

Compare and discuss your notes with a member of the opposite sex. Discuss your feelings about this form of marriage. Are you able to be culturally relativistic, or do your cultural ethnocentrisms creep in?

The original reasons societies became polygynous are unclear. Many hypotheses have been made, all having logic or data to support them, though few have been systematically examined. One exception is Melvin Ember's 1974 study that showed more women than men in societies that practiced polygyny—111 women for 100 men on average, compared to 94 women for 100 men in societies that were nonpolygynous (Pasternack, Ember, and Ember 1997: 90). This finding implies that an unbalanced sex

polygyny
Marriage of one man to two or more women.

A Muslim Rashaida Bedouin merchant and his three wives.

ratio led to the adoption of polygyny. Other studies seem to contradict this one. A difficulty in gathering data on origin hypotheses for any social custom such as marriage form is that correlations shown in the data don't necessarily mean that causation is established.

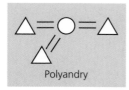

Polyandry

FIGURE 7.6
Polyandry

polyandry
Marriage of one woman to two or more men.

TRY THIS   *Hypothesize*

Try the intellectually stimulating exercise of seeing how many logical hypotheses you can devise to account for the high occurrence of, and preference among the world's cultures, for polygynous marriage. Compare and discuss your hypotheses with a classmate. Pick the most promising hypothesis and devise several ways to collect data to test it.

Polyandry   The form of marriage in which a woman has more than one husband is called **polyandry** (illustrated in Figure 7.6). Only three cultures out of a sample of four hundred (0.75 percent) practice this form of

A marriage of fraternal polyandry in Tibet.

marriage (Textor 1967: 124). In the cultures that practice polyandry, there *may* be a shortage of women resulting from practices such as female infanticide. There are conflicting reports on this issue (as noted in Chapter 1). A shortage of women may have been an issue, but it does not appear to have been the only, or even the major, cause. Rather, polyandry seems to be related to economics. Among Tibetans living in northern Nepal, when brothers share a wife, it is to keep large land holdings from being fragmented (Goldstein 1987).

Group Marriage   A group of individuals of both sexes married to each other is called group marriage. Although group marriage has surfaced in societies from time to time, such as the hippie communes of the 1960s, it is reported to be legal in only one society. This culture is the Kaingang in Brazil, where 8 percent of the population practiced this marriage form during historic times. The remainder of the population practiced

Kaingang

FIGURE 7.7
Cousins Ego's parallel cousins (MoSiCh and FaBrCh) are shown in red. Ego's cross-cousins (MoBrCh and FaSiCh) are shown in blue.

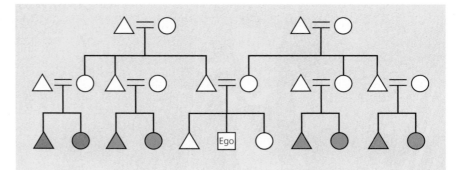

monogamy (60 percent), polygyny (18 percent), or polyandry (14 percent). Obviously there are diverse ideas about marriage among the Kaingang (Murdock 1949: 24).

Sister Exchange Marriage

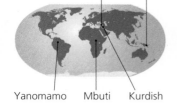

Turkic   Gebusi

Yanomamo   Mbuti   Kurdish

A type of marriage termed **sister exchange** is found in many cultures including the Mbuti pygmy, the Turkic, the Kurdish, the Gebusi, and the Yanomamo. In speaking of a form of such exchange known as *berdel* in southeastern Turkey, anthropologist Serpil Altuntek has said "Berdel, cousin marriage, and similar arrangements are better viewed as part of a family's strategy to forge and maintain favorable political and economic alliances" (Ersen 2002: 75). Such alliances are part of the security network created by marriage ties.

While sister exchange may constitute a society's ideal marriage, other spouses are allowed as long as exogamous rules are obeyed. As anthropologist Bruce Knauft notes in his ethnography of the Gebusi, "the notion that Gebusi sister-exchange is 'preferential' means just that: sister-exchange is preferred 'if possible.' But if not, that's life. In actuality, just over half of all first Gebusi marriages (52 percent) were sister-exchanges" (Knauft 2005: 61).

Sister exchange typically involves the marriage of **cross-cousins** (MoBrCh or FaSiCh). Examine Figure 7.7. Although it may seem complicated to most North Americans to keep track of whether a cousin is a cross-cousin or **parallel-cousin** (MoSiCh or FaBrCh), the distinction isn't difficult for people who have been enculturated to use different terms for parallel-cousins and cross-cousins. Parallel-cousins are often called by the same word and treated the same as one's siblings. Cross-cousins are called by different terms and therefore are the only eligible marriage partners in one's own generation (providing lineage exogamy is practiced). The *sisters* who are exchanged represent all women in the category, not just a man's true sisters. Keep in mind that early ethnologists and ethnographers coined the terms *parallel-cousin* and *cross-cousin*. From an insider's view, members

sister exchange
A common type of marriage consisting of the marriage of cross-cousins. Men exchange their sisters as marriage partners.

cross-cousin
Ego's mother's brother's child and father's sister's child.

parallel-cousin
Ego's mother's sister's child and father's brother's child.

Newlyweds in south-west Turkey pose for a photograph. The two men from different villages have each married the other's sister. This custom, known as *berdel,* has economic and political advantages.

of a culture may, as Robin Fox (1983: 186) has suggested, view this *category* of people as possible marriage partners only because of generations of sister exchange marriage. In other words, they don't think about an eligible cross-cousin as a cross-cousin; they just exchange sisters.

TRY THIS *Consider*

How do you think about your relationship to your cousins? Do you think of them as your mother's brother's children, your mother's sister's children, your father's brother's or father's sister's children, or simply as your cousins? Does the etic view in this case truly represent the emic view?

◎ MATE CHOICE AND MARRIAGE FINANCE

Mate Choice

The ethnographic literature reflects three basic ways in which marriage partners are chosen: free choice of spouse, free choice with parental approval, and arranged marriage. In one small ethnographic sample, six societies allowed free choice of mates, six societies required the approval of parents or other kin, twelve societies showed a mix of free choice and arranged marriages, and sixteen had arranged marriages with occasional elopement (Stephens 1963: 198). To people enculturated to expect to choose their own marriage partner, data such as these can be puzzling, and thoughts of arranged marriages can trigger one's ethnocentric attitudes.

Arranged marriage was and is a common occurrence among humans. Many of the subcultures of India practice arranged marriages today, although financially independent young people of the urban middle class have more say in whom they marry. This custom extends to many people of Indian descent living abroad. When this topic is addressed in my classes, I nearly always have an Indian student who shares information about arranged marriages. Several students have brought in a copy of *India West*, a widely distributed North American Indian newspaper that contains matrimonial advertisements for those searching for suitable marriage partners. Indian students tell me that these ads are especially useful for Indian Americans with strong cultural ties to India and who wish to continue the practice of arranged marriages. The majority of the ads that I have read in this and other Indian publications begin with phrases such as "parents invite correspondence," "brother invites correspondence," or "uncle seeking . . . ." Desired traits sought in a mate and listed in these ads include "educated professional," "intelligent person," and "from a respectable family"; religion and caste are also often mentioned. These ads are aimed at initiating correspondence with potential mates. Though not limited to such societies, arranged marriage is quite common in societies in which large kin groups are important and households tend to be of the extended-family type. The entire kin group is important because of economic ties, and marriage finance is an important issue for everyone. My students tell me that large dowries are expected when marriages are arranged within the local Indian community (see the following discussion of marriage finance).

Where arranged marriage is the custom, families search and negotiate, often for years, for a mate for their offspring. Your family wants you to be secure economically and in a good marriage to someone from a stable family. They know you best and have your interests as well as their own in mind. Cultures that go through these laborious mate-selection processes must find traditional North American customs of mate selection flawed. Most North Americans marry strangers whom we meet at school, at work, in singles' bars, or while on a vacation. We know little about their families, and we seldom look at their bank accounts. Love, we say, will keep us together.

Marriage Finance

Important economic exchanges occur in many societies when marriage is proposed. To North Americans, **bridewealth** (gifts from the groom's family to the bride's family) and **dowry** (wealth brought with the bride when she marries) imply the treatment of women as objects. Although it

---

OLC

mhhe•com/lenkeit3

See Internet exercises.

bridewealth
A form of marriage finance in which valuable gifts are given by the groom's kin to the bride's kin.

dowry
A form of marriage finance in which valuable gifts are given by the bride's kin to the groom's kin.

is true that women have often been viewed historically and cross-culturally as property, the functions of marriage finance usually go beyond direct market exchange. The customary exchanges of property that take place during negotiations before marriage, at marriage, and after marriage cement relationships between families, lineages, and clans.

Bridewealth payments are often substantial. Today, among the Nuer of Africa, twenty-five to thirty head of cattle are given to the bride's family (with a value of US$100 to US$200 per head of cattle for a total of around US$5,000), (Holtzman 2000: 105; Hutchinson 1996: 263). For Nuer immigrants residing in the United States, cash payments are made instead of cattle. In one instance the payment was US$10,000 (Holtzman 2000: 105).

Arranging large bridewealth payments can be difficult. Everyone in a society is not of the same socioeconomic class or rank; thus everyone has different abilities to pay. And what if you are a fourth or fifth son in a family with no daughters? Will resources be available for you to make a bridewealth payment? Many societies developed variations on their ideal traditions to accommodate diverse socioeconomic circumstances. In past times the Yurok of the Lower Klamath River in northwestern California exhibited such a variation in their custom called **half-marriage.** In a full-marriage, a man paid bridewealth to the bride's family and took her to live with him in his house and community. Children of the union belonged to him and stayed with him if divorce occurred (unless the bridewealth was refunded). According to a 1909 census, three out of four marriages were of this form. Nearly one in four (23.4 percent) were of the half-marriage type, a statistic that remained consistent over five generations of Yurok marriage data (Waterman and Kroeber 1934: 1–5). A half-marriage involved a man making a reduced bridewealth payment, usually about half. The groom lived with the bride in her father's house, and children of the union belonged to the wife and her family. Men in such marriages were usually of low social rank and were poor. Other cultures made various arrangements for paying off a bridewealth debt. These often involved a man living with and working for the bride's family for an agreed-upon period of time and then bringing her back to his father's residence (see the discussion of matri-patrilocal residence later in the chapter).

Yurok

◎ FAMILY

What exactly is a family? Early definitions of *family* refer to a social group that includes people with biological or marriage ties, reciprocal group economic obligations, shared child-rearing obligations, and common residence. These definitions were typically based on sociological studies of families in Western cultures, that is, families based on monogamous marriage. When ethnographic data from anthropology began to accumulate,

half-marriage
A custom among the Yurok of northwestern California and other patri-centered groups in which a man pays partial bridewealth and lives with the bride's family, and the couple's children belong to the wife and her family.

Betsileo

⸎ TRY THIS ⸎
Analyze

Based on the functions of family listed in the text, would the Betsileo man and his wives constitute a family? Defend your response.

Maori   Maori

it became apparent that a rigid definition of what constituted family did not apply across cultures.

The criterion of common residence turned out to be a problem because in some cultures women and children live in one residence and men in another, yet both mother and father constitute an economic unit and share child-rearing responsibilities. Among the polygynous Betsileo of Madagascar, for example, a man and several of his wives live in different villages. A man resides most of the time with his senior wife and visits his other wives in other villages occasionally during the year. In still other cases, such as among the Maori of New Zealand and the Cook Islands, a child is often taken and reared by a grandmother in a distant household. I once had a conversation with a Maori woman while awaiting a plane at the small landing strip on the island of Aitutaki in the Cook Islands. She had an eight-month-old child with her, and she was on her way to another island to visit her daughter, the child's mother. Informants verified that this arrangement was a common occurrence and, in fact, that it was expected for grandmothers to claim the right to raise one or more of their grandchildren.

The criterion of shared child-rearing obligations is not fully met in some cases. In some societies that practice descent through females, a child's mother and father may reside together but the father does not have primary economic or social responsibility for *his* children but rather for *his sister's* children because they belong to the same matrilineage. This matrilineal group has strong economic and ceremonial ties (see the discussion of matrilineages in Chapter 8).

Later studies of the family began to focus on the *functions* of family units. The functions listed most often include group responsibility for rearing children and the group acting as an economic corporation in which all members have reciprocal obligations to one another. Keep these functions in mind as you read about the following family forms.

Traditional Family Forms

Family provides the most enduring relationships we have during our lifetime. A person is born (or adopted) into a kin group that we call *family*. In North America this consists of parents, brothers, sisters, grandparents, aunts and uncles, and cousins. These kin are what anthropologists call our **family of orientation.** This is the family in which you were a child, the family that orients, or enculturates, you. At the center of the family of orientation is the nuclear family. A nuclear family consists of a married couple and their children. It may be isolated and independent from other kin, or it may be part of a larger kin group. Because these members are related (or considered as if related) to one another by blood, they are referred to as **consanguineal relatives** or consanguines. The term *con-*

family of orientation
A person's childhood family, where enculturation takes place.

consanguineal relatives
Kin related by blood.

An Inuit nuclear family.

sanguine derives from the Latin roots *con*, meaning with, and *sanguineus*, meaning blood.

Consanguinity can be a thorny issue when addressing kinship. Anthropologist Robin Fox noted, in his classic study of kinship systems, that "a consanguine is someone who is defined *by the society* as a consanguine, and 'blood' relationship in a genetic sense has not necessarily anything to do with it, although on the whole these tend to coincide in most societies of the world" (Fox 1983: 34). Today most humans are sophisticated about the role of egg and sperm in producing offspring. As noted in the earlier discussion of exogamy, not all peoples shared this understanding in the distant past, when various kinship groups were conceptualized. All peoples acknowledge a mother and her child, but there were cultures where the father was considered to be the mother's husband (and not the child's biological father). In such cultures, Ego's mother's husband was acknowledged by a term that designates this male as mother's husband and does not necessarily mean that the male is Ego's father (in the manner that modern peoples conceptualize the relationship). In some cultures, such as

FIGURE 7.8
Diagram of a Kinship System

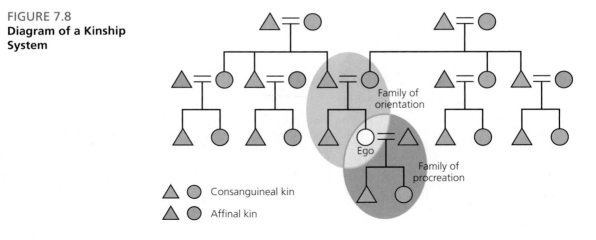

Family of orientation

Ego

Family of procreation

△ ○ Consanguineal kin

△ ○ Affinal kin

that of the Trobriand Islanders of Melanesia, a child is viewed as having been created wholly by the mother with the help of some of the mother's lineage spirits (Weiner 1988: 55). Modern Trobrianders have scientific understanding of the biology of inheritance yet maintain traditional kinship organization. North Americans would view mother, father, and child as constituting a nuclear family of blood relatives (consanguines), but the traditional view of Trobriand culture would be that the father is related only by marriage. This is why, as noted earlier, the use of diagrams with symbols is helpful in the study of these matters so that linguistic confusion is minimized.

Most people also belong to a **family of procreation** during their lifetime. By definition, a family of procreation is the family in which you become, or have the potential to become, a parent—you procreate. When you join a mate to form a family of procreation, you also acquire a whole set of nonblood kin, persons who are often called in-laws in North American society. Individuals who are related to you by marriage are called **affinal kin** (or affines).

The complex system that results from people belonging to these two family types during their lives (a family of orientation and a family of procreation) and the role expectations for each person in these families is called a **kinship system.** In other words, a kinship system consists of the group made up of people who are considered consanguines and affines and the shared understanding as to how each should behave toward the other (Figure 7.8).

The term *extended family* is also used in anthropology. An extended family is defined as two or more nuclear families who are related in some way by blood and who live together in the same household, village, or ter-

family of procreation
A kin group consisting of an individual and the individual's spouse and children.

affinal kin
Kin related by marriage.

kinship system
The complexity of a culture's rules governing the relationships between affinal and consanguineal kin.

extended family
Two or more nuclear families that are related by blood and who reside in the same household, village, or territory (e.g., a man and wife, their sons, and their sons' wives and children).

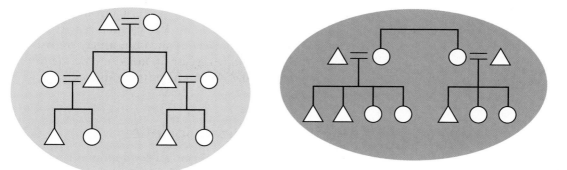

FIGURE 7.9
Diagrams of Two Extended Families

A three-generation
extended family.

ritory. Descent relationships are the most common blood ties between members of extended families, and the eldest man or woman is the head of the family. About half of the world's societies view extended families as the ideal. Figure 7.9 shows that an extended family may or may not be generational. Historians often use the term *extended family* differently. They use it to mean whoever is living under the same roof—kin, hired help, and apprentice workers; so be certain that you have the anthroplogical definition

household
A common residence-based economic unit.

in mind as you read the anthropological literature. Currently the term **household** is being used by many disciplines. A household is a group that resides together and acts as a corporate economic unit; it may consist of a family but it may also include, or fully consist of, nonkin. The use of this term for a living group that includes nonkin helps to avoid confusion with the usage of *extended family*.

Family Forms in Industrialized Societies

The industrialized world has been experiencing a revolution in family patterns in recent decades. Terms such as *expanded families* (families that include persons who are not kin), *blended families* (the result of divorce and remarriage), *matrifocal families* (in which the mother is dominant, with husband-father absent or present—typically the result of economic conditions such that the husband is unable to support the family [Pasternak, Ember, and Ember 1997: 246]), and *single-parent families* appear in local newspapers as well as international periodicals. The many variations in family types are not a new phenomenon. In the past, in Western industrialized societies, new families were often formed after death and remarriage; today, in the United States, an increasing divorce rate is the primary reason for varied family types. A cross-cultural perspective on the rate of divorce can offer insight. In one study of forty *preliterate* societies in North and South America, Africa, Asia, and Oceania, divorce was allowed in thirty-nine of the societies. Moreover, according to one analysis, the divorce rate in about 60 percent of preliterate societies was, at the time of the study, higher than in the United States (Murdock 1950, cited in Hutter 1981: 437).

Changes in family focus have often resulted from industrialization, which has been hypothesized as a causative factor in the decline of extended families and the rise in the numbers of socially isolated nuclear family units. This change occurs because people must move to where jobs can be found, and roles change as nuclear families have fewer local extended family support systems. We cannot, however, jump to hasty conclusions about the effect of industrialization on families. Many of these conditions and changes have occurred, but studies in West Africa and sub-Saharan Africa have found that the extended family system is in place and growing stronger since the removal of colonial governments (Hutter 1981: 111–35). However, data from contemporary studies of migration, such as that of the Nuer moving from Sudan to Minnesota, result in men or couples living apart from kin in independent nuclear families where they must resolve problems without the benefit of supportive kin (Holtzman 2000: 106). There is an extensive body of literature, from both anthropology and sociology, on the subject of family patterns associated with industrialized modern societies. The bottom line seems to be that human cultures continue to adapt.

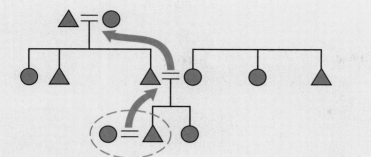

FIGURE 7.10
Patrilocal Residence
The newly married
couple reside with
or near the groom's
father. The groom's
father brought his
bride to live with his
father. This results in a
patrilocal extended
family.

◎ RESIDENCE PATTERNS

Customs about where one lives after marriage are known as residence patterns. It is easy to identify residence patterns by noting the roots to each word. The inclusion of the word *local* (meaning *place*) in each type of residence is a flag that tells you that the word refers to residence.

The pattern regarding place of residence after marriage in which the newly married couple set up their own household away from both sets of parents is called **neolocal residence,** which is the residence custom most often practiced in North American culture. This is a popular residence pattern in industrialized societies, but it is the preferred residence pattern in only about 7 percent of all societies (Murdock 1949: 194). Whether in a contemporary urban culture or a foraging culture, neolocality is marked by economic independence and privacy for the newly married couple. The emergence of this residence pattern as societies became industrialized is one reflection of the adaptive nature of culture—people moved to be near their workplaces. This functioned well for one-income families. It seems less adaptive today for two-income families and single-parent families.

The residence pattern known as **patrilocal residence** (*pater* meaning *father*) refers to the custom in which the newly married couple go to live with the groom's father (Figure 7.10). The term **virilocal residence** (living with the husband's group) is also used to designate this form of residence and some anthropologists prefer this term. *Patrilocal residence* (the term used in this text) can mean living in the same house as the groom's father (the groom's mother is living there too, of course), on the father's property, or in the village of the father. Any pattern in which the new bride moves away from her family to live with or near the groom's father's group is considered patrilocal residence. This is overwhelmingly the most popular residence custom, with 58 percent of cultures practicing it (Murdock 1949: 194). One function of the bride moving away from her natal group is that it creates alliances between groups.

neolocal residence
A postmarriage residence rule that requires the bride and groom to set up an independent household away from both sets of parents.

patrilocal residence
A postmarriage residence rule that requires the bride and groom to live in or near the residence of the groom's father.

virilocal residence
The custom of living with the husband's relatives after marriage.

A large family based on polygynous marriage in Amman, Jordan. Patrilocal residence is practiced in this society. What type of descent would you expect them to practice? Why?

TRY THIS
Analyze

You are a person from a traditional culture that practices a strict post-marriage residence rule of patrilocality. How would you view the North American custom of neolocal residence? Why?

The patrilocal residence pattern is found most often in societies in which descent is traced through males and where property is passed through the male line. The predominant hypothesis to explain patrilocality is that it keeps men together where males work together for mutual profit. Another hypothesis to explain residence rules has emerged from an analysis of the cross-cultural data. A high correlation exists between the type of warfare practiced by a society and residence patterns. Societies with internal warfare, that is, where groups within the same society fight with one another (different villages or clans), usually practice patrilocal residence. It is argued that patrilocal residence keeps fathers, sons, and brothers together as a warring unit. It must be remembered, though, that correlation does not equal causation. Patrilocality and internal warfare may be a coincidence.

The Yanomamo practice the custom of patrilocal residence. When a man marries, it is to a woman of a descent group different from his (such groups are exogamous among the Yanomamo). Because two or three descent groups usually are represented in a village, marriage to a man who lives in the same village would merely mean that the woman would move to her husband's part of the village when she marries. A village consists of a series of living spaces under one roof, and families occupy a section of the village, or **shabano** (the native term for the village). Descent group members locate near each other. If a man marries a woman from a different *shabano*, a practice that is encouraged because it aids in alliance formation, the woman would move to her husband's village.

shabano
A Yanomamo village.

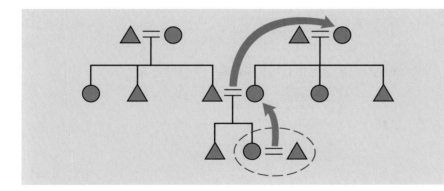

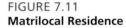

FIGURE 7.11
Matrilocal Residence
The newly married couple reside with or near the bride's mother, who in turn is living with or near her mother. This results in a matrilocal extended family.

Matrilocal residence means that the newly married couple live with the bride's mother (*matri* meaning *mother*) (Figure 7.11). The term **uxorilocal** is also used for this residence form. Uxorilocal refers to living with the wife's group. The term *matrilocal* is used here.

This form of residence is found in 15 percent of cultures and is typically associated with societies in which descent is traced through women and property is passed from mother to daughter (Murdock 1949: 194). This residence pattern also has an economic function. Because the women-centered group owns the land or herds, it is logical that they would remain together and their husbands would move to live with them at marriage.

The Hopi, who farm and herd sheep, demonstrate matrilocal residence. A Hopi household consists of a woman, her daughters and their husbands and children, plus her unmarried sons (you no doubt recognize this as an extended family). Married sons usually live nearby and occasionally help out with farming. Her husband would also reside there if she is still married (divorce is an easy matter). Women have a great deal of influence among the Hopi; they control access to the land and own the harvest (Fox 1983; Keesing and Strathern 1998: 194).

A correlation also exists between type of warfare and this residence pattern. Matrilocal residence correlates with cultures in which warfare is external. Men leave to fight a different group and must travel away from home for periods of time. Recall the Nayar case discussed earlier in this chapter. Has the preceeding discussion helped you to respond to the Try This box on the previous page?

A woman and her children residing without co-residence of a husband is called **matrifocal residence.** This pattern is a result of economic conditions in which the husband leaves the residence because he is unable to support the family. In other words, matrifocal residence is a form of residence, but technically it is not a traditional pattern of residence in any society. Some anthropologists and sociologists place this as a form of family—the matrifocal family—rather than as a type of residence. Where would you place it?

matrilocal residence
A postmarriage residence rule that requires the bride and groom to live in or near the residence of the bride's mother.

uxorilocal residence
The custom of living with the wife's relatives after marriage.

matrifocal residence
A residence group consisting of a woman and her children residing without co-residence of a husband.

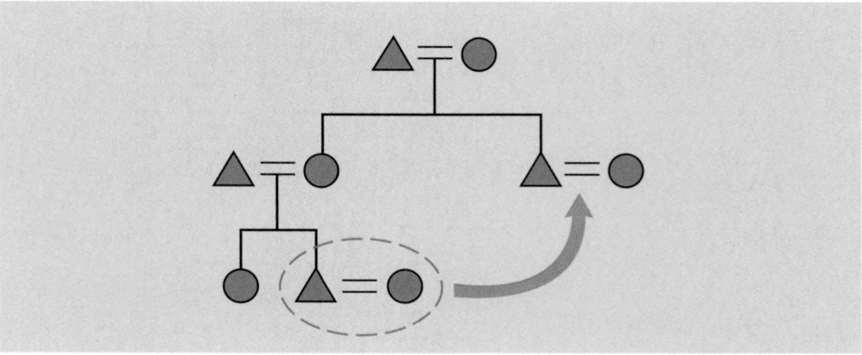

FIGURE 7.12
Avunculocal Residence   The newly married couple reside with the groom's mother's brother. This is found in matrilineal societies.

avunculocal residence
A postmarriage residence rule that requires the bride and groom to reside with or near the groom's mother's brother.

bilocal residence
The condition in which a newly married couple reside either with or near the groom's parents or the bride's parents.

ambilocal residence
See *bilocal residence.*

matri-patrilocal residence
A temporary residence form in which the groom moves to live with the bride's family until bridewealth payments are complete and the couple take up permanent patrilocal residence.

Each residence pattern is associated with specific adaptations for the culture with which it is found. **Avunculocal residence** (representing 3 percent of the cultures in Murdock's sample) occurs when the newly married couple live with the groom's mother's brother (Murdock 1949: 194). This form of residence is often associated with sedentary, small-scale societies in which property is passed from generation to generation through females and males help to manage the resources of their sisters. Examine Figure 7.12. Note that Ego's mother's brother is in the same descent group (known as a lineage and discussed further in Chapter 8) as Ego and thus shares the benefits of the same property. It would make economic sense, then, for Ego to live and work with his maternal uncle.

Choice is the rule with **bilocal residence** (also called **ambilocal residence**). A newly married couple live with or near *either* the groom's parents or the bride's parents. This residence type occurs in just over 7 percent of a sample of 250 cultures (Murdock 1949: 194). Which family the couple lives with or near is negotiated with everyone involved and is often related to economics. Such is the case when one family has all daughters and negotiates to have one of the daughters and her husband live with them in order to have the husband's economic support.

Matri-patrilocal residence (a pattern named by Murdock [1949]) is really an interim residence form found primarily in societies in which bridewealth is paid. Similar to the case of the half-marriage of the Yurok discussed earlier, in matri-patrilocal residence the groom moves to live with the bride's family but this residence is temporary. In negotiating the marriage the groom agrees to live and work as an economic member of the bride's family until the agreed-upon period of time has passed, thus compensating for his inability to make the full bridewealth payment at the time of the wedding. Regular residence is patrilocal, which is the permanent residence once the bridewealth has been worked off. This then is a residence pattern that is an adaptive response to economic situations. Other patterns of residence exist but are practiced by few cultures and are not treated in this text. See the Suggested Readings at the end of this chapter for references that will lead you to more information.

SUMMARY

The rules and customs about mate selection and marriage differ widely around the world. Yet common patterns can be identified. There are both formal and informal rules regarding whom you can or should marry and whom you are forbidden to marry. Rules such as the levirate (brother-in-law marriage) and the sororate (sister-in-law marriage) provide security for a spouse and children should the other spouse die. Mate selection is either free choice or arranged. Marriage finance is often complex and includes bridewealth and dowry. There are several forms of marriage—one spouse (monogamy), multiple wives (polygyny), and multiple husbands polyandry). Each form has its unique adaptive advantages. Families result from marriage (affinal) ties and blood (consanguineal) ties as these are constructed by individual cultures. Customs regarding residence after marriage are varied, and the functions of such residence patterns reflect issues that are important within each culture, such as economics and political alliance formation.

Study Questions

1. Discuss how the Nayar case illustrates the difficulties that anthropologists have in listing the common features of marriage found across cultures.
2. Describe the various forms of marriage found cross-culturally. Explain the advantages of each from a woman's viewpoint and from a man's viewpoint.
3. Discuss and evaluate the adaptive significance of exogamy and endogamy.
4. What are common features and functions of families around the world? Why is it difficult to define *family?*
5. What is an extended family? What is a household?
6. Describe traditional family forms. How have these forms changed in industrialized societies?
7. Compare and contrast the functions of neolocal, patrilocal, and matrilocal residence patterns.

OLC
mhhe•com/lenkeit3
See Self quiz.

Suggested Readings

Chagnon, Napoleon A. 1997. *Yanomamo.* Fort Worth, Tex.: Harcourt Brace College Publishers. Chagnon discusses marriage and residence in the social organization chapter of this ethnography. Real situations illustrating ideal and actual behaviors are discussed and genealogies are diagrammed.

Fox, Robin. 1983. *Kinship and Marriage: An Anthropological Perspective*. Cambridge, England: Cambridge University Press (originally published in 1967). Fox offers one of the best introductory discussions of anthropological kinship analysis—widely used in most universities. Lots of detail but clearly written.

Knauft, Bruce. 2005. *The Gebusi: Lives Transformed in a Rainforest World*. New York: McGraw-Hill.

Malinowski, Bronislaw. 1929. *The Sexual Life of Savages*. New York: Harcourt, Brace, Jovanovich. A classic account of courtship, marriage, love magic, and sexual norms among the Trobriand Islanders.

Murdock, George P. 1949. *Social Structure*. New York: Macmillan.

Pasternak, Burton, Carol R. Ember, and Melvin Ember. 1977. *Sex, Gender, and Kinship: A Cross-Cultural Perspective*. Upper Saddle River, N.J.: Prentice-Hall. A good read. Addresses many questions that may have occurred to you when you read this chapter.

Shostak, M. 1981. *Nisa, the Life and Words of a !Kung Woman*. New York: Vintage Books. A personal account of this Ju/'hoansi San woman's life with her feelings about marriage and family.

Suggested Web Sites

http://www.umanitoba.ca/faculties/arts/anthropology/tutor/kinmenu.html
This superb tutorial site, created by Brian Schwimmer (University of Manitoba), covers all aspects of kinship descent, marriage, and residence supported with cultural data from seven different cultures (Akan of West Africa, Igbo of Nigeria, ancient Hebrews, a Turkish village, the Yanomamo of the Amazon forest, the Dani of New Guinea, and the Ju/'hoansi of the Kalahari).

http://anthro.palomar.edu/marriage/default.htm
This site provides a quick cross-cultural overview of kinship, marriage, and residence customs. It includes information regarding homosexuality.

8

Kinship and Descent
Are These the Ties That Bind?

I am a mother-in-law. Given all of the stereo-types about mothers-in-law in North American culture, I wear this label with some trepidation, though I believe that my son-in-law and I have a harmonious relationship. I always remember how a Native American student who was in one of my classes in Canada told of his culture's solution to the mother-in-law issue. He avoided her. This was the tradition. If she came to visit and he was in the bedroom, he either stayed put behind a closed door or he exited through the bedroom window. Contemporary North American culture gives few guidelines as to proper behavior for a mother-in-law. The *ideal* seems to be a role of support and harmony. The *actual* relationship seems to miss this mark considerably if we are to believe all of the jokes told about mothers-in-law.

Mother-in-law avoidance taboos were reported for 137 societies in a sample of 250 groups (Murdock 1949). Avoidance of a man's wife's mother ranged from informal avoidance of situations in which a male Ego might encounter his wife's mother (twenty-six cultures, or 19 percent of the sample), to respect or reserved behavior in her presence (thirty-three cultures, or 24 percent), to true avoidance (seventy-eight cultures, or 57 percent) (Murdock 1949: 277). In the cultures that practice true avoidance, a man cannot be in the same room with his wife's mother. He must leave the immediate area if he sees her coming. Murdock lists thirty different categories of avoidance relationships for a male Ego, including wife's brother's wife, son's wife, and mother's sister's daughter. Mother-in-law avoidance and other avoidance taboos seem to correspond with incest taboos (Murdock 1949: 277). One explanation offered for such taboos is that some societies need an external support and reinforcement of incest taboos. The various avoidance taboos provide this reinforcement. This is an example of behavior being directed by rules within the kinship system.

◀ A grandfather and granddaughter in Papua New Guinea.

A cross-cultural study of kinship provides insight into the flexibility of human adaptive strategies. Kin ties are often at the core of human culture, and anthropologists have learned that understanding them is often essential to a full understanding of a culture's economic system, political system, or religious structure.

If you are reading this book, you most likely live in an industrialized society. Many aspects of the lives of people in industrialized societies take place away from home and family. Friends and colleagues are usually not relatives. By contrast, nonindustrial societies revolve around kinship. As noted in Chapter 5, the archaeological record shows that societies based on subsistence strategies of foraging, horticulture, pastoralism, and early agriculture preceded large-scale societies. Thus we are able to gain glimpses of the possible roots of our own social organization by examining the kinship structure of societies today that have these subsistence strategies (always keeping in mind that present societies are not fossilized remnants of earlier ones). The following discussion is intended to provide you with the skills to read ethnographic accounts of the kinship organization of other cultures, including patterns of descent and terminological systems.

The objectives of this chapter are to
◆ Describe and analyze the functions of kinship systems
◆ Describe and discuss the types of descent systems found around the world
◆ Explain the functions of associations based on descent
◆ Discuss the cross-cultural patterns of kinship terminology

◎ FUNCTIONS OF KINSHIP SYSTEMS

See chapter outline and chapter overview.

Anthropologists have gathered detailed information about family and kinship from hundreds of different cultures. Although the specifics of the kinship systems differ, the goals of kinship are remarkably similar all over the world. Recall from Chapter 7 that a kinship system is the complexity that results from the affinal and consanguineal ties within a society and the traditions that govern how people in these relationships behave toward one another. Kinship systems achieve three major functions for their group members. As each function is discussed, think about how it applies to your culture's kinship system.

First, kinship systems function to organize people into groups. Families constitute one such group. Residence groups and descent groups are other types of organized kin groups within societies.

Second, kinship systems function to direct people's behavior. They do this because each of us is enculturated to know the **role** (the assigned behavioral expectations for a particular position within society and how it is acted out) for a particular kin classification. Role behaviors are reciprocal between *classes* of individuals within a kinship system. *Mother*, for example, is a class of people who are female parents (either by giving birth or by adoption). In North America, your role expectation when you interact with your mother is to show respect and love toward her. She, in turn, has a role to play in relation to you—to protect you, nurture you, provide for you while you are a child, and love you. The mother-in-law avoidance customs cited at the beginning of this chapter also illustrate how a kinship system's customs direct behavior.

Another aspect of the kinship function of directing behavior involves a person's **status** within the society. You are born into a kin group (or are adopted by the group) and automatically acquire the status of that group. Anthropologists call this **ascribed status.** Other forms of ascribed status include that conferred by virtue of gender, age, ethnic group, and subcultural affiliation. In most cultures, for example, an individual from a wealthy family is treated differently from a member of a poor family; elders have rights that children and young adults do not have. A person may also acquire status in a variety of other ways, for example, by developing skills as a midwife, hunter, gardener, mediator, and so forth. These forms of status are called **achieved status.** An individual's role in the society is how that person plays out or behaves in her or his position of ascribed and achieved status.

Third, kinship systems function to provide security for members of a kin group. The security can be economic—kin lend you money, share food, come to help you harvest crops. It can be security provided by support in the tasks of daily life—watching your baby while you run errands or helping you with household chores. The kin group also provides security and

role
The culturally assigned behaviors and expectations for a person's social position.

status
A person's position in society.

ascribed status
The status a person is given at birth and over which that person has no control.

achieved status
A status position that is earned through an individual's skills, actions, and accomplishments.

support during major life transitions—birth, marriage, divorce, death. The details of this security and the roles assigned to classes of kin often differ from one culture to the next. In small homogeneous societies, the kin group provides a person's only security. If a spouse dies, for example, specific relatives provide support for the remaining spouse and children. Social control issues, conflict resolution, and political decision making are other behaviors assigned to kin in such societies.

Kinship provides security in many of the same situations in complex heterogeneous societies. In such societies, however, governmental agencies, private agencies, and businesses have taken over the security functions of kinship in many situations. In North American culture, many people purchase life insurance policies so that their spouse and children will be financially cared for should they die. Or the state will take care of your children if you die without leaving any assets or designated guardians for them. Courts and professional mediators are designated to resolve conflicts in state societies.

> **TRY THIS**
> *Analyze*
>
> Think of three specific ways your nuclear family provides you with security. Discuss your list with a classmate.

◎ IDEAL VERSUS REAL PATTERNS OF KINSHIP

A word about ideal and real patterns of kinship, descent, and terminological systems must be made before we examine these systems. In Chapter 2 we discussed ideal and real (or actual) culture. When anthropologists describe a culture's kinship system, they are presenting the culture's ideal custom or the most common pattern. For example, monogamy is the ideal form of marriage in North American culture. In fact, most North Americans really *do* have only one spouse (at least only one at a time). This would be a case in which real and ideal cultural patterns are virtually the same. Nearly everyone, however, can recall a publicized case in which a man or woman had more than one spouse, though often the spouses did not know that their mate was married to someone else. There are also accounts of marriages in the United States in which men have several wives and each wife knows the other wives. Such cases, though rare, often receive a great deal of attention in the media because they are defined as illegal in all legal jurisdictions in the United States.

In the ethnographic literature, anthropologists most often discuss and present examples and analyses of ideal customs and behaviors. Real behaviors, and their variations, are also recorded in some but not all ethnographic accounts. Napoleon Chagnon's account of the Yanomamo Indians of Venezuela and Brazil first presents the reader with a discussion of the ideal model of Yanomamo society—exogamous patrilineages, bilateral cross-cousin marriage, and the classification of bilateral cross-cousins as wives (Chagnon 1997: 140). These terms will be explained shortly. Chagnon then diagrams and discusses a number of actual (real) marriages and kinship relationships that he encountered among the Yanomamo, and quite a few do not match the ideal pattern.

Variations and exceptions to the ideal within a society nearly always occur. The *knowledge* of proper, accepted customs is usually shared by most members of a culture, even if all do not practice the custom or behave in the ideal manner. Human beings are complex, and human cultures are equally complex. Variations and exceptions to ideal behaviors add spice to the texture of social life everywhere if you consider that these are often the topics of gossip, song, sermon, and story. Careful ethnographic descriptions based on participant observation over a long period reveal these variations and exceptions. The ethnological analysis of data from hundreds of cultures has revealed the common *patterns* discussed in the following sections, but keep in mind the notions of ideal versus real culture.

◎ DESCENT GROUPS

Descent groups are important in most kinship systems. A **descent group** consists of a group of people who share identity that is directly traced (or stipulated to come) from a common ancestor. As we established previously, all of our ancestors lived at one time in societies with economies based on foraging, horticulture, and pastoralism, and it was in these societies that ideas about descent began, although we will never know the details of how they originated. Most foraging cultures do not focus on descent groups; however, in societies with food-production strategies, where property is owned by corporate kin groups and populations are large and concentrated, the focus *is* on descent. These societies also exhibit the most variety and complexity in all aspects of kinship. We therefore think that ideas about descent likely began with food-producing societies. For these groups, property ownership led to the problem of how and to whom property would be left when one died.

Unilineal Descent Groups

Unilineal descent systems are often perplexing to individuals who have been raised in a society without such systems. Before reading about these kinship groups, you should set aside all thoughts of your own descent system and concentrate on the logic and functions of the unilineal systems presented. These systems reflect the ingenuity of humans in developing kin groups that made sense to them and that worked to each person's benefit.

As food-producing societies evolved, descent groups became something like modern business corporations, to use a contemporary analogy. Members of the corporate group act together and are governed by specific

descent group
A group of people who share identity and come from a common ancestor.

East African cattle-herding peoples such as these Masai have unilineal descent, specifically patrilineages. Look closely at these men practicing traditional dance. What examples of diffusion from other cultures can you see?

rights and duties. Because property ownership was an issue, large families created descent groups to manage property. The most basic descent group is the **lineage.** Members of a lineage descent group can trace their ancestors back through several generations to a common ancestor. The lineage holds property in common (e.g., land, sheep, or cattle). All members benefit from this property, all contribute to its maintenance in some manner, and all view the other members of their lineage as their closest, most important relatives. Furthermore, authority and power in group decision making and cohesiveness are important functions of lineages. The lineage continues over time even as its members change through births and deaths. These features are what lead some researchers to point out that the lineage functions like a modern corporation.

Unilineal descent groups recognize consanguineal ties as being passed through only females or males. It is not that other blood relatives are unknown but rather that *by cultural definition* they belong to a descent group different from Ego's. For example, the father may be recognized as the male parent (a consanguineal relative) but may not be considered as a *lineal* relative. This underscores that unilineal descent groups are culturally defined groups.

lineage
A unilineal descent group that traces its consanguineal relatives back to a common ancestor.

FIGURE 8.1
Ego's Patrilineage

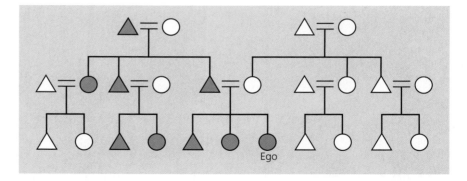

Patrilineal Descent   In a **patrilineage,** descent is passed through the male line. All members (both males and females) acquire their lineage from their father, but only males pass it on. This kin link through males is a link through what some anthropologists call **agnates** (a term in Roman law that is a synonym for members of a patrilineage) (Fox 1983: 45). Ego's agnates are all of the members of Ego's patrilineage (Figure 8.1). The term *agnates* is a specialized term, but it is used in ethnographic accounts such as that of the Yanomamo, so it helps to be familiar with it.

A major function of patrilineal groups is to keep property for the males who own and manage it. This is the most common form of descent worldwide; 42 percent of societies (in a sample of 250 societies) practice it (Murdock 1949: 194). Lineages are permanent, often tight, cohesive groups. Lineage membership provides an individual with an ascribed status and group membership that is kept throughout his or her life. Even when an individual marries or changes residence, lineage membership is retained. Of course there are exceptions. Occasionally an individual is adopted by another lineage. This might happen if a man has all daughters and negotiates to adopt one of his daughter's husbands so that his line will continue.

The enculturated role behaviors and expectations for lineage members are that first responsibilities are always toward one's own lineage members. This does not mean that an individual does not care about the relatives acquired through marriage. It simply means that the culture is organized in such a manner that those affines are being looked after by the members of *their* lineage. Exceptions do occur and are typically related to political or economic practicalities. Among the patrilineal Yanomamo, for example, a man's brothers-in-law are important political allies and are given priority consideration in many situations.

Matrilineal Descent   A **matrilineage** (or **uterine descent group**) is characterized by descent that is traced through females. In matrilineal descent, representing 20 percent of cultures (from a sample of 250), both males and

patrilineage
A unilineal descent group passed on through males and traced to a common male ancestor.

agnates
Members of a patrilineage.

matrilineage
A unilineal descent group with membership passed on through females and traced to a common female ancestor.

uterine descent group
See *matrilineage.*

Malay women of Negeri Sembilan, Malaysia. Numerous societies in Malaysia practice forms of matrilineal descent.

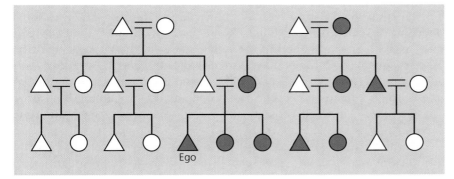

Ego

FIGURE 8.2
Ego's Matrilineage

OLC
mhhe•com/lenkeit3

See Internet exercises.

females acquire the lineage of their mother (Murdock 1949: 194). Only women can pass the lineage membership on to the next generation.

In matrilineal societies the women have inheritance rights to property, although within the corporate matrilineal group it is often their brothers (also members of the same matrilineage) who control it. The social organization of the Hopi of the southwestern United States is matrilineal, with the matrilineage acting as a corporate economic unit. Upon marriage a man joins the household of his wife and makes important economic contributions to farming and sheep herding but does not participate in the wife's lineage rituals. He still has ties to his mother and sisters through *his* lineage relationship and plays important roles in transmitting the ritual heritage of his matrilineage.

As you examine Figure 8.2, note that if the members of Ego's lineage were asked to name *their* lineage members, each would name exactly the same set of people. The same would hold true if you posed this same

FIGURE 8.3
Bilateral Descent

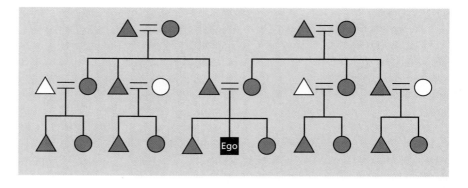

question to individual members of a patrilineage. The result is a closely knit permanent group.

Nonunilineal Descent Groups

The best-known and most common nonunilineal descent system is called **bilateral descent.** An individual Ego recognizes all consanguineal relatives on both the mother's and the father's sides of the family. She or he inherits equally from them. This system is found in North American society among persons of European ancestry and is common in foraging societies. Such a bilateral descent group consists only of siblings and their consanguineal kin. Ego's cousin, for example, does not share the same ancestor line as Ego (Figure 8.3).

Within bilateral systems, every Ego belongs to what is called a **kindred** group, which consists of Ego's relatives and their degree of relationship to Ego (e.g. aunt, great uncle, first cousin). An interesting feature of a kindred group is that only siblings share exactly the same kindred and set of relatives (at least until they marry). Another way to describe a kindred is that it consists of Ego's nuclear family and consanguineal members of Ego's extended family. Study the diagram in Figure 8.4. Note that in

bilateral descent
Descent that is traced equally through both mother and father.

kindred
A term associated with bilateral descent in which relatives calculate their degree of relationship to Ego. In a kindred, only siblings share the exact same set of relatives.

TRY THIS *Consider*

Imagine that you have a problem. You have a fence on your property that was knocked down in a recent storm, and you need help repairing it. In which descent system, unilineal (patrilineal or matrilineal) or nonunilineal (bilateral), would you expect to have the most relatives who would feel a real *obligation* to drop all of their weekend plans, cancel motel reservations and theater tickets, and come to your home to help with the fence repair? Discuss this with a classmate.

Look for examples of such support by kin group members in the other assigned readings for this course.

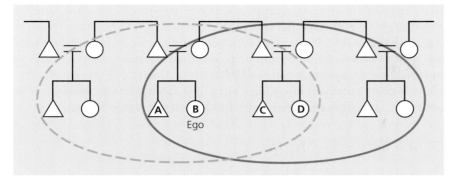

FIGURE 8.4
Kindred   The kindred
of siblings A and B are
shown with the broken
line. The kindred of
siblings C and D are
shown with the solid
line. If you follow the
kindreds back another
generation, you'll see
that A and B would
have a different kin-
dred from that of their
mother and father.

A large North Ameri-
can kindred group.
How many individuals
can you name in your
own kindred?

Ego's kindred, Ego and Ego's brother have the same parents, grandparents, aunts, uncles, and cousins. Ego and her brother have the same consanguineal relatives and the same bilateral descent group, and they share
the same kindred group. If you consider Ego's mother, her bilateral descent group includes Ego and Ego's brother and their children. However,
Ego's mother will not name her husband (Ego's father) as part of her kindred because he and all of his consanguineal kin are related to Ego's mother
affinally. In other words, kindred group members related to Ego do not

share exactly the same set of biological ancestors unless they are siblings. What they have in common is Ego herself as a member of their kindred (Fox 1983: 164–74). Kindred groups are useful in societies in which people need occasional support and help. For example they might participate in rituals involving Ego such as a wedding or funeral. Within a kindred, focus is more often on one's nuclear family. Compare this with a matrilineage or patrilineage where Ego's focus is on the whole lineage.

Other Descent Groups

Other types of descent groups are less common than patrilineal, matrilineal, and bilateral descent. Each could be placed under unilineal descent types or nonunilineal descent types—there are arguments for each. For the sake of simplicity, they are classified here as other descent groups. After reading the description of each group, decide whether you would classify them as unilineal or nonunilineal systems.

Double Descent   **Double descent** is a system in which two separate lines of descent are recognized at the same time. In this system some property is passed down only through females, and other property is passed down only through males. An example of double descent would be a system in which land could be passed only from mother to daughter, whereas cattle could be passed only from father to son.

Ambilineal Descent   **Ambilineal descent** is a system in which everyone belongs to a unilineal descent group that is acquired through *either* the mother or the father. In other words, some members of the society trace their descent through their mothers, whereas other members of the same society determine their descent through their fathers. Discussions are held and traditional, economic, political, or other issues are considered before decisions are made about which system to follow.

double descent
A descent system with two separate lines of descent that are both recognized at the same time.

ambilineal descent
A unilineal descent system in which some members of the society acquire and pass on descent affiliation through females, whereas others do so through males.

Associations Based on Descent

Descent-based societies are effective. The threads created by marriages between lineages (recall that lineages are usually exogamous groups) combine with the strong ties of lineage membership itself to weave a cultural fabric of interdependent units. Common culture and language, plus the associations created by affinal and consanguineal ties, hold such groups together. There is no centralized leadership or governmental system. Leadership (discussed more fully in Chapter 10) remains within the immediate family and descent group.

Anthropologists have recorded additional types of kin-based organization in horticultural and pastoral societies with large populations. These

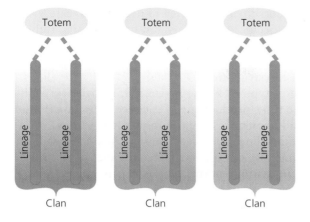

FIGURE 8.5
Second-Level Descent

are often called second-level descent groups because individuals first belong to a lineage. The second-level descent groups are clans, phratries, and
moieties (Figure 8.5). These groups are unilineal, and membership in them
is passed through either the female or the male line. In other words, you
are assigned membership in a clan because your mother is a member (in a
matrilineal society) or your father is a member (in a patrilineal society).

A **clan** is a group consisting of two or more lineages that share a common ancestor in the mythical past. A lineage, you will remember, is a descent group that can explicitly name ancestors back several generations.
Clan members cannot name their ancestors all the way back to a common
ancestor. In some societies, the ancestor of a clan is considered mythical
or a symbol and is called its **totem.** Mythic ancestors often figure in a culture's origin myths. Clans may or may not be exogamous. When they are
exogamous it forces members to seek spouses from other clans. The threads
of marriage ties thus reach farther away from Ego, while at the same time
Ego is bound closely by the clan association to members of other lineages
(i.e., those in her or his own clan).

Additional levels of descent associations also occur in some societies,
although these are rare. A **phratry** is a grouping formed by two or more
clans when there are at least three or more such groupings (Schusky 1972:
75). It is also unilineal, but the original association is often vague or is
based on some type of mutual relationship from past times in the culture's
history. Phratries are also usually exogamous groups.

Finally, moieties are sometimes found in nonindustrial societies. A
moiety association divides the society in half. Because a moiety is a unilineal association inherited through either women or men, it creates a
common bond with many individuals. Moieties are usually exogamous too.

To recap, exogamous rules commonly apply to the nuclear family,
lineage, clan, phratry, and moiety groups, thus forcing a complex network

clan
A descent group consist-
ing of two or more lin-
eages that trace their
origin to a mythical
ancestor.

totem
Mythical ancestor or
symbol of a clan.

phratry
A group of two or more
clans that have a tie to
one another, often based
on a historical relation-
ship; obligations and
rights are expected be-
tween clans in this
relationship.

moiety
An association that di-
vides a society in half.
Moiety affiliation is in-
herited unilineally and
carries obligations to
other members.

TRY THIS
Hypothesize

Suppose for a moment that you are an anthropologist. You have been reading about all of these unilineal, exogamous groups, here and in other assigned readings. Formulate a hypothesis that explains the purpose served by such associations. Share, compare, and discuss your hypothesis with a classmate. It might help you to study Figure 8.5 as you formulate your hypothesis.

Complete this hypothesis on another sheet of paper: If _____ exist within a society, then clans, phratries, and moieties serve to _____.

Now, determine two ways that you could test your hypothesis. Compare your hypothesis and tests with those of a classmate.

of marriage relations. Membership at each level of descent (lineage, clan, phratry, or moiety) carries specific obligations and expectations. Reflect on the functions of kinship listed at the beginning of this chapter. Imagine viewing the world through the lens of a person who is a member of a culture with this complex kinship structure.

Another rather common type of kin organization, **segmentary lineages,** found in some large food-producing societies seems to function in the same way as the clan and phratry. Instead of progressively larger groupings, however, the segmentary lineage system consists of smaller sublineage sets (Figure 8.6). Segmentary lineages are often found in large African tribes. The Nuer provide an example of this type of organization.

Nuer patrilineages consists of a large group of agnates who trace their descent to a common ancestor. Each major lineage is in turn segmented into minimal lineage segments. All property is owned and passed on through the males. All lineages are exogamous units. E. E. Evans-Pritchard (1940) noted that each Nuer could, when asked, readily name his ancestors back four to five generations. Lineages are usually three to five generations, and the major ones have ten to twelve generations. Evans-Pritchard graphically represents these lineages rather like a tree with thick branches that divide into smaller branches at the ends. The smaller, more recent lineage segments frequently further divide or recombine. Besides these actual traceable lineage relationships, termed *mar* (also spelled *maar*), the Nuer recognize another relationship termed *buth*. These *buth* relationships occur when there is believed to be a special relationship between two lineages but the actual links cannot be traced. The *buth* relationship would correspond to clans as discussed previously (Evans-Pritchard 1940: 192–200).

Voluntary Association Groups

Kinship groups are at the core of societies; they function to meet the needs of individuals and groups as discussed at the beginning of this chapter. Not all of an individual's needs may be met through various kin group associations, however. This is particularly true in large industrialized societies where kin group fragmentation often results from the mobility of individuals. An increase in voluntary association groups is one adaptation that is observed in such societies. Members of these groups fulfill some of the support roles once found only among family members, particularly in the realms of supporting one another in everyday activities and during life crisis situations. Examples of such associations in North America include formal groups such as the Boy Scouts of America, Rotary International, Elks, Jeep Owner's Club, AL-ANON, and the Canadian Kennel Club. Less formal groups also abound—quilters clubs, knitters clubs, book clubs,

segmentary lineage
A descent group consisting of sublineage sets.

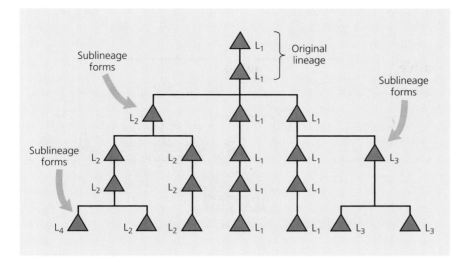

FIGURE 8.6
Segmentary Lineage
A lineage has segmented. Sublineages form when lineages get too large. Some members move and establish sublineages. They can still name lineage ancestors back four to five generations.

biking clubs, Web gamers, and even very informal groups such as the Friday morning coffee group or the pick-up basketball group that meets at the local park. Many voluntary association groups consist of local clubs that draw members from across a small geographic area, but the association may also create relationships across the larger society or even to individuals in other societies across the globe. Anthropologists use the term **sodality** for association groups that crosscut an entire society and whose membership is based on common interest rather than kinship or residence. Globalization has resulted in worldwide association groups, so perhaps we can speak of global sodalities. Among pre-industrial societies, voluntary association groups are fewer in number. See Chapter 10 for further discussion of sodalities as integrative mechanisms in tribes.

◎ PARALLEL-COUSINS AND CROSS-COUSINS REVISITED

To most North Americans of European descent, a cousin is a cousin is a cousin. This is because we use a type of kin terminological system in which all relatives in our own generation outside of our nuclear family are lumped and designated by a single term, *cousin*. So when we talk of a cousin who visited us yesterday, we are not giving much information about our relationship to this person. Is it our MoSiCh, our MoBrCh, our FaBrCh, or our FaSiCh? (See Figure 8.7.) The term doesn't even tell us if the cousin is female or male. Many cultures, most commonly those based on unilineal

TRY THIS
Consider

Name the voluntary association groups to which individual members of your nuclear family belong. What is one specific incident where one of these groups performed in a support role similar to what kin supply (or ideally are supposed to supply)?

sodality
A group that crosscuts a society and whose membership is based on common interest rather than kinship or residence.

FIGURE 8.7
Hypothetical Society with Only Two Patrilineages The rule of lineage exogamy results in the marriages shown. All parallel-cousins will be of Ego's lineage, whereas cross-cousins will be possible marriage partners. This suggests that traditions of marrying certain cousins may have its roots in societies with two unilineal descent groups.

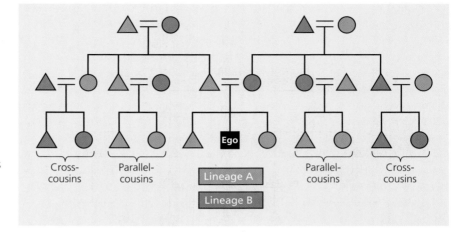

descent systems, recognize two types of cousins—**cross-cousins** and **parallel-cousins.** To appreciate the significance of these cousin types, you must set aside the knowledge that all cousins are equally related to you biologically. If one imagines a time when people may not have fully understood reproductive biology and genetics, the reasons some cousins are treated differently from others will be easier to comprehend. Traditional treatment of different types of cousins continues today, even when biological relationships are clearly understood. Why? In the emic view, the answer usually is, *tradition.*

As noted in Chapter 7, parallel-cousins are defined as the children of one's parent's sibling of the same sex, in other words, Ego's MoSiCh and Ego's FaBrCh. If you think of the word *parallel* and MoSi or FaBr, it may make more sense to you. These people's children are your parallel-cousins. Conversely, cross-cousins are the children of your parent's sibling of the opposite sex, or MoBrCh and FaSiCh. The cross can be remembered if you think of opposite sex of parent.

Knowing these distinctions between types of cousins is helpful in understanding some of the common terminological systems found in other cultures. Our own system does not make any distinction regarding cousins, but in some cultures, such as ones using the Iroquois terminological system, parallel-cousins are part of the incest taboo whereas cross-cousins are considered ideal marriage partners. One such system is called sister exchange marriage (discussed in Chapter 7), and it takes place between men who are cross-cousins. Each man arranges with a cross-cousin so that they marry each other's sisters. The Yanomamo tribe of Venezuela and Brazil practice sister exchange, as do the Mbuti pygmy bands of Africa.

cross-cousin
Ego's mother's brother's child and father's sister's child.

parallel-cousin
Ego's mother's sister's child and father's brother's child.

Therefore, one could suggest that cousin designations, and the rules surrounding them, function to control mate selection.

◎ TERMINOLOGICAL SYSTEMS

Terminology is an accompaniment to the kin structure. In foraging, horticultural, and pastoral societies, kinship is the primary manner in which people relate to one another. Furthermore, kin relations resulting from exogamous rules are central to the unity of the culture—they bind it together. It follows that kin roles and the obligations they carry are important. The complexity of terminological systems is relative. The system you have been enculturated to seems obvious and easy to you; other systems seem difficult and complex. A **kinship term** is a word that designates a culturally constructed social relationship between individuals who are related by blood or marriage (consanguines or affines). Kinship terminological systems are quite variable, but a comparative analysis shows that there are several basic terminological patterns. These patterns are most apparent in Ego's generation and Ego's parent's generation. These patterns have come to be called terminological systems. Several patterns that are repeatedly found in world cultures are Inuit (Eskimo), Iroquois, Hawaiian, Crow, Omaha, and Sudanese. Each system bears the name of the particular cultural group in which that terminological system was first recorded by ethnographers. These systems apparently developed independently in different parts of the world; that is, cultures in North America, South America, Africa, Asia, and Australia often independently developed the same *patterns* of terminology. Three of these terminological systems are discussed here: the Inuit, Hawaiian, and Iroquois.

The Inuit Terminology System

Terminological systems reflect recognized kin categories and often reflect values central to a culture. Cultures that use the Inuit, formerly Eskimo, terminology system (18 out of 250 societies, or 7 percent) focus on the nuclear family, in which each relative is given a separate term—Mo, Fa, Si, Br. Although this is not the most common terminological system, it is a good place to initiate an analysis of terminological systems because most North Americans use this one. Neolocal residence is often practiced in such cultures, thus making the nuclear family the central economic unit of the society (Murdock 1949: 249). Family band societies such as the Inuit (Eskimo) also typically exhibit this form of terminology. In these societies, kin outside of the nuclear family are lumped together terminologically. For example, MoBr and FaBr are both called by the same term (*uncle* in English),

> ❊ **TRY THIS** ❊
> *Question*
>
> Suppose you are being interviewed by an Amazonian anthropologist. She has just asked you the following question: Why do you use the same term for your MoBrCh, MoSiCh, FaBrCh, and FaSiCh? How would you respond? Ask someone else this question. Convey your seriousness in wanting a response. Discuss this question with a classmate.

kinship term
A word that designates a social relationship between individuals who are related by blood or marriage.

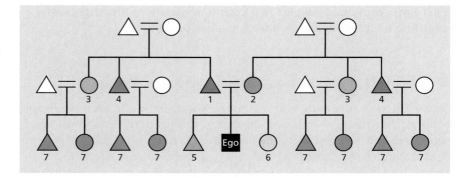

as are MoSi and FaSi (*aunt* in English). And all cousins are lumped with a single term (Figure 8.8). Of course, because each culture that exhibits the Inuit system speaks a different language, the words used are different. It is the *pattern* of usage that we are considering when we label a terminology as belonging to a particular system. Also, there are often cultures with variations on one of the basic terminological patterns that have been identified. For example, in Mexican culture the basic Inuit terminology system is used except that cousins are distinguished by sex (*primo* and *prima*). This variation is a reflection of the language (Spanish); that is, the male and female gender is built into all nouns. It does not appear that this distinction has any other significance. Such variations are minor, but they do point to the difficulty in precisely categorizing human cultures.

Now, toss aside your own cultural lens and through your imagination view the following systems. Pretend that you are looking through the cultural lens of a person who uses these terms. We are required to *really* think about the differences that our cultures have produced when we examine other terminological systems.

The Iroquois Terminology System

bifurcate
The distinction within kinship systems where father's side and mother's side of the family are labeled and treated differently, splitting mother's side of the family from father's side of the family.

fictive kin
Unrelated family friends who are addressed by kin terms.

The Iroquois system and its variations represent a common terminological pattern in the world cultures sample (33 societies of 250 sample, or 13 percent) (Murdock 1949: 249). Because it represents a common pattern of terminology that is quite different from the Inuit system, we'll consider it in more detail. Iroquois terminology is typically reported in cultures that practice unilineal descent and in which lineage affiliation is very important. In the Iroquois terminology pattern, members of Ego's nuclear family are each called by a separate term, but Ego's Fa and FaBr are called by the same term. Mo and MoSi are also called by the same term (Figure 8.9). Such a system is said to **bifurcate** (which means to separate into two categories). This means that Ego's mother's side of the family and Ego's

North American Kin Term Variations

What do you call your MoBr, FaBr, MoSi, or FaSi when speaking to them (using terms of address)? Studies show that many of us call these people aunt and uncle. We generally combine the kin term with the person's first name. Some of us drop the kin term when we are particularly fond of our aunt or uncle; others drop the kin terms when we don't like them and don't want to claim them as kin. Some Asian American's use only the kin terms and do not include the first name. Many of us use terms *aunt* and *uncle* for nonkin persons whom we are close to who are in our parents' generation. These people are considered **fictive kin.**

Even though North American kinship terminology follows the Inuit type, we do make choices when *applying* formal kin terms as in the case with *aunt* and *uncle.* Formal kin terms dictate the type of behavior expected of the *class of individuals* who are in a particular kin position. The *actual* North American kin term usage reveals that the terms we use reflect attitudes we have toward individuals and the nature of our personal relationship with them. Schneider and Homans (1955) label these two aspects or functions of kin terms as their "classifying" aspect and their "role-designating" aspect. The tone, pitch, and decibel level in which the kin term is vocalized also communicates a great deal of culture-specific information to the listener.

A variety of alternate terms are used in the North American system. Mother (Ego's biological female parent) is often called *mama, mommy, mum, mom,* or *mother* when Ego is addressing her. To the listener the term indicates that this is the speaker's female parent (the classifying aspect). The variation of the term used communicates information to us about the role-designating aspect. The term used often changes as Ego grows older,

though term usage may vary when certain social situations arise.

◎ What is the difference between the relationship and attitude of someone who addresses her parent as *mom* compared with *mother?* Does your use of a kin term variant reflect your attitude and feelings toward a kinsperson? Do the terms you use vary with the social situation? Do you have any fictive kin?

FIGURE 8.9
The Iroquois Termi-nology System
Each number in the diagram stands for a different term.

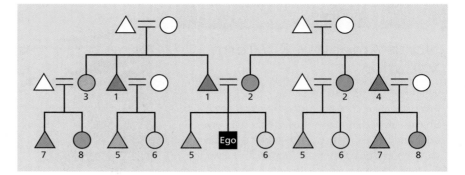

father's side of the family are treated differently, and this difference is reflected in the kin terms used. At the same time, this pattern is called a bifurcate-merging pattern because *classes* of kin in the same generation—for example, Mo and MoSi (women in the generation above Ego *and* on Ego's mother's side of Ego's family)—are called by the same term. Naturally peoples who use such a pattern of terms don't analyze it in this way. They have been enculturated to the usage, and for them it is the proper way to name relatives.

The usage of the same word for mother and mother's sister does not mean Ego thinks that they are exactly the same. As noted previously, these women belong to a class or category of individuals that are defined in the culture. Ego understands that he or she has a reciprocal relationship with all women called by the mother term. This relationship involves mutual obligations and expectations (remember the goals or functions of a kinship system discussed earlier). There is still a special relationship between Ego and her or his actual biological mother, and often there is a linguistic designation for one's biological mother that is outside the kin terminology pattern.

OLC
mhhe•com/lenkeit3
See Internet exercises.

It is evident from Figure 8.9 that this system has other interesting features. Cousins on each side of the family are distinguished by two sets of terms, one of which is the same as the terms for Ego's own siblings. Ego's parallel-cousins are the ones that Ego calls by the same terms used for Ego's own siblings. Cross-cousins are called by different terms. In some societies cross-cousins are Ego's ideal marriage partners. The Yanomamo, for example, use the Iroquois terminology system, and cross-cousins are Ego's ideal marriage partners. For a male Ego the terms *suaboya* (FaSiDa and MoBrDa) and *soriwa* (FaSiSo and MoBrSo) are used for cross-cousins. These terms translate into English as *wife* and *brother-in-law*. The Yanomamo terms represent *categories* of people, and for this male Ego, individuals in the *suaboya* category are possible mates. Each Yanomamo knows the difference between his actual wife and other individuals in the category of *suaboya* (wife).

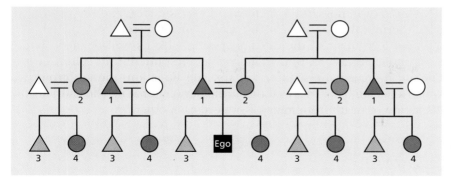

FIGURE 8.10
**The Hawaiian Termi-
nology System**
Each number repre-
sents a different term.

The Hawaiian Terminology System

The Hawaiian terminology system (used in 45 out of 250 cultures, or 18 percent) and its variations are more widely used than the Inuit or Iroquois systems (Murdock 1949: 249). More than the others, this system, as Figure 8.10 illustrates, lumps relatives by generation and sex. Hawaiian terminology is typically associated with societies that do *not* have strong unilineal descent.

The Hawaiian system is often called a *generational* system. Everyone in ego's generation is called by the same terms that Ego calls his or her siblings. Everyone in Ego's parents' generation is called by the same terms. For example, Mo, MoSi, and FaSi are called by the same term; and Fa, FaBr, and MoBr are called by the same term.

Other Systems

Other less common terminological systems are the Crow, Omaha, and Sudanese systems. And some cultures exhibit minor variations of each of the terminological systems described here. Because this is an introduction to the study of kinship, details of other systems are not included here. See the Suggested Readings list at the end of this chapter for readings with more information on terminology systems.

Each of the terminological patterns described in this chapter represents unique human adaptations that ethnographers have recorded. Anthropologists have used a great deal of ink and paper writing hypotheses to explain the patterns. Explanations of terminological patterns often center on unilineal descent groups, economic considerations, and the identification of proper marriage partners. The bottom line is that we are unlikely to know for certain how these systems originated, because there are no fossils or records of the origins of these customs. Still, it is challenging to try to explain them based on all of the data that we can accumulate.

These terminological systems represent the ideal and the manner in which terminology is applied and used by most members of the culture. The reinforcement of the existing system, with its well-defined obligations and expectations, is in an individual's best interest. In cultures without social security, insurance, welfare, and litigation, the kin groups to which a person belongs are all that stand between that person and possible starvation or death from injury. Kin need each other.

SUMMARY

Anthropologists have gathered ethnographic data on hundreds of different cultures from every corner of the world. Although there is great diversity, numerous consistent patterns emerge that show how people organize themselves and culturally define who they are related to and how—blood relatives (consanguines) and relatives by marriage (affines). The functions of kinship systems are common to a wide variety of cultures: People are organized into groups, behavioral expectations are dictated, and security is provided for group members. The North American system of bilateral descent groups known as kindreds is contrasted with unilineal descent groups known as patrilineages and matrilineages. Both types exhibit many of the same functions. The Inuit terminological pattern and the Iroquois terminological pattern illustrate how such systems dictate people's behavior toward their relatives.

Study Questions

OLC
mhhe•com/lenkeit3
See Self Quiz.

1. Compare and contrast the functions of kinship in societies that have unilineal descent and those that have bilateral (or kindred) descent. Give specific examples from your assigned ethnography or other readings and from your own culture.

2. Describe the kinship structure within another culture (use an ethnographic source that is assigned reading for your class), and discuss how the goals and aims of kinship are illustrated in this ethnographic account.

3. Compare and contrast the Hawaiian and Iroquois terminological systems.

Suggested Readings

Chagnon, Napoleon A. 1997. *Yanomamo.* 5th ed. Fort Worth, Tex.: Harcourt Brace College Publishers. Chagnon discusses kinship in the social organization chapter of this ethnography. Real situations illustrating ideal and actual behaviors are discussed and geneaologies are diagrammed.

Evans-Pritchard, E. E. 1940. *The Nuer.* Oxford, England: Clarendon. This ethnography is still considered a classic in the study of kinship.

Fox, Robin. 1983. *Kinship and Marriage: An Anthropological Perspective*. Cambridge, England: Cambridge University Press (originally published in1967). One of the best introductions to the details of anthropological kinship analysis. Lots of detail but clearly written.

Murdock, George P. 1949. *Social Structure*. New York: Macmillan. A detailed cross-cultural study of kinship including descent and terminological systems.

Pasternak, Burton, Carol R. Ember, and Melvin Ember. 1977. *Sex, Gender, and Kinship: A Cross-Cultural Perspective*. Upper Saddle River, N.J.: Prentice-Hall. A good read. Addresses many questions that may have occurred to you when you read this chapter.

Suggested Web Sites

http://www.umanitoba.ca/faculties/arts/anthropology/tutor/kinmenu/html
This superb tutorial site, created by Brian Schwimmer (University of Manitoba), covers all aspects of kinship, including descent and terminological systems. Cultural data from seven different cultures (Akan of West Africa, Igbo of Nigeria, ancient Hebrews, a Turkish village, the Yanomamo of the Amazon forest, the Dani of New Guinea, and the Ju/'hoansi of the Kalahari) provide specific examples.

http://anthro.palomar.edu/marriage/default.htm
This site provides a quick cross-cultural overview of kinship, marriage, and residence customs.

OLC
mhhe•com/lenkeit3
See Web links.

9

Gender and Sexuality

Nature or Nurture?

We were in a small bar on the island of Bora Bora in the Society Islands of Polynesia enjoying the music of local musicians. They entertained crowds at the bar nightly and usually drew both locals and tourists. The evening was well under way, and everyone seemed to be having a good time. Locals were asking tourists to dance, and many sang along with songs that were being played. Our attention was drawn to a nearby table where a group of local Tahitians began laughing heartily whenever a particular member of their

Bora Bora

group, a mature, rather stout, middle-aged woman, would get up to dance with one of the tourists. I recognized the woman as the person who was recommended to us as someone who did laundry for visitors as well as local residents. She was soft-spoken and friendly earlier in the day as we made the arrangements for our laundry. This evening she was attired the same way as other women her age, wore a flower in her hair, and smiled as she danced and chatted with the tourists. One male tourist in particular seemed to enjoy her company and kept asking her to dance. Each time he led her to the small dance floor, the other members of her party made a loud comment and they would break into song. I listened carefully but was unable to understand what was said. Finally, my husband bought a round of beers for the other table, and because we had talked to two of these men on other occasions and had established rapport with them, he asked them to share the source of their hilarity. The immediate response was that the tourist clearly did not know that he was dancing with a "he-she" (our informant said that this was an English translation for the Tahitian term; others have translated it as "half-man, half-woman").

◀ A young man carries a child in Laos.

They further remarked, matter-of-factly, that this person was one of the best dancers around.

We knew of the third gender *(mahu)* in Tahiti and Hawaii (different names are used for these individuals in other places in Polynesia), but this was the first time we had met one. We asked for more details on the gender, gender role, and status of he-shes. We were answered politely, but our interest clearly perplexed the residents. This third gender was simply a part of their society, and no one thought it unusual in any way. Deborah Elliston (1999) has written that social acceptance of the gender variant role in Tahiti is legitimized by a longtime participation in the role behaviors. Recent accounts have noted that the *mahu*, as part of male gender diversity in Tahiti, participate in women's work and adopt feminine dress, speech, and silent language gestures. They also adopt feminine dance styles (Nanda 2000: 60).

To what extent does our culture shape our behavior as a man or woman (i.e., nurture), and what does biology contribute (i.e., nature)? How are gender roles defined in other cultures? This chapter explores these questions.

The objectives of this chapter are to

◆ Distinguish between sex and gender cross-culturally

◆ Delineate factors affecting gender roles cross-culturally

◆ Give an overview of the variations in gender roles

◆ Explore human sexual behavior from a comparative perspective

◎ MARGARET MEAD AND EARLY GENDER STUDIES

OLC
mhhe•com/lenkeit3

See chapter outline and chapter overview.

Western societies assume two gender roles: male and female. However, three or four genders are often accepted in other societies. Gender refers to the socially and culturally prescribed and perceived ways that males and females are expected to behave (in other words, their culturally assigned roles). Issues relating to gender are interwoven into all aspects of our existence from the moment of our birth.

Gender diversity and the debate over nature versus nurture have been issues of interest to anthropology from its inception as a discipline. Early investigations on gender were called culture and personality studies and later became known as part of **psychological anthropology**—the study of the relationship between culture and personality. Ethnographies written in the early years of anthropology included descriptions of the division of labor—the gender roles assigned to males and females. Margaret Mead, one of the first woman anthropologists, brought gender diversity issues to public attention with her 1935 book *Sex and Temperament in Three Primitive Societies*. In this work, Mead profiled three groups living in the same region of New Guinea—the Arapesh (occupying mountain terrain), the Mundugumor (a group inhabiting a riverbank econiche), and the Tchambuli (lakeside dwellers). She focused on what she called the temperament of men and women in these three cultures. When Mead began her work, many people believed that men and women were biologically programmed to behave in certain ways and exhibit certain temperaments. Women were genetically programmed to be dependent, nurturing, gentle, and passive. Men were programmed to be independent, tough, and aggressive. Mead found that the Arapesh women fit this stereotype, but the men did not. Men, like women, were maternal. According to Mead, "they see all life as an adventure in growing things, growing children, growing pigs, growing yams and taros and coconuts and sago, faithfully, carefully, observing all of the rules that make things grow" (Mead 1963: 32). Mundugumor of both sexes exhibited stereotypically male behaviors, with an emphasis on selfishness, aggressiveness, and a high level of sexuality. The enculturation process, according to Mead, involved behavioral conditioning that treated boys and girls alike: "little girls grow up as aggressive as little boys and with no expectation of docilely accepting their role in life" (Mead 1963: 201). The Tchambuli had distinct roles for males and females, but these role behaviors were the opposite of what they are in North American society. Tchambuli males were described as less responsible and more dependent, vain about their appearance, and constantly involved in gossiping. Women were independent, competent, businesslike, concerned with providing for their family, and sexually aggressive. With rich detail in her narrative descriptions, Mead painted intriguing pictures of these cultural groups where enculturation instilled some very different

Arapesh
Mundugumor
Tchambuli

psychological anthropology
The study of the relationship between culture and personality.

Margaret Mead in New Guinea. Her 1972 autobiography *Blackberry Winter: My Early Years*, recounts her fieldwork experiences in New Guinea, Bali, and Samoa.

expectations and behaviors for men and women. It was a revelation for many to read of cultures that defined what it was to be male or female so differently from their own culture's definition of the natural order of things. Science builds its knowledge base through time, and although some details of Mead's work have not held up to later scrutiny, her work made the important contribution of stimulating further research and study.

Today, while biologists, biological psychologists, and other scientists work to reveal the biological bases of behavior, anthropologists sort through the many forms of gender identity and gender roles that are found in world cultures. We are joined by researchers in other fields, notably psychology and sociology, who share our interest in exploring gender diversity.

◎ SEX AND GENDER

Most people are assigned their biological sex at birth, based on the appearance of external genitalia. More technically, the term **sex** denotes whether an individual has two sex chromosomes that are alike in shape and size (the X chromosomes—XX, a female) or sex chromosomes that are not

sex
The biological aspect of being female, male, or other, assigned at birth based on external genitalia.

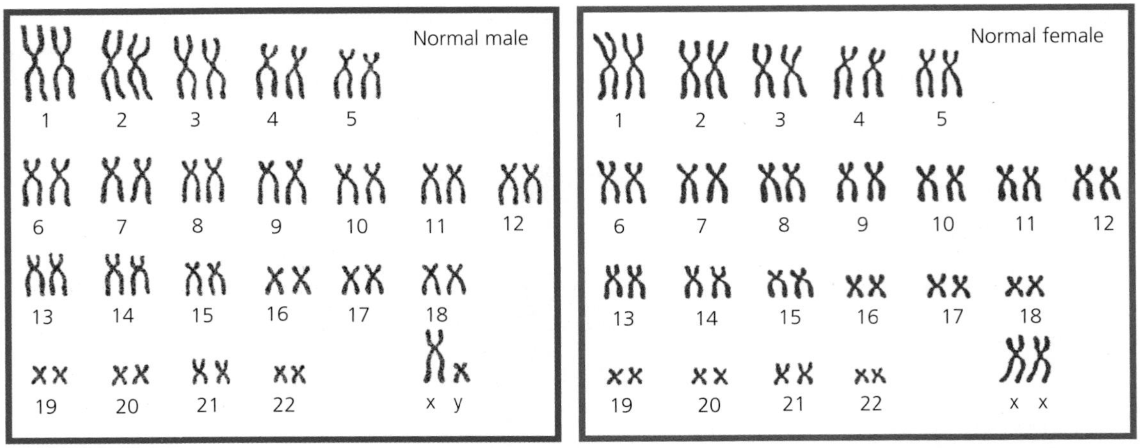

FIGURE 9.1
Notice that all of the pairs of these human chromosomes are similar in shape except the pair in the lower right. The normal male shows both a large X chromosome and a smaller Y chromosome. The normal female shows two X chromosomes.

sexual dimorphism
The biological and behavioral differences between males and females.

alike (an X chromosome and a Y chromosome—XY, a male) as shown in Figure 9.1. Sex, in other words, is a biological designation. This description is a simplification. There is, for example, a specific gene that has been identified on the Y chromosome—SRY (sex-determining region of the Y chromosome)—that controls biochemical reactions that result in the development of a male (anatomically and hormonally). However, nature is not quite as tidy as we might expect. Some individuals exhibit an extra sex chromosome—XXY, XXX, XYY—or a chromosome may be absent (X alone). Such chromosomal variations are not always easy to determine from the appearance of external genitalia. Few people have been genetically tested, so it is unclear how prevalent these variations are in the general population. Moreover, there is not much data on what effect such variation may have on the biochemistry of the individual.

Biological anthropologists have extensive data regarding biological variation and sexual dimorphism among humans and other primate populations. **Sexual dimorphism** refers to the biological and behavioral differences between males and females (Figure 9.2). Many physical measurements are available for contemporary populations, and these show ranges of variation for males and females, with the distribution curves on most characteristics overlapping. Some features show more distinction than others for biological sex differences. The pelvis, for example, is the most diagnostic skeletal feature for determining the sex of an individual. A female pelvis has wider openings and wider angles than a male pelvis. If only the skull is present, there may be difficulties in identifying the subject's sex unless one is very familiar with the population that the skull comes from. For example, among one ancient archaeological population from eastern Oklahoma, all individuals were very gracile (slender, lacking in ruggedness) in the appearance of the skull. None of the individuals in

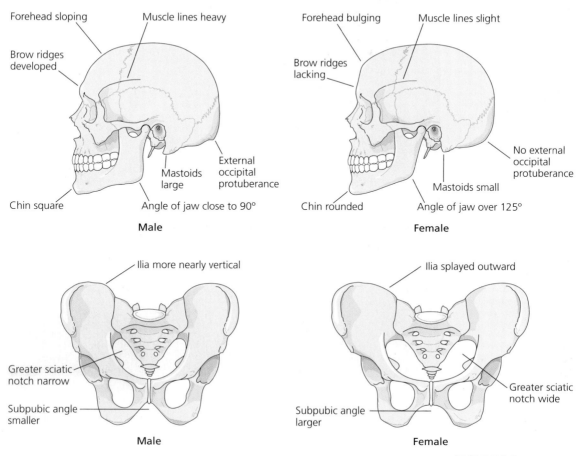

Forehead sloping
Muscle lines heavy
Brow ridges developed
External occipital protuberance
Mastoids large
Angle of jaw close to 90°
Chin square

Male

Forehead bulging
Muscle lines slight
Brow ridges lacking
No external occipital protuberance
Mastoids small
Angle of jaw over 125°
Chin rounded

Female

Ilia more nearly vertical
Greater sciatic notch narrow
Subpubic angle smaller

Male

Ilia splayed outward
Greater sciatic notch wide
Subpubic angle larger

Female

FIGURE 9.2
Sex differences in the skull and pelvis of humans.

this population was as robust in skull features as a typical female skull from a tribe of the northern plains. Therefore, it was initially difficult for archaeologists to differentiate females from males just by looking at the skulls. The point of this example is that skeletal dimorphism is present in our species, but there is overlap between measurements for males and females. Sexual dimorphism exists among many of our primate relatives and in many other animals. The common chimpanzee exhibits sexual dimorphism in anatomy, as does the gorilla. The dimorphic features present in these species are most likely a result of evolutionary selection. Males use their size, bigger canine teeth, and greater muscle mass to compete for access to estrus females, as well as in their efforts to maintain and defend their group. Estrus females are those who show signs of being fertile—the signs are recognized by and sexually stimulating to the males. The selective pressures that would produce greater sexual selection in our own

Heavy, muscle-building work is not consistently assigned to only one gender cross-culturally. Many cultures assigned strenuous work such as grinding corn to women, resulting in great upper-body strength. Here a Tarahumaran woman in Mexico is grinding corn the traditional way.

OLC
mhhe•com/lenkeit3

See Internet exercises.

species have been reduced because humans have used cultural adaptations as their primary adaptive mechanism for more than a million years.

Only women can bear offspring, and only men can produce sperm. Biological mechanisms continue to maintain these differences in sexual characteristics. Yet, as more contemporary women work out and participate in sports, some of the previous diagnostic features that mark skeletal differences between males and females will become less useful to forensic specialists as they work to identify fragmentary skeletal remains. Rough places on bones at the points of muscle attachments indicate degree of muscle mass development. In human societies where men do most of the "heavy work," it is reflected on their bones. Such details have been used to identify and confirm the sex of skeletal remains, but these clues can be misleading if the gender role behaviors do not conform to the stereotype expectations. Among Native American societies where women pounded and ground acorns or corn, great upper-body muscle mass developed—mass that was reflected in the rough places on bones where muscles attach.

But what about dimorphic features of behavior in human populations today? It is clear that there are few jobs that cannot be performed equally well by both females and males. Both can do mathematics, drive tractors, lay tile, cook, and change diapers. Cultural prescriptions of gender roles and behaviors are diverse and are becoming more diverse in the Western world as technology facilitates domestic tasks such as washing clothes, producing clothing, and cooking food. Therefore, the line that has defined the division of labor along gender lines has become more blurred.

Gender role refers to the assigned role of an individual within a society. **Gender** encompasses the behavioral, psychological, and sociocultural aspects of being female or male. Most societies assign one of two gender roles, male or female, although the details of expected behaviors vary. These assignments are made at birth, usually though not always based on what external genitalia imply about the sex of the new baby. Babies designated as "girls" are immediately described using terms that the society assigns the female gender role, and "boys" are described using terms the society associates with male gender roles.

◎ CULTURES WITH MORE THAN TWO GENDERS

The *mahu* gender discussed in the story at the beginning of this chapter is informally accepted in Polynesia. More formal third-gender roles have been assigned to individuals known as the *berdache* among the Zuni of the southwestern United States and to the *hijra* of northern India. The construct of variant genders is an example of the adaptability of human culture. As you read these examples, keep in mind that it is impossible to fully understand the cultural constructs about gender outside of a specific culture. Gender is interwoven into the total context of culture.

Zuni

The Zuni are a matrilineal, matrilocal society that recognizes a gender role for individuals who are not men and not women. Zuni boys who like to play with girls, who participate in the domestic activities of girls, who experience strange illnesses, and who have unusual dreams are identified as gender variants, or two-spirits. These individuals often begin adopting women's dress and hairstyle during adolescence. These men-women often have marriagelike, long-term relationships with men and perform the roles of traditional women. This alternative gender was and is accepted as such by Zuni and other American Indian cultures.

Early anthropological literature used the term *berdache* to refer to these individuals; the word has a long and involved history of usage. American anthropologist Ruth Benedict and others worked among the Zuni and recorded data about this group of individuals who did not fit into a two-gender, male-female system. She and others used the term *berdache*, and it is still used in the literature. Today, gender researchers prefer to use more neutral reference terms such as "gender variant." The term "two-spirit" is preferred by some, but it implies that the gender variants are

gender role
The task and behavior assigned by a culture to each sex.

gender
The sociocultural construct of masculine and feminine roles and the qualities assigned to these roles.

Today both women and men are often employed in jobs that are not traditional to their gender. For example, this woman is a firefighter in San Francisco, California.

made up of feminine and masculine. The gender variant of the *berdache* among the Zuni today is viewed as neither man nor woman; it is not viewed as merely part male and part female but is considered a separate gender that is a normative part of the culture.

The *hijras* of India offer another example of a third gender role that is integrated into the fabric of life. *Hijras* are a religious community of individuals who are culturally defined as neither man nor woman. These persons are born as males. They undergo voluntary ritual surgeries of emasculation (either in childhood or adulthood) that transform them into a third sex and gender category (Nanda 1999). The ritual surgery (which is potentially life-threatening) is performed by a "midwife" *hijra*, and both the penis and testicles are severed. Indian law prohibits this surgery, but it is secretly performed. Not all *hijras* undergo this surgery, though the cultural definition of *hijras* is that they are emasculated men. They dress, behave, and take occupations of women, including the taking of husbands. The major way that they are not men is that they do not sexually function as males during intercourse and reproduction. *Hijras* are distinct from males who seek same-sex partners and take the receptive role during sex. Anthropologist Serena Nanda has extensively researched the lives of *hijras*. She writes of their gender roles: "While hijras are 'man minus man,' they are also 'man plus woman'" (Nanda 2000: 30). *Hijras* take feminine names, dress in women's clothes, and imitate women in facial expressions, walk, hairstyles, and language. They view themselves as objects of men's sexual desires and have only male sex partners. At the same time, they are not

A *berdache* of the
Native American
Crow tribe.

like the traditional Indian female gender because they are aggressive in
their sexual demeanor and use coarse speech. They are not women because they are unable to have children.

Hijras receive a call from their goddess, the Hindu Mother Goddess, to
undergo the emasculation operation and change their gender by dressing in
women's clothing and wearing their hair long. Males who become *hijras* are
sexually impotent, and they themselves attribute this to a defective penis.
Hijras are considered between sexes. They are neither men nor women as
defined by Indian society, where marriage and reproduction are highly valued. The *hijras* renounce their families and sexual desires. To survive they
depend on charity (alms) and earnings from performing rituals.

One of the *hijra's* societal roles is to participate in a ritual performance on the occasion of the birth of a son to a family. The *hijra* blesses
the child and provides entertainment for the assembled family and friends.

These *hijras* are blessing a child, one of their societal roles.

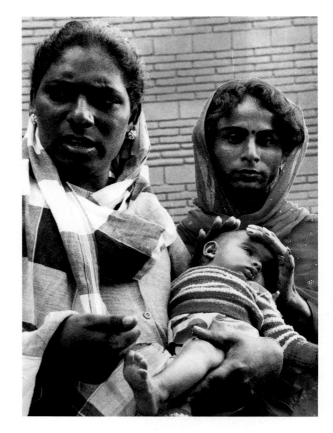

During this ceremony the *hijra* inspects the baby's genitals, confirms its sex, and blesses it for having the ability to procreate and thus continue the family line (Nanda 1999, 2000). *Hijras* also perform at marriages. People have ambivalent attitudes toward *hijras* because they have chosen this different path in life and because they can bestow both blessings and curses. Often *hijras* perform as prostitutes. They also have long-term relationships with men whom they call their husbands. This sexual behavior is not approved of by all *hijras* as it runs counter to the role of *hijras* in Indian society. *Hijras* are supposed to lead a life of self-discipline and abstinence.

◎ FACTORS AFFECTING GENDER ROLES

Many factors affect gender roles, and the issues surrounding gender are complex. This section highlights various facets of economic resources, kinship, and ideology as they relate to gender roles. There are excellent books that explore these topics in the detail they deserve and, most significantly, look at gender roles within the context of a whole society. It is not possible to include such complete coverage in a book of this nature, but I hope to interest you in further reading or possibly in taking an entire course in which this important topic is thoroughly explored.

Kinship

Kinship rules of descent and their associated residence patterns affect gender as it is perceived and constructed by a society. Recall from Chapters 7 and 8 that in patrilineal societies with patrilocal residence rules, men enjoy high status. Their gender owns the property and makes decisions for the group.

In traditional patrilineal (and patrilocal) Chinese society, gender roles are clearly defined. Males enjoy higher status than females, who serve only to produce sons. When a girl marries, she leaves her parents' household. She has no allies or friends among her in-laws. She becomes strong only in relationship to how many sons she bears. The gender bias is reflected even in personal names. Males acquire a variety of names over their lifetime, names that reflect deeds and accomplishments. Women do not. When a woman marries and moves to her husband's household, her name is not used. Rather, she becomes her husband's wife, a daughter-in-law, a sister-in-law.

Economic Resources

The example of "female husbands" among the Nandi of Africa can be used to illustrate how a number of African societies have integrated gender roles to accommodate special circumstances within the culture. The Nandi practice patrilineal descent; and wealth, primarily in the form of cattle and land, is inherited through the male line. The marriage of one woman to another woman, where one of the women takes the role of a husband, is a cultural adaptation that allows a woman without male heirs to transmit property. Men manage land and cattle. Women in the Nandi system of polygynous marriages are entitled to a share of the property owned by the house that they are part of. But traditionally that property could be transmitted only to male heirs.

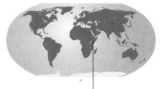

Nandi

A woman who does not have a male heir has no one to whom she can leave property (her share of a household or other property that she has acquired). Several options are open to women in this situation. One option is to adopt a child, though this is difficult because few children are available for adoption. Another option is for the youngest daughter of a woman with no sons to stay at home rather than taking up the customary post-marriage residence pattern of patrilocality. This daughter's sons will inherit the house's property. The most common option for a woman without an heir is woman-to-woman marriage, in which the woman with no male heir becomes a husband to another woman. In a sample taken from one community of 286 Nandi households, just under 3 percent of the households were headed by female husbands (Oboler 1980: 69–88). Children born to this couple are considered heirs of the female husband. In other words, when the "wife" has a child, that child is considered to be the heir of the female husband.

Gender roles for female husbands are based on normative male behavioral expectations in the division of labor. The female husband should participate in cattle herding and cultivation along with her wife, as both sexes are involved in these activities. Female husbands often reinterpret these activities to be male work in order to affirm their status as males. Plowing, fencing, house frame building, thatching, digging of drainage ditches, and slaughtering are jobs reserved for men. Women cook, wash utensils, collect firewood, and carry water. Because female husbands are older, they do not often do heavy work, but informants told anthropologist Regina Smith Oboler (1980) that generally the division of labor is the same in female husband and wife relationships as it is for male husband and wife relationships. Female husbands and wives do not engage in a sexual relationship with one another. The female husband does not have sex with men or with other women either. The two occupy separate dwellings, which allows the wife in this relationship to maintain sexual relationships with other men.

The primary and most consistent factor that distinguishes a female husband from a woman and that makes her the same as a man is the legitimate right to transmit property to heirs. There are reported variations in other behaviors of the female husband among the Nandi, but there is conformity to male behavior in contexts associated with management of property. The Nandi have created a gender situation that is economically adaptive for a segment of their population—older women who are infertile or do not have male heirs. The gender of the female husband is culturally configured as a man. Variations on this type of woman-to-woman marriage are widespread in African societies.

Division of Labor   The division of labor as it relates to economic factors, such as systems of production and ownership of property, also reflects gender issues. Ernestine Friedl, a former president of the American Anthropological Association, has suggested that the control over scarce resources—determined by gender roles—is related to status and power in societies. Among foraging peoples such as the Washo and the Dobe Ju/'hoansi, gender roles are defined along traditional lines in which men hunt for food and women gather it. The distribution of meat through generalized reciprocity is important and creates obligations. Men control the process of dividing and giving meat, and through these activities they gain status and power. Even among foraging societies where it is documented that women provide, by their gathering activities, more than half

The division of labor is by gender among the Dugum Dani of New Guinea. This photograph shows men working cooperatively to scoop fertile silt from garden irrigation ditches. The silt is spread on garden beds before planting.

of the food in the diet, they do not have much power, nor do they have the same status as men. In these societies, the source of power is in the hands of males because they control the scarce commodity of meat protein. Such societies have defined females as the gatherers, though the strength and endurance that women have developed in their walking and carrying the gathered foods (as well as small children) certainly would qualify them to be hunters.

In foraging groups such as the Inuit, where men provide the vast majority of the food through hunting of seals and caribou, women are subordinate to men. When women contribute more to the process of food procurement, as in the case of the Washo (where women work beside men in gathering and fishing), the society is more egalitarian. Friedl's hypothesis seems to fit the data—gender roles affect who controls valued resources, which in turn determines who has status and power.

In contemporary urban industrialized societies, household equality arises when women and men both bring income to the relationship (assuming their earnings are about equal). If one individual stays home and does

TRY THIS
Analyze

How are gender roles defined? What is the division of labor? Who controls valued resources? Who has power? Find the answers to these questions in the following contexts: (a) a culture described in an ethnographic account that is part of a class assignment or that you have found on the Web, and (b) your own nuclear family.

not work and the other partner works to bring in the money that is then used to buy food and housing, the earning partner generally has the power within the home. Interestingly, research indicates that the division of labor within North American households differs along gender lines. The division of labor is most unequal in heterosexual relationships, it is fairly equal in gay male relationships, and it is most equal in lesbian relationships.

Ideology

Ideologies prescribe a culture's values and serve many purposes (Chapter 11 discusses the many functions of belief systems). A culture's value system is founded in its belief system, which contributes in major ways to the enculturation of gender role expectations. Hinduism, for example, acknowledges many variants as well as the basic male and female oppositions. Ancient Hindu origin stories and ritual arts feature an array of variant mythical ancestors, including ones with androgynous (both male and female features and personalities) and hermaphroditic (again, having both male and female qualities) images such as male deities with breasts. India's *hijras* identify with the Hindu Mother Goddess, as Nanda writes:

> Popular Hindu mythology (and its hijra versions) abounds in images of the aggressive Mother Goddess as she devours, beheads, and castrates—destructive acts that nevertheless contain the possibility of rebirth, as in the hijra emasculation ritual. This dual nature of the goddess provides the powerful symbolic and psychological context in which the hijras become culturally meaningful as an alternative sex/gender. (Nanda 2000: 32)

The ideology of the Yanomamo tribe reinforces the relative positions of men and women. Men and women have separate origin myths. One origin myth holds that men came from Moon's blood (Figure 9.3). Moon was shot in the belly by an original human ancestor (the Yanomamo are unclear as to where these came from, but they were part human, part spirit, and part animal, and they were distinct from living humans). Moon's blood fell to earth and changed into men. This is why men are fierce. There were no women, and the men wanted a woman to have sex with. One day the men were out collecting vines. One of the vines had a wabu fruit attached to it. The fruit was opened, and it had eyes on it. The man who saw it thought that it was what women looked like. One of the men tossed the wabu fruit onto the ground, where it changed into a woman and developed a long and hairy vagina. At first the men didn't notice her, but when they did, they were overcome with lust and took turns copulating with her. Eventually she had a daughter, and as each daughter came out the men copulated with her, and that is how all of the Yanomamo came to be (Chagnon 1997: 104–5).

The Yanomamo believe that everyone has a *noreshi* in addition to a multifaceted soul. A *noreshi* is a person's animal counterpart. The animal

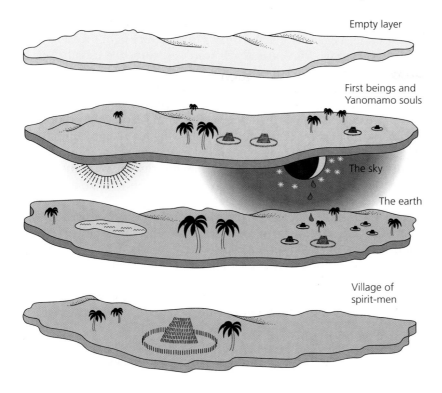

Empty layer

First beings and
Yanomamo souls

The sky

The earth

Village of
spirit-men

FIGURE 9.3
The Yanomamo cos-
mos contains these
four layers. One ver-
sion of the origin story
of the Yanomamo tells
of an ancestor shoot-
ing Moon in the belly,
whereupon Moon's
blood fell to earth and
transformed into men.

lives in the forest but at the same time is a component of the person's psy-
che or body. Women inherit their *noreshi* from their mother, men from
their father. Female *noreshi* are animals that are ground dwellers, like dogs
and snakes; males have *noreshi* that are found in high places, such as hawks
and monkeys. This creates a duality with men above women, and it is reflected in the division of labor. Women do all the menial tasks such as collecting firewood and fetching water, whereas men hunt, make war, and
become shamans and headmen. The male above can also be seen in the
traditional placement of hammocks—a woman's hammock is hung below
her husband's.

◎ PERSPECTIVES ON HUMAN SEXUAL BEHAVIOR

Sexuality refers to erotic desires and sexual practices. The term is also
used to refer to sexual orientation. Sexuality is an interesting topic to consider from a comparative perspective. I had two goals in mind when I
started to write this section: to emphasize the great diversity in attitudes
toward sexuality and to describe some of the variations in accepted sexual

behaviors from an emic viewpoint. I also had some concerns about presenting this topic, especially given that this discussion might evoke strong ethnocentric reactions. Our attitudes toward sexuality are usually based on our cultural values, which in turn are based on ideology and tradition. These are the aspects of culture about which people are usually least able to maintain an attitude of cultural relativism. Another concern was that much of the cross-cultural data on sexuality come from old ethnographies, many of which are incomplete. The following discussion draws from both contemporary reports and the earlier ethnographies. The ethnographic present (how a society did things at the time it was studied) is used for consistency. The amount of available data is not ideal, but it can give us a sense of the diversity in human sexuality.

Interest by anthropologists in sexuality can be traced in part to *The Sexual Life of Savages in North-Western Melanesia*, an important work on Trobriand society by Bronislaw Malinowski, published in 1929. Malinowski carried out ethnographic research in the Trobriands between 1914 and 1918. Until this study, most ethnographic research involved a few weeks or months, as anthropologists were in a hurry to gather data before aboriginal traditions were altered by outside contacts. Malinowski was interested in and critical of Freudian psychoanalysis. He was also critical of the then popular view of the origins of human institutions. Several theorists had explained the evolution of human institutions as originating in "savage" society, where promiscuous hordes of natives participated in unbridled sexual activity. Such explanations fed Western ethnocentrism.

Malinowski wrote in a special foreword to the third edition of *The Sexual Life of Savages*: "My aim in this book, however, was to show that from whichever side you approach it, the problem of sex, family, and kinship presents an organic unity which cannot be disrupted" (Malinowski 1987: lviii–lix). He had tried to focus attention on the holistic nature and integration of sexuality and adolescent sexual freedom with traditions of courtship, marriage, and family. He was disappointed that readers focused on "sensational details" of the "technicalities of love-making" (Malinowski 1987: lix). Herein lies the problem of presenting short examples of human sexuality in an introductory text. As I've pointed out before, context is important in studying any aspect of culture. So keep this in mind as you read the following brief overview.

Humans everywhere learn about what is sexually stimulating by watching, listening, and imitating those around them as they grow up. Some societies are permissive about sexuality and premarital sex. Sexuality is learned early in some societies, with adults either ignoring sexual experimentation or encouraging it. Among the Trobriand Islanders, Weiner reports that "By the time children are seven or eight years old, they begin playing erotic games with each other and imitating adult seductive attitudes. Four or five years later, they begin to pursue sexual partners in earnest. Young

TRY THIS
Analyze

Find a classmate with the same cultural background that you have. Discuss between yourselves and come up with a list of ways that the ideological foundations of your culture have influenced expectations of what constitutes the number of genders and acceptable gender role behaviors for your group.

TRY THIS
Recall

Recall how you learned about sexuality. How did you learn what was appropriate behavior and what was not? Do children in your culture experiment with sexuality? How do adults regulate children's sexual behavior? Discuss this with a classmate.

people change partners often, experimenting first with one person and then another" (Weiner 1988: 66).

Nisa, a Dobe Ju/'hoansi woman, was interviewed about her life by anthropologist Marjorie Shostak. The interview included the topic of sexuality, and Nisa described how children learn about sex. She notes that they lie in their parents' hut and hear everything that is happening with their parents when they make love. When they get a little older, they experiment. "At first, boys play that play with other boys—poking their genitals around one another's behinds—and girls play that play with little girls. Later, if a boy sees a little girl by herself, he takes her and "has sex" with her. That's how little boys and little girls learn" (Shostak 1981: 114). Nisa also tells Shostak that adults don't necessarily approve of all of the experimentation, but they ignore it.

Other societies are restrictive regarding sexual experimentation and premarital sex. The East Bay people of the South Pacific are very concerned about sexual propriety. Children are discouraged by scolding and ridicule from touching their genitals in public. By age five, they are very conscious of lapses in modesty and have learned to avoid all physical contact with the opposite sex (Pasternak, Ember, and Ember 1997: 20).

◎ SEXUAL ATTRACTION AND BEHAVIOR

There are no universal standards of sexual attractiveness. Early cross-cultural literature focused primarily on physical features of females (this was likely due to the Euro-American cultural preoccupation with women's bodies). The attractiveness of the male, if mentioned at all, was usually attributed to his skills and status rather than his physical attributes. The Chukchee, Maricopa, and Hidatsa reportedly like women with plump bodies, whereas the Dobuans and Masai prefer women with a slim body build. Among the Siriono of Bolivia, corpulence is stimulating and desirable. Holmberg, who studied the Siriono, writes, "Besides being young, a desirable sex partner—especially a woman—should also be fat" (Holmberg 1946: 181; Ford and Beach 1951: 97).

Sex play varies considerably across cultures. Kissing, for example, includes sucking on the lips as well as deep kissing involving thrusting the tongue into the partner's mouth. This behavior is popular in contemporary Western societies, where motion pictures and television programs show this as the ideal for erotic sex play. Other societies include this form of kissing too, with the Kwakiutl, Trukese, and Trobrianders sucking the partner's lips and tongue. The Tinguian place their lips near the partner's face and suddenly inhale rather than kissing lip to lip. At the time of first contact with Europeans, some cultures did not kiss (the Chamorro, Balinese, Manus, Tinguian, Siriono, and Thonga). The Thonga remarked ethnocentrically

✿ TRY THIS ✿
Hypothesize

Most colleges in the United States today have courses on human sexuality taught in the psychology departments. Hypothesize why these courses were added to the curriculum in the 1970s. Compare your hypothesis with that of a classmate, and discuss ways to test your hypotheses.

✿ TRY THIS ✿
Analyze

Identify several factors that have been responsible for changing sexual attitudes and behaviors among people in prestate societies and in modern state societies. Discuss this with a classmate.

Actors Minnie Driver and Matt Damon in the film *Good Will Hunting*. Kissing in this manner is considered disgusting in some cultures, particularly if it is done in public.

when they first saw Europeans kissing, "Look at them—they eat each other's saliva and dirt" (Ford and Beach 1951: 58–59). The Mehinaku of the Amazon also consider kissing to be disgusting (Gregor 1985).

Genital stimulation is widespread among human groups. Manual stimulation of both female and male genitalia is common prior to intercourse. Oral stimulation by both men and women occurs in numerous societies but not in others. Choose any behavior associated with sex and you will find that there is much variation across cultures, and sexual practices change over time too.

◎ SEXUAL PROHIBITIONS

Diversity also surrounds attitudes about sexual prohibitions. For many societies there are no prohibitions on sexual practices, except that in most groups sex is supposed to take place in private. Among the Mbuti pygmies, sex can take place during menstruation, pregnancy, and lactation. Other societies, such as the Onge of Little Andaman, do not have sex during menstruation—they believe that swelling of the arms and legs would occur if they did. The Chinese consider women to be polluting during menses and avoid intercourse at that time. Variations are found in attitudes about allowances and prohibitions of sex during pregnancy and after childbirth. It seems to come down to general attitudes toward sex. If

❀ **TRY THIS**
Interview

Interview both a male and a female elder in your culture. Ask them to tell you how views of acceptable nonmarital sexual behavior as portrayed on television have changed since they were teenagers. Discuss your interview with a classmate and together write a hypothesis as to why presentations of nonmarital sex on television have changed.

the culture views sex positively, it is enjoyed frequently and with few prohibitions. Where people think of sex as dangerous, as among the Mae Enga of New Guinea, it occurs minimally and has many prohibitions. The Mae Enga view sex as dangerous, and men are afraid to have sex with women even in marriage. Men believe that they have vital fluids that are in their skin and that make them handsome and full of vigor, and the fluid is also in men's semen. Ejaculation, it is thought, depletes a man's vitality.

Mae Enga

Extramarital sex is fairly common across cultures, and it is ignored by many as long as affairs are carried out with discretion. The Dobe Ju/'hoansi are an example of a society where tolerance of extramarital affairs exists: "In many Ju marriages the partners are strictly faithful to one another, while in a large minority there is evidence of extramarital affairs. . . . At one waterhole with about 50 married couples between the ages of 20 and 50, we recorded 16 couples in which one or another was having an affair. Both husbands and wives take lovers; there is no double standard among the Dobe Ju/'hoansi" (Lee 1993: 91).

OLC
mhhe•com/lenkeit3
See Internet exercises.

◎ SEXUAL ORIENTATION

Another dimension of sexuality is sexual orientation, the pattern of attraction, both sexual and emotional, that is based on the gender of one's partner. **Heterosexuality** refers to sexual attraction between men and women. **Homosexuality** is sexual orientation that involves same-sex attractions. These terms are used more broadly in contemporary European and American culture to mean a person's social identity, which is all-inclusive of self and personality. In Western cultures we speak meaningfully of gay, lesbian, and bisexual identities and communities. In other cultures, homosexual and heterosexual labels do not underscore an entire social identity or indicate community affiliation based on sexual orientation. In other words, the problem of taking Euro-American constructs and using them as categories to describe the behaviors and attitudes of other cultures could result in incorrect interpretations (at least from an emic perspective).

The cross-cultural incidence of homosexuality is difficult to estimate. The literature shows many societies that deny the occurrence of homosexuality; whether this is real or ideal behavior for these cultures is unclear. In other cases ethnographers do not mention the topic of sexuality; therefore, there are no useful comparative data. Perhaps not surprisingly some ethnographers have reported that they repeatedly asked about issues related to sexuality but received evasive answers. Ford and Beach (1951), in their comparative study of sexual behavior, had information on homosexuality from seventy-six societies. Homosexual activities were considered as normal and socially accepted for certain members of the group in

heterosexuality
Sexual attraction between members of the opposite sex.

homosexuality
Sexual attraction between members of the same sex.

64 percent of these societies, whereas homosexual activities were reported to be absent, rare, or carried on only in secrecy in the remainder. Some societies in this latter group strongly disapproved of any homosexual behavior, whereas others claimed that it never occurred. Anyone who reads a newspaper is aware of the variety of opinions about same-sex sexual orientation in contemporary North American culture.

Historical records indicate that ancient Greeks accepted same-sex relationships as natural. According to Greek cultural values, same-sex relationships between two males were considered to be the highest form of love. Sexuality was only one aspect of this relationship. It typically involved an older man and a youth whom the older man courted. The two had a close emotional relationship, and the older man was a mentor to the young man. This homosexual relationship coexisted with heterosexual marriages—marriage was viewed as necessary to produce children and continue the family.

The pattern of an older man with a younger man has been called transgenerational homosexuality. This form of homosexuality has been studied most thoroughly in New Guinea and Melanesia. Some 10 to 20 percent of New Guinea cultures have traditions that are similar to those of the Sambians, whose practices can be used to illustrate this point. The Sambian males go through a series of sexual encounters as they grow up. Young boys, seven or eight years old, begin sexual activities with older boys. Sambians believe that boys can grow to manhood only by ingesting semen—they say it is like mother's milk. During adolescence, boys engage in both homosexual and heterosexual relations. Betrothals are arranged between adolescent males and preadolescent girls. The betrothed couple engages in sexual activities. Meanwhile, these adolescent males provide semen to young boys so that they can develop into men. When the girls that they are betrothed to mature, the boys stop their involvement with other males and usually participate in heterosexual relationships from then on. Here, then, is a culture where all males participate in homosexual relationships during early phases of their lives and it is considered essential for the growth of boys into men (Herdt 1981, 1987).

Only a few accounts of transgenerational lesbianism are in the literature. In the Easter Islands, for example, middle-aged women are reported to seduce young women, but these relationships are not ritualized or participated in by all women (Greenberg 1988: 29). Ford and Beach (1951)

Sambia

ANTHROPOLOGY AROUND US

Does Gender Affect Attitudes About Circumcision?

Female circumcision (and other forms of female genital cutting) and male circumcision are topics regularly covered in college human sexuality courses and often in anthropology courses. Female circumcision refers specifically to the removal of the clitoral prepuce (the foreskin covering the clitoris). Male circumcision involves the removal of the foreskin (the loose skin that covers the head of the penis). Various forms of these and other practices of genital cutting for both men and women are found throughout the world.

The outcry against female genital cutting in any form by the World Health Organization and various human rights groups is often reported in newspapers, women's magazines, and on television. These topics arouse strong reactions. Kirsten Bell, in a June 2005 article in the journal *Medical Anthropology Quarterly,* examined these practices anew after she consistently found her university students outraged at practices of female circumcision; they were even more outraged that Bell compared this practice to removal of the male foreskin. Her students argued that male circumcision was innocuous and even beneficial to one's health. Why, Bell wondered, did students have these attitudes? Bell's research and review of the historical and current literature on circumcision in Europe and North America led her to conclude that these attitudes are based on learned, culture-bound opinions regarding the differences between men and women. She demonstrates that "Medical and commonsense constructions of the human body are not divorced from cultural beliefs and values . . ." (Bell 2005: 140).

In cultures that practice it, female circumcision, like male circumcision, is considered an essential part of a child's socialization. Moreover, female circumcision ensures that daughters will be sought after as desired marriage partners. Yet most North Americans consider this operation to be mutilation and argue strongly against it. At the same time hundreds of baby boys are circumcised every day, and the claims that these operations are also a type of mutilation do not get much attention. Why? Note that the American Academy of Pediatrics says that the studies of the medical benefits and advantages of male circumcision are inconclusive and not sufficient for it to be routinely recommended. There are many activist and advocacy groups against circumcision for males, and even a journal, *Foreskin Quarterly,* that addresses related issues.

◎ What do you think? The photo shows a village in Nagar, Senegal, where a play is being performed to raise awareness about the dangers of female genital mutilation. Do you think that such activities can change enculturated values?

found only seventeen societies in their sample of seventy-six with specific information on female homosexuality.

It should be apparent, even from this brief account, that homosexuality is viewed permissively and as part of nature in some cultures and is restricted and viewed as abhorrent behavior in others (and in some cultures there are mixed views). Attitudes depend on cultural constructs of sexuality.

SUMMARY

Gender, gender roles, and issues of human sexuality are of interest to people everywhere. Gender is the culturally assigned role given to individuals identified as male, female, or other. Gender roles are the prescribed ways that individuals identified as males, females, or others are expected to behave. Most societies recognize two genders, whereas some societies recognize a third and sometimes a fourth gender. Factors affecting gender roles include kinship, economics, and ideology.

Gender role expectations vary widely, as do issues associated with human sexuality. Sexuality—erotic desire, sexual practice, and sexual orientation—varies widely throughout human societies. Some are permissive, some restrictive. Premarital and extramarital sex are often approved and often disapproved. Sexual orientation and sexuality are best viewed and understood within the cultural context of which they are a part.

Study Questions

OLC
mhhe•com/lenkeit3

See Self Quiz.

1. Distinguish between the terms *sex* and *gender.*
2. Discuss an example of a gender variant and the role taken by these individuals.
3. Compare the ideology of your culture to the ideology of the Yanomamo with respect to gender.
4. How does studying Nandi female husbands, the *hijras, berdache,* or *mahu* contribute to the understanding of gender as a cultural construct?
5. What generalizations can be made about human sexuality across cultures?

Suggested Readings

Herdt, Gilbert. 1990. *The Sambia: Ritual and Gender in New Guinea.* Belmont, Calif.: Wadsworth. This book underscores the importance of culture in establishing sex and gender roles in a society. The ethnography is an excellent vehicle to critically evaluate our own cultural perceptions of sex and gender.

Herdt, Gilbert. 1999. *Sambia Sexual Culture: Essays from the Field.* Chicago: University of Chicago Press. A collection of essays that cover the twenty years of fieldwork conducted in the Eastern Highlands Province of Papua New Guinea.

Herdt's reflection of his time spent with the Sambia underscores how sexual behavior, gender politics, and ritual are integrated in a culture's worldview.

Nanda, Serena. 1999. *Neither Man Nor Woman*, 2nd ed. Belmont, Calif. Wadsworth. This is an excellent, short, focused introduction to the topic of gender diversity across cultures, and it has a good bibliography for further reading.

Pasternak, Burton, Carol R. Ember, and Melvin Ember. 1977. *Sex, Gender, and Kinship: A Cross-Cultural Perspective.* Upper Saddle River, N.J.: Prentice-Hall. This book is full of specific ethnographic examples and quotations to illustrate these topics, and major theoretical issues associated with each topic are covered.

Womack, Mari, and Judith Marti. 1993. *The Other Fifty Percent: Multicultural Perspectives on Gender Relations.* Prospect Heights, Ill.: Waveland Press. Gender is examined within marriage, politics, economics, and religion with data from case studies.

Suggested Web Sites

http://www.un.org/womenwatch/site/map
This site concentrates on the proactive and watchdog role of the United Nations regarding women's issues. An outgrowth of the 1995 Fourth World Conference on Women (Beijing).

http://www.engenderhealth.org
This sixty-year-old nonprofit nongovernmental organization addresses gender and health issues for both men and women in at least thirty countries on five continents.

http://www.hsph.harvard.edu/organizations/healthnet
The Global Reproductive Health Forum, affiliated with the Harvard School of Public Health, encourages a critical discussion on the Internet about global gender and reproductive health issues. Forums exist for West Africa, South Asia, reproductive technologies, and women of color.

OLC mhhe•com/lenkeit3
See Web links.

10

Political Order, Disorder, and Social Control

Who Decides?

The shade of the large ironwood tree provided an ideal spot to sit and look out at the crystal-clear lagoon. I was chatting with a local Maori woman and asked about the pig that awakened everyone before dawn (again!) as it overturned garbage cans. She said that it shouldn't be a problem much longer as it was nearly fat enough to be given as a gift to the chief. My husband and daughter and I had been in the Cook Islands of Polynesia for a month as part of a sabbatical that included research on the culture of the Maori people. We had noticed pigs of varying sizes on many properties on the small island. They were nearly always tethered to a tree or a stake driven into the ground and often wallowed under a simple shelter of four posts and a tin roof. We surmised that these pigs were being raised as food for the resident family.

To my query about the many tethered pigs, the woman replied that most were being raised as gifts for the local paramount chief of the district, the Ariki. The Ariki granted favors such as giving a newly married couple a house and land. (Individuals did not own land; it was owned by the entire group and was under control of the chief.) It was exciting to learn of customs that until now I had only read about. To my further questions about the role of the Ariki and how he was chosen, my informant gave me a lecture on both the history of the paramount chief system and the genealogy of the local Ariki. She told of the hereditary system of selecting the chief, noting that the person always comes from one family and that although the chief is usually a man, since 1881 two women had been chosen to be chief by members of the family. Really warming to her topic, my informant proceeded to give me a history lesson on how the chief system was incorporated into the governing system with the arrival of Europeans before 1900. She emphasized that the information she was giving me was for the local district chief. She thought that the chiefs of the other districts were chosen in the same way, but she wasn't certain.

This Maori woman was telling me about how decisions were made in her community, and how, with the giving of fat pigs, people both showed appreciation to the Ariki and perhaps tried to influence his (or her) decisions. She was telling me about politics, the topic of this chapter.

The objectives of this chapter are to

◆ Examine concepts used in the cross-cultural study of political systems

◆ Describe the cross-cultural forms of political organization

◆ Describe social stratification in societies

◆ Explore societal approaches to social control

◀ Voters in Michoacan, Mexico, choose their political leaders through election.

Britain's Queen Elizabeth delivers a speech to Parliament. Heads of state in many societies use speeches to wield their power. What type of power does the queen have?

◎ POLITICS

OLC
mhhe•com/lenkeit3
See chapter outline and chapter overview.

What exactly is politics? Defining what is meant by the word *politics* is a difficult problem because people tend to define it based on their own perspective—what their culture considers political. To people living in contemporary industrialized societies, politics comprises the process of selecting rulers who are empowered to make decisions for our **community** (an association of people who share a common identity, including geographic boundaries, common language, and culture). Political scientists seek to understand the structures and practices, including rules, that communities use and enforce. They study government and how it works. They examine power and authority, how these are distributed within the community, and how decisions are made.

Anthropologists study these same issues and concepts across cultures. Territorial groups and the activities that pertain to them are the focus of political organization studies by anthropologists. But it is not an easy task, because in non-Western cultures the political systems vary tremendously.

community
An association of people who share a common identity, including geographic boundaries, common language, and culture.

What is considered political in one society may not be in another. Using the lens of our own culture to examine other cultures may cause us to miss what is there or to distort it by trying to make it fit into our preconceived categories. Still, we must try to observe objectively and analyze cultural phenomena such as politics with an attitude of cultural relativism. The concepts presented in this chapter provide a place to begin.

◎ POWER AND AUTHORITY

Power is the ability to influence people or cause them to do things they would not do otherwise. Two basic types of power are common: coercive power and persuasive power. Coercive power involves the use of force, whereas persuasive power involves the use of argument, reciprocity, wealth, ideology, reputation, and other personal attributes. **Authority,** by contrast, is the exercise of legitimate power, *legitimate* meaning that the society or community has invested the rulers with the right to rule and that the people will be obedient to the rules. In other words, the members of the society have agreed to and accept the right of the rulers to rule, be they presidents, chiefs, or queens. In non-Western societies, particularly foraging, horticultural, and pastoral groups, power is present but authority often is not. A Yanomamo headman, for example, wields his personal power by influencing the behavior of others, but he has no authority to force their compliance with his wishes. In societies with a chief, the chief has both power and authority. In state societies, authority and power are intertwined. The president of the United States, for example, has authority but must often use the powers of the office and personal persuasion to convince members of the U.S. Senate and House of Representatives to pass legislation that the president favors. Power is not equally distributed in any society, and it is not always easy to determine the sources of power.

TRY THIS
Analyze

Name one person in your college community who has authority. Identify what the authority is and where it comes from. Name one person in your college community who has power. Why does this person have power, and how does she or he use it? Discuss who, what, where, why, and how with a classmate.

◎ FORMS OF POLITICAL ORGANIZATION AND LEADERSHIP

Several dimensions of political organization have been used to classify human societies. These dimensions are based on the criteria set out by Elman Service (1978) in the evolutionary-ecological model discussed in Chapter 5. Recall that, in my view, paradigms such as Service's provide a starting point to examine the various aspects of human culture. The dimensions of Service's scheme include (1) the type of authority within the system and the way it is focused within specific roles, (2) the degree to which political institutions are distinct within the structure of the society,

power
The ability to influence or cause people or groups to do certain things that they would not do otherwise.

authority
The exercise of legitimate power; the right to rule invested by members of the community in its leaders.

ANTHROPOLOGY AROUND US

Who Has the Power?

In the workplace, in our communities, and in the media *power* is generally misunderstood. Most people really mean *authority* when they speak of power, and they don't distinguish between persuasive and coercive power. When it is said that a CEO of an organization is a powerful woman, we tend to mean that she makes decisions and gets things done. Her decision making is a reflection of her authority—authority vested in her by the board of directors of the corporation. She is authorized to make decisions related to the corporation, and this authorization is explicitly delineated in her employment contract. She can also try to persuade people that the course of action that she thinks best is the course that they should follow. If they respect her and she has a good track record, they might be persuaded to support her plan. But she also has coercive power—in the form of sanctions. If an employee does not fall in line with the CEO's plan, she can block the employee's next raise or promotion. The bottom line is that she has the authority to make decisions, regardless of whether others support her.

Lessons about decision making in the workplace abound in news reports. Recent articles on alleged illegal activities by corporations such as Enron with regard to stock values attest to the confusion over authority and power. Each employee blames others for inappropriately reporting data and falsifying documents. The CEOs claimed that they delegated authority to others and were not responsible. Corporations contain layers of employees with varying degrees of authority and power, as all who work in them understand. Even if one articulates these con-

cepts or uses the terms correctly, every worker quickly learns these realities. No one talks of the CEO's use of authority or power, but it is the elephant in the room.

◉ **What examples of a boss's use of authority and power have you experienced in the workplace? Is the authority you have over others clearly spelled out in your employment contract? Have you ever kept quiet about unethical or illegal behavior in your workplace for fear of a boss exercising his or her authority in a manner that would make your life difficult?**

and (3) the amount of political integration—the number of individuals and size of the territorial group that must be managed by the political structure.

Each of these dimensions may be viewed as features of political adaptations, or how people make decisions relating to their communities. Service delineated four basic types of political structure—the band, the tribe, the chiefdom, and the state, which he described as levels of sociocultural

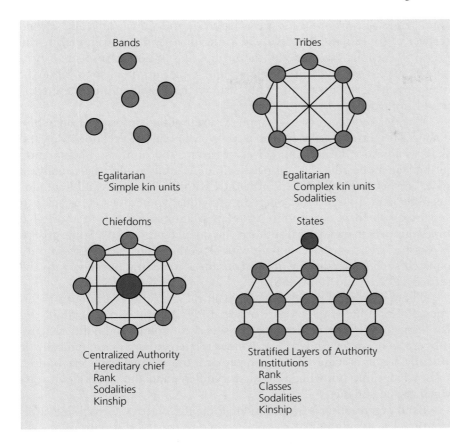

FIGURE 10.1
**Organizational Bases
of Societies**

integration, acknowledging the interrelationships of all parts of culture. The food-procurement patterns of societies, for example, influence the carrying capacity of land, which in turn influences the size of communities and necessitates types of integration and decision making for the adaptive success of the group. Keep in mind that societies are continually changing, and to give any example it is necessary to use the ethnographic present (the point in time when the culture was described). Today, the nonstate forms listed here have been incorporated in various ways into state systems. Still, by discussing them we can think about the array of human political adaptations (Figure 10.1).

Band Societies

Band societies are marked by an egalitarian social structure. In band societies there is no social stratification. Everyone within the same category such as age or gender has equal access to status mechanisms. There

band
A type of society common in foraging groups and marked by egalitarian social structure and lack of specialization.

is no single authority; leadership is based on individual skills and earned respect. People with these valued traits have some power within the group. Decisions are made by the group, and although respected individuals may sway others, the bottom line is that no one has to follow or obey anyone else's decisions. Thus we say that leadership in these societies is informal.

The Washo band (see Chapter 5) exemplified informal leadership. The Washo turned for leadership to those who had special knowledge and skills as advisors, healers, midwives, warriors, and hunters. Their tenure in the leadership role was not predictable. A family leader was usually an older, respected, and trusted individual who knew people and had connections over a large area. Such an individual sometimes emerged as a spokesperson for a community of related families, though in aboriginal times this person had no real authority (as defined previously). Some groups of Washo, after extensive contact with settlers of European descent, recognized such leadership by group consensus for doing business with the settlers (D'Azevedo 1986: 488).

There is no separate, identifiable political institution within band societies. Political life is fully a part of social life. All aspects of social life are familistic in orientation, meaning that social, economic, and political activities are associated with kin. Everyone is related either consanguineally or affinally. Status is achieved through personal traits—an exceptional hunter, a knowledgeable midwife, a good storyteller—and the status disappears when the person dies.

Band organization is found among foraging societies. Group size varies from nuclear family units of several people to patrilocal groups of around fifty members. Each of these bands is a productive unit unto itself. The integration within bands occurs only as a result of kinship ties. A number of bands that share common language and culture are loosely integrated as a result of affinal ties created by exogamous marriages. Foraging bands are thought to represent the earliest form of societal organization.

Tribal Societies

tribe
A type of society marked by egalitarian social structure, based on horticultural and pastoral economies, and integrated by various types of kinship organizations and sodalities.

The term **tribe** has a long and complex history both in anthropology and in general usage. One practice was to use the word as a catchall term for *primitive* people; that is, it was used as an ethnocentric term for *others*—meaning nonindustrialized, non-Western societies. Even some nineteenth- and early-twentieth-century anthropologists used it to mean *primitive*, a point of some embarrassment for contemporary anthropologists because we profess to acknowledge that all cultures are equally worthy of respect. Even today the term is often used in a pejorative manner to describe the political system of a non-state society.

The Ju/'hoansi of Botswana and Namibia, shown here at a camp among mongongo trees, follow informal leaders.

Another usage of the term is as a stage in cultural evolution that came after bands and before chiefdoms. There have been variations over time within this usage, and debate continues today. Most views are tied to a particular paradigm, and differences of opinion about what constitutes a tribe are contingent on the veracity of the model. Because this text uses an evolutionary-ecological model to organize the discussion of systems of food procurement and resource allocation, the organization of political systems follows this approach for consistency.

Tribal societies are similar to band societies in their forms of leadership, and they are egalitarian. Significantly, and in contrast with chiefdoms and states, tribes do not have a single leader with authority, and leaders generally do not have any form of coercive power to supplement an individual's achievements and personality traits. Instead, leaders rely on their persuasive power. **Headmen** and **Big Men** exemplify leadership in such societies. Among the Siuai of the Solomon Islands, leadership is acquired by becoming a *mumi*. Generosity and the use of wealth in giving feasts is the traditionally accepted way to gain prestige, status, and power—to become a *mumi*, a Big Man. Leadership depends on an individual's ability to organize friends, relatives, and neighbors to help give feasts, which are held to observe times of life crisis, to pay favors (balanced reciprocity), to solicit favors (asking for help to build a clubhouse, for example), and to honor a neighboring *mumi* (in fact, to test the neighbor's reciprocal power).

Siuai

headmen
Types of leaders found in tribal and chiefdom societies whose leadership is based on persuasive power. (See *Big Men*.)

Big Men
Alternate term for *headmen* common in Polynesian and Melanesian societies. (See *headmen*.)

Displays of generosity help Big Men, such as this one in Papua New Guinea, gain prestige.

OLC
mhhe•com/lenkeit3

See Internet exercises.

Giving feasts requires much preparation, and the aspiring *mumis* have to acquire wealth—much of it in the form of live pigs—so that they can demonstrate their generosity. Initially this preparation involves constructing pens for the pigs and then giving a feast for those who helped to build the pens. The aspiring *mumi* then must manipulate others to collect pigs—pigs that will be eaten and given away during feasts—by giving piglets to men who have been persuaded to help by raising the pigs. Or a reserve of pigs may be built by socially cultivating trade partners, friends, and kin. Alliances are formed as a result of the various activities of the aspiring *mumi*, and the clubhouses that the *mumis* eventually build serve as centers of social activities for their supporters. In the end, the man who has achieved *mumi* status through his generosity has acquired prestige and power in the community. Although his power to influence may be great, he still has no authority.

Political institutions are indistinct in tribes, just as they are in bands. Tribal societies are territorial groups who share a common language and

A Nuer man, working at a Chevron plant in the Sudan, exhibits tribal initiation scars on his face.

culture and are based on food-procurement strategies of horticulture and pastoralism. These procurement strategies, you will recall from Chapter 6, result in much larger populations. Property ownership is in the hands of lineages and clans. The integration of large tribes, sometimes numbering hundreds of thousands of people, is still based primarily on kinship. Lineages and clans are the most common types of kin groupings in tribes, and the complexity of relationships that result from exogamous marriages of these groups weaves the society together. In other words, the network of kin relationships is an integrative agent that holds the society together.

One other integrative agent in tribal societies—the **sodality**—is a group whose membership is based on common interest rather than on kinship affiliation or residence group; they may or may not be voluntary. Sodalities function to unite and integrate geographically dispersed local groups. They are also found in chiefdoms and state societies, where they serve similar functions. The most common sodalities within a tribe are the age-set groupings made up of males who were initiated into manhood at the

sodality
A group that crosscuts a society and whose membership is based on common interest rather than kinship or residence.

FIGURE 10.2
The integrative mechanisms in tribal societies are based primarily on lineage and clan affiliation. Exogamous marriage also integrates people. Finally, sodalities such as age sets unite people across the tribe.

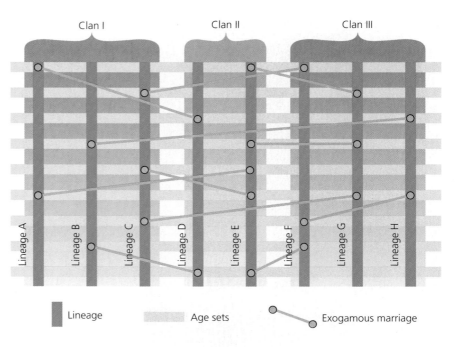

same time. Age-set sodalities are often termed pan-tribal sodalities, and these may not be voluntary. These initiation groups are formed across the entire tribe when initiations are held every few years. Among the Nuer tribe of cattle herders in east Africa, male initiates between the ages of fourteen and sixteen are put through a series of rituals and ordeals, including cuts across their foreheads that result in scarification, which is an outward symbol of manhood. Because the initiations take place about every four years, the age-set system creates groupings of males that cross-cut the tribes' lineages. Boys who have been initiated together into these age sets have a lifelong comradeship (women take on the association group of their husbands). Additionally, men of an age set may act as a military unit during conflicts with neighboring tribes. Pan-tribal sodalities functioning in this manner were found in Africa and among Plains Indians in colonial America.

One can visualize a tribal society being rather like a cloth that is created by a series of many lineages (threads running in one direction) and clans that are woven together by exogamous marriage ties (threads that run in the other direction). The cloth is further made whole by wide swaths of groupings of different-colored threads that run across the entire cloth (representing age sets). Figure 10.2 illustrates this vision of societal integration. One additional tribal binding agent has been noted. The group's response to external conflict and to resource scarcity or abundance also works to bind tribes together (Braun and Plog 1984).

A Trobriand paramount chief visits the home of one of his two wives. Chiefs in some cultures practice polygyny as a right of their office.

Chiefdom Societies

Chiefdoms differ from tribes primarily in the office of chief, which is most commonly hereditary. This office bestows authority on the person who holds the office. Often the chief is believed to have a direct connection to the supernatural and is thus unique. Moreover, this supernatural connection provides the chief with a means to enforce judgments and punish individuals who break rules. The members of the society recognize and acknowledge the chief's authority. The leadership position of the chief gives the person holding the office not only authority but also prestige and status. By association, the chief's immediate family members also have prestige, status, power, and sometimes wealth. Because this ascribed status is not available to other members of the society, the chiefdom is not egalitarian. Rather, social ranking is present, consisting first of the chief and the chief's family members and second of the other members of the society.

chiefdom
A type of society with a hereditary office of chief, most commonly hereditary, social ranking, and a redistributive economy.

The office of chief demands that tribute be paid to the chief, usually in the form of food surpluses and goods. Surplus tribute is redistributed to the community through communal feasts or a subsidy. Tribute serves as a way for individuals to show their support for the chief, and his redistribution of surplus functions to ensure that everyone has food. The reciprocity (both generalized and balanced) of bands and tribes can be found in personal exchanges within the chiefdom. The centralized office of chief and the redistributive system that arises from it serve to orchestrate economic production and encourage specialization. This specialization may take the form of different sections of the larger community specializing in the production of a particular type of food. The redistributive system will result in everyone receiving some of everything produced, so such specialization is in everyone's interest. Another way to specialize is for an entire group to work communally on food production, knowing that each will benefit and receive a portion of the foods produced.

Much variation occurs in chiefdom societies, as with other societal types. Yet the basic tenet of the office of chief and a redistributive economic system is always present. This system serves as the integrative mechanism for the society—it weaves the various groups together and makes them interdependent. Additional integration is provided by the complex of kin ties based on descent and marriage (exogamous lineages and clans are present in chiefdoms).

State Societies

State societies are the most recent form of political organization to emerge in the history of humanity. **States** exhibit tremendous variety—there are democratic states, parliamentary states, authoritarian states, and communist states, to name a few. They all exhibit common features as well as differences. A state constitutes itself legally; that is, there are laws, and these laws are administered by the state. Specifically designated people are authorized and empowered to enforce the laws; in other words, policing is institutionalized. Ruling bureaucrats have varying degrees of authority and power, and political and economic classes stratify the society. Wealth is not equally distributed. There is specialization at every level. Food producers carry out intensive agriculture that results in surplus crops, and these surpluses support the bureaucracy. The merchant class is part of an extensive market system of distribution, both within the state itself and with other state societies. Cities become common as states grow, and these cities eventually develop into vast urban centers.

Today we often speak of nation-states. Technically a *nation* is a group that has a symbolic identity, sharing some or all of the following: geographic location, culture, history, religion, and political structure. The term *state* designates a type of political structure. **Nation-state** refers to a group

❈ TRY THIS ❈
Analyze

Review the definition and discussion of sodalities given in the section on tribes. How many such integrative interest groups can you identify in modern North American state society? Compare your list with a classmate's.

state
A type of society characterized by a political structure with authority that is legally constituted.

nation-state
A group that shares a common cultural heritage, territory, and legitimate political structure.

that shares both—a common cultural heritage and territory plus a legitimate (acknowledged by the people and willingly accepted) political structure. This is, of course, an ideal description.

◎ RANK AND STRATIFICATION

A slightly different approach to classifying societies with regard to their organization originated with the work of anthropologist Morton Fried (1967). It is based on social structure and people's access to wealth, prestige, and power. This classification includes four types of societies: (1) egalitarian societies, (2) rank societies, (3) stratified societies, and (4) stratified state societies. The focus of such comparisons within these types is on equality and inequality. Because power is an aspect of the criteria for Fried's classification, it is included in this chapter. This classification does not precisely parallel Service's scheme (bands, tribes, chiefdoms, and states) because rank societies include both tribal and chiefdom groups. It does provide another lens for etic viewing of cultures.

Egalitarian Societies   In an **egalitarian society,** as noted earlier, everyone has equal access to wealth, prestige, and power within categories, usually based on age and gender. Foraging bands fit this category, where the economy is based on generalized reciprocity. The Washo, Dobe Ju/'hoansi, and Inuit, as discussed earlier, are considered egalitarian societies.

Rank Societies   In a **rank society** individuals gain prestige and wealth by the use of persuasive power. In other words, there are inequities in the society—the number of rank positions is limited so that not everyone, even those with the talent to achieve the status of the position, can do so. Rank may be associated with economics in the control of production, distribution, and consumption. It may be associated with the sociopolitical aspects of society such as authority to punish people who break rules. It may be ceremonial—inequity of access to ritual and the supernatural. Most tribal and chiefdom societies fit this category.

The Trobriand society profiled earlier is ranked. Clans, villages, and individuals are ranked by prestige. Rank is seen primarily in terms of etiquette. High-ranking individuals' heads must be higher than others, and these individuals have titles and the right to wear certain ornaments. High-ranking individuals, such as village headmen, are paid tribute in the form of garden produce at the time of harvest. A headman may gain wealth in this way, giving him more prestige. It is, however, not personal wealth—he redistributes it to pay for services he receives and to feed people at feasts and ceremonies. These social obligations outweigh the economic aspect of the headman's position (Malinowski 1922; Weiner 1988).

egalitarian society
A society in which individuals within the same category of age and gender have equal access to wealth, prestige, and power.

rank society
A society in which the individual's access to prestige and wealth is limited by the number of positions available. A society may be stratified by rank, such as in a chiefdom.

Hawaiian and other societies throughout Polynesia exhibit a range of ranks. The Hawaiians had three basic levels of rank, the high chief of an island (often called the paramount chief), a second-level chief who had less rank but who administered for the chief and was a distant relative of the paramount chief, and a third level of commoners who were most numerous. Other island societies such as the Maori of New Zealand and the Cook Islands had a rank system based on descent and segmentary lineages. One's rank depended on degree of nearness to the main line of descent (Sahlins 1958). Most chiefs in such societies enjoyed prestige and power but usually did not gain great wealth because they redistributed the majority of what they received from those of lower rank.

Stratified Societies   A **stratified society** is one in which individuals within the equivalent age and same sex status group do not have equal access to resources. In other words, these are societies based on inequity. Pure stratified societies were hypothesized as a level between rank societies and states, but these were likely unstable and quickly became state societies. While stratification is not theoretically limited to state societies, that is where it is exhibited today.

Stratified State Societies   A **stratified state society** consists of institutions in which coercive power and authority are determined in ways other than those of kin relationships, and social stratification is manifest in the institutions. The dimensions of **social stratification** include (1) economic status or wealth, (2) power status, (3) prestige or social status (recall that status is both ascribed and achieved; see Chapter 8 to review these concepts). Strata groups are known as classes, and inequities exist between classes with respect to these dimensions of stratification. A **class** is a group of people who have a similar relationship to the mechanisms of wealth, power, and social status. A ruling class, for example, is composed of people who have wealth and power. The access to resources by members of other classes within the same society—lower or underprivileged classes—is limited by the privileged ruling class, thus creating inequities.

Opinion about what constitutes a class is somewhat controversial. Some anthropologists say that for a class to exist it must be recognized from an emic viewpoint; that is, members of the class must themselves recognize this identity. Others note that from an etic view a class can exist whether members are conscious of it or not, if the outsider can identify the group based on the inequities that they have in common.

To anthropologists, states are by definition stratified into classes. They are not egalitarian, as are bands and tribes. Neither are chiefdoms stratified societies because the status system is based on whether one is a relative of the chief. In states, the strata consist of unrelated groups. So the type of *group* and its members collectively are the focus. To many sociologists, all societies are stratified, because the sociologists define stratification differ-

stratified society
A society with unequal access to resources within the same gender and status group.

stratified state society
A society in which institutions are based on coercive power and authority. Inequality exists within social groupings.

social stratification
Ascribed and achieved differences between two classes within a society.

class
A group of people who have a similar relationship to wealth, power, and prestige.

Police in state societies are clearly identifiable by their uniforms. This visibility alone helps maintain order. Can you identify the country where this image was taken?

ently, with a focus on *individuals* and the inequalities that societies exhibit from one person to another. For example, an adult has advantages over a child, a man has advantages over a woman, a skilled worker has advantages over an unskilled worker.

Classes in some societies, such as Canada and Sweden, are mobile; that is, people can move from one class to another. This mobility in contemporary societies is often the result of an increase in the availability of education. In other societies, such as Japan, mobility is more restricted. Caste-based societies are the most restricted. A **caste** is a ranked group with membership determined at birth. Because marriage is restricted to members of one's own caste, it is impossible for children to acquire another caste. India was once legally bound to a caste system. Today, it is possible for individuals to move up in the caste system economically, but religious and other traditions prevent marriage between members of different castes, so the caste hierarchy continues.

Class boundaries are based on traditions and customs, and each generation learns these traditions. The attitudes that each of us holds toward an upper or lower class are another example of how culture shapes us.

◎ DISORDER AND SOCIAL CONTROL

Within every society, conflicts occur that lead to conditions of disorder. Conflicts arise when individuals or groups disagree with others, when people are murdered or injured, or when property is damaged or stolen. In other words, disorder occurs when people deviate from the accepted

caste
A ranked group with membership determined at birth.

TABLE 10.1 Murder Rates (per 100,000 per year) in Metropolitan Areas of the United States and in Other Societies

Society or Metropolitan Area	Murder Rate per year During Time Period	Time Period
Samoa (Western and American)	9.9*	1977
!Kung (Ju/'hoansi)	41.9*	1920–1955
Tepoztlan, Mexico	59.0*	1920–1955
Yanomamo, Venezuela	165.9*	1970–1974
Gebusi, New Guinea	419.0*	1963–1982
Fargo, North Dakota	1.1†	2003
New Orleans–Metairie–Kenner, Louisiana	25.5†	2003
Houston–Baytown–Sugarland, Texas	8.0†	2003
Denver–Aurora, Colorado	5.3†	2003
Philadelphia, Pennsylvania	10.1†	2003

Sources:
*Knauft 1987: 464 (Table 4).
†Federal Bureau of Investigation. Uniform Crime Reports—2003. Table 6, Crime in the United States, Metropolitan Statistical Area, 2003—Murder and Nonnegligent Homicide. Accessed July 12, 2005, at http://www.fbi.gov/ucr/cius_03/xl/03tbl06.xls.

OLC
mhhe•com/lenkeit3
See Internet exercises.

social control
A process involving a structure and mechanisms to ensure that people do not violate the society's accepted forms of behavior.

deviance
The violation of an ideal pattern of behavior within a society.

norms and rules of the society. **Social control,** an issue that must be addressed whatever the type of political organization—band, tribe, chiefdom, or state—refers to the way a society ensures that people behave themselves. Social control involves structures and mechanisms whose purpose is to ensure that people do not violate accepted forms of behavior. Both formal and informal means are used to address issues of **deviance** (violation of a society's ideal pattern of behavior). In prestate societies most conflicts took place between individuals or kin groups. As large state societies developed, beginning around six thousand years ago, economic and social stratification occurred, which included the development of an elite group of leaders who wielded power and authority. The lack of direct involvement in decision making by large segments of such societies resulted in new types of conflict, both internal and external.

Homicide is an example of a deviant behavior that occurs in every human society. The killing of another human being is a serious deviation from normative behavior that is highly disruptive. We can view the disruption caused to families and communities as we watch nightly television news broadcasts, and we are appalled by crime statistics that put murder rates in the United States for the year 1997 at 7.4 persons per 100,000 population (Table 10.1).

Anthropologist Bruce M. Knauft (1987) has presented dramatic data on murder rates for prestate societies. Knauft's data are drawn from various ethnographic accounts, including his own work among the Gebusi of New Guinea. These data showed a homicide rate for the Dobe Ju/'hoansi of the Kalahari Desert for the year 1979 to be nearly three times that of the murder rate in the United States (Knauft 1987: 458). Knauft's genealogical research on clans of the Gebusi of New Guinea revealed that between 1963 and 1982 by extrapolation the homicide rate was calculated to be equivalent to at least 419 per 100,000 per annum (Knauft 1987: 463). One must keep in mind that many prestate societies have small populations. Knauft therefore had to mathematically extrapolate the homicide numbers for each society in order to have comparative data. The FBI must do the same for towns and cities with varying population size. Knauft also notes that homicide reports in state societies rarely give totals from all sources. Rather, "Killings are tabulated separately (and in different types of reports) depending on whether they took place in warfare, nonlegitimate interpersonal aggression within the society or legitimate violence (e.g., killing in self defense, killing by officials in the line of duty, and legal executions)" (Knauft 1987: 463).

Gebusi

All disruptive behaviors must be dealt with by a society. In prestate societies with a lack of centralized authority, the means of social control are informal, whereas state societies focus on formal systems of social control.

Informal Means of Social Control

In societies such as bands and tribes, where there is no political entity with authority and there are no formal laws, informal sanctions must serve to provide control. The most common informal means of social control take place through the use of social pressures, including ridicule, gossip, and ostracism. These methods can be very effective in small-scale societies. When everyone with whom one interacts is making both direct and subtle negative comments about one's behavior and character, the pressure is difficult to ignore. Colin Turnbull's account of the treatment of Cephu, a member of a foraging Mbuti pygmy band, illustrates the effectiveness of group pressure to control behavior. The hunter Cephu had, in effect, stolen meat from the entire group by placing his hunting nets in front of the communal hunting net. Successful net hunting requires that everyone participate, and afterward the meat is shared by all. After stealing the meat, Cephu did not share it either. Back at camp the jeers began. Kenge said, "Cephu is an impotent old fool. No, he isn't, he is an impotent old animal—we have treated him like a man for long enough, now we should treat him like an animal. Animal!" (Turnbull 1987: 104). Youths ignored traditional rules of deference to elders and did not relinquish the chairs that they occupied as Cephu approached the communal fire. When he pointedly stood by a chair that was occupied by a younger man, he was

Mbuti

Among these Mbuti pygmies and other small scale societies informal means of social control are effective.

told that "Animals lie on the ground" (Turnbull 1987: 105). After more name calling and oratory in which Cephu's behavior was blamed for the bad hunt and the bad camp, Turnbull records that Cephu was humiliated and defeated. "He apologized profusely, reiterated that he really did not know he had set up his net in front of the others, and said that in any case he would hand over all the meat" (Turnbull 1987: 107).

TRY THIS *Analyze*

Describe the informal means of social control that students employ within a class for the following offenses (assume that the instructor has been ignoring the offenses):

1. A student's cell phone, carried in his backpack, goes off once during each class meeting of the first two weeks of class.
2. Three students constantly talk among themselves during lectures.

Ridicule and ostracism, or the threat of ostracism, and gossip can be effective in small groups in any society—as most of us will recall from our childhood and early school experiences. However, the larger the society, the easier it is for individuals to withdraw from any uncomfortable situation and join other groups, thereby limiting the effectiveness of these informal means of social control.

Formal Means of Social Control

Law refers to cultural rules that are formulated by societies and backed up by sanctions. Formal means of social control involve consistent systems of sanctions that are applied when rules are violated. Some political anthropologists take the position that law should be defined more strictly. They would argue that law exists only when there is a codified system that involves judges and courts. Others take the broader view outlined here. Formal means of social control range from systematic sanctions found in prestate societies, such as the formal song duels used as a means of conflict resolution among the Inuit or the moot of many African societies. A moot is like an informal court where disputes are settled. Most disputes that are aired in the moot are those between kin and neighbors. There is a great deal of variation on when, where, and how the moot is held, but its function seems to be to get the issues out in the open, air differences, and reach an agreement. Often small fines are levied against the guilty party, some restitution is awarded the wronged party, and a public apology is made.

Inuit song duels are essentially contests in which derisive, biting, witty songs are composed secretly by two individuals who are involved in a dispute. The dispute could be over adultery, sorcery, or theft. If informal means have not solved the issue, and gossip and insults are escalating rather than solving the issue, a song duel is performed in front of the entire community. These duels are ritualized with strict procedures; for example, the songs have to be in verse form. The opponents present their songs in turn. The songs bring the conflict into the open. Aggression is vented, and the entire group who hears the song acts as arbiter in the conflict. It is reported that the songs often deal with the whole personalities of the opponents rather than focusing on the specific grudge. After the performances, the audience decides who has presented the best song. The merits of the dispute are not the deciding factor, but rather the construction of the song and performance. Once the group has passed judgment, the issue is considered resolved. Song duels have not always ended the dispute; sometimes the disagreement has continued and led to fistfights, with the winner of the fistfight being declared the winner and the matter settled.

Law and adjudication in state societies are founded on penal systems with specific written rules and consequences for violation of these rules. Laws of this sort are often founded in religious value systems, such as the

law
The cultural rules formulated by a society and backed up by sanctions.

The Dugum Dani of New Guinea wage war.

commandment "Thou shalt not steal." Because we have been enculturated with such laws, we feel that they are morally right and we avoid
breaking them for that reason rather than because we fear legal punish-
ment. It should be apparent from this example that law and social control
are intertwined with other aspects of a society. In other words, the holistic approach must be applied if one is to fully understand and appreciate
issues such as social control in any society.

◎ EXTERNAL RELATIONS: WAR AND PEACE

When conflict arises between groups and the result is aggressive behavior
and killing, it is usually called war. War is one form of conflict resolution
that has been used by humans throughout history, and it likely occurred in
prehistorical times as well. Societies often seek peace, but it seems elusive.

Anthropologists have written a great deal about warfare. This is a complex topic that is beyond the scope of this introductory book. Even definitions of what constitutes warfare differ from one account to another.
Generally, there seems to be agreement that war involves conflict between

groups of people, and it involves the use of weapons and organized force. Finally, it involves the killing of the enemy. Internal warfare occurs when the warring takes place between groups within the same tribe or nation-state, and external warfare takes place between distinct states (in a territorial and political context). Anthropologist Les Sponsel, who has written extensively on issues of war, peace, and nonviolence has stated:

> Although there may be some utility and even validity in a simple, broad definition of warfare, it does not seem to be very meaningful to group together under the same category called "warfare" the Yanomami, Cheyenne, Kwakiutl, Iroquois, Dani, Mae Enga, Maori, Ilongot, Nuer, Zulu, and other societies when the types, frequency, and intensity of their aggression are so extremely different. Neither would it seem to advance understanding to lump together Yanomami raids, Indian-White wars in colonial America, the American Civil War, the Vietnam War, the Gulf War, and wars in Somalia, former Yugoslavia, Afghanistan, and so on. (Sponsel 1998: 107)

SUMMARY

The issues of who makes decisions for a society and how order is maintained are of concern to all people. Some fundamental differences between state societies and prestate societies such as bands, tribes, and chiefdoms are as follows: Leadership in bands and tribes is informal and is based on personal qualities of the leaders. Such individuals may have the power to persuade, but they do not have authority or coercive power to make people comply with their wishes. In chiefdoms, authority is vested in the office of chief, and in state societies authority is vested in the leaders. Authority is the exercise of legitimate power—power that has been agreed upon and accepted by the members of the society. Inequities in access to wealth, power, and prestige result in rank and stratified societies. Societies have developed both informal and formal means of dealing with conflicts and the disorder that results from conflict. Informal means of social control include ridicule and ostracism. Formal means of social control include formalized laws and sanctions. Methods for judicial settlement of such laws range from the formal song duels of the Inuits to the formal court system of the United States.

Study Questions

1. Distinguish between power and authority.
2. Compare and contrast the features of the leadership of bands, tribes, chiefdoms, and state societies.
3. Compare and contrast rank-based societies and stratified state societies.

OLC
mhhe•com/lenkeit3

See Self Quiz.

4. Discuss the dimensions of social stratification and how these dimensions define state society.

5. What means are used in various societies to maintain social control? Cite examples to support your generalizations.

Suggested Readings

Chagnon, Napoleon. 1997. *Yanomamo*, 5th ed. Fort Worth, Tex.: Harcourt Brace. Chagnon's work among the Yanomamo spans more than thirty years. It is one of the best ethnographies covering the politics of conflict within and between tribal groups.

Cohen, Ronald, and Elman R. Service, eds. 1978. *Origins of the State: The Anthropology of Political Evolution.* Philadelphia, Pa.: Institute of Human Issues. Several well-known anthropologists look at the evolution of political systems. Cohen offers an excellent review summary of the topic.

Fried, Morton. 1967. *The Evolution of Political Society.* New York: Random House. Detailed explanation of the essential features of Fried's model of egalitarian, rank, and stratified societies.

Heider, Karl G. 1997. *Grand Valley Dani: Peaceful Warriors*, 3rd ed. Belmont, Calif.: Wadsworth. Until recently the Dani participated in ritualized warfare with neighboring groups who speak the same language and share the same culture. Heider's ethnography is readable and a useful adjunct for exploring topics introduced in this chapter.

Keesing, Roger M. 1983. 'Elota's Story: *The Life and Times of a Solomon Island Big Man.* New York: Holt, Rinehart and Winston. This is an interesting account of politics among the Kwaio, a Melanesian society in the Solomon Islands, South Pacific. It is essentially a life history account and includes the etic descriptions of Kwaio culture by Keesing but also many of 'Elota's own comments.

Maybury-Lewis, David. 2001. *Indigenous Peoples, Ethnic Groups, and the State.* Boston: Allyn and Bacon. A timely book that uses case studies to examine the history, politics, and conflict of interethnic situations, particularly between states and ethnic minorities.

Suggested Web Sites

OLC
mhhe•com/lenkeit3

See Web links.

http://www.bestplaces.net/crime/
This commercial Web site uses data collected from the Federal Bureau of Investigation's Uniform Crime Reporting Program to provide statistical data regarding homicides (per 100,000 population) in over twenty-five hundred U.S. cities.

http://www.aaanet.org/apla/index.htm
The Association for Political and Legal Anthropology, a subgroup of the American Anthropology Association, focuses on political and legal issues surrounding nationalism, citizenship, political and legal processes, the state, civil

society, colonialism and postcolonial public spheres, multiculturalism, global-ism, immigration, refugees, and media politics. The association's Web site links to a regular column in the monthly publication *Anthropology News*.

http://sosig.esrc.bris.ac.uk/roads/subject-listing/World-cat/polanthro.html
This is a searchable site organized by the Social Science Information Gate-way that accesses an extensive electronic library of ethnographic, ethnological reports in the sociopolitical field of anthropology.

11

Belief Systems
How Do We Explain the Unexplainable?

The Sikh temple of Punja Sahib in Hasan Abdal, Pakistan.

We sat on benches in the small white wooden clapboard church on the island of Raiatea in French Polynesia, as the voices rose and fell in what to me were hauntingly beautiful hymns. The words were in Tahitian and I didn't understand them, but the rhythms reminded me of a lively Southern Baptist choir. The older women parishioners of this Christian Mission church were dressed in mumu style dresses of brightly colored print fabrics. Each wore a hat of finely woven palm fibers. All of the hats were different but had a similar style, and each hat held a band of small cowry shells around the crown.

Rituals associated with this church service were similar to the church services of my childhood, yet they were different. Feelings of euphoria permeated the gathering, and these mixed with the fragrance of the plumeria blossoms that grew outside the open windows on either side of the church. I was reminded of how belief systems can and do diffuse from one culture to another and how local belief systems often accommodate new ideas. I was also reminded that religious beliefs and the rituals associated with them differ widely around the world, but the adherence to a pattern of moral guidelines is essentially the same. And sitting in that church many thousands of miles from my own community reminded me of the long tradition in anthropology of studying religion and belief systems.

One of the earliest anthropology books, *Primitive Culture*, by E. B. Tylor, published in England in 1871, addressed the issue of belief systems in various world cultures. Supernatural beliefs and practices are found among all human groups and serve important roles by integrating the social, economic, and political components of a culture. Supernatural beliefs and practices also help regulate and shape the choices a culture makes about its social, economic, and political institutions. In other words, the values generated by and based on belief systems are at the core of cultural decision making.

Unfortunately, many of the examples cited by Tylor in 1871 were used to feed ethnocentric views of peoples in other parts of the world. Supernatural beliefs present, from the emic view, logical explanations of events that are an integral part of the culture. A quotation from an Islamic religious text, the Kasidah of Haji Abdu al Yezdi, is a favorite of mine for underscoring our own group-centered attitudes regarding the topic of the supernatural and belief systems.

> All faith is False, all Faith is true:
>   Truth is the shattered mirror strown
> In myriad bits; while each believes
>   his little bit the whole to own. (Burton: 1991)

My experiences that day in the little church on Raiatea brought these words to mind. I was using an outsider's (etic) view when I evaluated the behaviors I saw, and this is what scientifically oriented anthropologists often do. This view is reflected in this chapter.

The objectives of this chapter are to

- Define the supernatural world as it is viewed cross-culturally
- Discuss why people develop belief systems
- Describe the functions of supernatural belief systems and practices
- Describe the common types of beliefs found in most cultures, including supernatural beings and forces
- Describe supernatural practices and types of practitioners

BOX 11.1 Definitions of Religion

Religion is the belief in Spiritual Beings. (Tylor 1958: 424)

Religion [is] . . . a set of beliefs and patterned behaviors concerned with supernatural beings and forces. (Ferraro 1998a: 284)

[Religion is] a set of beliefs and practices pertaining to supernatural beings or forces. (Lehmann, Myers, and Moro 2005: 491)

[Religion is] an institution consisting of culturally postulated superhuman beings. (Spiro 1966: 96)

[Religion] is . . . all that is not natural, that which is regarded as extraordinary, not of the ordinary world, mysterious or unexplainable in ordinary terms. (Norbeck 1961: 11)

A religion is a system of symbols which acts to establish powerful, pervasive, and long lasting moods and motivations in men by formulating conceptions of a general order or existence and clothing these conceptions with such an aura of factuality that the moods and motivations seem uniquely realistic. (Geertz 1973: 90)

Religion [is] . . . that instituted process of interaction among the members of that society—and between them and the universe at large as they conceive it to be constituted—which provides them with meaning, coherence, direction, unity, easement and whatever degree of control that they perceive as possible. (Klass 1995: 38)

◎ DEFINITIONS OF THE SUPERNATURAL

OLC

mhhe•com/lenkeit3

See chapter outline and chapter overview.

Why use the term *supernaturalism* rather than the term *religion*? The moment you read the word *religion*, myriad symbols and ideas seep into your mind, each evoking thoughts and associations based on what *you* have been enculturated to believe. These images set the stage for ethnocentric reactions to other belief systems. The term *supernaturalism* is more neutral. It suggests that there are natural things in the universe and supernatural things, beyond or outside of the natural. There are things and events that can be explained, tested, and demonstrated, and there are things and events that cannot. Those that cannot be explained, tested, or demonstrated must be taken on faith. Hence, we may label them supernatural things and events. The selection of several anthropologists' definitions of religion listed in Box 11.1 all acknowledge or imply the dichotomy that is drawn in belief systems between what is natural and what is beyond the natural. These definitions also address other aspects of belief that will be examined later in the chapter.

What is considered natural to members of one culture may be in the realm of the supernatural in another culture. A thunderstorm may be explained as the result of high- and low-pressure zones in the atmosphere, or as the hurling of boulders by an angry god. Abdominal pain and diarrhea may be explained as having been caused by eating bacteria-tainted food or as the result of a magical spell cast by an enemy. This is a difficult issue to dissect because one might argue that it is ethnocentric to label an event or belief by others as being supernatural while labeling one's own culture's belief natural. Nonetheless, the present discussion embraces this dichotomy and defines a **supernatural belief** as any belief that transcends the observable, natural world. Several of the definitions in Box 11.1 (Norbeck, Geertz, and Klass) also include some of the functions served by belief systems. Because the functions of supernatural beliefs are central to any comparative discussion of this topic, they are addressed before the various types of beliefs are introduced.

◎ WHY PEOPLE DEVELOP BELIEF SYSTEMS

Belief systems and practices explain the unexplainable. This is their over-arching function—they give us explanations of what happens, why things happen, why we are on the earth, where we came from, and what happens after we die. Although they provide answers to these questions for individuals, supernatural practices and beliefs also serve the social group as a whole, and these functions have been labeled the *social* and *psychological* functions of supernaturalism. These are useful broad categories for the analysis of the functions of beliefs. The social functions take an etic view of how a society interacts as a whole and with its external social environment. The psychological functions take an outsider's look at what the belief system provides for individuals as they struggle with answers to the questions posed above.

I prefer to focus on specific functions based on an expanded version of what the early student of human behavior Emil Durkheim cited as the functions of religion in his book *The Elementary Forms of the Religious Life* (Durkheim 1961). Durkheim directed his analysis at Western religious practices, but his approach clearly may be applied to all supernatural belief systems, and I like his categories because they are specific (refer to Table 11.1 for a comparison of these two approaches).

Cohesion and Support

The cohesive and supportive functions of supernaturalism apply to both individuals and groups. People come together for ceremonies and rituals. Individuals are provided with social, economic, and political support from

supernatural belief
A belief that transcends the observable, natural world.

Muslims pray together before a soccer game in Saudi Arabia. Prayer serves both a cohesive and a supportive function for participants.

Dani

other group members during trying times. Each individual feels connected to the group, bound together by common beliefs and actions. Specific symbols—such as a cross or a specific animal form—make it possible to quickly recognize fellow members of a belief system.

Among the Dani of New Guinea, deceased members are cremated. The Dani believe that the soul is released in the smoke of the funeral fire. If a loved one dies, others offer support by their actions and words during this ceremony. Comfort is found in this ritual, and it is supportive for the entire group because all of the participants are in effect saying that this is the right ritual to send the soul to the next place. Moreover, because it is obvious that all humans will die, the activities you perform for others will also be performed for you when you die. The ritual of the funeral supports and solidifies the values of the culture. Such rituals are the glue that holds the system together, providing a cohesive and mutually supportive base for individual members of the group. These two functions are obviously both psychological functions (serving the individual) and social functions (serving the group).

Education and Discipline

The educational and disciplining functions of supernaturalism are often interwoven. The Ten Commandments of the Judeo-Christian religions serve as an example. Children are taught group history about the origin of these governing rules and how their deity gave the commandments to

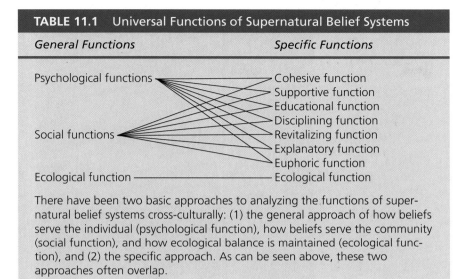

TABLE 11.1 Universal Functions of Supernatural Belief Systems

General Functions	Specific Functions
Psychological functions	Cohesive function
	Supportive function
	Educational function
	Disciplining function
Social functions	Revitalizing function
	Explanatory function
	Euphoric function
Ecological function	Ecological function

There have been two basic approaches to analyzing the functions of supernatural belief systems cross-culturally: (1) the general approach of how beliefs serve the individual (psychological function), how beliefs serve the community (social function), and how ecological balance is maintained (ecological function), and (2) the specific approach. As can be seen above, these two approaches often overlap.

Moses, an important early ancestor. At the same time, the commandments serve to discipline because there are consequences for breaking them. Often-repeated origin stories, rules of behavior, and admonitions against committing transgressions become the growing child's foundations of ethical codes of behavior that shape the choices that are considered right and wrong. During the enculturation process, young children are told accounts of how specific individuals' lives changed because they did, or did not, follow the appropriate rules established by deities. Again, the more general functional categories of psychological and social functions apply to each of these more specific functions.

TRY THIS
Compare

Talk to a classmate who has a belief system different from yours, and identify and compare how your respective belief systems meet the cohesive and disciplining functions of supernaturalism.

Revitalization and Euphoria

The revitalizing function of supernaturalism involves regular and repetitious rituals and practices that result in a renewal and revitalization of the belief system, which serves to motivate and lift the mood of the individual participants as well as the entire group. When you observe the *molimo* ceremony of the Mbuti pygmies of the Congo region of Africa, the revitalizing function is clear. This ceremony serves to reawaken the forest in which the pygmies live. The forest, they say, is like their mother and father, and it must care for them. When the hunt has been going badly, someone will suggest that perhaps the forest is sleeping and that they should have a *molimo* to awaken the forest. Colin Turnbull quotes his informant and friend Moke as saying, "So when something big goes wrong, like illness or bad

A funeral celebration on Siar Island, Papua New Guinea.

hunting or death, it must be because the forest is sleeping and not looking after its children. So what do we do? We wake it up. We wake it up by singing to it, and we do this because we want it to awaken happy" (Turnbull 1987: 92). Turnbull's description of the ceremony itself, and the elevated mood of the participants afterward, clearly demonstrates the revitalizing function. During one *molimo*, as participants sang around the fire, the *molimo* trumpet could be heard moving through the forest imitating the sounds of leopards, elephants, and buffalo. (*Molimo* trumpets were originally made of wood, but while Turnbull was with the Mbuti, they were using a trumpet fashioned from a metal drainpipe.) Turnbull writes, "it was a mysterious thing . . . alive and awe-inspiring and wonderfully beautiful; something that made the eyes of young and old alike light up with pleasure as they heard it sing" (Turnbull 1987: 89).

The euphoric function of supernaturalism is that believers experience a sense of well-being when they participate in the supernatural rituals.

A Pentecostal church service in Los Angeles, California. An etic description of this scene by an American anthropologist would state that these people are experiencing euphoria.

Individual and group anxiety is relieved, and a profound sense of joy and happiness occurs because the appropriate actions have been taken. Individuals who have experienced this euphoria describe it in terms such as elation, ecstasy, bliss, and rapture. Observe participants at a Christian tent revival meeting and you will see examples of this euphoria. You will also witness it during ritual trance in Bali and *hekura* chanting among the Yanomamo.

Ecology

The ecological function of supernaturalism was not discussed by Durkheim, but it is clearly one of the functions of many belief systems. The ecological function involves any belief or ritual that contributes to the maintenance of the society's environment or resource management. For example, the Hindu religious system of India prohibits killing or eating cattle. Although cattle are a good source of protein-rich meat, they are also sources of fertilizer and fuel (dung), and they provide power for pulling plows. Anthropologist Marvin Harris has argued that the taboo against killing cattle makes sense in the long term as an ecological adaptation (Harris 1966).

Explanation

The explanatory function of supernatural beliefs serves both the individual and the group. Encoded within the belief system and its symbols, in texts and stories, revealed through prayer, trance, and divination are explanations

TRY THIS
Analyze

Select two functions of supernaturalism from the text discussion, and identify specific examples of how they apply to your own belief system. Identify a specific example of how the same two functions apply to an article or ethnography you are reading as a class assignment.

that are culturally sanctioned and approved. Reasons for life. Reasons for death. Reasons for good times. Reasons for bad times. It is comforting to have explanations for questions, large and small. Humans everywhere desire to understand why bad things happen, especially when they happen to good people—members of the culture who play by all of the rules. Answers given to the why questions include "It is the will of Allah," "It is Karma," "It is God's will." These are explanations that are acceptable to those with faith. We may not understand the reason for a specific unfortunate event, but we feel better because the belief system provides an answer.

◎ TYPES OF BELIEFS

Each culture includes a variety of beliefs that are interwoven in the fabric of that culture. The details of belief systems are rich and varied. Over a century of anthropological study has revealed that common categories of belief are found in most cultures. The two categories of **supernatural beings** and **supernatural forces** are the most obvious. Native members of a culture do not themselves separate or categorize their beliefs in this way. It is, however, a useful dichotomy for a cross-cultural study of supernaturalism.

Supernatural Beings

OLC
mhhe•com/lenkeit3

See Internet exercises.

Belief in invisible beings who exhibit form, personality, attitudes, and powers is found in all cultures. These beings are able to do things that humans cannot do. Humans can and do petition many of these beings, particularly gods and goddesses, to assist with life's difficulties. The beings may or may not respond to such petitions. Many supernatural beings are concerned with humans, but for reasons that are not revealed to us, they may not do what we ask. Their existence is taken on faith; it cannot be proven using scientific methods. A wide spectrum of such beings exists with great variation in the powers they wield. Some of the types of beings found in many different cultures include the following, though this is by no means a complete listing.

supernatural beings
Invisible beings that exhibit form, personality, attitudes, and powers.

supernatural forces
Unseen powers that are not personified and may be manipulated to achieve good or evil.

polytheistic
A belief system consisting of many supernatural beings of approximately equal power.

monotheistic
A belief system that focuses on one all-powerful supernatural being.

Gods   A wide array of gods (male gender beings) and goddesses (female gender beings) are to be found in most cultures. **Polytheistic** systems consist of belief in many of these beings, who are often of nearly equal powers, whereas **monotheistic** systems focus on one all-powerful god or goddess. Even within a monotheistic system, careful scrutiny will usually reveal more than one supernatural being that exhibits the features of a god or goddess. Gods and goddesses are often ancestral in nature. They are the source of human beings, or they have spent time living among humans. They are typically concerned with what humans do and often have given

Common functions of rituals can be identified even when specific details of belief systems differ. Buddhist monks in Thailand (left) and Hasidic Jews in Israel (below) pray.

humans rules for behavior. They have many powers or few. Often, as in the belief system of the ancient Greeks, the supernatural beings are placed in a hierarchy with specific tasks or responsibilities associated with each being.

Sedna is a goddess of the Inuit, and her story was one of the ethnographic recordings made by anthropologist Franz Boas in the 1880s. Sedna was responsible for sending marine animals such as seals to be captured by the Inuit (seal meat was a primary food source for these aboriginal people). Sedna's story begins when, a long time ago, she left her father to live with a seabird that promised her that she would have plenty of food and that she would always be warm. Sedna soon discovered that the seabird had misrepresented his situation. Sedna's father came to rescue her and killed the seabird. A terrible storm caught the father and Sedna as they traveled by boat back to her home. Fearing that the seabirds wanted Sedna back, the father threw her into the ocean. Sedna clung to the boat, and the frantic and frightened father cut off her fingers. These became seals and other sea creatures. Believing Sedna to have drowned, the seabirds left and the storm abated. Sedna did not drown but survived to once again live with her father. Angry at her father for his behavior in the boat, Sedna directed her dogs to attack him and eat his hands and feet while he slept. Soon the father, the dogs, and Sedna were sent to the ocean bottom to live. From the depths, Sedna came to reign over the creatures of the sea. She makes decisions about whether to send creatures for the Inuit to kill (Boas 1964).

There have been numerous variations on the story of Sedna, as is often the case with origin myths. In each variation, however, the main elements remain—Sedna is ancestral, she has power that ordinary Inuit do not have, and what happened to her explains why she is not always generous to humans. Much of Inuit seal hunting ritual involves appeasing Sedna so that she will continue to send seals to the Inuit. For example, before butchering a seal the Inuit offer it a ritual drink of water.

Inuit

TRY THIS   *Analyze*

Find a religion that is unfamiliar to you in the yellow pages of your local telephone book. Log on to an Internet search engine such as Google or Yahoo! or Excite and search for information about this religion. Discover whether there are any gods or goddesses in this belief system that are ancestral to humans in some manner. What function (or functions) does the belief in the ancestral nature of beings have for a society?

Demons   The word *demon* is used to denote a negative, evil being. Most systems that have gods or goddesses also have one or more demons. Demons may try to steal the souls of people and force them to commit evil, anti-social acts. They are powerful and can change form, and they often do so to trick and lure humans. They provide a culturally appropriate explanation for people's inappropriate behavior. Demons are responsible for bad events that befall humans. In the Christian belief system, the devil is a demon who tempts humans to stray from the right path and commit sins.

Souls   The soul is considered the supernatural component of humans and sometimes other animals. This component is believed by most peoples to be what gives life and makes us what we are. The soul's existence is taken on faith, and the teachings of many of the world's belief systems describe how the gods and goddesses give humans their souls. There are many debates, even among theologians, as to when souls arrive in the physical body—at the moment of conception, when the fetal heart begins to beat, or at the moment of birth. Some cultures believe that the soul arrives at a designated point after birth. Elaborate parties and celebrations are held at that time, and a name is bestowed upon the child. It has been noted that societies that believe in late soul arrival are often societies with high infant mortality rates.

There are also many variations of beliefs regarding what happens to the soul at death. Among the Yanomamo Indians of Brazil and Venezuela, the central part of the soul escapes the body at death and goes to a layer that exists, according to Yanomamo cosmology, above the earth. We can see the underside of this layer (the sky) from earth. Arriving there, this part of the soul travels down a path until it reaches a fork in the trail, where a spirit inquires whether the soul has been generous or stingy. Stingy souls are sent on a path to the place of fire, and generous souls go on another path, to a place of tranquility (Chagnon 1997: 112). The Yanomamo soul concepts are elaborate. Another portion of the soul is released at cremation and continues to live on earth and wander in the jungle.

The Berawan of Borneo believe that at death a person's soul undergoes a transformation into a spirit that will pass to a place where only the dead reside. Because there is a period of time before a person's body completely disappears (putrefies) and only bones remain, the soul must also slowly change. Until the body is nothing but bones, the soul will linger and be responsible for causing illness among the living (Metcalf 1978: 6–12).

Berawan

Ghosts   After the death of the physical body, souls are believed by many societies to transform into ghosts. Many societies, though not all, use the term *ghost* in place of the term *soul* after death. Ghosts are often viewed as beings with the potential to cause harm to the living. Anthropologists have suggested that this is one of the reasons for funeral rituals—a send-off for the soul, now a ghost, to the next place before it can cause trouble

TRY THIS
Analyze

Make a list of supernatural beings that are believed in by a subculture (or portion of the subculture, such as children) with which you are familiar. Identify the subculture that holds these beliefs. What powers do these beings have? Consider how someone from a different subculture might view these beings and beliefs.

among the living. Drawing on the functions of supernaturalism outlined previously, we could suggest that belief in ghosts serves as an explanation for bad things that happen, just as the Berawan attribute difficulties for the living to the lingering, transforming souls of the dead.

Tricksters   Most societies have one or more beings that fit this category. Tricksters are beings that play tricks or practical jokes on people. They typically mean no real harm and are more bothersome than anything. The trickster known as Coyote (or Old Man Coyote, or Old Man) lived among Native American cultures from the Pacific to the Great Plains. This trickster being was believed responsible for wickedness such as seducing women or being deceptive so that he could win races. He is also sometimes virtuous and often stupid. One story tells of Coyote diving into water to retrieve food that he sees there. The food he sees in the water is actually a reflection of the food he is carrying. Coyote also served as a negative role model, or how a person should not behave in life.

Witches   In a historical and cross-cultural analysis, witches are supernatural beings. As such, these beings have power to affect the lives of humans, often in negative ways, but they never admit that they are witches. Even when condemned to death, real witches will deny being witches. At the present time, Hollywood films and the current interest in neopagan Wiccan groups has muddied the understanding of witches. An individual who practices supernatural arts of magic and spells is not a witch in the historical and cross-cultural meaning of the term. The understanding of what constitutes a witch is a good example of how language and culture change over time. For more on the anthropological, historical, cross-cultural perspective, see Lucy Mair's book listed under Suggested Readings at the end of the chapter.

Supernatural Forces

Supernatural forces are typically neutral and surround us the way air does. These forces cannot be seen or felt, but their powers may be harnessed to accomplish good or evil ends. Individuals can learn to manipulate these forces directly by studying and learning from those who have gone before. Amateurs can and do manipulate these forces, but most believe that an individual with training or a special intuitive knack for such manipulations will achieve better results. Supernatural beings may also manipulate the supernatural forces.

mana
An impersonal supernatural force that flows in and out of people and objects.

Mana   **Mana** is a supernatural force that is part of cultures throughout Polynesia. Other cultures also believe in a similar force but call it by different terms. Mana is everywhere, though it is often concentrated in objects,

A member of the Iban tribe of Malaysia carries a mana object. Possession of such an object brings the owner the power of supernatural forces.

or people, or even a part of a person. It may be harnessed by practitioners; it may flow into or out of objects and people. Some people are born with it, just as some objects naturally contain it. Mana may be drawn into objects, such as a pebble, by a practitioner who has the skills to manipulate it. Mana is a neutral but very powerful force. As such, it is potentially dangerous, and care must be taken with its use. If one obtains an object containing mana, it is believed to enhance one's behavior or opportunities; placing an object containing mana in one's garden, for example, is believed to ensure a good crop.

Magic   Magic is not actually a supernatural force. Rather, **magic** refers to the techniques used to manipulate various supernatural forces and sometimes supernatural beings. Individuals may use magical recipes or formulas, or they may call upon someone with special knowledge of these formulas to perform them. A **shaman** is such a person—a part-time practitioner who, by training or inheritance, has special powers to deal with the unseen

magic
The techniques used to manipulate supernatural forces and beings.

shaman
A part-time practitioner of the supernatural who has special powers to mediate between the supernatural world and the community.

universe. The following section on supernatural practitioners has more details on shamans.

Magic shares some features with science. Specifically, magical formulas have been acquired by trial and error. For example, over time various practitioners may have given different herbal teas to people complaining of a headache. The herbs that relieved the most headaches were retained in the arsenal of magical curing formulas, and others were discarded. With much trial and error, a practitioner, over time, came to use certain herbs consistently to cure headaches. So, in essence, a hypothesis was formulated—this herb may relieve headache pain. It was tested—many people were given the herb for the complaint of a headache. The hypothesis was evaluated—most people given this herb reported a reduction in headache pain. Of course, shamans did not use formal, modern scientific methodology with control groups and blind tests, and they did not know the details of physiology and chemistry that modern scientists know. Their approach, in its broad terms, however, was what we would call scientific in that they were attempting to explain and control their environment and the events that affected them.

Anthropologist Sir James Frazer published a popular study and analysis of magic in 1911 and introduced the concepts of imitative magic and contagious magic to the reading public. He formulated two laws that are the governing principles of magic—the Law of Similarity and the Law of Contact. The Law of Similarity, or what is now called **imitative magic,** states that *like produces like.* The idea is that a drawing of a person, animal, or event (an imitative image or representation) can connect with an unseen world through the supernatural to influence what happens to that person or animal. A drawing of a deer with an arrow piercing its body would thus influence the outcome of a hunting expedition (Figure 11.1). The Law of Contact, or **contagious magic,** operates under the same law but has as its premise that something that has contact with a person or animal contains some of the essence of that person or animal. Hair, a footprint, nail clippings, an article of clothing, excrement—all are used as part of formulas to affect the being that has had contact with the material. Voodoo practitioners often employ imitative and contagious magic. A little doll created to look like an enemy, dressed with a scrap of fabric torn from the enemy's clothing can be used in a magical ceremony to cause injury or illness to the person. The practitioner who sticks pins in the doll would cause pain to the person. Typically someone lets the victim know that such a ceremony is in progress, or the person *believes* that magic is being worked against him. From an unbeliever's view the pain is caused by the psychophysiological processes associated with believing in the efficacy of magic.

Magic is effective. It works—if you do it correctly and believe it works. And this is one of its major appeals. In terms of the functions of belief sys-

TRY THIS
Analyze

A person owns a scarf once worn by a rock star and carries it with him at all times for good luck. Is this an example of imitative magic or contagious magic? Why?

imitative magic
A type of magic based on the notion that working magic on an image of an animal or person will cause the same effect on the actual animal or person.

contagious magic
A type of magic based on the idea that something that has contact with a person or animal contains some essence of that being and that magic performed on the item will have the same effect as if performed on the being.

Types of magic   **Functional analysis**

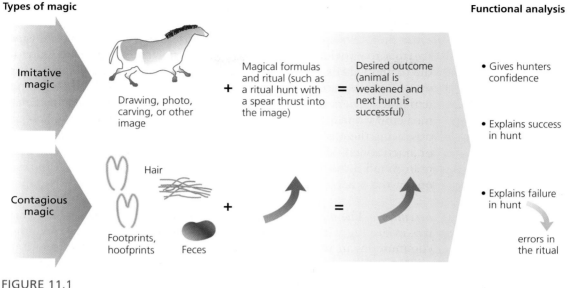

FIGURE 11.1
How imitative and contagious magic work.

tems, magic explains things. A relative's illness can be blamed on someone working evil magic. If the illness is cured by the magical practitioner, it is because the correct formula was used. If the ill person worsens or dies, it is attributed to one of several reasons: the diagnosis was in error and thus the wrong formula was used in the cure, or the curing formula was done incorrectly or incompletely, or another individual was using more powerful magic. Shamans often involve many people and steps in a curing ceremony. A skeptic might say that this is done so that there are many avenues of blame if the cure fails—someone gathered the wrong herbs from the wrong place, or someone did not observe the behavioral taboos called for by the practitioner (e.g., abstinence from sexual activity during a specified period).

> ❋ **TRY THIS** ❋
> *Compare*
>
> Compare the explanation given here for the failure of a magical cure with the explanation given by modern doctors when an attempt at a cure fails. Discuss your comparison with a classmate.

Supernatural Practices and Practitioners

Living in a community, whether large or small, brings universal dilemmas that must be addressed by the members of that group:

> Why did someone become ill, and who or what was responsible?
> What caused someone to die, or who was responsible for the death?
> Why were we unsuccessful hunting?
> Why are the crops failing?
> When will it rain (or stop raining)?

Anthropologists refer to the individuals who address such concerns for a community as the supernatural specialists. They are specialists because they have special abilities to diagnose these kinds of problems and are able to provide culturally acceptable explanations and solutions for them. Individuals who act as intermediaries between the supernatural world and the natural world are found in every culture. These supernatural practitioners are called by many terms—witch doctor, medicine man, medicine woman, rabbi, pastor, prophet, sorcerer, parson, monk—and classifying them is difficult. To anthropologists there are two major classes of practitioners: shamans and priests. Nearly all practitioners of supernaturalism fall into these two categories and exhibit the general features of one or the other.

Shaman   The most common form of specialist is a shaman, who specializes in dealing with supernatural beings and forces. Shamans serve their communities in many capacities, often acting as healer, counselor, and mediator. Shamans are part-time practitioners. They aid their society by using their special skills, but they do not make a living from these activities. They live day to day like everyone else in the society except when called upon to interface with the supernatural.

The use of the term *shaman* is quite tangled in today's society, much like the term *tribe* that was discussed in Chapter 10. It is often broadly applied to *anyone* who deals with the supernatural, including New Age practitioners who focus on treating their own individual needs through drumming, dancing, and trancing. Alice Kehoe (2000) takes issue with such current broad uses of the term. She points out that among the Tungus-speaking cultures of Central Siberia where the term originated, the term *shaman* refers specifically to those who mediate with the supernatural on behalf of their *community*. Mari Womack (2001) argues that language changes over time, and most anthropologists use the word *shaman* to describe a specific behavior complex (discussed in the following paragraphs).

A shaman is culturally perceived as being supernaturally chosen for the role. The spirits have selected this individual to act as an intermediary between two worlds—the natural (or known) world and the supernatural (unknown or beyond the known) world. Shamanistic individuals are often identified because they have survived some extraordinary event such as being struck by lightning or escaping a dangerous situation that would have likely resulted in death or severe injury to most people. Some individuals become shamans because of what we might call their unstable personalities, to use a modern label. Or it may be that they have a culturally ambivalent sexuality or are either gay or lesbian. These events or conditions are an indication to the group that there is something unique and special about the person. It should be remembered that humans have often lived in communities with small populations. In such communities,

A Dobe Ju/'hoansi shaman trances to contact supernatural forces and beings that will help him diagnose the other man's illness.

someone who does not conform to the narrowly defined social and cultural expectations of behavior stands out readily. A person's differences can be channeled into a positive role within the community by labeling that person as *chosen* by the supernatural. An older shaman may apprentice such an individual. In this manner the knowledge and the appropriate techniques and strategies are transmitted to the next generation. An additional feature of many shamans is that they have a particular specialty in dealing with the supernatural. This might be a special relationship with a specific supernatural being or force. When that shaman dies, the connection is broken.

A shaman makes contact with the spirit world in a variety of ways. The Yanomamo use mind-altering drugs to contact spirits, whereas Chuckee shamans interpret their dreams as an indication of contact with the spiritual universe. Prolonged and physically demanding dancing or listening to rhythmic music (often drumming) is used by the Dobe Ju/'hoansi to trance and contact spirits. Specific spiritual beings may then enter the shaman's body and speak to the community through him or her. Spirits will, in this way, provide an explanation of why something has happened. The appropriate course of action (or treatment) will then be explicated.

Aguaruna   Chuckee

Shamans use a variety of techniques. A deep knowledge of the medicinal qualities of the local flora is used to cure common problems such as fevers or digestive ailments. Psychosomatic techniques are also used, and these are often very persuasive. Sucking a foreign object out of an afflicted person's body is a technique used by the Yanomamo. The *object* is often a small piece of bone or stone or even an internal organ from a small animal that has been kept hidden from the patient. When the shaman spits out this object, it provides evidence of the cause of the person's problem. Alternatively the shaman may pull a contaminating spirit from a patient into his or her own body. The conflicting spirits—the shaman's and the contaminating spirit—will then engage in a vigorous struggle. This struggle often demonstrates through very dramatic body movements and gestures that the shaman's spirit is superior, and the contaminating spirit is subdued or cast out.

The shaman has most often been viewed as a key player ministering to the physical and mental well-being of a community, and anthropologists have always considered that role to be of utmost importance. The shaman can create and enforce a set of behavioral standards that will serve to create and maintain social order (remember the disciplining function of supernatural belief systems discussed earlier). However, as Michael Forbes Brown has shown, the shaman can also have a malevolent or dark side that is used to explain misfortune for a community; that is, the shaman is made the scapegoat (Brown 1989). Among the Aguaruna of northeastern Peru, illness and misfortune are believed to be attributable to the spirit darts that are sent by shamans from other communities. When someone in a community falls ill or dies, the shaman is able to identify the person responsible and thus set the stage for a victim's family to achieve reprisal and revenge.

Priests   The term **priest** is used by anthropologists to describe a special type of supernatural practitioner. Priests are often called by other terms—chaplain, pastor, or monk, for example. All of these practitioners have the same basic character and function, whatever they are called. Priests are supernatural specialists who hold a well-established place in societies that have centralized authority. Typically priests are part of organized agricultural societies. Agricultural societies, you will recall from Chapter 10, are stratified societies with central leadership and authority. Priests are specialized, full-time practitioners who are supported economically by the

priest
A full-time supernatural practitioner who is part of a bureaucracy.

The ritual of blessing the cows is a traditional part of the *festa* celebration held by Portuguese Americans in Modesto, California. This celebration is a rite of intensification for this group.

groups they serve. They perform regular calendrical rites and rituals that are fixed and serve the entire community. That is, the rituals follow a prescribed pattern and are always performed the same way. A priest learns rituals, protocols, and doctrines from other priests and typically performs rituals in a place of worship such as a temple, shrine, or sanctuary. Unlike the shaman, who is born with special qualities or has a special connection with the supernatural, the priest must *learn* how to be an intermediary to the supernatural world. The key difference between shamans and priests, then, is that priests undergo structured, formal training. Priests are part of a large bureaucracy, and there are often hierarchies of priests within their belief system such as that of the Catholic Church with the pope, cardinals, bishops, and priests.

Among societies with chiefs or kings (centralized political authorities), these officeholders may also have priestly functions. They may perform rituals associated with planting and harvest, or attempting to control the weather. In other words, they serve as the political authority and at the same time are the primary supernatural authority. In other chiefdom and state societies the political and religious organizations and roles are separate.

◎ RITUAL

Ritual is behavior that is formalized, is regularly repeated, and has symbolic content. It connects the natural and supernatural realms for individuals and for groups. Most anthropologists use the term as an analytical tool and primarily in association with religion. However, not all participants of formal, regularly repeated behaviors that include symbolic content "believe" in the supernatural. Some observers have suggested that behaviors associated with the supernatural should be called sacred rituals and others should be called secular rituals. Ceremonies such as Christmas, birthday parties, new year celebrations, homecoming, and anniversaries incorporate rituals. For some cultures (and some individuals) the rituals associated with such events encompass the supernatural; for others they do not.

Ritual occurs in two major categories of ceremonies across cultures: **rites of passage** and **rites of intensification.** A critical difference between the two categories is that rites of passage focus on the *individual* and rites of intensification focus on the *group*. These rituals reinforce group solidarity — the cohesive and supportive functions discussed earlier — for both the individual and the society.

Rites of Passage   Rites of passage mark culturally defined biological and social phases that humans pass through in their lives — birth through puberty, adulthood, and death. None of us can avoid these phases as we move through what can be referred to as the *arc of life*. Ceremonial rituals are created to mark movement from one socially defined role (behavior) and status (social position) to another. Remember that as an individual moves from one biological or social stage to the next, that person's social role and status within a group change. For these reasons, rituals associated with rites of passage, although they focus on the individual, also involve the group. The group may be an entire culture, or a smaller unit within the culture such as the family, a religious group, a sorority, or business associates. Group involvement in such rites is necessary because the group members must be able to change the way they interact with the individual in the future.

All cultures, for example, have different role and status expectations for individuals who are viewed as *children* and those who are viewed as *adults*. Likewise, when a person dies, the group is obligated to alter its relationship with the deceased. Everyone in the group is affected by the

TRY THIS
Analyze

Identify three rites of passage in your culture or subculture that are identified and defined culturally rather than biologically. Remember to use criteria such as change in status or role.

ritual
Behavior that is formalized, is regularly repeated, and has symbolic content.

rites of passage
Rituals associated with the social movement of an individual from one culturally defined role and status to another during the passage from birth to death.

rites of intensification
Rituals, often seasonal, that reinforce group solidarity, cultural values, and group social and political status relationships.

ANTHROPOLOGY AROUND US

Thanksgiving as a Rite of Intensification

Thanksgiving, the national holiday of the United States, is held in late November. It is thought of as a time for people to give thanks for their many blessings. Millions of people are caught up in preparations for this event. Travel plans are made to come together at a family gathering, everyone discusses the menu, and the buying and preparation of special food takes place. More people travel during the Thanksgiving holiday than during any other holiday of the year. Federal and state offices close, and many businesses show their solidarity by also closing and giving employees the day off from work. Differences and disagreements within families are put aside for the day. These ritual preparations show our unanimity as families and as a nation.

Cultural values are reinforced when we give thanks to the deities of our subculture's belief systems. Some acknowledge their good fortune by saying a ritual blessing at the feast table or going to their place of worship for a special religious service. Some reinforce the value of helping those less fortunate than themselves by spending the day feeding the poor and homeless—people who have less to be thankful for.

The foods that are placed on the tables across the nation reflect and reinforce our many ethnic cultural heritages—turkey, ham, roast beef, lamb, enchiladas, kippered herring, curry, borsch, potatoes, rice, pasta, tortillas, sweet potato pie, pumpkin pie, lemon meringue pie, flan.

Status relationships within the family are reinforced when respect is paid to elders who prepare special dishes and regale the assembled family with tales of past gatherings and events. Seat placement at the feast table(s) is important, and it reflects and reinforces the social status of each family member (many adults remember when they were first allowed to leave the children's table and sit with the adults).

We prepare for a change in behavior as we shift into the winter season of celebrations—Hanukkah, Christmas, New Year's. Many Americans are distressed by the appearance of decorations and songs that celebrate these holidays *before* Thanksgiving. Yet the day after the Thanksgiving ritual is historically the busiest gift shopping day of the year.

◎ **What rituals can you identify that are part of your family's Thanksgiving celebration? What acts of solidarity and reinforcement of cultural values are associated with the rite of intensification known as the Fourth of July?**

TRY THIS
Hypothesize

The rituals associated with rites of passage in small-scale societies are often clearly defined. Some transitions in the arc of life among industrialized urban peoples lack such definition. Cite an example of a poorly defined status or role change in your culture (where specific cultural rituals are absent). Now write a hypothesis that might account for this lack of definition or associated ritual.

Ndembu

change. Involvement in the activities and ceremonies of others, either as a participant or an observer, prepares you for your own movement through the arc of life phases.

It is often easier to view these rituals by breaking them into three more or less distinct phases: separation, transition, and reincorporation. During the *separation* phase the individual is usually removed or separated from her or his present group. The *transition* phase is marked by a change of some sort happening to the person—circumcision, for example, in a puberty rite, or loss of virginity on the wedding night as part of the wedding ritual. *Reincorporation* occurs when the ceremonies reintegrate the person into the society as a member of a new group. For example, in the initiation rites of passage that occur among the Ndembu of East Africa, the initiate is often secluded and is considered ritually polluted (separation phase). During this period of seclusion the individual is stripped of clothing and possessions and is shown secret objects, given sacred knowledge, and undergoes circumcision rites (transition phase). Finally, the initiate is reintroduced to society as an adult (reincorporation). Some analysts further subdivide the phases of rites of passage to show that they are not always clearly separated. Rather, the phases often blend from one to another. I have shortened the Ndembu rites considerably for purposes of illustration, and I've omitted discussing the rich symbolism associated with their rituals.

Rites of Intensification   Several features of rites of intensification are recognized. They involve rituals that reinforce (1) group solidarity, (2) values of the culture, subculture, or microculture, and (3) social and political status relationships within the group.

Paul Kutsche (1998) has also suggested that these rituals, which are often seasonal, prepare the group for a pronounced change in their environment such as the end of the harvest season or the arrival of migratory fish or birds.

The Day of the Dead celebration in Mexico (*Día de los Muertos*) may be analyzed as a rite of intensification. It is celebrated during two Catholic holy days—November 1, All Saints' Day, and November 2, All Souls' Day. Symbolism is incorporated into the rituals of the celebration, particularly ones in the form of skeletal caricatures in a variety of media including masks, effigies, and edible candy skeletons. The celebration is a blending of traditional Aztec beliefs and practices that honored the dead with rituals introduced by Spanish priests in the sixteenth century.

The Day of the Dead celebration illustrates the major features of rites of intensification, plus those features delineated by Kutsche. Mexican people travel great distances to return to their natal villages for this celebration that honors and remembers deceased relatives (reinforcement of solidarity). Many families create altars (*ofrendas*) in the home to honor the dead. Special foods that were favorites of the deceased are prepared for the home altar and are taken to the cemetery (more solidarity). At the cemetery a Catholic priest holds a mass (reinforcement of cultural values). The presence of the Catholic priest also affirms the status and role of the church in explaining events such as what happens at and after death (status affirmation). The timing of the celebration in the fall prepares people for the seasonal environmental changes ahead.

◎ REVITALIZATION MOVEMENTS

Throughout human history there have been organized **revitalization movements,** which have been identified by various terms: nativistic movements, revitalization movements, or millenarian movements. Examples of these include the Ghost Dance religion (1869 and 1889) in North America, the Mau Mau religion (1950s) in Kenya, and Vailala Madness (1920s) in Papua New Guinea. More recently such groups as the Branch Davidians (1990s) have exhibited features common to revitalization movements.

OLC
mhhe•com/lenkeit3
See Internet exercises.

Considerable literature has analyzed these movements, and classifications and theories about them abound. Regardless of the details and differences, various common features and themes are found. One frequent theme is that they often arise during times of a perceived crisis, such as a loss of traditional cultural values, or a time of economic distress, or an increased awareness of inequalities within the social structure. A charismatic leader will articulate the specific concerns for the group—often after having received a special communication with a god or having had a personal encounter with the supernatural. Such a leader is often called a **prophet.**

The leader, or prophet, will outline a set of behavioral changes or a program that will return the group to a better, revitalized state. These changes often require the members to be physically or emotionally isolated from the rest of society. Members will often change their residence, manner of dress, diet, or even their name. Each of these acts underscores the attempt to leave the present set of cultural traditions and values and return to a former set of traditions and values.

The classic example of such a movement is the Ghost Dance religion that spread among Native American cultures of North America. This movement actually arose twice—first in 1869 and again in 1889—from the same tribal source, the Paiute near Walker Lake, Nevada. A Paiute prophet claimed that revelations had been made to him during a trance. In the trance state he visited the spirit land of the dead and was told that if certain rituals were followed there would be universal peace between Native Americans and the Euro-Americans. Many people believed that the

revitalization movement
An organized movement that occurs during times of change that involves perceived loss of traditional cultural values. A prophet or charismatic leader predicts a revitalized society if a program is followed.

prophet
A person, usually charismatic, who has had direct communication with a god. Often receives a message that articulates a plan of action for the group.

Men from the Island of Tanna in Vanuatu participate in a revitalization movement. By mimicking the behavior of Western soldiers (using bamboo poles as rifles) they believe that they can attract a messiah who will bring them material goods.

Paiute

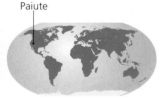

prophet was a messiah sent by God. The message was modified as it spread among different Native American groups. Some groups believed that the Euro-Americans would disappear and their dead ancestors would return. The Plains Indian cultures that adopted this movement held the belief that there would be a return of the vast bison herds of the past. This movement spread through many of the tribal groups that had been impoverished and marginalized by more than two hundred years of contact with the new Americans from Europe. When the promised changes did not occur after several years, the intense participation in the rituals declined and the movement largely died out. Alice Kehoe (1989) has suggested that the American Indian Movement of the 1970s could be viewed as a continuation of the Ghost Dance movement.

If we analyze such movements based on the previously discussed functions of religion, their popularity can be understood. The rituals and beliefs offer participants a cohesive and supportive group of like-minded, frustrated, and often unhappy people. Their cultural traditions are revitalized, and there is an opportunity to reinforce the group's history. Explanations are given for why conditions are as they are, and euphoria is achieved with the promise of deliverance from the current social and economic circumstances.

A group of Arapaho participates in a Ghost Dance in the year 1893.

SUMMARY

Humans throughout the world distinguish between the natural and supernatural. Belief in the supernatural world, both supernatural beings and supernatural forces, provide answers to many of the questions of life—why we are here and why events happen. Belief systems function to support, educate, discipline, and explain for both individuals and groups. Supernatural practitioners such as shamans and priests serve both individuals and communities in their dealings with the supernatural. Rituals such as rites of passage focus our attention on biological and cultural transitions, whereas rites of intensification reinforce cultural values and promote group solidarity. When economic turmoil and rapid cultural changes occur, human groups often create revitalization movements, which can solidify group cohesion and offer the promise of positive change. From the perspective of participants, a revitalization movement usually means a return to older values. Such movements tend to dissipate when the change is not forthcoming.

Study Questions

OLC
mhhe•com/lenkeit3
See Self Quiz.

1. Describe the functions of supernatural beliefs cross-culturally, and cite a specific example of each from your other assigned readings for this course.

2. Define ritual and describe in detail a common ritual that is practiced by you or members of your subculture.

3. Compare and contrast the general features of a belief system employing supernatural beings with one employing supernatural forces.

4. Describe the features of revitalization movements. Recount an example of such a movement and point out how it exhibits the features common to such movements.

Suggested Readings

Bowie, Fiona. 2000. *The Anthropology of Religion: An Introduction*. Malden, Mass.: Blackwell. Readable introduction to the topic with excellent coverage of historical and contemporary scholarly analyses and an extensive bibliography.

Evans-Pritchard, E. E. 1976. *Witchcraft, Oracles and Magic Among the Azande*. Oxford, England: Clarendon Press. (Originally published 1937.) This is an abridged version of the classic ethnographic account of Azande practices.

Kehoe, Alice B. 1989. *The Ghost Dance: Ethnohistory and Revitalization*. New York: Holt, Rinehart and Winston. The definitive treatment of this topic. Addresses history of the movement including the events surrounding the 1890 massacre at Wounded Knee Creek, South Dakota.

Lehmann, Arthur C., James E. Myers, and Pamela A. Moro. 2005. *Magic, Witchcraft, and Religion*, 6th ed. New York: McGraw-Hill. This collection of readings on supernatural topics serves as a good introduction to the topic. Extensive bibliographies are offered under topic headings that present a potpourri of interesting readings for more depth on any one topic.

Mair, Lucy. 1969. *Witchcraft*. New York: McGraw-Hill. This is an excellent short cross-cultural and historical review of witchcraft.

Suggested Web Sites

OLC
mhhe•com/lenkeit3
See Web links.

http://religiousmovements.lib.virginia.edu
This well-maintained, easily navigated site focuses on religious movements around the world; it addresses cult controversies and provides clearly stated profiles of world religions.

http://www.uwgb.edu/sar
Created and maintained by the Society for the Anthropology of Religion (of the American Anthropological Association), this site contains nearly one hundred annotated links covering all aspects of belief systems (academic organizations, bibliography, journals, museums, history, religious practices, and more). It also contains a useful "Lists of Links" from around the world.

http://hirr.hartsem.edu
   This research clearinghouse has links to over two hundred denominational home pages maintained by the Hartford Institute for Religion Research (Hartford, Connecticut).

http://anthro.palomar.edu/religion/default.htm
   This community college tutorial provides a quick cross-cultural overview of the many variations of the human religious experience.

12

Expressions

Is This Art?

Wet colors!!! The entire ceiling in the hall of bison looked as though it had just been painted. I had read, of course, about how fresh the paintings looked but was not prepared for this. None of the other caves that I have seen have paintings with this appearance. The colors are so vibrant. It has something to do with the particular type of seepage pattern of this cave, with the ceiling having a very slight incline to one side along which the seeping groundwater moves.

The above passage is my journal entry describing my first of three visits to the cave of Altamira in northern Spain, where artists painted wonderful images of animals fourteen thousand years ago. I have had the privilege of visiting more than a dozen of the caves in France and Spain where Upper Paleolithic artists expressed themselves, often in vivid color, on the cave walls and ceilings. To many artists and anthropologists today, these Upper Paleolithic caves represent the beginnings of human artistic expressions. Of course, there were likely many forms of expression that preceded these paintings, but they have not been preserved in the archaeological record.

The categories of expression that are surveyed in this chapter represent only a small sample of human expressive forms—prehistoric cave art, wood carving, textile art, and music. These topics were chosen based on inquiries made by my students, and it is my hope that they will pique your interest in finding out more about the cross-cultural nature of an expressive form of interest to you.

The objectives of this chapter are to

◆ Delineate the parameters of human expression

◆ Describe the earliest known human expressive images from the Upper Paleolithic period

◆ Present a sample of aboriginal and contemporary expressive forms—carver's art, textile art, and music

◆ Explore the functions of these human expressions

◀ A Cuna woman of San Blas, Panama, sews creative designs onto a blouse.

267

Apprenticeship is an important element in learning many forms of expressive arts. Young pupils learn the fine points of arm positions at the Joffrey Ballet School in New York City, and a master teacher instructs a dancer in Bali, Indonesia.

◎ PARAMETERS OF HUMAN EXPRESSION

OLC
mhhe•com/lenkeit3
See chapter outline and chapter overview.

Forms of human expression are often the first aspects of another culture that we encounter. Our senses have come to recognize and feel comfortable with the sights and sounds that have surrounded us during our enculturation. The familiar becomes our yardstick in assessing the aesthetic quality of expressions. Since its inception, anthropology has brought the diversity of human expression to our attention. Human expressions—images, decorative arts, music, dance, storytelling, and the myriad other forms they may take—are cultural universals. Some forms of expression are found in all known human cultures. Many who study expressive arts cross-culturally and through time have concluded that they are fundamental to the completeness of human life.

Prepare to step outside of your own cultural perceptions once again as you contemplate the material presented in this chapter. Those of us who were raised in a society where artists exist as specialists who earn a living (or try to) by practicing their art tend to view and experience art, dance, and music in discrete categories of time and place. Art in contemporary North American culture is usually peripheral to other aspects of life. We visit galleries and museums to view art, and it is placed in our homes to decorate our living space. A poster on the wall is pleasing to look at; a rock concert is an entertainment event. In many other societies the arts are often more wholly integrated into everyday life and institutions, particularly those associated with the supernatural. For example, the intricate *mola* textiles of the Cuna Indians of Panama are created to decorate utilitarian clothing, specifically women's blouses. Among the various groups of African pygmies, songs accompany many daily activities as well as ceremonial events.

Expressive arts may be examined in several ways. One method takes the close-up approach of technical analysis, dissecting the content of decorative pigments or the structure of musical scales. Another looks at the functions of the expressive arts within the context of the culture that creates them. Both of these methods give an outsider's (etic) analytical view, which is emphasized here. Another approach is to try to understand or appreciate how expressive arts are experienced and viewed by those who create them (an emic view). Keep this approach in mind, and draw on your own experiences to represent this perspective.

> **TRY THIS**
> *Define*
>
> Define *art* and make a quick list of features that you associate with art.

◎ EXPRESSIVE BEGINNINGS: ART IN THE UPPER PALEOLITHIC PERIOD

The beginnings of human artistic expression are unknown. By the Upper Paleolithic, the archaeological period that dates from about 40,000 to 12,000 B.P. (before present), anatomically modern people in the Franco-Cantabrian region of Europe (France and northern Spain) began to produce what has been called parietal art (from the French *art parietal*) and mobile art (French *art mobilier*). **Parietal art** refers to all art executed on permanent features: walls, ceilings, and floors of rock shelters and caves. The term also applies to art on large blocks of limestone in or near inhabited rock shelters. **Mobile art,** as its name implies, is not fixed to any place and can be moved or carried about.

This discussion considers the images from the Upper Paleolithic as art—that is, things created for aesthetic purposes. Long-standing debates about the definitions of art (Conkey et al. 1997: 2) are not considered here. Parietal art is difficult to date, but recent developments in accelerator mass spectrometry have allowed the dating of paint samples. The paint pigment used in these caves can be dated in this way because some of it

Franco-Cantabrian region

parietal art
Art executed on permanent features such as cave walls, rock shelters, and large blocks of rock.

mobile art
Art forms that are not fixed to any place and can be moved or carried.

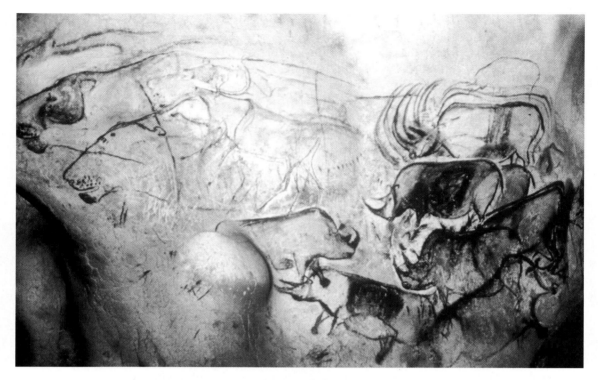

The Upper Paleolithic Period French cavern Grotte Chauvet (above) is filled with images of lions, rhinoceroses, and bears, whereas the Spanish cave of Altamira (right) contains images mainly of bison and deer. Anthropologists do not have an explanation for this different emphasis in subject matter.

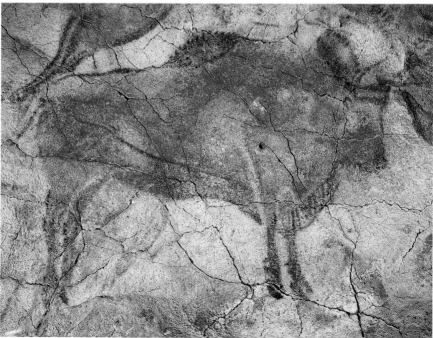

The deer on the ceiling of Altamira cave in northern Spain illustrates the use of distortion by Upper Paleolithic artists.

was made from compounds that included carbon-based material such as charcoal. In a recent analysis of thirty-four samples from six different cave sites, dates range from 12,180 ± 125 B.P. to 32,410 ± 720 B.P. (Davidson 1997: 149). Dates for isolated pieces of mobile art are between 26,000 B.P. and 32,000 B.P. (Davidson 1997).

The well-preserved parietal art forms are firmly established in the Upper Paleolithic. Therefore, it is logical to presume that earlier forms existed but have not been discovered or have not survived in the archaeological record. The Upper Paleolithic cave art that has survived was sealed in limestone caves when the cave entrances collapsed. As recently as the early 1990s, a spectacular new cave, Grotto Chauvet, was discovered in France. Of the several caves discovered early in the twentieth century, most have suffered great damage due to the intrusion of bacteria, algae, and high levels of carbon dioxide created by human visitors. Most of these caves have been closed, or visits have been severely restricted, to preserve the paintings.

One of the most intriguing aspects of Upper Paleolithic cave art is the range of styles represented. Realism and naturalism are dominant, but abstraction, exaggeration, fantasy, portraiture, caricature, and elaborate decoration are found. Although many animals look slack and immobile, others appear in realistic and lively postures, such as the swimming stags of Lascaux Cave in France or the feline engravings from La Marche, also in France, that look as though they are in the middle of a roar. Bison predominate in the paintings at the cave of Altamira near the coast in northern

TRY THIS
Analyze

Defend the following statement: "Cave art represents a biased view of human expression during the Upper Paleolithic." What data would you need to back up this statement?

OLC
mhhe•com/lenkeit3

See Internet exercises.

Spain. The most spectacular frescoes in this cave are on the ceiling of one gallery, where twenty-five figures—crouching or lying bison in the core group surrounded by standing bison and a red deer—are found covering an area of about 45 feet in length. These figures range from 4.5 feet to 6 feet in length. This ceiling has been hailed as the Sistine Chapel of prehistoric art and is viewed by some as coming close to an arranged composition (Conkey 1981: 24).

The bison at Altamira are very natural in appearance and attest to the competence of the artists in the use of what is labeled *tone*. Tone includes three properties—color, intensity, and value (the lightness or darkness). Other analytical aspects used in describing art may also be applied to the animals at Altamira. The use of line (which defines shape and form) and mass (the solidity of shapes) is apparent here. The bison were first outlined with a fine black line, and then color (reds, browns, and black) was applied. A washing or scraping technique was used to create shadings of the colors. Features such as eyes, nostrils, horns, and hooves were emphasized by incising the limestone surface. The effect was to model the bison's body with the use of light and shade. Also, natural rocky protuberances and bulges on the ceiling surface were incorporated into thighs, rumps, backs, and heads of the animals, making them even more realistic. There is harmony and balance to the paintings as well.

At the back of the Altamira gallery, on the ceiling behind the crouching bison, is a painting of a red deer. This doe was painted in the most subtle shadings of brown, taupe, and pale chamois. Amid the intense colors of the bison, it is an interesting contrast. There is another interesting aspect to the deer. She is in perfect proportion when viewed from the entrance to the gallery, but if one views her from directly below this section of the ceiling, her head is too small and her rump seems huge. This use of exaggeration of proportion was used by sixteenth-century artist Michelangelo in his statue of David (1501–1504 A.D.). The head and upper torso are out of proportion to the lower body if the statue is viewed from directly in front of it, but when viewed from below, with the statue on a pedestal, the head appears proportional to the lower body. This planned use of exaggeration by Upper Paleolithic artists is also found in other caves.

Author James Michener's comment when he first viewed the ceiling at Altamira focuses on the feature of this cave that most inspires those who view it:

> The thing that surprised me most, as I recall this amazing room, was the series of bulls constructed around rocky protuberances which jutted down from the ceiling. Mostly these extrusions are elliptical, but some are circular; they project eight or ten inches or perhaps even a foot, forming kinds of rocky hummocks standing forth from the rock pasture lands. On these humps the ancient artists, using a trickery not surpassed by Salvador Dalí, drew sleeping animals, wonderfully curled, with their feet tucked under

Small female images carved of ivory, bone, horn, and stone are examples of Upper Paleolithic mobile art. Such images may have served various purposes—as goddess symbols, magical amulets to ensure a safe pregnancy, fertility magic, or simply representations of female forms. This figure, called the Venus of Willendorf, is 4.5 inches high.

them and their heads resting on their forelegs . . . the bulls look as if at any moment they might rise from their slumber. (Michener 1968: 616–17)

Each time I think about the art of these ancient ancestors I remember my first experience at Altamira, and I ponder their lives of fourteen thousand years ago. We know that these peoples were technologically sophisticated, as attested to by the thousands of artifacts and ecofacts that have been recovered by archaeologists. The artists sought various minerals, particularly ochre and ferrous and manganese oxide, which give gradations of color from light yellow through red, brown, black, violet, vermilion, orange, and gray. Technical analysis of prehistoric paint chips proves that these people mixed compounds to create just the right color of paint. The colors were sometimes mixed on stone palettes, which have been found with samples of colors spread in much the same way a modern artist would do (Marschack 1979: 100). They made brushes of juniper twigs, and they would even blow pigments through hollow bird bones to create the first airbrush painting. This latter technique achieved hazy outlines of a contour or space such as appears in the manes of horses at Lascaux. They built scaffolds inside of the cave of Lascaux in order to raise the artists to the part of the cave wall with the most desirable surface, and they lit the caves with stone lamps that held tallow and twisted juniper wicks.

We know what these people looked like and what they wore. More than four hundred drawings of humans have been found, although this achievement is dwarfed by the thousands of animal paintings and carvings of species such as bison, horses, ibex, red deer, roe deer, mammoth, elephants, lions, and bears. We know from the mobile art that they had a rich decorative tradition in the form of jewelry and carvings on utilitarian items. Despite knowing all of this, we do not know why they made these expressive forms. The same may be said of much of both aboriginal and contemporary art. We may analyze it according to content, form, type, and other comparative categories, but it is difficult to accurately know why people express themselves through art.

◎ WHY DO ARTISTS CREATE ART?

Many of the hypotheses offered to explain the reasons or purposes for cave art are the same as those offered to explain the art of contemporary peoples. Archaeologists can't ask informants why people did things, so the approach of drawing analogies between past and contemporary cultures is used. One must keep in mind, however, as archaeologists do, that by drawing analogies we are making only educated hypotheses, and we may never know whether our hypotheses as to why prehistoric people created art are correct.

Art for Art's Sake

The idea of creating art for its own sake is based on the argument that Paleolithic humans liked beautiful things and that the luxurious Upper Paleolithic environment provided the leisure time to develop art. Critics of this hypothesis argue that if Paleolithic humans liked art for aesthetic reasons, they would not have painted deep in caves that were difficult to get to. Others suggest that paintings are found in dark recesses simply because they first filled up wall spaces in the sheltered areas near cave mouths and progressively moved farther back in the caves. Unfortunately there is no real supportive evidence for this argument—some paintings are associated with living sites near cave entrances, but in some caves the paintings and engravings are found only deep within inaccessible areas of the cave. Studies have looked for correlations between location of art and a number of variables, but none has proven particularly successful.

Imitative Magic

One of the earlier hypotheses given for why prehistoric people created cave art was that the art was used for magic. The magic hypothesis is still popular today. In essence this hypothesis states that drawings represent attempts by prehistoric humans to control their world through the use of imitative magic. There are numerous ethnographic examples of imitative magic from around the world in which drawings are used in ceremonies, as with pygmy hunters drawing a picture of an antelope in the sand and shooting it prior to embarking on the hunt (Frobenius and Cox 1937: 22–23). This in itself, however, does not prove that the Upper Paleolithic drawings represent magical practices. In addition, quantifiable data to support this hypothesis are lacking. The number of animals that appear wounded or marked with projectiles in the European Upper Paleolithic caves is only 10 to 15 percent (Hadingham 1979: 207; Leroi-Gourhan 1967: 34).

Cave Art as a Backdrop for Ceremonies

Ceremonies, such as rites of passage, have been suggested as possible reasons for the creation of cave art. Most proponents of this hypothesis cite as evidence the fact that rock paintings and engravings play important parts in the initiation ceremonies (rites of passage) of groups in both Australia and Africa. In these areas the engravings and paintings are used to instruct, explain, and teach.

Further, it has been suggested that if caves were used for ceremonies they would have been considered as sacred places by the cultural groups who lived in the area. Although this may be true, ethnographic parallels are lacking. Among the Australian aborigines, for example, anyone is free to admire the representations painted on the walls (Ucko and Rosenfeld 1971: 251). Among the Tiwi of Australia, children are expected to be present at all ceremonies, and they play by carrying out mock ceremonies in which adult behavior is mimicked (Goodale and Koss 1966: 198).

Some data support the argument for caves being used for ceremonies during the Upper Paleolithic. At the French cave of Tuc D'Adoubert, six rows of heel prints begin deep in the cave and fan out toward the entrance. At all known sites with footprints, both adults' and children's prints are present. For example, at Niaux Cave between one-third and one-half of the more than five hundred prints are considered to be those of children (Pfeiffer 1982: 177–79). This, it has been suggested, might indicate that children were brought to the caves for initiation ceremonies.

TRY THIS   *Hypothesize*

Offer an alternative hypothesis that might explain the presence of both adult and child footprints in caves where Upper Paleolithic art is found. What other data might there be to help support your hypothesis?

Art as Symbol

A number of researchers have suggested that prehistoric art such as that found in the Upper Paleolithic caves of Europe represents an early form of symbolism (Leroi-Gourhan 1967; Marshack 1997; Otten 1971; Ucko and Rosenfeld 1967). Symbols in the form of art are suggested as a means of the transmission of information. Some scholars who have argued for this interpretation have been quite ambitious in counting and mapping cave art figures. Researcher Leroi-Gourhan, for example, spent years visiting 66 out of 110 art caves and rock shelters in the Franco-Cantabrian region. He claimed to have identified pairings of animals in the art, such as horses with bison, and concluded that these were symbols representing males and females. His works have been heavily criticized on the basis of his statistical and other methodologies. Nonetheless, the idea of art as symbol is popular both in the interpretation of prehistoric art and in understanding contemporary art.

As noted earlier, one of the goals of archaeology is to establish chronological sequences (see Chapter 1 for review). Currently there is much interest in looking at prehistoric expressive material culture (art forms) within properly established chronological sequences (Morales 1997). This has not been accomplished in the past. Once we are able to sort out more precisely *when* particular cave images were made, we will be better able to integrate these peoples' expressive traditions with other cultural adaptations and variations at specific times and places, as well as view the process of artistic changes through time. In other words, when we can place the images within their proper temporal, cultural, and ecological contexts, we should be able to make more valid hypotheses about the reasons for the creation of prehistoric images. In the meantime these cave art images, at the very least, provide us with a window through which we can appreciate our rich and complex cultural ancestors.

◎ DECORATIVE ARTS

In cultures around the globe there are an abundance of decorative art forms, which include decorative utilitarian objects, objects of adornment (such as jewelry), body art (tattoos, scarification, and body piercing), and sculpture. Examination of a sample of such decorative art, and its role in the cultures that create it, illustrates the importance of this type of human expression today.

Carving

The wood, bone, and antler carving traditions of the native peoples of northwestern California illustrate expressive art that is an integral part of life. The purpose of this decorative art in these cultures is well known from ethnographic research. For the Yurok, the Karuk, the Hupa, and the Tolowa peoples of the Klamath River drainage region, the carving of wood, bone, and antler transcended the aesthetic function of adding beauty and pleasure to their world. Everyday use and display of the highly valued carvings also served an important social function by validating a person's inherited rank (Jacknis 1995). Emphasis on accumulated wealth and inherited social status was not unique to this group of Native Americans but rather was part of a long cultural tradition among the many coastal populations stretching from northern California to southern Alaska.

Tolowa
Yurok
Karuk
Hupa

Members of the Yurok, Karuk, Hupa, and Tolowa cultures used a variety of objects to reinforce their social position. Valued items included large obsidian blades (up to thirty inches in length), white deerskins, and acorn woodpecker scalps. Decorated everyday household items, such as elaborately carved acorn cooking paddles and elk horn serving spoons, were also valued. Such possessions reinforced an individual's social status. The items could be purchased using strings of dentalium shell money, which was stored in intricate purses made from elk horn.

Artisans, almost always men, carved the acorn mush paddles and elk horn spoons with intricate geometric designs. Men of high social rank purchased and collected the elk horn spoons to serve their guests on ceremonial occasions. Low-ranking or poor individuals possessed far fewer elk horn spoons or used plain, undecorated spoons and acorn mush paddles.

Like any other element in a people's culture, art is continually changing. Too often anthropologists have inadvertently conveyed to the public the idea that the early cultures of North America changed little before their contact with Europeans. In fact, ideas and technologies were constantly being borrowed from peoples with whom they came in contact—other cultures within trade networks, for example. The early cultures of North America also borrowed from the nineteenth-century Anglo-Europeans who moved into their territories. This can be seen among the Yurok, Karuk, Hupa, and Tolowa carvers, who used European iron-cutting tools to supplement and replace their own stone tools. The artistic tradition continues to evolve today as tribal carvers use modern band saws, gouges, chisels, files, and knives to complete their carvings.

Today carvers are also expanding the scope of their art by studying at contemporary art institutes and universities. The artists are borrowing indigenous designs from a century ago and combining them with new

The carvers' art can be appreciated in the designs of these spoons carved from elk horn by the tribes of northwestern California.

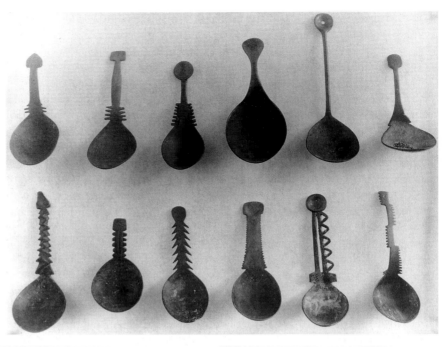

(Below) These paddles carved by the tribes of northwestern California were used to stir acorn mush.

A woman cooks acorn mush using a mush paddle.

innovations to create an evolving tradition. The creations of present-day carvers are not confined to traditional places within the cultures of the Klamath River drainage; they have found a new appreciative audience in the larger art world. The bold geometric designs of the wooden acorn mush paddles, elk horn serving spoons, and purses reflect a continuous link between the past and the future (Jacknis 1995).

Textiles

The Cuna (also spelled Kuna) of the island archipelago of San Blas, Panama, have a rich and varied expressive art in the form of *molas* (the Cuna word for a woman's blouse). These blouses are made of cotton, and the design is short-sleeved and boxy, something like a T-shirt in outline. Intricate patterns of geometric designs, stylized plants, animals, and humans are sewn on the front or back panels (or both) of the *molas*. The designs are a form of appliqué that involves from two to several layers of different colored cloth. The layers of cloth are basted together, and the design elements are formed by cutting through a top layer of cloth and folding under the raw edges of the cut. Cut edges are then sewn down

Cuna

A totem pole in Prince Rupert, British Columbia, has just been completed and is being carried out to a display area.

These contemporary Maori carvers in New Zealand apprentice at an art co-operative.

with hidden stitches. In this manner the color of the lower layer is exposed and the design is revealed. The traditional background color is black or a dark blue-black with designs in bright red, blue, yellow, orange, and green. Other colors are used but these are the most popular. Care is taken by the artists to create balance and harmony in their designs.

The origin of the *mola* appliqué technique is not known, but it developed after the introduction of manufactured cotton cloth, scissors, and metal sewing needles around 1900 (Salvador 1976: 171). The designs are believed to have evolved from traditional forms of body painting. The subject matter of the *mola* pictorial designs is taken primarily from the natural environment, but subjects include a girl's puberty celebration, recreational activities, religious themes drawn from missionaries, and political themes. Panamanian political candidates come to the islands to campaign, for example, and Cuna women create *molas* based on political party designs or even portraits of the candidates. *Mola* panels are often cut out of the *mola* blouse after a woman has gotten tired of it and sold to become a collectible art form in the United States and elsewhere. Cuna women take pride in the quality of their work and in showing it off. According to Mari Lyn Salvador (1976) *tourista molas* are sometimes made and sold, but these are done quickly, the quality suffers (i.e., stitches are too large, colors are wrong, and design elements are not properly balanced), and the women who make them are criticized. A co-op was formed to create *molas* for sale, and it has a quality-control board.

Throughout the world, traditional cultures are producing their art for outsiders, which can make good economic sense. Today Cuna women may choose to wear either contemporary Panamanian-style dress or the traditional *mola* and skirt. The *molas* that many of them make are still a functional art allowing aesthetic expression and storytelling; they are also considered a commercial fine art because *"they adhere to culturally embedded aesthetic and formal standards"* (Graburn 1976: 6). In contrast, souvenir-produced art, produced solely to make money, is considered to lack quality and does not reflect traditional aesthetics or standards of the culture.

TRY THIS *Surf the Web*

Log on to a search engine such as Google, Yahoo!, or Excite. Type in a specific country's name (e.g., Panama, Peru, Tanzania, Mali) followed by prompts such as art, traditional folk art, primitive, ethnic (and more specific prompts that interest you, such as wood carving, textiles, rock art, body art, tattoos). See what you can find about a particular expressive art form. Share what you find with a classmate. Did any of the search results discuss the traditional reasons for the particular form of expression? Was mention made of the art being sold commercially?

These *molas* show popular bird motifs and once decorated the front of women's blouses. Note the layers of colored cloth that have been exposed to reveal the design.

ANTHROPOLOGY AROUND US

Storytelling Festivals

The art of storytelling is enjoying a rebirth. All over North America and the world, modern peoples are discovering that there is drama, poetry, wisdom, and just plain fun in tales told. At my college the annual storytelling festival begun several years ago now includes workshops as well as performances.

Long before the written word, storytelling was a key device used by peoples to convey their history, values, etiquette, and religion, and to entertain. Theodora Kroeber in her book *The Inland Whale*, a classic collection of stories of the tribes of California, concludes that such stories with their patterns and structures represent the roots of later written literature.

Storytellers perform as they retell a tale. They use voice, gestures, facial expressions such as widening or rolling of the eyes, and body language to emphasize or embellish the narrative. A good storyteller draws the listener into the story as it unfolds. Johnny Moses, a Tulalip Native American from Vancouver Island, British Columbia, Canada, exemplifies the master storyteller. In his story about how the daily cycle of night and day came to be, for example, he weaves imagery, colors, and humor into a story that also teaches about values and the world around us. In this story, Ant Lady is in a contest with Bear Man. Ant Lady wants day-night cycles to continue; Bear Man wants a year of night so that he can sleep. Her steady, calm persistence during the contest helped her prevail over the large, fierce, and arrogant bear. That is why we have night and day. The storyteller's art joins with other forms of human expression to create a mosaic of that which makes us human.

◎ Recall a story told to you as a child. Did you realize as a child that the story embodied cultural values? Do you recognize as an adult that the story had a message?

◎ MUSICAL ARTS

Expressive Beginnings

The oldest musical instruments from archaeological sites are flutes and flute fragments that range in age from 12,000 to 36,000 years old. The early agricultural site of Jiahu in the Henan Province in Zhengzhou, China, has yielded six complete flutes made from the ulnae of cranes. There are another thirty fragmentary flutes from this site as well. Radiocarbon dating has established that the flutes are 9,000 years old. The best-preserved flute has been played and the sounds analyzed. This flute and the other five complete ones have seven main holes. On the flute that was played, the tone of one hole had been corrected by a small hole drilled next to it. Further testing of replicas of each of these bird-bone flutes is expected to allow comparison of the musical scale produced by these flutes and the current Chinese six-tone scale and seven-tone scale (Zhang et al. 1999: 366–68).

Ethnomusicology

The study of the music of a contemporary society within the context of that society is called **ethnomusicology.** Some anthropologists study musical sound structures, the people who make the music, and the cultural context in which the music is played. There are also specialists from the field of music who study world music within the context of its making. Both are considered ethnomusicologists. Ethnomusicologists have both the perspectives and interests of the social sciences and the humanities.

Music, as it is created by humans, is different from natural musical sounds such as birdsong. One difference is that human music involves tonality—fixed scale systems. In Western music the tonal scale involves seven basic tones. In non-Western cultures, five-tone scales are common, and seven-tone scales are sometimes used. The seven-tone scale uses tonal intervals different from the European seven-tone system. Arabic music has smaller intervals between tones, resulting in scales with seventeen steps, and there are many other tonal variations. When you have been enculturated to hear one set of tones, other systems sound strange or out of tune, and it is often difficult to pick out melodies (sounds that are produced in a sequence).

OLC
mhhe•com/lenkeit3
See Internet exercises.

ethnomusicology
The study of the music of a contemporary society within the context of that society.

TRY THIS *Analyze*

Consider your own experiences with music. Where is it played and listened to? Who plays it? How many different types of music can you identify that you can listen to on your radio?

Pick the lyrics of a favorite piece of music from your subculture or a microculture to which you belong. What story does it tell? What emotion does it evoke? How does it define the subculture or microculture?

Rhythm (a steady succession of beats) and harmony (sounds produced at the same time) are other aspects of music that vary widely from culture to culture and even within the same culture. In Western music a waltz has one kind of rhythm, a tango another. Some modern pop music has a number of different rhythms that shift. In other cultures, two musical rhythms may be carried on at the same time. These are some of the more technical aspects of musical analysis. When, where, and why people play and listen to music is also of interest to ethnomusicologists.

Our music helps to define who we are, whether we are composers, performers, or listeners. It contains history and social commentary and elicits emotional responses from joy to sadness. Music is integrated into our systems of worship, and it is used as a rallying point for political activities.

Folk music was once the only music. A family—or a group of families—got together and with or without the accompaniment of hand-crafted instruments joined in and sang. It was a bonding time, a time for the enculturation of values, a time to socialize, and a time to have fun. Singing also accompanied work and play and ritual. Colin Turnbull, for example, emphasized how central singing was to the Mbuti of the Ituri Forest. They sang songs during the honey harvest, during the joyous monthlong *elima* (female puberty rite), and while celebrating a successful elephant hunt. It was when they sang the simple refrain "The forest is good" (Turnbull 1987: 84) during a *molimo* that Turnbull began to understand—singing was essential to the pygmies and their relationship with the forest.

There are, of course, many other forms of human expression—verbal arts such as the telling of stories and legends, poetry, and dance—and there are subcategories within each of these. I encourage you to choose a category of expression that you participate in and investigate it on the Internet. The more you know about other peoples, the more you will come to celebrate not only human diversity but also the important commonalities among cultures.

SUMMARY

Human expressive arts are ancient. They date archaeologically to the Upper Paleolithic period, beginning around 32,000 years ago with carving, sculpting, and painting. It is likely that they date to much earlier times, but so far we have not recovered direct evidence of them. Many hypotheses have been put forward to explain why people create visual arts and music. These explanations suggest that the arts serve as expressive outlets for individuals, as a means of identity and solidarity for groups, as educational tools, and as a means of connecting with the supernatural.

Study Questions

OLC
mhhe•com/lenkeit3

See Self Quiz.

1. Describe three features of Upper Paleolithic cave paintings that are also found in contemporary paintings.

2. Discuss two hypotheses that explain the purpose of prehistoric cave art, such as that at the Spanish cave of Altamira. What evidence is there that these are valid explanations for prehistoric art? Are they valid explanations for contemporary art?

3. Using either the example of wood carvings of northwestern California native peoples or the Cuna Indians of Panama, describe how expressive art is integrated into the everyday lives of a society. Compare and contrast this with art in your own life.

4. What do ethnomusicologists study?

Suggested Readings

Conkey, Margaret W., Olga Soffer, Deborah Stratmann, and Nina Jablonski, eds. *Beyond Art: Pleistocene Image and Symbol.* Memoirs of the California Academy of Sciences, number 23. San Francisco: California Academy of Sciences. This is an excellent collection of papers that cover a range of topics about prehistoric art. Particularly impressive are the four articles that discuss the analytical methods, from dating to technologies of image making, and articles in section 4 that explore the interpretive process, including a consideration of context as an important part of interpretation. This selection also provides an excellent bibliographic source for additional reading.

Green, Thomas A., ed. 1997. *Folklore: An Encyclopedia of Beliefs, Customs, Music, Tales, and Art.* Santa Barbara, Calif.: ABC-CLIO. An essential reference work. Leading scholars address over 240 topics in the folklore genre. Each article is fully referenced and looks at historical, anthropological, literary, and psychological components.

Layton, Robert. 1994. *The Anthropology of Art,* 2nd ed. Cambridge, England: Cambridge University Press. Considered to be an outstanding introduction to non-Western art forms, this book addresses the difficult problem of what constitutes art across the diversity of artistic expressions found cross-culturally. Layton makes continual reference to an understanding of the cultural context in grappling with this dilemma.

Rosenberg, Donna. 1997. *Folklore, Myths, and Legends: A World Perspective.* New York: Glencoe/McGraw-Hill. Covering all parts of the world, the 120 verbal stories introduce a novice to the historical and cultural context of stories about heroes, fools, tricksters, parents, children, and animals. Her introduction offers an essential conceptual framework for an academic analysis of myths, legends, and folktales.

Suggested Web Sites

http://www.culture.gouv.fr/culture/arcnat/lascaux/en

This easily navigated site includes a virtual tour of the famous French Lascaux Cave and a great deal of background information about this and other prehistoric cave art locations.

http://www.maori.org.nz

This broad-ranging site covers Maori (New Zealand) culture, history, and current events. It includes easily navigated links to a variety of Maori artistic traditions including tattooing, weaving, and carving.

http://lcweb.loc.gov/folklife/other.html

Maintained by the U.S. Library of Congress, The American Folklife Center includes links to directories, academic programs, archives and museums, journals and newsletters, and much more pertaining to various folklore media. A wide-ranging site with excellent information pertaining to collecting folklore information and fieldwork techniques.

http://www.story-telling.com/References/Resources.htm

This site contains a large listing of storytelling organizations, collections, and resources in the United States and elsewhere.

OLC
mhhe•com/lenkeit3

See Web links.

PART THREE

APPLYING THE ANTHROPOLOGICAL PERSPECTIVE

THE UNIQUE PERSPECTIVE OF ANTHROPOLOGY HAS BEEN USED TO FOCUS ON how culture changes. Archaeological and ethnographic data, together with outcome analyses of programs of directed change, contribute to our understanding of the *processes* of change. We have learned, for example, that the human factor of cultural values and traditions may undermine the success of change programs.

Much of anthropology involves academic research, but we are also applying our findings to situations outside of academia. The anthropological perspective is relevant and useful in our everyday lives—I hope that you have seen this as you've analyzed, hypothesized, compared, and pondered in the various Try This boxes. The following chapters offer a glimpse of specific ways that anthropology can be applied, and how it can aid our understanding of the processes of culture change both locally and globally.

Chapter 13 offers what we understand of the processes of culture change and globalization and how this understanding can be used in our communities, jobs, and lives. Chapter 14 offers glimpses of the specific ways that anthropology can be applied by summarizing several case studies in which anthropology made a difference. The chapters are grouped together because this is the "So What?" part of the book. You have read about anthropological perspectives, methods, and theories, plus cross-cultural data in many categories in Part I and Part II. Part III is about how all of the foregoing can be *used* to make a difference in our lives.

◀ All aspects of culture are dynamic. The Chinese city of Shenzhen illustrates how older sections of the city give way to new construction. What other aspects of their culture will be affected by the new construction?

13

Culture Change and Globalization:
What Have We Learned?

Culture change is evident in this image from Dubai, United Arab Emirates, that shows camels crossing a road in front of the city's fully equipped, modern camel hospital.

The warmth of the sand beneath our toes, the sounds of waves lapping the beach, and the companionship of old friends lulled us into reminiscences. We had been away nearly four years, though we had kept in touch by mail and the occasional phone call. The beach was the same. As one looked north toward the small harbor one saw the same three fishing boats moored at the quay. The rocky cliffs to the west still held the monument to Christopher Columbus (local legend claimed that this coast was Columbus's first sighting of land upon his return from his explorations of the New World). To the east the high cliffs were as inspiring as they were when we regularly hiked along them.

The view to the south was a different matter. I stood and turned my back to the waves and faced a skyline that I barely recognized. There were several new high-rise apartment buildings. Two tall cranes were in constant motion lifting prefabricated wall sections up to the third floor of another condominium complex under construction. According to our friends, their quiet little village had been "discovered," and a real estate boom was on. This, of course, meant a boost to the local economy. But the negative side of this was that most of the building was for holiday residences whose owners spent only the month of July or August in the village. The year-around residents still numbered less than 2,000. During the summer 10,000–12,000 people converged on the area, bringing around-the-clock partying and trash along with their *pesetas* to spend. Our old landlord expressed concern and dismay that so much of the change was haphazard and unplanned, spurred by outside interests and money. A thoughtful man, he looked beyond the improved economic climate and worried about the long-term effects on the traditional culture of locals. Similar issues face people all over the globe. My local newspaper has carried headlines about parallel issues for the past six months. The lack of foresight has resulted in major problems with infrastructures such as parks, sewers, schools, and roads to accommodate the traffic brought by the significant numbers of new residents to the area.

Cultures are constantly changing. Some change is accidental; some is by choice; and some is forced on people, as during colonial rule, war, or occupation by postwar victors. The pace of culture change seems to be accelerating everywhere, as it is in the Spanish village where I conducted fieldwork, and as it is in my hometown. In my community, as in the community in Spain, it is the lack of planning and short-sighted attempts to see the unforeseeable consequences of changes that are causing problems. The anthropological view of the processes of culture change can help us keep a perspective on what is happening around us and can be used to assist in planning programs for change, both near and far. This chapter addresses some of these issues.

The objectives of this chapter are to
- Describe how culture changes and methods for studying change
- Consider lessons learned from directed change programs
- Discuss issues of globalization
- Examine issues of culture change in urban settings

◎ HOW CULTURES CHANGE

Data from studies in archaeology and cultural anthropology point to two primary sources for culture change: internal sources and external sources. Ideas and material culture items are recycled every so often within a culture (fluctuations), and new ideas or combinations of already existing ones (innovations and inventions) are generated within a culture and add to it. The areas of such changes range from technology to ideology.

Diffusion is responsible for most change and is a primary example of an external source of change. Many agents act to bring about diffusion (borrowing) between cultures—contact on territorial borders, contact during trade missions, contact during colonialism, contact during war and imperialism. In the distant past all diffusion occurred as a result of people's movements. Whenever people come into contact with one another, there is the possibility that one group will borrow an idea from the other group and incorporate it into their own customs, traditions, behaviors, technologies, and ideologies. A small personal example: Some years ago a visitor from New Zealand shared a backyard barbeque with my family. He was so excited by our Weber kettle barbeque that he declared that he would look into importing such grills to New Zealand.

The process of diffusion that is termed **acculturation** involves the borrowing between cultures as a result of prolonged contact—the borrowing may be by choice or the result of a dominant society forcing the diffusion. We have evidence of this process in the earliest written records and continuing throughout historical times. There is also much archaeological evidence of the diffusion of material culture in prehistoric times. Today, with the advent of global electronic communication, the process of diffusion and acculturation has accelerated. It occurs through exposure to new items and ideas presented on the Internet as well as in motion pictures, television, print media, missionary work, international business, tourism, and the activities of NGOs (nongovernmental organizations) such as the World Bank, Cultural Survival, and Oxfam.

The rapidity of culture change and the study of change itself dramatically increased with the economic and infrastructural rebuilding that was initiated following World War II. The genesis of such global changes began earlier, of course. The Industrial Revolution, for example, was a starting point of much global change and increased the contact between widely separated geographic regions. Prior to the industrial phase (discussed in Chapter 6), people survived primarily by foraging, hunting, gathering, simple horticulture, and animal husbandry. With the industrial age came labor and market specialization and work for wages. Slowly people the world over became more and more part of a world system, due to economic trade that grew with technological developments in transportation, manufacturing, and communications. In the 1980s media and

acculturation
The borrowing between cultures as a result of prolonged contact.

communication networks accelerated global culture contacts, causing new ideas and material culture to rapidly diffuse.

◉ HOW CHANGE IS STUDIED

There are numerous approaches to studying culture change. Each has its advantages and drawbacks. A combination of these approaches may give us the best view. A careful scrutiny of the *archaeological record* can reveal patterns and trends of culture change. For example, the diffusion of methods for raising domestic plants has been documented archaeologically. Research and analysis of *historical records* provide documents about change over time in such public aspects of culture as politics and economics. But other aspects of culture, such as the lives of everyday people, or women, may not be represented.

The ethnographic approach of taking *life histories* enables us to learn about culture change by talking to elder members of a culture and asking them to recount aspects of their lives. This information may be, in the absence of written documents or archaeological evidence, the only available way to gain some idea of how a culture has shifted and readjusted through time. Of course, selective memories may render some of this information suspect.

Documentation of change can come from *ethnographic restudies*, although restudy does not tell us what happened during the time between the studies, nor does it point to the processes of change. Finally, **impact studies** use ethnographic methods to look at a situation during and/or after a program of planned cultural restructuring has been implemented. Such studies often lead to an understanding of how change occurs, particularly with ongoing research. Such analytical approaches suggest impediments or stimulants to culture change, particularly if patterns emerge when studies are compared.

> ### ✖ TRY THIS ✖
> *Critique*
>
> Point out how and why the data acquired through historical records and life histories may not be accurate. Compare your thoughts on this with those of a classmate.

◉ CULTURE CHANGE: A BRIEF HISTORICAL OVERVIEW

The discipline of anthropology began in the 1860s when European colonialism and imperialism was well under way. Theoretical perspectives at the time reflected an emphasis on social evolution, influenced by Charles Darwin's theory of biological evolution written in 1859. The **unilineal** (single line) **evolutionist's** perspective of early anthropologists, such as E. B. Tylor, who wrote his classic *Primitive Culture* in 1871, and Lewis Henry Morgan in his *Ancient Society* (1877), emphasized that every culture proceeded through a series of successive stages. Morgan stated that "The

impact studies
Ethnographic study of a situation to document effects of change. May take place during and/or after a program of cultural restructuring.

unilineal evolution
Early theoretical school that postulated that all cultures proceeded through a series of successive stages.

latest investigations respecting the early condition of the human race are tending to the conclusion that mankind commenced their career at the bottom of the scale and worked their way up from savagery to civilization through the slow accumulations of experimental knowledge" (Morgan 1963: 3, originally published 1877). No stages were skipped. Morgan's cultural evolutionary stages of savagery, barbarism, and civilization focused on cultural differences in food procurement strategies and the technology that accompanied these at each stage. He proposed that all cultural groups progressed, or evolved, through these stages, and he gave specific criteria for each stage, such as cultures in the stage of savagery procuring food through foraging, hunting, and gathering and using tools such as the bow and arrow. Barbarism included the innovation of pottery, the domestication of animals and cereal plants, and in the later part of this stage, the smelting of iron ore. Civilization was marked by the invention of the alphabet. *Ancient Society* also included detailed discussions on kinship and political organization of societies and how these altered as subsistence strategies changed. Note that at the top of this sequence, and that of others proposed by the unilineal evolutionists, were the culture groups of the researchers themselves, which were considered "civilized." This means, of course, that an ethnocentric perspective guided the analysis.

These early models attempted to explain the quickly accumulating data regarding the many differences and some of the similarities between cultures. Unfortunately much of the data was incomplete, and field methods were inconsistent; indeed much of the information used in early evolutionary models came from letters, memoirs, and accounts of European and American missionaries, the military, explorers, and merchant seamen. Remember that the development of anthropological methods was just beginning. From our perspective today, we understand the early paradigms to be somewhat simplistic and incomplete. I like to consider, however, that Morgan and others of his time were making bold attempts to understand the world's cultures and how they developed over time. Additionally, Morgan, at least, had spent years working among the Iroquois (first as an attorney representing them in a legal dispute over land and later doing fieldwork) so he had some firsthand knowledge. Alas, we know today that such evolutionary models were used by governments, bureaucracies, and individuals to fuel colonialism. From the indigenous peoples' view, this anthropological model was used to suppress and exploit. And we are more than a bit embarrassed that early anthropology contributed to this, although it was not the intention of our founding scholars to do so.

Responses to the models of the unilineal evolutionists came from two theoretical schools that rejected the evolutionary perspective: **diffusionism** and **historicalism** (also labeled **historical particularism**, or **American historicism).** The diffusionists focused on explaining the origin of artifacts and ideas and how cultures developed through time. They saw

diffusionism
Early theoretical school that explained the origin and spread of artifacts and ideas through borrowing between cultures.

historicalism
Theoretical school, established by Franz Boas, who hypothesized that each culture had its own particular history that could be documented through repeated ethnographies. Comparisons of many such histories could uncover underlying principles of culture change. Also termed historical particularism; American historicalism.

the mechanism as diffusion, the notion of the borrowing between cultures as they came in contact with one another. One diffusionist group known as the **heliocentric diffusionists** thought that historical and archaeological evidence pointed to ancient Egypt as the center of cultural innovations and inventions, and those innovations and inventions spread from the Egyptian cultural center to other cultures, eventually reaching around the world. These diffusionists viewed Mayan temples as evidence of diffusion from the great pyramids of Egypt. With hindsight we can say that this hypothesis failed to account for the complexity of intercultural contact and diffusion and ignored the possibility of independent innovation or invention by geographically distant cultures. Another major problem we recognize in hindsight is the incompleteness of field data. Nonetheless, this was an attempt to explain how cultures changed over time. Today we acknowledge the diffusionist contribution because the borrowing between cultures is an important aspect of how cultures change.

Historicalism began in the early 1900s with Franz Boas (1858–1942), an important early figure in American anthropology. Boas began the first anthropology department in the United States at Columbia University and taught most of the first-generation anthropologists in this country. Among his noteworthy students were A. L. Kroeber, Robert Lowie, Margaret Mead, Ruth Benedict, and Edward Sapir, all considered foremothers and forefathers of today's anthropology. Boas received his university degree in physics, but redirected his life's work to anthropology. He brought scientific rigor and methodology to bear on his new profession of anthropology. He insisted that data should be gathered in the field through participant observation and the detailed recording of a specific culture's features—customs, practices, rituals, tools, clothing. He dismissed earlier stage models of cultural evolution primarily because they lacked sufficient field data to support their claims about how cultures evolved. He argued that each culture had its own particular history of change and that these were researchable through repeated and fact-laden ethnographic studies. He further suggested that if such repeated ethnographies were done over extended periods of time, with many cultures, we might then compile ethnological data to uncover underlying principles of cultural change.

Meanwhile, archaeologists were busy accumulating different kinds of evidence of change through time via the material record. Unfortunately, those early researchers were hampered by a dearth of accurate dating methods and thus could not always determine whether widely separated geographical regions and sites were older, more recent, or contemporary with one another. This lack of time frame made investigations of cultural evolution elusive.

The radiocarbon revolution in the 1940s provided a time framework for archaeological sites and made possible investigations of culture change

heliocentric diffusionism
Diffusionist school that pointed to ancient Egypt as the center of cultural innovations and inventions that spread around the world.

FIGURE 13.1
The insights of anthro-
pology can aid the
success of planned
change programs.

in prehistory. Similarly, in biological anthropology, with discoveries in genetics, there was a shift from describing human variation and fossils to explaining why and how change had occurred. Cultural anthropology followed suit, moving away from data gathering and description as an end in itself, and shifted to a greater focus on *cultural process*. You will recall that Chapter 2 discusses how this shift was embraced by anthropology as the discipline fine-tuned definitions of culture to include the processes of acquiring culture.

At the end of World War II, European countries focused their economic and social resources on rebuilding their war-devastated cities. The United States became involved in rebuilding efforts and sought to help peoples around the world. Many were surprised at the high failure rate of programs to assist change. Anthropologists conducted impact studies and gathered data to document the successes and failures. We began to understand both barriers and stimulants to change and to appreciate fully the holistic nature of culture and how its parts are integrated (Figure 13.1).

An important contributor to our understanding of the process of diffusion and acculturation was George Foster. He presented his analysis of what stimulated the modification of cultural behavior patterns and what forces prevented change in his seminal book *Traditional Cultures and the Impact of Technological Change* (1962). His analysis and the contributions of many others ultimately led to the specialty of applied anthropology. Anthropologists provide a theoretical perspective and they can act as a catalyst for change in a culture's customs and practices.

But wait. Are attempts to effect change compatible with the anthropologists' ethical position? Quite a spectrum of anthropological opinion exists on the whole issue of activism. Some believe that as scientists they should stay objectively neutral and not become involved in any planned and directed manipulation of a culture. At the other extreme are what some have labeled **action anthropologists,** who believe that they have a moral obligation to take the side of indigenous populations whenever such peoples' rights to self-determination are violated. Still other anthropologists take a middle ground with efforts to educate all sides in any issue. Regardless of whether one believes that anthropologists should be advocates or even agents of culture change, our discipline was and is at the forefront of understanding change processes from within.

◎ LESSONS LEARNED FROM DIRECTED-CHANGE PROGRAMS

Before turning to a consideration of anthropology's role in the study of global change today, I believe that a review of the highlights of Foster's work will give important insights. Foster found that many change programs were initiated at the request of members of the culture. Yet change programs in agriculture, health care, and economic development regularly failed and often made everyone uncomfortable. Foster documented the patterns of barriers and stimulants to the modification of customs, ideas, and behaviors. The barriers that emerged from his compilation of global development studies centered on cultural issues, plus some social and psychological issues. Technological and economic issues were not, he found, significant barriers to change, though both were often stimulants. Current globalization impact studies verify Foster's analysis regarding many of these barriers and stimulants. The following provides a quick sketch of Foster's work with specific examples analyzed. The issues he identified are directly relevant to issues of globalization today as discussed later in the chapter.

Cultural Barriers to Change

Different cultural values and attitudes are important barriers to change, including

> fatalistic outlooks (*Everyone dies; what will be will be.*)
> tradition (*This is the way my father and his father tilled the land.*)
> ethnocentrism (*We know more about mother earth than any college-educated city dweller; our way is best.*)
> relative values (*I know motorcycle helmets save lives, but I like to feel the wind in my hair; I acknowledge the benefits, but I prefer my way.*)
> norms of modesty (*I just could never have a male doctor examine me; I'd die of embarrassment.*)

action anthropologist One who believes that he or she has a moral obligation to take the side of indigenous populations whenever such peoples' rights to self-determination are violated.

Relative values are often barriers to culture change. Many bikers choose not to wear protective helmets, as seen at this Harley-Davidson party in Milwaukee, Wisconsin.

The structure of cultures can themselves create barriers to change. First, there may be logical incompatibilities in the structure of cultures. An agricultural pest-control program, for example, might advocate the use of insecticides. The Buddhist belief system prohibits killing any life form, and therefore a program that introduced chemically based pest management to a society that practiced Buddhism would be incompatible with Buddhist cultural values. The belief system would be a barrier to the proposed pest-management program, and the program would likely fail.

Second, there may be unforeseen aspects of the culture's structure that could create barriers to change. These occur simply because the change is not compatible with the structure of the culture. Foster cites the case in the lowlands of Bolivia, where a new maize was introduced with the intention of improving people's diet. It had many advantages over the indigenous crop—higher yield, better nutrition, and rapid maturation. It also turned out to be difficult to grind and process for consumption. Nonetheless, it was very popular—but not for the reasons it was introduced. Rather, its popularity was due to the fact that it made an excellent commercial alcohol that sold well and at high prices (Foster 1962: 85).

The patterned ways people use their bodies can also create barriers to change. Many people of the world cultivate the soil by standing and bending at the waist, whereas others squat or rest on their knees. If an agricultural aid program to a country with these traditional body positions includes typical North American long-handled tools, the aid program may fail.

Such aid is rejected because using the long-handled tools, and having to stand up straight to do so, results in back and shoulder pain.

Social and Psychological Barriers to Change

Group dynamics within a culture may be a source of barriers to change. Women who enjoy the dynamics of small-group interaction while cooking may be frustrated and unhappy if the North American architect of a new housing project for natives in a developing country places the stove in a corner, facing a wall, away from the center of social activities (a common configuration in modern apartments in North America). Such cross-cultural errors have been made more than once and have derailed many projects. The reader has undoubtedly sensed the cultural ethnocentrism emanating from the architect in the preceding example. This is not to say that such errors are planned, but rather they result from a genuine lack of cross-cultural awareness and sensitivity in most instances.

Perceptions and miscommunication can provide barriers to change too. Of course the social and psychological barriers are extensions of cultural barriers, because both types of social groups and perceptions are learned and transmitted by individual members of cultures. The early days of the contraceptive pill illustrates these problems. There were many tales of errors in both perceptive differences and miscommunication regarding pill usage in Europe, North America, Africa, and elsewhere. Clients did not always understand the nature of an oral contraceptive and sometimes inserted the contraceptive pills into their vaginas or took them only when they had sex. Such mistakes usually were traceable to failure of health care workers to clarify the use of the pills. After all, until this time all contraceptive techniques directly involved the genitalia or consisted of herbal potions that induced abortion.

Stimulants to Change

Desire for economic gain is perhaps the biggest stimulant for change. Individuals themselves may identify a part of their lives that they want to change, especially if they perceive a positive economic outcome. Information and aid from the World Health Organization has been sought by people who want to plan the size of their family. Such people have themselves recognized that there are positive economic advantages to family planning. If an agricultural program demonstrates that different agricultural practices will lead to higher yields per acre, and thus to more crops to sell, traditional practices of cultivation will generally give way to new innovations. When planned change is directed at issues such as health, economic advantages may not be as obvious to the recipients. Motivators such as desire for prestige, pride in nationalism, or intracommunity competition

---

❆ TRY THIS ❆
Explore

To experience just how your culture dictates the way you use your body, try sitting for a half hour on the floor with your legs stretched straight out in front of you (Inuit style), or try squatting balanced on your toes (Vietnamese style) for the same length of time.

❆ TRY THIS ❆
Hypothesize

Read the community or metro section of your local paper, or read letters to the editor. Identify a controversial topic in your community regarding a proposed change (this might have to do with issues such as recycling, urban growth, the outlawing of leaf blowers—any local issue). Write a hypothesis about why the planned change is meeting opposition. Phrase your hypothesis in terms of one or more of the barriers discussed here. How might you test your hypothesis?

TRY THIS *Analyze*

Suppose that health care workers from another technologically advanced society have come to your community. They tell you that they have overwhelming scientific evidence that sitting on the typical North American toilet is bad
for your circulation and is an unnatural position for a bowel movement. Sitting and the necessary straining that often results is a primary cause of piles
(hemorrhoids). Squatting with legs bent and weight on flat feet (as is the tradition in a good number of world cultures) is how you should take care of
bodily elimination. (The raised toilet would have to be replaced with just a
hole in the bathroom floor. To accommodate North American sanitary requirements a lid could be designed to drop over the hole when not in use.)

Discuss which of the three categories of cultural barriers discussed in the
text might play a role in the rejection by you and your friends of this attempt
at culture change. How different is this from North American experts in agriculture going to other cultures and offering superior ways to grow crops?
How would you go about changing people's attitudes and behaviors?

OLC
mhhe•com/lenkeit3

See Internet exercises.

may stimulate the target population to try the new approach or product or
idea. All of these stimulants or motivators have been used by both insiders
and outsiders—for reasons of altruism, politics, or religion—to bring about
changes that are seen as desirable.

◉ HUMAN PROBLEMS IN CHANGE

First, I am going to relate a very early study in technological change that
involves the introduction of hybrid corn to farmers in New Mexico. I've
selected this case because it is a direct example of the human cultural element that can impede a program of planned change—even one in which
the people involved want the change. If you consider it closely, you will
see many parallels to attempts by the government, the health care community, and educators to introduce change in your own culture. Next, I'll
summarize a more recent case involving camel herders and economic
change. In this case, outside factors are forcing difficult decisions that affect a people's traditional values. Keep Foster's barriers to change in mind
as you read these accounts, and see if you can anticipate the problems that
affect the process of change.

A Case Study of Hybrid Corn

Background.   A community of Spanish American farmers in the southwestern United States grew a native variety of corn known as Indian corn.
Seed was saved each year from the harvest for planting the next year's

Culture change often involves the blending of old and new. A camel cart with rubber tires transports goods past parked trucks in the city of Ahmedabad, Gujarat, India.

crop. Yield of the corn was twenty-five bushels per acre. Soils were fertile, and fertility was maintained by the addition of some manure each year. Abundant water for irrigation of small fields came from the nearby river. The corn was used primarily to make tortillas, a diet staple for the people. Corn, in the past, had been ground by hand using a *mano* (handheld grinding stone) on stone mortars called *metates*. Currently the grinding was done commercially at a local mill. Surplus corn, as well as corn stalks, was fed to animals (Apodaca 1952).

Introduction of the Hybrid Seed. The local U.S. Department of Agriculture farm extension advisor, who spoke Spanish in the same way as the local farmers, had worked in the area for several years. He was familiar with all of the local farming practices and had good rapport with the farmers. He felt that the introduction of a hybrid variety of disease-resistant high-yield (about one hundred bushels per acre) corn would benefit the farmers. He discussed this proposal with local leaders of the village, who acknowledged that the traditional seed strain was weak. A meeting was held, and everyone in the village was invited. At the meeting a movie about the hybrid corn was shown, and community leaders themselves discussed its advantages. A demonstration plot of corn was grown near the village so that farmers could see for themselves the increased yield from the hybrid variety compared to the local Indian corn (Apodaca 1952: 35–37).

The Result.   At first the program seemed to be going well. Of the eighty-four growers in the village, forty planted a small amount of the hybrid corn and doubled their production of corn compared to the preceding year. The next planting season sixty farmers grew the new hybrid. The extension agent felt that the newly introduced hybrid corn was a success. Again the harvest yield was high. But the following year only thirty farmers planted the hybrid variety. By the next year the number of farmers planting the new hybrid had dropped to three (and these were farmers the extension agent considered to be progressive). Everyone else was again growing the traditional Indian corn, and there had been no diffusion of the hybrid variety to any surrounding villages (Apodaca 1952).

None of the farmers reported any problems with growing the new hybrid corn. They were pleased with the higher yields. There was a market for the surplus. There had been no difficulty in obtaining the seed to plant. Farmers even indicated that the Indian corn was clearly a weaker variety. Yet they had gone back to growing it. Why?

Unanticipated Barriers.   The farmers' wives did not like the new corn. They had complained from the first harvest. The new hybrid did not have the proper texture, and it made poor tortillas that did not hang together well. They did not like the color of the tortillas that were produced from the hybrid corn flour, and they did not like the taste. Farmers continued to grow the new corn anyway for the first two years because it resulted in high yields and could be fed to animals. But their wives were very unhappy and in the end persuaded the farmers to return to the old Indian corn. In other words, in the terms laid out by George Foster, cultural values and attitudes, particularly tradition and relative values, had been barriers to the change.

A Case Study of Economic Change Among Pastoralists

Background.   The Raikas, of the state of Rajasthan in India, are pastoral camel herders. They belong to a Hindu caste whose members breed livestock and are well known as expert camel breeders, though they also keep cattle, sheep, and goats. Their expertise includes knowledge of selective breeding. They keep track of pedigrees of their animals, and they sell only male animals. Their traditional knowledge of diseases and the treatment of them is extensive. For example, the Raikas developed a technique for vaccinating camels against camel pox by taking skin from an infected camel, mixing it with water, and rubbing the solution into a small cut in the nose of the animal they wanted to protect from the pox.

TRY THIS
Analyze

You are an anthropologist who has been hired to look at the hybrid corn case and offer suggestions for future programs of planned change. From the anthropological view, make a list of what the extension advisor did correctly to introduce the new corn in this cultural setting. Then, make a list of additional steps that should have been taken to increase the likelihood of success in this case.

Camel caravans at one time linked India to prosperous markets in Asia, Mongolia, and Europe. Today camel herders in Gujarat and Rajasthan offer camel safaris for tourists.

Raikas live in permanent houses near villages where women, children, and elderly live year-round. Men travel up to one hundred miles herding their camels to pasture. Human population has dramatically increased in the region, and traditional open grazing land is decreasing as cultivated land increases. Historically, local maharajahs kept camel herds, maintained by the Raikas, in order to have a supply of camels for their warriors. Today there is a strong market for camels as draft animals, primarily for pulling carts. These carts are equipped with large used airplane tires and can traverse even roadless terrain. Because these camel carts do not require imported fuel, they are the preferred form of transport.

Traditional Values Among the Raikas.   Raikas believe that the Hindu god Lord Shiva created them from his own skin and sweat to care for camels. They follow a strict taboo against killing and eating camels. Fresh camel's milk is consumed, but in their belief system there is a prohibition against making yogurt and cheese from the milk. They also do not believe that milk should be sold.

Raikas

The Problem.   Grazing land is diminishing, and underfed female camels mature later, are less fertile, and often abort. Because the birth interval for well-fed, healthy camels is a calf every two years, a reduction in fertility is a serious issue. Camel herds that numbered 10,000 animals fifty years ago were down to 1,000 in 1995 (Kohler-Rollefson 1995).

Possible Solutions.   The slaughtering and selling of animals that are old or unproductive would be advantageous to the Raikas, and there is a market for camel meat. Other possible solutions include the selling of fresh camel's milk and the use of excess milk to make milk products that keep longer than fresh milk, such as cheese and yogurt.

Processes of Change.   Just when the future of the Raikas seemed most bleak, because of the many cultural barriers to change, word came of successful camel's milk sales among a caste closely related to the Raikas who lived in an adjacent territory. Twenty years earlier, these camel herders had begun to sell milk to tea stall owners (milk being considered an essential ingredient of tea in India). Camel's milk was found to keep longer and was cheaper than cow or buffalo milk. Sales had expanded over the years, and the supply was currently short of the demand. Raikas began to hear about the success of the other caste, and some Raika breeders began looking into changing their attitude about selling milk. The economic demand for camel's milk could save the Raika herds. Of course, underfed camels do not produce large quantities of milk, but the Raikas began seeking advice as they made this transition, and the Camel Husbandry Improvement Project has been formed to help them (Kohler-Rollefson 1995).

This case shows that cultures can and do adapt and change. In this case, diffusion played a big role. It helped the Raikas to see that traditional values could change to accommodate circumstances. Remember that George Foster recognized desire for economic gain as a stimulant to change. Although this may not always be enough of a reason, as in the case of the hybrid corn, change in traditional values and attitudes may occur when economic survival is at stake, as in the case of the Raikas. Additional perspectives on change have been gained in the years since Foster's analysis, and these are discussed in the following sections. Keep the basic issues that he identified in mind, however, because those issues impact how diffusion and acculturation occur.

◎ ANTHROPOLOGY AND GLOBALIZATION

Imperialism, colonialism, hegemony, and globalization are buzz terms among cultural anthropologists, and one or more of them appear in many current titles and articles in the *American Anthropologist*, *Anthropology News*, and *Current Anthropology*, as well as in papers in AAA publications and papers presented at national and international meetings. Looking back over the past two centuries, and particularly since the inception of anthropology as a discipline (1860s), we recognize that much of the change that has occurred in indigenous cultures (often called traditional or undeveloped, or Second or Third World cultures) was brought about due to actions on the part of First World nation-states in Europe and North America. Nation-states on these continents dominated territories and peoples economically, politically, socially, and culturally for extended periods of time as they exploited the natural resources of their territories. The term **imperialism** was used to describe influence and authority of one nation over another, often associated with the exploitation of natural and human resources. The proliferation of Coca-Cola, Shell Oil Corporation, Sony Corporation, and McDonald's around the globe is an example of economic and cultural imperialism. **Colonialism** describes influence and dominance of one nation over another for the purpose of exploiting raw resources. Additionally the dominant nation-state establishes a physical presence in a territory and places a colonial government there—for example, the European governments in many parts of the African continent. The terms are often used as synonyms. We recognize that imperialist and colonial contact with the West is responsible for a great deal of what is currently termed hegemony. In the analysis of contemporary cultural change, this term appears to be replacing the terms *imperialism* and *colonialism*. **Hegemony** may be defined as the ideological domination by one cultural group over another through institutions, bureaucracy, education, and sometimes force. The term's use ranges from the analysis of the activities of nation-states in international relations to the analysis of class structure within a culture. The term is enjoying new popularity today among writers and scholars, but it has a long history of use beginning with the ancient Greeks. An example of hegemony is China's dominance over much of East Asia for long periods. I hope that this serves to alert you to some of the vocabulary you will encounter. Writers often assume that the reader understands the meaning of such widely used terms. Unfortunately, authors themselves sometimes attach slightly different meanings to their usages, so watch for this in your readings.

Anthropologists have joined many other disciplines in studying the culture change resulting from hegemony that began with imperialism and colonialism. It continues today with what are termed globalization studies. Since the 1980s, anthropologists have been increasingly interested in the dynamics of **globalization** and its impact on world cultures. Other disciplines—economics, sociology, geography, political science, health, communications, and others—also study globalization.

What exactly is globalization? The term is defined in a number of ways, each with a slightly different nuance, depending on the discipline involved; the vast literature on globalization makes a concise definition difficult. The term as most commonly used in anthropological writings

imperialism
Influence and authority of one nation over another, often associated with exploitation of natural and human resources. See *colonialism; hegemony.*

colonialism
Influence and dominance of one nation over another for the purpose of exploiting raw resources. The dominant nation-state establishes a physical presence and a colonial government. See *imperialism; hegemony.*

hegemony
The ideological domination by one cultural group over another through institutions, bureaucracy, education, and sometimes force. See *imperialism; colonialism.*

globalization
In anthropology, the rapid spread of economic, social, and cultural systems across continents.

Evidence of globalization can be seen at a mall in Saudi Arabia.

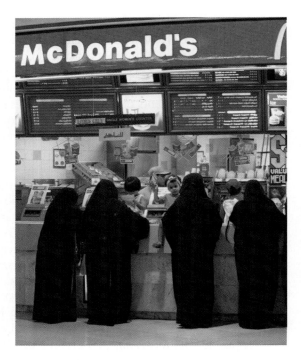

refers to the rapid spread of economic, social, and cultural systems across continents. Issues of both time and space are relevant in the study of globalization. Time refers to the speed with which change occurs, and space refers to the spread of change between cultures and across traditional geographical and political boundaries.

In anthropology, cultural processes and their effects on individuals are the focus of most of our studies of global change. Jonathan Xavier Inda and Renato Rosaldo note that anthropologists interpret various approaches to aspects of globalization through "the prism of the cultural" (Inda and Rosaldo 2002: 9). I like this analogy. A prism breaks light into its component parts, and anthropology sees globalization's effect on culture as having many facets—among them economic, political, and social—that are reflected at the same time. The following sections will offer a sample of several types of anthropological research on global change. See the Suggested Readings at the end of this chapter for more details on this subject.

Globalization, Tourism, and the Spread of Capitalism

Capitalism is rapidly diffusing to even the most isolated regions of the earth and is responsible for much acculturation—remember that Foster identified desire for economic gain as a strong stimulant of change. Most

Hula dancers in Kailua, Hawaii, perform for tourists and local residents on the arrival off the canoe Hokule'a at the island. The Hokule'a was patterned after ancient voyaging canoes used by the Hawaiians and Tahitians. It has completed numerous long-distance voyages throughout Polynesia using traditional celestial navigation.

such research on this phenomenon draws heavily from and focuses on economic theory, but we focus on the effects on individuals and their culture. The study of global tourism offers one focal point for such research.

Tourism is big business, unquestionably the largest global industry. The diffusion of a desire for possessions (materialism) has contributed to the development of the tourist trade. Indigenous peoples have discovered that wealthy people will pay to experience authentic "native" culture. So they produce it. It is part of the globalization of capitalism.

There are two main approaches to anthropological tourism research—academic and applied. Academic researchers, particularly in the beginning of tourism studies, focused on tourism's negative effects on traditional indigenous communities. The viewpoint that tourism has negative impact was brought to our attention in the 1970s. Tourist money creates a new hegemony that some term *neocolonialism* (Douglass and Lacy 2005). I think that the bottom line is that anthropologists saw tourists as seeking the glamour of contact with small indigenous cultures as a form of conspicuous consumption—the tourists gained status at home by talking about and showing pictures of their travels. Tourists (and tour companies) had little interest in or concern for indigenous cultures or their problems and were oblivious to the impact they made.

Applied researchers hold the view that both negative and positive outcomes to tourism are possible and that anthropologists "can contribute to neutralizing the negative aspects of tourism development projects without losing their wariness over the potential for harm that unrestrained tourism can cause, especially in smaller communities" (Wallace 2005: 10). Some argue that carefully conceived tourism projects may help to preserve aspects of indigenous culture. Applied anthropologists may work as advisors and consultants to the tourist industry, as well as researchers and even mediators. Of course ethical issues are of concern with applied work.

Ethical Dilemmas.   Tourism research, academic or applied, requires navigating various ethical dilemmas with local hosts. Kathleen M. Adams writes of numerous ethical issues that surfaced during her field research on tourism in Indonesia. In one case a host wanted to use her to help sell local tourist art. The host believed that Adams's presence would help attract potential buyers, which it did (Adams 2005: 46). This placed Adams in a quandary because she wanted to have rapport with all of the villagers, not just one family, and felt that her helping one vendor in this manner would make others angry. Yet, she also felt indebted to her host. She helped her host one time but then managed to steer her way out of this awkward situation.

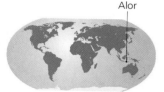

Alor

Adams also had the opportunity to observe tourists to Indonesia as a lecturer on a cruise ship. The ship made a stop in Alor, a location made famous by Cora Dubois in her ethnography *The People of Alor* (1944). Adams discovered that her anthropological presentation about the people of Alor as a contemporary cultural group with a complex, dynamic society was contradicted by the presentations given by the shipboard tour director. The tourism director presented the Alorese as a sensational, exotic, primitive culture. This approach was underscored when a dance troupe greeted the ship upon arrival at Alor. Barefoot dancers performed welcome, hunting, and headhunting dances. She later learned that the dancers were from different island ethnic groups that had been "schooled by a local tourism official who believed that the imagery of primitiveness was a surefire way to captivate tourists" (Adams 2005: 56). The shipboard tourists looked to Adams to authenticate or question the dances, which placed her in a complicated ethical predicament.

Ecotourism.   Amazon ecotourism was studied by Palma Ingles, who, as an addition to her research, joined various tour companies as a tour guide. This gave her a unique view of both tourist and indigenous villager. Ingles became curious about the authenticity of dances that were performed for tourists and wondered if the dancers found it demeaning to sell their culture in this way. She discovered that the villagers had a positive view of tourism. They used the tour visits to sell locally made crafts directly to the tourists, and they could keep some of their traditions alive by staging the dances. Additionally, the money from tourism helped to preserve the ecology of the region because it increased household income and reduced the ecologically damaging aspects of slash-and-burn agriculture (Ingles 2005:

222–23). The desire to join in capitalistic enterprises by indigenous peoples is echoed in the work of Adams on the island of Alor, where she found the villagers to be quite open in communicating their hopes that the publicity from Adams's anthropological writings would bring more tourists (Adams 2005: 54–55).

A strong desire for economic gain motivates people to change traditional ways of making a living, from tourism in the Amazon jungle or on an Indonesian island, to global locations where cheap labor entices business from countries like the United States to build factories. The Coca-Cola and Nike corporations, for example, have gained attention for their factories in Third World countries, and this wage-based employment is often desired by those who participate. Our outsider's ethnocentrism regarding the "poor" working conditions, "injustices," "exploitation" of women and children, and the disruption of traditional cultures often do not represent the economic position of those indigenous peoples who want to provide for their families. On the other hand, such situations can be viewed as examples of hegemony resulting from economic globalization.

Technology, Mass Communication, and Transportation

Each of these issues stimulates change. Studies in these areas analyze the rapid spread of materials, technology, and ideas around the globe, but they also tell us that values may not diffuse with the same rapidity. I offer a topically narrow example to illustrate. Eric Michaels studied the Warlpiri Aborigines and looked at the impact of Hollywood videotapes on this group of traditional aboriginal Australians. During his three years of fieldwork, Michaels documented that the Warlpiri quickly adopted various components of electronic media. Videotapes were introduced to the aboriginal camps in the 1980s and satellite television a bit later. Both have been readily integrated into aboriginal life. Four-wheel-drive vehicles and rifles are the only other rapidly accepted contemporary Western technologies.

Aborigines are enthusiastic about Hollywood videos but view them through their own cultural lens. Kinship relationships between characters in television programs, such as *The A-Team*, interest the Warlpiri, and they speculate about what the family relationships might be if the story doesn't have that information; they look for supernatural reasons to explain events such as an individual's death. Both kinship ties and supernatural explanations are important focal points within Warlpiri culture. When they create their own videotapes, their tales emphasize extended landscape shots, and the stories appeared to move very slowly to someone enculturated in a Western culture. But as Michaels states, "what are to the European observer semantically empty landscape pans are explained by Aboriginal producers and viewers as full of meaning. The camera in fact traces 'tracks' or locations where ancestors, spirits, or historical characters traveled" (Michaels 1994 in Inda and Rosaldo 2002: 320). In other words, to the Warlpiri the scenes are full of meaning when viewed through their own cultural lens.

Similar studies worldwide indicate that electronic media are readily embraced (as in the Warlpiri case), but the message or values represented may, in fact, not be part of an acculturation; the message may not be crossing cultural borders. The television show *Dallas*, widely televised outside of the United States, garnered various interpretations of the story line from international audiences. For example, when the *Dallas* character Sue Ellen left her husband (JR) and moved in with her lover, Israeli Arabs reported that she returned home to her father's house (Hannerz 1989: 45). Egypt banned the program because of its perception that the show gave a negative view of capitalism (Michaels 1990), and Dutch women interpreted the program using their feminist agenda (Hunter 2000: 3).

Films written and produced in the United States carry a particular worldview and value system. Films that are produced and disseminated by countries such as Taiwan, India, and Mexico carry other culture-specific values. From a global media viewpoint it could be said that these provide peoples with "alternatives that permit them to fashion modern forms of existing in the world without being weighed down by the ideological baggage of western cultural imperialism (Inda and Rosaldo 2002: 309)." Yet, none of the values presented in films of whichever culture of origin may be absorbed by the people who view them.

◎ URBAN SETTINGS AND CHANGE

The anthropological study of urban lifeways is an integral part of anthropology today, and many of these studies involve the identification of patterns of change and adaptation. Urban places have their own social institutions that set them apart from small-scale societies. One feature of cities is that they are heterogeneous places with many segments that are quite distinct from the features of homogeneous foraging or horticultural societies. Moreover, the cross-cultural comparative studies of such places have revealed that there are differences in cities. In other words, the notion that a city is a city is a city is simply not true. There are many different types of cities, and they can be classified by their segments, focus of activities, geography, and so forth. Anthropologist Richard Fox has distinguished such city types as administrative cities, industrial cities, colonial cities, mercantile cities, and city-states (Fox 1977).

Numerous approaches have been taken toward developing an understanding of urban settings, and each has asked different questions. One approach is referred to as urbanism studies. A holistic conceptualization is

OLC
mhhe•com/lenkeit3

See Internet exercises.

the focus of this approach. The city is viewed as an integral part of a larger society (often referred to as a folk-urban continuum), and its place and influence are investigated. A second approach is that of studies of urban poverty. Urban poverty studies focus on ghetto populations, the homeless, urban alcoholic nomads, and Native American urban populations, to name a few. A third approach, known as **urbanization studies,** looks at the adaptations made by rural peoples as they move to cities. Much anthropological work in urbanization has centered on Latin America and Africa.

An example of the information that has come from urbanization studies is the change it has brought to what we know about family and kin in urban settings. Before fieldwork-based urbanization studies were undertaken, the literature focused on the breakdown in social relations within extended families when a move was made to an urban center. It was thought that the transplanted rural family became a self-contained urban nuclear family, a family that was isolated from other kin. The importance of reciprocal economic, social, and emotional relationships were said to diminish. In the past, this was the prevailing thought on the subject. Ethnographic data from more recent urbanization studies do not support this view. Susan Emley Keefe's work among urban Mexican Americans and Anglo-Americans in southern California demonstrates this finding. Keefe found that these two groups differed only in the *proximity* of kin. For Mexican Americans, kin were found to be geographically local, whereas for Anglo Americans, kin were more dispersed. In both groups, extended family continue to be important to them as they live, work, and adapt to the urban environment (Keefe 1996).

A combination of these approaches is obviously useful. And, of course, many other social scientists, such as sociologists and social psychologists, study urban populations. These researchers use data-gathering methodologies that focus on the use of surveys and standardized interview schedules and statistical analyses. These methodologies have been honed by sociologists and are useful for the study of large populations. After all, thousands of people live in urban settings, and the participant-observation approach favored by anthropologists when studying small-scale societies,

---

TRY THIS   *Hypothesize*

Ask six acquaintances how many times per week they communicate with kin who are outside of their nuclear family. You might want to distinguish between each form of communication—face-to-face, telephone, e-mail, text message, and letters. Do you live in a city? Based on your small sample, develop a hypothesis about the importance of extended kin relationships in your city. How would you go about gathering data to test your hypothesis?

urbanization studies
Studies of the adaptations made by rural peoples as they move to cities.

ANTHROPOLOGY AROUND US

Mother's Milk

Data from both biological and cultural anthropology present us with information about breast-feeding. The contributions from primatologists, medical anthropologists, nutritional anthropologists, ethnographers, and ethnologists combine to support the view that mother's milk is best for infants and that family, friends, doctors, employers, business, and government should be joining in an all-out effort to support nursing mothers.

The biological facts are clear—breast milk is for most babies the ideal source of nutrition. Besides being food, breast milk is also, as reported by the University of Pennsylvania Health System (Hoke 1997), a bioactive compound containing important antibodies, hormones, and growth factors that defend against infection and aid the infant's immune system to fully develop. Numerous studies of thousands of infants show significantly less infant mortality among breast-fed infants. Also, children who were breast-fed had significantly fewer middle ear infections (otitis media). The protection offered by breast-feeding continues as long as the child is breast-fed.

Ethnographic data tell us that across cultures, prior to the widespread use of infant formulas, children were nursed two to four years. Katherine Dettwyler has compared data on nonhuman primate growth, age at weaning, and other life history variables and concludes, "If humans weaned their offspring according to the primate pattern, without regard to beliefs and customs, most children would be weaned somewhere between 2.5 and 7 years of age" (Dettwyler 1995: 66).

By the year 2010, the surgeon general of the United States has a projected goal to have 75 percent of American women breast-feeding at the time of hospital discharge after giving birth, with 50 percent of them still breast-feeding at six months (U.S. Department of Health and Human Services 2000: 16–19). According to La Leche League, in 1998 just 62 percent of new mothers tried breast-feeding and only 26 percent of them were still

breast-feeding at six months. Breast-feeding issues are not confined to the United States. In Hong Kong, for example, a Department of Health survey found 30 percent of women who begin nursing stop because of work (Hong Kong Department of Health 2002).

With all of the data to support the positive value of breast-feeding, why don't more American mothers breast-feed and why don't they do it for more than a few months? In the United States today the cultural context of breast-feeding includes the focus on female breasts as sexual objects (a view found to be amusing and perplexing from the perspective of many other cultures) and the attitude that breast-feeding should be limited to very young infants and should not occur in public.

◎ **What other cultural views do Americans hold toward breast-feeding? Which of Foster's cultural barriers to change can you identify with respect to having more American women breast-feed and do it longer? How might these barriers be overcome?**

such as foragers and horticulturalists, has its limitations. Still, ethnographic interview techniques in which long-term contact takes place between an informant and the anthropologist provide texture and dimension to urban studies that simply are not present in a statistical survey approach. Each urban studies methodology complements the whole.

SUMMARY

Diffusion and acculturation are responsible for most culture change. Anthropologists use a number of approaches to study culture change, including scrutiny of the archaeological record, analysis of historical records, life histories, ethnographic restudies, and impact studies. Theories about how cultures develop and change began with the schools of unilineal evolutionism, diffusionism, and historicalism. Comparative studies of change programs after World War II led to the work of George Foster and his analysis of cultural barriers to change, such as traditional values and attitudes. Hegemony, the ideological domination by one cultural group over another, and the dynamics of globalization are current focal points for the anthropological study of change in world cultures. Finally, anthropology contributes to the study of change and adaptation in urban studies.

Study Questions

1. What are the major barriers to change, as delineated by Foster?

2. Present an argument to support the thesis that cultural barriers to change are the most important barriers because they are the least obvious and the most difficult to overcome. Support your argument with specific examples from the case studies presented here and in other course assignments.

3. What methods have been used to study culture change? Critique each method.

4. Discuss the focus of globalization studies in anthropology and cite a specific example from the study of tourism or mass media to illustrate.

5. What have urbanization studies revealed about the nature of kin relationships for Mexican American and Anglo American families living in the Los Angeles area?

OLC
mhhe•com/lenkeit3

See Self Quiz.

Suggested Readings

Bodley, John H. 1999. *Victims of Progress*, 4th ed. Mountain View, Calif.: Mayfield. Looks at the impact of Western institutions and industrialization on small-scale societies.

Gmelch, George, and Walter P. Zenner. 2001. *Urban Life*. 4th ed. Prospect Heights, Ill.: Waveland Press. This collection of readings in urban anthropology presents interesting and timely examples of cultural adaptations and change within urban settings.

Holtzman, Jon D. 2000. *Nuer Journeys: Nuer Lives*. Boston: Allyn and Bacon. Chronicles the changes in traditional Nuer society as refugees adapt to life in Minnesota.

Hutchinson, Sharon E. *Nuer Dilemmas*. 1996. Berkeley: University of California Press. Detailed ethnographic account of how the Nuer have coped with the political and social dilemmas resulting from war in Sudan.

Kottak, C. P. 2006. *Assault on Paradise: Social Change in a Brazilian Village*, 4th ed. New York: McGraw-Hill. Traces the changes that have occurred over two decades of the author's work in the village of Arembepe, Bahia, Brazil. A readable, personal account that connects the events in Arembepe to larger, global issues of culture change through the 1990s.

Stuart-Macadam, Patricia, and Katherine Dettwyler, eds. 1995. *Breastfeeding: Biocultural Perspectives*. New York: Aldine DeGruyter. A data-packed book of contributions that demonstrate how a holistic perspective can illuminate a topic. Chapter 2, by Katherine Dettwyler ("A Time to Wean: The Hominid Blueprint for the Natural Age of Weaning in Modern Human Populations"), is particularly insightful for information to support culture change issues about breast-feeding.

Suggested Web Sites

OLC
mhhe•com/lenkeit3
See Web links.

http://www.cwis.org/wwwvl/indig-vl.html
Organized and maintained by the Center for World Indigenous Studies (Olympia, Washington), this site contains over two hundred links, organized by geographic region, devoted to ethnic advocacy groups and nongovernmental organizations addressing specific social, political, and economic concerns. There are additional links to nearly fifty Web virtual library sites.

http://www.culturalsurvival.org/newpage/index.cfm
This excellent site supports and gives voice to the world's indigenous peoples.

http://www.undp.org
This United Nations site contains information pertaining to sustainable human development. It offers a collection of information with a focus on knowledge, experience, and resources available.

http://www.usaid.gov
This site, for the U.S. Agency for International Development, contains information relevant to anthropology and development projects. It describes the economic aid and humanitarian assistance available that furthers the foreign policy goals of the United States.

14

Applying Anthropology
How Does It Make a Difference?

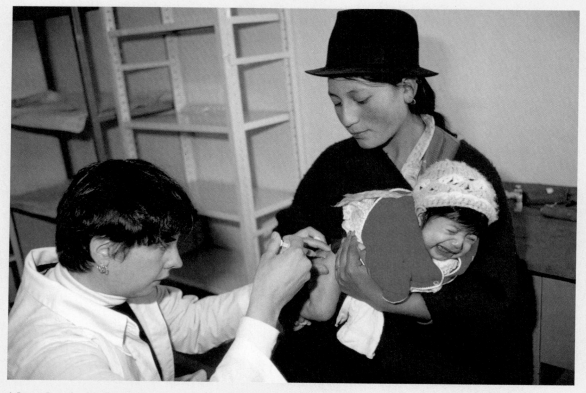

A Peace Corps health clinic in Ecuador provides immunizations. Medical anthropologists consult and work with health care professionals to provide culturally sensitive care in a variety of settings.

" I wish I had taken this class before I began working at the hospital," said the student sitting across from me. He had stopped by to ask about an assignment, and he suddenly blurted out the preceding statement. Further conversation revealed that he worked as a hospital orderly. He told of his frustration (plus the frustration of the nursing staff) over an elderly non-English-speaking Chinese patient. Numerous relatives were in the patient's room around the clock and refused to leave, plus many visitors each day brought food and gifts. This made it difficult for the staff to do their jobs. Additionally, several nurses felt that family members watched them as if they might do something harmful to the patient. The relatives brought food prepared at home for the patient, and they insisted on administering his oral medications. They also bathed him. The student related that a number of heated verbal exchanges had occurred between staff and family. He described how the staff talked in negative terms about *those* people interfering with the care of the patient.

The student did some independent research and discovered that the view about health care and the role of family in health care is quite different in traditional Asian cultures than it is in traditional Anglo-American culture. Among the peoples of China, Japan, Vietnam, Laos, Korea, and their many subcultures, it is typically considered a family responsibility to care for relatives, particularly in meeting their personal needs. Medical professionals are expected to provide medical care only. Armed with this information the student shared with other staff members what he had learned. He said that several staff members indicated that they had never thought of such situations from a cultural perspective. The student further said that he hoped the hospital would offer more cultural awareness in-service classes and that he had made this suggestion to his supervisor.

I often tell students to consider that they are in an alien microculture when they or a relative are hospitalized. In a hospital setting, culture shock can set in quickly for the patient and the patient's family, and cultural ethnocentrism easily develops. After all, the hospital's natives (the staff) understand the culture, its language, and traditional behaviors, and they are comfortable in this environment. The visitors (patient and family), by contrast, are not natives. Combined with worry and stress over the patient's condition, this situation adds to the difficulties they experience.

To view the world through the anthropological lens is to have awareness of our human commonalities *and* our differences. This approach helps us to be flexible in our interpersonal relationships, whether they are encountered in the workplace, at play, in our neighborhoods, or when visiting other cultural environments near or far. This chapter focuses on how professional anthropologists use anthropology outside of academia. It is my hope that you will consider how and where *you* can apply anthropology to your everyday life, just as this student did in his hospital job.

The objectives of this chapter are to

- Explain the application of anthropological methods and perspectives outside of academia
- Describe how the anthropological approach is used in business
- Describe the applications of anthropology in health care
- Describe how anthropological knowledge is used to develop social programs

◎ WHAT IS APPLIED ANTHROPOLOGY?

OLC
mhhe•com/lenkeit3
See chapter outline and
chapter overview.

The perspectives and methodologies of anthropology are used and should be used at many levels. I have placed this chapter at the end of the text not because applied anthropology is an afterthought but rather because I see it as the culmination of acquiring the basic tools of anthropology. **Applied anthropology** is the use of the various perspectives, methods, theories, and data of anthropology to identify, evaluate, and offer solutions to human problems. Anthropologists who work outside of academia and focus on the application of anthropology make up a growing percentage of anthropologists, and their expertise is increasingly in demand. A recent article in *USA Today*, for example, was titled "Hot Asset: Anthropology Degree" (Jones 1999) and chronicled the popularity of applied anthropology in corporate America. The Society for Applied Anthropology and the National Association for the Practice of Anthropology (NAPA) are the professional organizations to which applied anthropologists belong. These organizations support members by providing forums for information sharing, which aids members in honing their skills and marketing their services.

OLC
mhhe•com/lenkeit3
See Internet exercise.

What do applied anthropologists do? They help businesses and corporations solve problems, from management issues to customer complaints. They help develop programs in public health and nutrition and family planning. They tackle problems in agricultural development. They work in programs of natural resources management. They work in education and in government at all levels—local, state, and federal. Practicing anthropologists often do not refer to themselves as anthropologists; rather, they call themselves consultants, usually because most people do not understand the scope of what anthropology is all about—most people think of anthropologists as those people who dig up pottery and fossils and work at a university or a museum. This popular idea of what anthropologists do is likely due to all the media attention given to biological anthropologists, who hunt fossils, and anthropological archaeologists, who uncover cultural evidence of the human past. Consulting anthropologists may be part of an academic community, or they may work entirely as part of the business community.

◎ USEFUL CONCEPTS IN APPLIED ANTHROPOLOGY

applied anthropology
The branch of anthropology that focuses on the application of anthropological methods and approaches to the solution of problems, as distinct from academic anthropology.

Several central concepts introduced in this text—Culture with a capital *C* and culture with a lowercase *c*, cultural relativism, and cultural ethnocentrism—are at the core of applied anthropology. Ethnographic field methods, including a focus on participant observation, are applied as means of understanding issues. A holistic perspective is maintained and the com-

The study of corporate culture by applied anthropologists would include attending meetings such as this Nike Corporation ethnic diversity meeting.

parative method is used whenever possible. And applied anthropologists, like academic anthropologists, use the scientific method as they work to solve problems. Three areas of applied anthropology are profiled in the following pages: anthropology in business, anthropology in health care, and anthropology in economic development projects.

Specialized upper-level courses that examine the applications of anthropology are available at most universities, and I encourage you to consider those courses that contain material relevant to your future career. You do not have to have a degree in anthropology to use its perspectives and basic methods any more than you must be a computer science major to use computers. Basic knowledge allows you to use the tools. It is also important that you know enough to hire an expert (in this case a consulting firm with anthropologists on staff) when problems warrant input from a specialist.

◎ ANTHROPOLOGY IN BUSINESS

The world of business has borrowed and embraced the idea of culture. Business management books now use phrases like *corporate culture*, *organizational culture*, *Japanese culture*, and *German culture*. Yet definitions of culture that are found in business management texts are often incomplete from the anthropologist's perspective (Harris and Moran 1996: 125; Morey and Morey 1994: 17). Most such definitions center on ideas such as those found in the group A definitions of Chapter 2, namely lists of what constitutes culture, with a strong emphasis on traditional behaviors such as handshakes, bows, eye contact, attitudes toward time, appropriate dress, and so forth. In other words, manners and customs are the focus. Such behaviors, as you know, are a part of culture, but as you also know, the concept involves much more. An additional conceptual area associated with the term *culture* that businesspeople often fail to recognize is in the distinction between *Culture* (capital *C*, abstract culture or culture in general) and *culture* (lowercase *c*, a specific culture). When businesspeople use the term *corporate culture* (culture with a capital *C*, from the anthropologist's view), they typically discuss its features as if it were culture with a lowercase *c*, in other words, a specific culture or subculture (Jordon 1994b: 11). When the anthropological consultant helps to sort out these distinctions, those involved gain a better understanding of the problem's sources. This in turn leads to solutions.

Numerous aspects of business are studied in the process of problem solving, from management levels to support staff. When anthropologists study business organizations, we say that we are studying organizational culture. We look at an organization as if it were a culture, and the goal is to understand behavior within the organization. As with the study of any culture or subculture, an organizational culture is viewed holistically as an integrated unit. Applied anthropologists look for patterns of behavior in the organization, just as fieldworkers do when conducting research in New Guinea or in an urban neighborhood.

An important tool used in business consulting is ethnography. Ethnographic methods, including participant observation, result in types of *qualitative* information and data that cannot be gathered in other ways (review Chapter 3 for a refresher on ethnographic methods). At the onset of any such study, the consulting anthropologist advises the client that she or he must adhere to the anthropological code of ethics developed by the American Anthropological Association and the anthropologists' *Ethical Guidelines for Practitioners* that was developed by NAPA in 1988. The latter contains guidelines for clarifying issues such as responsibilities to the client as well as the research subjects (these may be the client too) and the protection of the rights of everyone who may be affected by the work. The anonymity of research subjects is assured. Rigid adherence to the protection of anonymity in gathering information through participant observation can result in much useful and important data about the culture of the organization.

Some have challenged whether an organization such as a corporation should be called a culture, because one does not acquire this culture from childhood through the enculturation process. Although this is technically correct, if one carefully considers the issue, many parallels to enculturation can be seen.

✸ TRY THIS ✸
Analyze

Make a quick list of ways that learning about a job you have held is like being enculturated into your ethnic subculture. How did you learn to do the tasks required and to get along with coworkers and bosses? Compare and discuss your list with that of a classmate.

TRY THIS *Surf the Web*

Go to
http://www.practicinganthropology.org/about/?section=ethical_guidelines
and carefully read the National Association for the Practice of Anthropology's
Ethical Guidelines for Practitioners.

A Case Study of Anthropology in Business

This case study illustrates the usefulness of the anthropological perspective and is one of my favorites. I like it because the manager herself used anthropological tools to help solve a problem. David McCurdy (2000) reported on this case of applying anthropology, and I direct you to his excellent article for more details.

This situation occurred at a large multinational corporation that is diversified into manufacturing, research, and customer services, with customers in public, private, and government sectors. An educational division offers courses and programs to businesses and individuals who want special training or information—for example, special computer training for employees. One department within the education division produces learning materials such as books, pamphlets, and audiovisual materials that are used in the various courses and programs. Materials are shipped from a storage warehouse to customer outlets around the country. Difficulties with the shipment of course materials was the focus of the problem (McCurdy 2000).

A new manager was asked to take over the division responsible for the shipment of course materials. This manager had started as an employee and had just advanced to management. Her new assignment came with a provision. She was told to solve a problem with the warehouse inventory and improve customer service. The specifics of the problem were vague, but she soon discovered that there was a serious problem. Computer inventories often did not match actual numbers of books and pamphlets in the warehouse. Customers received more or fewer books than they ordered and were disgruntled, especially when the company computer indicated that the correct number had been shipped.

Other managers in the company believed that the problem in the warehouse resulted from workers' poor attitudes. They even referred to the warehouse workers as being without a good work ethic, described them in disparaging terms, and said that they were not loyal to the company. They suggested to the new manager that she couldn't do anything with these workers and that she would be lucky just to contain the problem and keep it from getting worse. Others told her that the customers were the main problem because they were a bunch of complainers.

	TRY THIS *Consider*	

Suppose you are the new manager in this case and have been assigned to solve the problem in the warehouse. What steps would you take based on your anthropological background? Review ethnographic field methods (Chapter 3) and outline your approach. Compare yours with the actual approach outlined below.

Traditional management techniques are often fueled by an *us versus them* attitude. New managers set up new procedures and work rules and rarely ask workers for their opinions, because the managers believe that to do so would show weakness and lack of control in leadership. Problem situations are often dealt with by offering retraining classes, developing employee work quota competitions (with rewards), or providing motivational pay incentives. Such solutions do not address the basic causes of problems, so they often fail in the long run. In this case, the new manager did not take the role of a traditional manager; rather, she utilized the perspective and approaches of anthropology and sought creative solutions.

The new manager was not a professional anthropologist, but she knew some ethnographic field techniques, including how to conduct field interviews (informal and formal) and how to observe and analyze behavior. She spent six weeks discovering what workers did in the warehouse. She observed and talked at length to employees, customers, and salespeople. She asked for advice on how to solve the problems. She listened. As she remarked, "And people were excited because I was asking and listening and, by God, intending to do something about it instead of just disappearing again" (McCurdy 2000: 393).

A number of specific problems were discovered: Orders took too long to get to the warehouse, quantities of materials shipped were often incorrect, customers were unhappy because they were billed for what they ordered regardless of what they received, and books arrived in poor condition with gouges and frayed edges.

The on-site ethnographic techniques used in the warehouse revealed the causes of the problems. Workers filled orders by going to the warehouse shelves, handpicking books, and placing them in boxes. Because counting large orders took time, the employees disclosed that they usually picked up what looked to be a stack of about the right number based on their experience. These estimates were, it turned out, usually incorrect. Yet they would then go to the computer and enter the number sent as the number ordered, which created errors in billing as well as errors in the computer inventory database. It was also revealed that shipments were often delivered to the ground floor lobbies of multistory buildings. Staff would open the boxes in the lobby and carry armloads of the books and pamphlets in the elevator up to the office. Observations revealed that people entering the building would help themselves to a copy of the book or pamphlet while the open shipping box was left unattended in the lobby.

When the manager was searching for a solution to her warehouse problem, shrink-wrapping was a new packaging process. She decided that the few cents more that it would cost to have the books shrink-wrapped into packages of five and ten books before they arrived at the warehouse was a good investment. Most customers ordered books in units of five and ten, so counting was more accurate as orders were filled. Further, she kept shipment boxes to a maximum of twenty-five pounds (previous packing boxes accommodated one hundred pounds), and she had these packages marked for *inside delivery* so that boxes would be delivered directly to the customers' offices upstairs.

Customers were happy with the results of these changes. Books arrived in good shape and in correct numbers. Warehouse employees were more efficient in filling orders, and because they could work more quickly to count out orders, they were able to spend more time making accurate computer entries. Morale improved in the warehouse as employees took pride in the service they provided. Customers responded positively and let people at the corporate headquarters know how they felt. Managers with previously negative attitudes about the warehouse workers were now asking questions about what was happening and joking about the warehouse workers taking vitamins. The new manager attributed her success in problem solving to the use of ethnographic methods.

◎ ANTHROPOLOGY IN HEALTH CARE

Medical anthropology focuses on the application of anthropological methods and perspectives to issues of health and illness. It seeks solutions to problems in areas such as maternal and child health, nutrition, public health, folk or ethnomedicine, epidemiology, and health care provider services. Medical anthropologists have backgrounds and degrees in both biological and cultural anthropology. They use a holistic perspective and eclectic and multidisciplinary approaches. They often play a number of roles—ethnographic researcher, consultant, and program developer. These professionals are employed full time at medical centers and clinics, or they work on a contract basis for consulting firms. Numerous aspects of the usefulness of anthropology in health care are demonstrated in the following case study of lead poisoning from folk remedies in Mexican American communities.

medical anthropology
The study of illness and health care from the perspective of anthropology.

ANTHROPOLOGY AROUND US

Folk Illness and Medical Anthropology

Folk medicine refers to the perceptions of ordinary people about health, illness, treatment, and cures. Stereotypes about folk medicine are that only poor and uneducated people use it. In fact, most people grow up learning ideas about sickness and health and use the remedies taught them by family members. We treat what we define as minor illness at home.

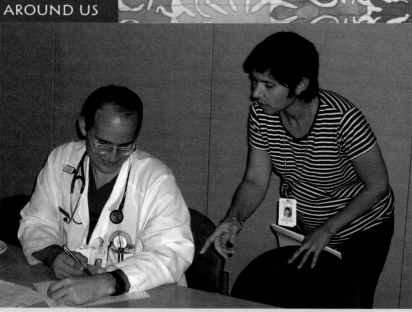

The work of medical anthropologists such as Elisa J. Sobo (shown above right) has revealed the complexity of issues related to illness and health, including folk medicine. The use of multidisciplinary approaches and participant observation gives unique perspectives. Numerous studies of folk medicine among Hispanic populations in the United States, Latin America, and Mexico underscore this complexity.

A common folk illness found among Hispanics is *susto* (fright, magical fright, or fright sickness, where the soul is believed lost from the body). It

---

TRY THIS *Analyze*

Suppose you are a head nurse in a large urban hospital where a situation is causing problems for your nursing staff. You have obtained a sizable grant that will allow you time away from your normal hospital duties to study this issue. Consider the data presented below and outline how you might approach this problem using anthropological perspectives and methods.

The situation: Rom Gypsies (an ethnic minority numbering several hundred thousand people in the United States) have a reputation of being difficult hospital patients. Their behavior when hospitalized causes conflict and disruption for hospital staff. They are uncooperative patients, and the presence of a crowd of family and friends in the patients' rooms has led to unpleasant confrontations with nurses. Outline how you would proceed to investigate this issue. Be as specific as possible.

develops when a person has had a sudden shock — for example, a close relative's death, an accident, an intense argument, or watching a child nearly drown. Symptoms of *susto* include nervousness, daytime sleepiness, nighttime insomnia, depression, and diarrhea. Diagnosis includes the finding of a cluster of the above symptoms and the noting of a recent traumatic event in the person's life. Severe cases (often called *espanto*) are potentially fatal, and studies have shown higher death rates among long-term sufferers (cause of death is commonly attributed to diabetes mellitus, liver disease, or cancer). Folk healers treat *susto* with "sweeping" ceremonies, in which various herbs are passed over the body and the frightened soul is coaxed to return. Repeated ceremonies are required. Because such ceremonies are often effective in relieving symptoms, *susto* has been labeled a culture-bound psychological illness.

Medical anthropologist Arthur Rubel together with Carl O'Nell and Rolando Collado-Ardon designed a controlled multidisciplinary study to investigate *susto*. Three culturally distinct and historically independent communities in Mexico were subjects of the study. The project involved the use of participant observation, interviews, and questionnaires designed to test a series of hypotheses. Lifestyle, social stress, and levels of psychiatric impairment were variables under consideration as causes of *susto*. A sample of matched pairs of fifty individuals, one group with *susto* and the other consisting of individuals who did not have *susto*, were scrutinized, including medical examinations (Anderson 1996: 117).

The primary hypothesis was that *susto* is a unique culture-bound syndrome caused by social stress. The survey provided only weak evidence that this hypothesis was correct. The medical examinations showed people with *susto* actually had a measurably greater number of biological diseases than the control group. Both culture (social stresses) *and* biology (actual disease states) were responsible for the symptoms of *susto*. This project underscored the usefulness of medical anthropology to aid understanding of folk illness.

◎ What folk remedies did you learn from your family? Are there folk illnesses and remedies of others in your community about which you react ethnocentrically?

A Case Study of Anthropology in Health Care

This case illustrates how the consultant works as part of a team to investigate health issues and develop culturally sensitive solutions to problems. An investigation into an alternative cause of lead poisoning in children was launched as a result of a case in Los Angeles, California, that involved a child whose stomach was pumped in a hospital emergency room. A bright orange powder was found in the stomach contents, and a laboratory analysis established that the powder had an elemental lead content of over 90 percent. Health professionals interviewed the child's mother and were able to determine that she had given the child a folk remedy called *azarcon*. This remedy was used to treat a folk illness called *empacho* — a combination of constipation and indigestion. A public health alert was sent out based on this case. The health alert resulted in a nurse uncovering another case of *azarcon*-caused lead poisoning in Greeley, Colorado. Alerted by the Los Angeles case, the nurse asked the parents if they were treating the child for *empacho* given that they claimed the child had not had access to lead-based paint. The remedy that the Colorado mother had given her child also turned out to be *azarcon* (Trotter 1987).

Lead poisoning most commonly affects children, and media messages often draw attention to the major causes of lead poisoning: lead-based paint chips eaten by babies and small children, and eating off of pottery decorated with improperly treated lead-based glazes. In these cases the usual sources of lead poisoning could not be established. The folk remedy called *azarcon* was a dangerous new source of lead poisoning, and health officials were concerned, especially when some initial research uncovered widespread knowledge of the remedy.

Robert Trotter, an anthropologist who had done research on Mexican American folk medicine, was brought in as a consultant on this case. He had not heard of *azarcon* in his previous research. Trotter's investigation began with research on *azarcon* in four Texas towns with large Mexican American populations. He searched herb shops (*yerberias*) and talked with folk healers (*curanderos*) but did not locate anyone who knew of *azarcon*. Meanwhile, the Los Angeles County Health Department discovered alternative names for the remedy. After receiving this information, Trotter returned to the towns and looked for *azarcon* under other names, such as *greta*. This remedy, which had the same amount of elemental lead content as *azarcon*, was sold in the herb shops as a remedy for *empacho*. Further investigation uncovered a wholesale distributor in Texas that was supplying more than 120 herb shops with *greta*. Most of the people buying and selling *greta* and *azarcon* believed them to be herbal compounds, probably because herbal remedies are common home remedies for Mexican Americans (Trotter 1987: 158).

Based on this initial research, Trotter began working on a health education project that ultimately served six clients, including the U.S. Food and Drug Administration and the regional office of the U.S. Department of Health and Human Services in Texas. Each of his clients wanted specific types of information about the use of *azarcon* and *greta*, or they contracted for Trotter to develop culturally sensitive materials on health awareness that would reduce the use of these remedies without attacking the local systems of folk medicine.

Open-ended questions used in survey instruments plus formal and informal interviews were used to gather data and information for the various clients. For example, a short ethnography was produced on herb shops where *greta* was sold, and it focused on how *greta* was used, what it was used to treat, and the dosages prescribed. Another of Trotter's strategies involved a survey administered to people along the border between the

Folk herbalist shops like this one in Hong Kong, China, are sources for traditional herbal medicine in many parts of the world.

United States and Mexico. This survey focused on what was known about *greta* and *azarcon* and who used these remedies. A comparative survey to determine the different levels of *greta* and *azarcon* use between the clinic population and the local population was developed for another client. Each of these approaches alerted the health care providers to the need for health education for their clients.

Trotter was asked to help develop health education programs that focused on sources of lead poisoning. Media exposure included Spanish radio stations that broadcasted public service announcements. Information packets about the hazards of *greta* and *azarcon* were sent to clinics that served immigrants. And a poster designed by Mexican American art students was placed in over 5,000 clinics and other public places in states with concentrations of Mexican Americans (other Hispanic populations were not targeted because research revealed that *greta* and *azarcon* were not part of their folk remedies). Although no follow-up scientific research was carried out, two years after the education project the two dangerous compounds were hard to find (Trotter 1987: 154).

This case demonstrates the usefulness of anthropological research methods and knowledge in solving health care problems that are culturally related. Subsequent work showed that remedies similar to *greta* and *azarcon* were causing lead poisoning in Hmong, Saudi Arabian, and Chinese communities.

Reforestation in Haiti.

◎ ANTHROPOLOGY IN ECONOMIC DEVELOPMENT

The United States has a long history of providing both financing and technical expertise in programs of economic development around the world. With the recognition that the anthropological approach enables the anticipation and avoidance of common barriers to culture change (as discussed in Chapter 13), anthropological consulting in economic development programs is on the increase.

A Case Study of Reforestation in Haiti

Haiti

The U.S. Agency for International Development (AID) funded a reforestation program in Haiti, which was administered by the Haiti Ministry of Agriculture. Problems with this program led to the involvement of anthropologist Gerald Murray, who was asked to assess the program. His report resulted in his being asked to head a program of reforestation that would also provide economic benefits to farmers. The following is a brief summary of Murray's consultant work (Murray 1987).

Haiti had a serious deforestation problem that occurred as a result of critical levels of population growth and a history of colonial exploitation. Colonial Spaniards and French exported trees and cleared land to grow sugar and coffee. More recently, hardwoods were cut and exported by foreign lumber companies. It should be noted from a holistic perspective that archaeologists from the University of Florida demonstrated that deforestation and regrowth cycles had been part of Haiti's history long before the first Europeans came to the island. And for a time, after population devastation by European diseases, there was actually a period of regrowth of forests. From the colonial period onward, however, the forests were devastated. Though periods of political upheaval made the task difficult, AID funded a program for reforestation in Haiti that was intended as an economic development program whereby peasants could supplement their income by growing and harvesting trees on their lands.

The project was not successful. In the capital city of Port-au-Prince, for example, numerous jobs were created in conjunction with the project, but this did not result in an increase in the production of seedlings. The seedlings that were produced often never reached peasant landholdings. Peasants perceived that the state owned and would profit from the tree planting project. They purposely let their goats and other livestock forage on newly planted trees, resulting in the death of most of the trees.

Evidence of the failure of the project and the political misdirection of funds caught the attention of a U.S. congressman, who exposed the graft and mismanagement of the AID reforestation project. In the process he became interested in the problems of overpopulation and deforestation in Haiti and threatened a worldwide freeze on AID funding if results were not soon forthcoming in Haiti.

Murray had conducted his doctoral research in Haiti. His focus was on how internal population growth had affected peasant land tenure over time. Because of his knowledge of Haitian land tenure and culture, Murray was able to look at the problem of why peasants were not embracing the reforestation project from an anthropological perspective. He was asked to evaluate current and previous programs, and in his report he noted that the existing system of land tenure, crop production, and livestock were compatible with the undertaking of reforestation efforts. At the time this was the opposite of views held by others. Murray's report included a section in which he speculated on how an anthropologist would organize and administer a reforestation project. He even jokingly told people involved with the AID program that he could administer a successful program with fifty thousand dollars and a jeep. Moreover, he claimed that peasants working in conjunction with his program would plant more trees than were being planted under the multimillion dollar program currently run by the Ministry of Agriculture (Murray 1987).

Murray was working in academia two years later when he was notified that a $4 million project for reforestation had been approved. The project was presented as he had outlined it in his earlier report. Murray was offered the job of administering the project, and he accepted the challenge. The technical issues and solutions associated with Murray's program (known as the Agroforestry Outreach Project, or AOP) were as follows:

First, Murray needed to identify fast-growing drought-resistant trees that produced wood suitable for construction and that produced good charcoal (a market existed for both products). Suitable tree species were found, and several had the added benefit of restoring nutrients to the soil. Some, such as *Eucalyptus camaldulensis*, would produce new growth from stumps, thus allowing multiple harvests from a single planting. The trees chosen would produce four-year harvest rotation times in optimal humid lowland environments. Slower rotation times occurred in less optimal arid areas.

Next, the program had to produce microseedlings that were lightweight and could be produced in quantity and transported easily. The previously used seedlings were bulky and heavy. For example, only 250 traditional seedlings could be transported in an AOP project truck, whereas 15,000 of the new lighter microseedlings could be carried in the same truck. Clearly, a peasant planter could carry more seedlings as he planted. Microseedlings also required less soil preparation for planting.

Murray needed to develop ethnographic information on cropping patterns and solicit input from the peasants themselves. This helped to develop strategies in which planting trees, even on small holdings, was feasible. Trees were planted on perimeters and intercropped in ways that did not reduce the land occupied by other crops.

Meeting several potential barriers to the project head on (you might review the various barriers to culture change that were delineated in Chapter 13) was critical to project success. One barrier was the perception by peasants that trees took a long time to grow. This delay in receiving benefit from the plantings made the project undesirable to them. Fortunately, there were four-year-old stands of several of the project tree species already in Haiti. Taking groups of peasants to see what four-year-old stands of the trees looked like changed their perceptions.

Another barrier was the perception that too much space would be taken up by the trees. Farmers believed that growing trees would prevent them from growing other cash crops. By creating a demonstration plot that showed the space needs of seedlings, farmers learned that they could plant other cash crops between the rows of tree seedlings for several years before the trees created too much shade.

AOP technicians also had to overcome the perception that somehow the project or the government would actually own the trees. Murray clearly communicated and presented the project in the form of a contract agreement. The project would furnish the trees. Each planter had to agree to plant five hundred seedlings and to allow AOP workers to make periodic survival counts on the trees. The AOP would not pay any wages for the work of planting, but they guaranteed that the planter owned the trees. No permissions would be needed to cut trees; there would not be penalties if trees died.

TRY THIS   *Analyze*

Choose a problem at a place where you work or have worked. Think about things **you** complain about or listen to the complaints of coworkers to get ideas for a problem focus. Then list three specific ways that you could use the tools of anthropology to search for a solution to the problem.

Finally, Murray's team actually calculated with peasants the income that they would derive from the sale of wood and charcoal. These profit figures clearly offset any loss from decreased production of other crops.

The AOP tree planting project was a huge success. By the time the four-year funded project ended, close to 20 million trees had been planted. By the end of the fourth year, trees were being harvested and money was being made (Murray 1987).

Murray's application of anthropological methods and theories when he conceived of and administered this program was at the core of its success. This project exemplifies the many successful projects that have drawn upon the expertise of anthropological consultants.

⊚ ANTHROPOLOGY AND YOU—ON THE JOB AND IN THE COMMUNITY

It is my hope that you have learned enough about the basics of anthropology that you will use its perspectives and methods in your work and life. If you are going to be a teacher, you will deal with students of diverse subcultures. No place in North America is so isolated as to not have some cultural diversity, and such diversity can be the source of misunderstanding and conflict in a formal educational setting. Teachers, administrators, and parents of students will benefit from viewing diversity through an anthropological lens. Those of you entering careers in the business world will be able to use these same concepts and perspectives as you deal with clients, competitors, employees, and managers domestically and internationally. Health care careers increasingly require awareness and sensitivity to diverse subcultural groups for the effective delivery of health care programs.

OLC
mhhe•com/lenkeit3

See Internet exercises.

SUMMARY

Recently there has been a growing awareness of the application of anthropological perspectives and methods to the solution of practical problems. Corporations, both domestic and international, are calling on consulting anthropologists to study, analyze, and make recommendations for solving problems when traditional management techniques have failed. Private and government agencies are using anthropology to solve everyday problems. Participant observation and a focus on issues of culture can help to view situations through lenses that are unavailable with other approaches. Applying anthropology is not about standard lists of memorized approaches and facts; rather, it is about using the tools of anthropology to uncover the cultural issues unique to each situation.

Study Questions

1. What are some areas of practical application of anthropology?
2. How can an understanding of the culture concept be useful in solving problems in business, health care, and development programs? Cite a specific example.
3. Select an assigned reading from another text and discuss how the following anthropological methods were utilized in addressing the problem situation: culture, participant observation, the natives' view (emic) of the situation, the anthropologists' view of the situation (etic), and informal and formal interviews.

Suggested Readings

Anderson, Robert. 1996. *Magic, Science and Health: The Aims and Achievements of Medical Anthropology.* Belmont, Calif.: Wadsworth. Provides an overview of medical anthropology. Includes discussions of theoretical models, methodologies, and case studies.

Ervin, Alexander M. 2000. *Applied Anthropology: Tools and Perspectives for Contemporary Practice.* Boston: Allyn and Bacon. Overview of history of applied anthropology, ethics, policy analysis and practice, needs assessments, program evaluation, social impact assessment, and methods for applied research. A thorough presentation of what applied anthropologists do.

Fadiman, Anne. 1997. *The Spirit Catches You and You Fall Down: A Hmong Child, Her American Doctors, and the Collision of Two Cultures.* New York: Farrar, Straus and Giroux. Extraordinary account of Western medicine attempting to address epilepsy in an immigrant Hmong child. Both cultures learn a great deal about and from each other.

Ferraro, Gary P. 1998. *Applying Cultural Anthropology.* Belmont, Calif.: Wadsworth. This is an excellent selection of readings in applied anthropology with thirty-nine articles encompassing medicine, business, education, law, government, and economic development. Ferraro is a professor of anthropology and the director of the Intercultural Training Institute at the University of North Carolina at Charlotte.

Suggested Web Sites

http://www.aaanet.org/careers.htm

This site is the American Anthropological Association's online career center with a searchable job database, tips for job seekers, and helpful information on a career using a degree in anthropology.

http://carbon.cudenver.edu/public/sma

This site, organized by the American Anthropological Association's Society for Medical Anthropology, identifies and provides links to medical anthropological organizations, journals, newsgroups, and libraries. It also contains informative links to ethnomedicine, population nutrition, and the role of culture in shaping health care issues.

OLC

mhhe•com/lenkeit3

See Web links.

APPENDIX A
How Do You Read an Ethnography?

The following guide to reading ethnographies is intended to aid your reading and study of ethnographic material. It is directed at book-length ethnographies, but the approach may also be used to read, study, and assess shorter, topic-specific ethnographic accounts such as those often found in collections of readings.

◎ WHAT TO DO AS YOU READ

I. Determine When the Fieldwork Was Conducted and When the Resulting Ethnography Was Published

When you first pick up an ethnography, check the dates. When was it published? When was the fieldwork accomplished? The fieldwork may have occurred on more than one set of dates. Often the author of an ethnography has returned repeatedly to the same group and been with that group for varying lengths of time. Franz Boas emphasized that this was the only appropriate way to record the history of a culture, with revisits and restudies of the same group. One drawback to this approach is that one does not know from firsthand observation what happened between visits. The only sources for that information would be the recollections of the native members of the culture. Awareness of the dates is also important because the ethnography may be old. It is a snapshot of a group of people at the time of the study. You may want to do additional research to find out how the group has changed and adapted over time.

II. Identify the Perspective Guiding the Author

The approaches taken by the author should be clear. Identifying the author's perspective before your more careful reading of the text will be helpful as you analyze the data presented. The perspectives described here offer valuable information about other cultures, but it can be difficult to compare the data presented in accounts that use different perspectives.

Scientific Method Approach or Reflexive Approach? Look for a statement by the author of the perspective used or favored: the scientific method approach (see Chapter 1) or a reflexive approach (see Chapter 3). If the ethnography is based on the scientific method, it will include careful definition of terms and statements about the parameters of the research. It will often include one or more hypotheses being tested, plus the methods used in gathering data relevant to the testing of hypotheses. Finally, data will be presented quantitatively. In other words, every attempt is made to apply the scientific method (keeping in mind that it is difficult to control variables in a field setting the way one is able to control them in a laboratory setting).

If the ethnography is based on a reflexive approach, it will include discussions of how the ethnographer felt about what was observed and experienced. It may include material presented in the voice of the culture's native members. Dialogue between ethnographer and native members of the culture may be included. The ethnographer's personal reflections about not only the process of the fieldwork but also the ethics of the situation may be included. Data usually focus on an in-depth consideration of a few specific personal interactions rather than the presentation of quantified information.

Traditional Ethnography or Problem-Oriented Ethnography? Traditional ethnographies attempt to give a complete picture of an entire culture based on the ethnographer's experience living in that society for at least a year. In the past this was a major goal of ethnography, but recognition over time of the complexity of culture and society led anthropologists to reassess this approach. Today many ethnographers take problem- or issue-oriented approaches to fieldwork, concentrating on one aspect of the culture. Such work is often longitudinal, with repeat field stays and ongoing field research that may span decades. Teams of researchers are often involved.

III. Note the Table of Contents

Before you begin reading, compare the chapter headings in the ethnography's table of contents with the table of contents in this book. Also compare the topics with those in a second ethnography. You may learn quite a bit by doing this. Specifically you will see what topics are focal points of the ethnography. This may give you insight about the author's perspective.

Carefully consider how each major topic is defined or explained. Definitions sometimes differ (sometimes the differences are quite small). These differences affect the data and how they are interpreted. Consider this, for example: If two authors use different definitions of what constitutes a family, what difficulties will occur when you attempt to compare their data?

IV. Look for Notes on Fieldwork

Does the ethnography contain a "Fieldwork" section? This is usually one of the first parts of an ethnography. Inclusion of fieldwork sections in original ethnographies, and fieldwork editions (a republishing of an original ethnography with the addition of a section on the fieldwork experience), have been popular since the 1960s. Prior to 1960 many ethnographic accounts were published without any mention of the ethnographer's personal fieldwork experience.

When reading the fieldwork section, look for evidence of how the ethnographer (1) entered the community, (2) established rapport with the people, (3) coped with physical challenges of adapting to this environment, (4) experienced culture shock, (5) dealt with ethical issues, and (6) carried out research. How did this account illustrate the method of participant observation? Did the ethnographer use key informants, use formal or informal interviews, gather genealogical information, collect life histories, collect botanical samples, or collect myths and stories? Did the ethnographer discuss her or his personal interactions with the native members of the culture?

V. Write in the Margin

As you read, jot notes to yourself in the margin. Actively connect your readings in the ethnography with your text reading assignment in this book. Most ethnographic accounts give only cursory definitions of terms. It is expected that the reader of an ethnography understands common anthropological terms and concepts, the word *culture*, for example. If you are given reading assignments in this book and in an ethnography, always read the text first. This way you will be prepared with an overview of a topic before you read a specific illustration. By using this technique, you should also find yourself analyzing and comparing as you read. For example, if you read about a person preparing for a marriage celebration, the ethnography may not always identify this as part of a ritual known as a rite of passage. If you have just read the text section about different types of rituals found in cultures, you can identify this as a rite of passage and jot that in the margin.

◎ ETHNOGRAPHIES WITHOUT INDEXES

Some ethnographies do not contain an index. These ethnographies are often written from a reflexive perspective. Because the author is telling of her or his experiences, what was seen and learned, the author does not expect that this information will be used in comparative scientific studies. Therefore, there is no index. This makes it difficult for the reader to quickly locate material. I strongly recommend notes in margins (for example, *marriage custom*). In addition I suggest that you "flag" pages with small colorful sticky notes (you can even use some form of color coding — green for food-procurement data, yellow for beliefs, red for rituals, blue for marriage and kinship).

◎ YOU AND THE ETHNOGRAPHY

Reading an ethnography involves the examination of how people in a society live. It is also an exercise in reflection. You *read* about a custom rather than learn about it firsthand through participant observation. As you read, you will likely encounter customs or behaviors that will bring forth an inner voice that says, That is stupid, or, These people are ignorant. Or you may read of a custom that you consider wrong ethically and morally. You may be confused by these feelings. These are the same issues of ethnocentrism that the ethnographer must face while living in a cultural setting different from his or her own. You may find that you have similar reactions when you change jobs, or move to a new neighborhood, or travel to a different country — in other words, when you are in a new subculture. You must grapple with that inner voice. You must try to step back to a neutral place and examine both the ethnographic culture and your own culture. Remember that you are reading about a cultural and social system that works for these people. To appreciate it and respect it, you must push away your own provincialism and move, for a time, outside the walls of your familiar sociocultural environment.

Jot down notes regarding how you feel about what you read. This can be an uncomfortable process, even painful. But an education is about expanding horizons. In the end you will have a new recognition of your own way of life as well as a new respect for another way of life. This does not mean that you will or should change your own viewpoint. It simply means that you are exploring a different way of knowing and being. Keep in mind that had you been adopted as an infant and raised by parents in the other culture you would be of that culture, and all of its customs and behaviors would seem correct and morally right to you. If you follow these suggestions as you read, you will likely learn as much or more about your culture and yourself as about others.

◎ HOW TO COMPARE TWO OR MORE ETHNOGRAPHIES

You will find it helpful to make a table when you need to process a lot of information. I recommend making a table as an excellent way to organize data and to prepare for comparison and contrast questions on exams. First, begin by making a table or grid for yourself. Second, choose major topics and concepts based on those in this book, your professor's lectures, and the table of contents of the ethnography. Place these topics along one axis of your table and the names of the ethnographies and ethnographers along the other axis. Finally, add information to this table each time you read. You can easily expand your table by taping 8½- by 11-inch pieces of paper together. These can then be folded and placed in a folder. Use this table as a quick source to study, to quiz yourself on the information, and to compare and contrast the ethnographies by topic. Note that this technique works well for materials in other courses too. Here is an example of such a table:

Topics	[Ethnography—name of society]	[Ethnography—name of society]
Dates of fieldwork		
Environment		
Subsistence strategy and technology		
Resource allocation		
Marriage pattern and residence		
Kinship and descent		
Political organization		
Belief systems		

APPENDIX B
How Do You Make
String Figures?

String figures have been reported in the ethnographic literature from cultures in every part of the world. They are known by various names around the globe—cat's cradle (England), string talking (Japan), well-rope (China), the ladder game (South Celebes), wolf talking (Korea). Each culture seems to have its own descriptive term (Jayne 1962). A person creates most figures alone, but some figures involve two or even three sets of hands. Some figures are widely known—whether as a result of diffusion or independent invention is unclear, because they usually bear different names and sometimes include variations in the steps required to produce them. Other figures are specific to one culture. Anthropologists began collecting these figures in the 1890s.

My husband and I first encountered string figures in the anthropology lab at the University of California at Santa Barbara. One of our professors, Thomas Harding, was making preparations to go to New Guinea to do fieldwork and was learning string figures because they are popular and well known there. Students and faculty would drop in to the lab for coffee and to share the latest string figures that we had mastered. Quite a bit of competition went into poring through the ethnographic literature to find and master obscure figures. This serendipitous activity was to become a lifelong hobby, one we have shared with thousands of students in our introductory anthropology courses. As you perform the various figures, you can reflect on the wonder of sharing and transmitting these figures that have diffused to our culture from all over the world.

String figures are primarily a form of entertainment. Words, stories, or chants sometimes accompany the creation of a figure. The main categories of string figures as outlined by Caroline Jayne (1962) include (1) patterns, where the purpose is to form a pattern in the final step; (2) tricks, where strings are pulled in the final move so that a movement is accomplished in the final step; and (3) catches, which as the name implies result in a catch of a finger or hand. I often refer to this third category as escape figures. Try your hand at making the following figures, and then to find out more about string figures, see the Suggested Readings and Web sites at the end of this appendix.

◎ HOW TO BEGIN

You'll need about six feet of medium-weight cotton string. The thickness of string typically used to tie packages is a bit thick but will suffice. You might want to experiment with various weights. Our favorite is the cotton string used for macramé or fancy ship knotting. Peoples of native cultures have used strips of hide or skin, finely braided human hair, and various types of fiber cordage such as coconut fiber or grass fiber. Measure your string, and then tie it in a loop by knotting the two ends together. Trim the loose ends close to the knot so that they will not interfere with your figures. The following directions will refer to your fingers as follows: thumb, index, middle finger, ring finger, and baby finger (Figure 1).

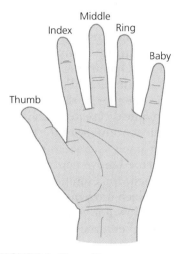

FIGURE 1 Finger Terms

◎ BASIC POSITION

The creation of the majority of figures begins with the basic position. Hold your hands in front of you with the palms of your hands facing each other. Bend your elbows and bring your hands up until your thumbnails are facing your chest (Figure 2). *You* are the point of reference in all of the directions. A near-thumb string means the one closest to your chest, and a far-thumb string means the one farthest from your chest.

FIGURE 2 Basic Position

Between each move as you create a figure, check to see if your hands are in this basic position, with palms facing each other. The string should always be a bit taut. If you let it go limp, it will make following the directions more difficult and you will more easily drop a string or loop. Figure 3 shows some of the common direction terms that you will use.

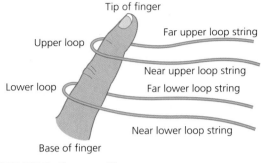

FIGURE 3 Common Terms

There are several "openings" used in creating string figures, of which Opening A is the most common. Practice this opening so that you can quickly create it, and then continue with the directions for the completion of the figures for the Outrigger Canoe and its variations. Then try the Fish Spear. Look for mirrored movements in several of these figures; that is, steps that are performed, for example, first with the right index finger and then with the left. Such movements create balanced patterns in the final form of the figure. Now get your string, make a loop, and try your hand at this ancient form of entertainment!

◎ OPENING A

1. A single loop runs behind the thumb and across the front of the palm and behind the baby finger of both hands. This is called first position (Figure 4).

FIGURE 4 First Position

2. With your **right index** finger, pick up the left palm string from underneath (Figure 5a) and return to the basic position with the string just below your fingernail. Let it slip down to base of your finger (Figure 5b).

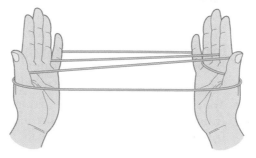

FIGURE 5A First Move of
Opening A

FIGURE 5B Second Move of Opening A
(hands return to basic position)

3. With your **left index** finger, pick up the right palm string below your right index finger from underneath. Make certain that you pick up the string by going between the two index finger strings (Figure 5c), and return to the basic position with string at base of your finger. This completes Opening A.

FIGURE 5C

Opening A

All directions for the following figures will use these descriptions to indicate which string to move or pick up. With the string in the completed Opening A position and hands placed in the basic position, look at your strings and identify each string as you read the descriptions.

- Your thumb has a "near" string (closest to your chest and positioned at base of thumb).
- Your thumb has a "far" string (on the far side of the thumb, crossing the opposite thumb, continuing to the opposite index finger, and becoming the "near index" string).
- Your index has a "near" string (close to your chest) and a "far" string (on the far side of your index finger, crossing the opposite baby and becoming the "near baby" string).
- There are no strings on your middle and ring fingers.
- Your baby finger has a "near" string (close to your chest, running from the far side of the opposite index finger) and a "far" string (running straight between the baby fingers).

◎ OUTRIGGER CANOE

The Outrigger Canoe, from New Caledonia (an island in the South Pacific), is classified as a pattern figure.

1. Begin with Opening A.
2. Both thumbs go *over* the near index string and pick up the far index string on the back of thumb and return to the basic position. Note that you now have two strings on the thumbs: an upper string (that crosses midway between your hands) and a lower string (that runs straight between your thumbs).
3. Pick up the bottom thumb string with your teeth, lift it over the thumbs, and release it. Be careful not to disturb or drop the upper thumb string.
4. Release your baby fingers by letting string slip off of them. Move your hands away from each other while keeping them in the basic position. Now look at this figure. You'll see the canoe shape between your thumbs. The outriggers stick out at both ends on one side of the canoe and go to your index fingers.
5. To release the figure, drop all but the baby finger string and slowly spread your hands apart.

Now that you've mastered the Outrigger Canoe, you can try the following variations.

◎ CUP AND SAUCER

After creating the Outrigger Canoe, rotate your hands (still in the basic position) so that your fingers point down and thumbs point away from your chest at right angles. You will see the cup (or bowl) sitting on the saucer.

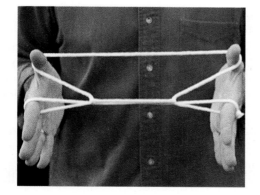

The Cup and Saucer figure shown here is a variant of the Outrigger Canoe figure from New Caledonia. Note that the hands are rotated down from the basic position.

◎ ROCKET SHIP

After creating the Cup and Saucer, grasp the top rim of the cup (near the thumb string) with your teeth. Keep your thumbs in place as you gently move your hands downward until your fingers are pointing toward the floor. Gently release your thumbs. Now you are holding the top (or nose) of the rocket ship in your teeth, and the base is between your index fingers. Someone facing you will see the rocket ship clearly. Spread your hands apart slowly to make the rocket ship "blast off."

◎ FISH SPEAR

This figure, which is widely known in New Guinea and North America, is classified as a **trick figure** because movement is involved to form the final effect.

1. The string loop runs behind your thumbs and across the front of your palm and behind the baby fingers. This is the string in first position (step 1) of Opening A.
2. Your right index finger goes *under* the left palm string. Twist once a full 360 degrees with the right index finger and return. It may help you perform this move if you pretend you are tracing a clock face with your index finger. Begin with your finger pointing at 12 o'clock and move your finger in a clockwise direction past 1, 2, 3 . . . 10, 11, and back to 12. You will now have a loop around your index finger that has a twist in

the string on the palm side of the loop. Return your hands to the basic position.

3. Your left index finger goes *under* the right palm string at the base of your right index finger between the far and near index strings. Return to the basic position. (Note that the movements thus far are those of Opening A *except* that you have made a twist in the loop of the right index finger.)

4. You are now ready to both form and throw the spear. Simultaneously release your right thumb and right baby finger and *quickly* pull with your right hand and move your hands apart (still in the basic position). The fish spear forms and becomes progressively smaller as the hands are pulled apart. The Trobriand Islanders describe how the spear gets smaller as it travels farther away.

5. To release the figure, drop your left thumb and baby finger loops and spread your hands apart.

The Fish Spear figure is widely known by groups in New Guinea and North America.

Suggested Readings

Ball, W. W. Rouse. 1971. *Fun with String Figures.* New York: Dover. A good introduction to some easy figures with easy-to-follow directions.

International String Figure Association. 1999. *Fascinating String Figures.* Mineola, New York: Dover. (Materials first published by *String Figure Magazine*, ISFA Press, Pasadena, California, in 1996 and 1997). Easy-to-follow instructions with illustrations. ISFA members actively collect and publish figures from world cultures and modern figures created by members.

Jayne, Carolyn Furness. 1962. *String Figures and How to Make Them*. New York: Dover. Originally published in 1906, this is the resource to have if you are serious about string figures.

Suggested Web Sites

http://www.isfa.org/
 This is the Web site for the International String Figure Association. It contains on-line directions for making figures and many links.

http://www.virtual.yosemite.cc.ca.us/lenkeitr/string%20anth%20web.htm
 This is Don and Roberta Lenkeit's Web site for making string figures. It continues with instructions where Appendix B (String Figures) leaves off.

OLC
mhhe·com/lenkeit3

See Web links.

GLOSSARY

acculturation The borrowing between cultures as a result of prolonged contact.

Acheulean hand axes Part of an African and European tool tradition associated with *Homo erectus* and *Homo ergaster.* The tradition also includes cleavers and some flake tools.

achieved status A status position that is earned through an individual's skills, actions, and accomplishments.

action anthropologist One who believes that he or she has a moral obligation to take the side of indigenous populations whenever such peoples' rights to self-determination are violated.

affinal kin Kin related by marriage.

agnates Members of a patrilineage.

agriculture A subsistence strategy based on intensive, continuous use of land for the production of plant foods. It typically includes one or more of the following: cultivation of soils, use of fertilizers, and irrigation.

ambilineal descent A unilineal descent system in which some members of the society acquire and pass on descent affiliation through females, whereas others do so through males.

ambilocal residence See *bilocal residence.*

anthropology The science or study of *Homo sapiens* using a holistic approach.

applied anthropology The branch of anthropology that focuses on the application of anthropological methods and approaches to the solution of problems, as distinct from academic anthropology.

applied archaeology The use of archaeological methods to study the material culture of contemporary societies. Data can be used to develop social programs.

archaeology The systematic study of the artifacts and ecofacts from past cultures as a means of reconstructing past lifeways.

artifacts Objects made by humans.

ascribed status The status a person is given at birth and over which that person has no control.

attribute A discrete characteristic of an artifact. Attributes include shape, size, design elements and their placement, and techniques of manufacture.

authority The exercise of legitimate power; the right to rule invested by members of the community in its leaders.

avunculocal residence A postmarriage residence rule that requires the bride and groom to reside with or near the groom's mother's brother.

balanced reciprocity Exchange and gift giving with the expectation of a return of equal value within a reasonable period of time.

band A type of society common in foraging groups and marked by egalitarian social structure and lack of specialization.

barter Exchange of products that does not involve currency.

behavioral archaeology An area of applied archaeology that focuses on the relationships between material culture and people's behavior.

bifurcate The distinction within kinship systems where father's side and mother's side of the family are labeled and treated differently, splitting mother's side of the family from father's side of the family.

Big Men Alternate term for *headmen* common in Polynesian and Melanesian societies. See *headmen*.

bilateral descent Descent that is traced equally through both mother and father.

bilocal residence The condition in which a newly married couple reside either with or near the groom's parents or the bride's parents.

biological anthropology A subfield of anthropology that studies humans as a biological species. Also called physical anthropology.

biped An animal that walks on two legs.

bridewealth A form of marriage finance in which valuable gifts are given by the groom's kin to the bride's kin.

carrying capacity The maximum population that a habitat can sustain.

caste A ranked group with membership determined at birth.

chiefdom A type of society with an office of chief, most commonly hereditary, social ranking, and a redistributive economy.

clan A descent group consisting of two or more lineages that trace their origin to a mythical ancestor.

class A group of people who have a similar relationship to wealth, power, and prestige.

cline The variation of a biological trait along a geographic continuum. Human skin pigments show distribution along a cline from the equator north and south.

colonialism Influence and dominance of one nation over another for the purpose of exploiting raw resources. The dominant nation-state establishes a physical presence and a colonial government. See *imperialism; hegemony.*

commodity money Currency in the form of valued objects such as shells or gold.

community An association of people who share a common identity, including geographic boundaries, common language, and culture.

comparative method The methodological approach of comparing data. Anthropologists use the comparative method.

consanguineal relatives Kin related by blood.

contagious magic A type of magic based on the idea that something that has contact with a person or animal contains some essence of that being and that magic performed on the item will have the same effect as if performed on the being.

contemporary human variation studies The study of the biological variation in living humans.

cross-cousin Ego's mother's brother's child and father's sister's child.

cultural anthropology A subfield of anthropology that focuses on human sociocultural adaptations.

cultural ecology The study of the processes by which a society adapts to its environment.

cultural evolution A model for the development of society that delineates a sequence of cultural change over time.

cultural relativism The perspective that any aspect of a culture must be viewed and evaluated within the context of that culture.

cultural resource management (CRM) The conservation and management of archaeological sites to protect them.

culture The sum total of the knowledge, ideas, behaviors, and material creations that are learned, shared, and transmitted primarily through the symbolic system of language. These components create a pattern (that changes over time) and serve as guides and standards of behavior for members of the society. The term *culture* is used in the abstract as well as to refer to a specific culture.

culture shock A label for the resultant feelings of homesickness, disorientation, helplessness, and frustration that occur after prolonged exposure to an unfamiliar culture.

descent group A group of people who share identity and come from a common ancestor.

descriptive linguistics The part of anthropological linguistics that focuses on the mechanics of language.

deviance The violation of an ideal pattern of behavior within a society.

diffusion The voluntary borrowing and exchange of items or ideas between cultures.

diffusionism Early theoretical school that explained the origin and spread of artifacts and ideas through borrowing between cultures.

displacement The ability of humans to communicate symbolically about distant time and space.

double descent A descent system with two separate lines of descent that are both recognized at the same time.

dowry A form of marriage finance in which valuable gifts are given by the bride's kin to the groom's kin.

ecofacts The remains of plants, animals, or naturally occurring nonorganic substances.

ecological model A model that views a culture as part of a larger global ecological system with each aspect of the system interacting with all of the other parts.

egalitarian Refers to members of a society having equal access to status, power, and wealth.

egalitarian society A society in which individuals within the same category of age and gender have equal access to wealth, prestige, and power.

emic An insider's view of a culture. This perspective in ethnography uses the categories and ideas that are relevant and meaningful to the culture under study.

enculturation The process of learning one's culture while growing up in it.

endogamy A cultural rule that dictates that one must marry within a designated group.

ethnic group A type of subculture characterized by members sharing a culture of origin, often one originating in another country.

ethnocentrism Making value judgments based on one's own culture when describing aspects of another culture.

ethnography A written description of a culture based on data gathered from fieldwork.

ethnolinguistics A field of study in linguistics that analyzes the relationship between a language and culture.

ethnology The comparative study of cultures with the aim of presenting analytical generalizations about human culture.

ethnomusicology The study of the music of a contemporary society within the context of that society.

etic An outsider's view of a culture. This perspective in ethnography uses the categories of the anthropologist's culture to describe the culture under study.

evolutionary-ecological model A paradigm of human culture that combines both the neo-evolutionary and ecological perspectives.

exogamy A cultural rule that dictates that one must marry outside of a designated group (e.g., outside of one's lineage, clan, or village).

experimental archaeology An aspect of archaeology in which experiments are performed to learn how prehistoric artifacts and features were made and used.

extended family Two or more nuclear families who are related by blood and who reside in the same household, village, or territory (e.g., a man and wife, their sons, and their sons' wives and children).

family band A type of band organization consisting of nuclear family units that move independently within an area. Joins others when resources are plentiful; travels alone at other times.

family of orientation A person's childhood family, where enculturation takes place.

family of procreation A kin group consisting of an individual and the individual's spouse and children.

features Nonportable evidence of technology at archaeological sites, such as roadways and fire hearths.

fiat money Paper currency backed by a nation-state's claim of its value.

fictive kin Unrelated family friends who are addressed by kin terms.

folate A metabolite essential for sperm and embryonic neural tube development that is destroyed by UVB.

foraging A food-procurement strategy that involves collecting wild plant and animal foods.

forensic anthropologist An applied biological anthropologist concerned with legal issues. Frequently focuses on the identification of skeletal material and the cause of death.

formal interviews An ethnographic research method in which planned, scripted questions are asked of informants.

gender The sociocultural construct of masculine and feminine roles and the qualities assigned to these roles.

gender role The tasks and behaviors assigned by a culture to each sex.

genealogical method The ethnographic method of recording information about kinship relationships using symbols and diagrams.

generalized reciprocity Institutionalized gift giving and exchange between close kin; accounts are not kept, and there is no expectation of immediate return.

globalization In anthropology, the rapid spread of economic, social, and cultural systems across continents.

half-marriage A custom among the Yurok of northwestern California and other patri-centered groups in which a man pays partial bridewealth and lives with the bride's family, and the couple's children belong to the wife and her family.

headmen Types of leaders found in tribal and chiefdom societies whose leadership is based on persuasive power. See *Big Men.*

hegemony The ideological domination by one cultural group over another through institutions, bureaucracy, education, and sometimes force. See *imperialism; colonialism.*

heliocentric diffusionism Diffusionist school that pointed to ancient Egypt as the center of cultural innovations and inventions that spread around the world.

heterogeneous culture Cultural group that shares only a few components. Typical of large societies such as states, where there are many subcultures such as ethnic groups.

heterosexuality Sexual attraction between members of the opposite sex.

historical archaeology A subfield of archaeology that studies the remains of cultures that existed during the time of written records but about which little was recorded.

historical linguistics The study of the history of languages, including their development and relationship to other languages.

historicalism Theoretical school, established by Franz Boas, who hypothesized that each culture had its own particular history that could be documented through repeated ethnographies. Comparisons of many such histories could uncover underlying principles of culture change.

Also termed *historical particularism; American historicalism.*

holistic An integrated perspective that assumes interrelationships among the parts of a subject. Anthropology studies humans from a holistic perspective, including both biological and cultural aspects.

homogeneous culture Cultural group that shares most ideas, values, knowledge, behaviors, and artifacts. Typical of small cultural groups such as foragers.

Homo sapiens The taxonomic designation for humans.

homosexuality Sexual attraction between members of the same sex.

horticulture A food-procurement strategy based on crop production without soil preparation, fertilizers, irrigation, or use of draft animals.

household A common residence-based economic unit.

humanistic anthropology A label for research that focuses on individuals and their creative responses to cultural and historical forces.

ideal culture What people believe they should do.

imitative magic A type of magic based on the notion that working magic on an image of an animal or person will cause the same effect on the actual animal or person.

impact studies Ethnographic study of a situation to document effects of change. May take place during and/or after a program of cultural restructuring.

imperialism Influence and authority of one nation over another, often associated with exploitation of natural and human resources. See *colonialism; hegemony.*

informal interviews An ethnographic research method using open-ended questions that allow informants to talk about what they deem important.

informants Native members of a society who give information about their culture to an ethnographer.

innovation Something totally new.

invention Something new that is created based on items or ideas that already exist.

judgment sample A sample that is chosen based on the judgment of the ethnographer. Key informants are chosen using this method.

key informant An ethnographic interview subject who has been selected by judgment sample; a knowledgeable native who plays a major role in teaching the ethnographer about the informant's culture.

kindred A term associated with bilateral descent in which relatives calculate their degree of relationship to Ego. In a kindred, only siblings share the exact same set of relatives.

kinesics The use of the body to communicate— gestures, posture, and facial expression.

kinship system The complexity of a culture's rules governing the relationships between affinal and consanguineal kin.

kinship term A word that designates a social relationship between individuals who are related by blood or marriage.

law The cultural rule formulated by a society and backed up by sanctions.

lexigrams Geometric figure symbols used to teach apes symbolic communication.

levirate A marriage custom in which a widow marries her deceased husband's brother.

life history The ethnographic method of gathering data based on extensive interviews with individuals about their memories of their culture from childhood through adulthood.

life shock A sudden unexpected experience that causes one to faint, become hysterical, or vomit. More likely to occur when immersed in an unfamiliar setting.

lineage A unilineal descent group that traces its consanguineal relatives back to a common ancestor.

linguistics A subfield of anthropology that includes the study of the structure, history, and social aspects of human language.

low energy budget The expenditure of minimum energy to acquire the basic needs for survival.

magic The techniques used to manipulate supernatural forces and beings.

mana An impersonal supernatural force that flows in and out of people and objects.

market exchange The trading of goods and services through the use of currency.

matrifocal residence A residence group consisting of a woman and her children residing without co-residence of a husband.

matrilineage A unilineal descent group with membership passed on through females and traced to a common female ancestor.

matrilocal residence A postmarriage residence rule that requires the bride and groom to live in or near the residence of the bride's mother.

matri-patrilocal residence A temporary residence form in which the groom moves to live with the bride's family until bridewealth payments are complete and the couple take up permanent patrilocal residence.

medical anthropology The study of illness and health care from the perspective of anthropology.

melanin A pigment in the outer layer of the skin. It is responsible for skin color and blocks UVB from damaging lower layers of the skin.

microculture The smallest subgroup within a culture that shares specific cultural features such as values or behaviors.

midden Archaeological term to designate an area of discard; a trash heap.

mobile art Art forms that are not fixed to any place and can be moved or carried.

moiety An association that divides a society in half. Moiety affiliation is inherited unilineally and carries obligations to other members.

monogamy A form of marriage in which one woman is married to one man.

monotheistic A belief system that focuses on one all-powerful supernatural being.

morpheme The smallest combination of sounds in human speech that carry a meaning.

multilinear evolution An evolutionary model of culture emphasizing different development patterns for societies in different habitats.

nation-state A group that shares a common cultural heritage, territory, and legitimate political structure.

negative reciprocity An economic exchange aimed at receiving more than is given.

neoevolutionary model A model of cultural evolution based on types of food-procurement strategies and the sociocultural adaptations that resulted from them.

neolocal residence A postmarriage residence rule that requires the bride and groom to set up an independent household away from both sets of parents.

nomadic pastoralism A herding adaptation that makes the most of available forage for animals by frequent habitat moves.

nuclear family A group consisting of a married couple and their children.

Oldowan tools A very early African tool-making tradition associated with the first members of *Homo*.

optimal-foraging model A model that aims at understanding how foragers optimize the gathering of food.

paleoanthropology The study of human biological evolution.

pan-tribal sodality An association group that crosscuts a tribe and unites tribal members, not always voluntary. See *sodality*.

parallel-cousin Ego's mother's sister's child and father's brother's child.

parietal art Art executed on permanent features such as cave walls, rock shelters, and large blocks of rock.

participant observation The process of an anthropologist doing ethnographic fieldwork.

participant observer The role of an anthropologist doing ethnographic fieldwork.

pastoralism A food-producing strategy based on herding.

patrilineage A unilineal descent group passed on through males and traced to a common male ancestor.

patrilocal band A type of band consisting of related males and their wives and children who stay together and forage as a group.

patrilocal residence A postmarriage residence rule that requires the bride and groom to live in or near the residence of the groom's father.

phoneme The smallest unit of sound in speech that will indicate a difference in meaning.

phonology The general study of the sounds used in human speech.

phratry A group of two or more clans that have a tie to one another, often based on a historical relationship; obligations and rights are expected between clans in this relationship.

physical anthropology See *biological anthropology.*

plasticity The pliability or malleability of a biological feature. An individual's genetic growth potential is malleable depending on nutrition, maternal health, and exposure to sunlight.

polyandry Marriage of one woman to two or more men.

polygamy Multiple spouse marriage.

polygyny Marriage of one man to two or more women.

polytheistic A belief system consisting of many supernatural beings of approximately equal power.

postmodernist One who uses the paradigm of postmodernism.

postmodernism A complex theoretical perspective that applies a humanistic approach to ethnography with a focus on individuals and their voices.

power The ability to influence or cause people or groups to do certain things that they would not do otherwise.

prehistoric archaeology The analysis of the material remains of cultures that existed before the time of written records.

priest A full-time supernatural practitioner who is part of a bureaucracy.

primates Animals in the order Primates; includes humans, apes, monkeys, and prosimians.

primatology The study of nonhuman primates.

prophet A person, usually charismatic, who has had direct communication with a god. Often receives a message that articulates a plan of action for the group.

proxemics The study of the use of space in communication.

psychological anthropology The study of the relationship between culture and personality.

quadruped An animal that walks on four limbs.

race Biologically: a group within a species that shares a cluster of genetically determined traits. No such trait clusters occur among *Homo sapiens.* Culturally: a social construct based on perceived cultural differences.

random sample A sample method in which all members of a population have a statistically equal chance of being chosen.

rank society A society in which the individual's access to prestige and wealth is limited by the number of positions available. A society may be stratified by rank, such as in a chiefdom.

rapport A harmonious relationship.

real culture What people can be observed to do.

reciprocity A form of exchange that involves the mutual giving and receiving of food and other items between people who are socially equal.

redistribution A system of exchange in which wealth is reallocated; found in chiefdom and state societies.

reflexive ethnography An approach to fieldwork that focuses on the personal experiences and perspectives of the ethnographer, as well as the voices of the native members of a culture.

revitalization movement An organized movement that occurs during times of change that involve perceived loss of traditional cultural values. A prophet or charismatic leader predicts a revitalized society if a program is followed.

rites of intensification Rituals, often seasonal, that reinforce group solidarity, cultural values, and group social and political status relationships.

rites of passage Rituals associated with the social movement of an individual from one culturally defined role and status to another during the passage from birth to death.

ritual Behavior that is formalized, is regularly repeated, and has symbolic content.

role The culturally assigned behaviors and expectations for a person's social position.

Sapir-Whorf hypothesis A hypothesis about the relationship between language and culture that states that language constructs perceptions.

segmentary lineage A descent group consisting of sublineage sets.

sex The biological aspect of being female, male, or other, assigned at birth based on external genitalia.

sexual dimorphism The biological and behavioral differences between males and females.

shabano A Yanomamo village.

shaman A part-time practitioner of the supernatural who has special powers to mediate between the supernatural world and the community.

silent language All of a culture's nonverbal symbolic systems of communication, including kinesics and proxemics.

sister exchange A common type of marriage consisting of the marriage of cross-cousins. Men exchange their sisters as marriage partners.

site The location of archaeological remains such as artifacts and features.

slash and burn The removal of plant materials by cutting and burning preparatory to planting. Also called swidden horticulture.

social control A process involving a structure and mechanisms to ensure that people do not violate the society's accepted forms of behavior.

social stratification Ascribed and achieved differences between two classes within a society.

sociolinguistics A subfield of linguistics that analyzes the relationship between language and culture with a focus on how people speak in social contexts.

sodality A group that crosscuts a society and whose membership is based on common interest rather than kinship or residence.

sororate A marriage custom in which a widower marries a sister of his deceased wife.

state A type of society characterized by a political structure with authority that is legally constituted.

status A person's position in society.

stratified random sample A random sample with divisions into categories such as by age or socioeconomic level.

stratified society A society with unequal access to resources within the same gender and status group.

stratified state society A society in which institutions are based on coercive power and authority. Inequality exists within social groupings.

string figures A type of entertainment in which designs, or figures, are created by weaving string on the fingers. Patterns, tricks, and catches are performed and are often accompanied by stories.

structured interviews See *formal interviews*.

subculture Smaller group within a large cultural complex. Behaviors, values, attitudes, and artifacts are shared by group members.

supernatural beings Invisible beings that exhibit form, personality, attitudes, and powers.

supernatural belief A belief that transcends the observable, natural world.

supernatural forces Unseen powers that are not personified and may be manipulated to achieve good or evil.

syntax The manner in which minimum units of meaning (morphemes) are combined.

technology The knowledge, tools, and skills used by humans to manipulate their environments.

totem Mythical or symbolic ancestor of a clan.

traditions Cultural choices consistently made by a society and practiced generation to generation.

transhumance A variety of pastoralism in which herds are moved seasonally.

tribe A type of society marked by egalitarian social structure, based on horticultural and pastoral economies, and integrated by various types of kinship organizations and sodalities.

ultraviolet radiation A part of the electromagnetic energy from the sun that is not visible to the human eye.

unilineal evolution Early theoretical school that postulated that all cultures proceeded through a series of successive stages.

unstructured interviews See *informal interviews.*

urbanization studies Studies of the adaptations made by rural peoples as they move to cities.

uterine descent group See *matrilineage.*

UVB Ultraviolet radiation from the sun in the B wave length.

uxorilocal residence The custom of living with the wife's relatives after marriage.

virilocal residence The custom of living with the husband's relatives after marriage.

 CREDITS

Associates; **p. 150,** © Carol Beckwith & Angela M. Fisher/National Geographic Society Image Collection; **p. 151,** © Thomas L. Kelly/Woodfin Camp and Associates; **p. 153,** © Sebnem Evas/Atlas Geographic; **p. 157,** © Momatiuk/Eastcott/Woodfin Camp and Associates; **p. 159,** © Ellen Senisi/The Image Works; **p. 162,** © George Chan/Photo Researchers, Inc.   **Chapter 8 p. 168,** © Maureen Mackenzie-Taylor, Courtesy Msquared Design; **p. 173,** © Patrick Bennett/Corbis; **p. 175,** © Michael Peletz; **p. 177,** © Paula Lerner/Woodfin Camp and Associates, Inc.; **p. 185,** © Michael Newman/PhotoEdit   **Chapter 9 p. 190,** © Joel Halpern/Anthro-Photo; **p. 193,** Courtesy of the Institute for Intercultural Studies, Inc. New York; **p. 196,** © Lindsay Hebberd/Corbis; **p. 198,** © Rachel Epstein/PhotoEdit; **p. 199,** Courtesy National Museum of the American Indian. Smithsonian Institution. (Neg. #N34256); **p. 200,** Courtesy Dr. Serena Nanda; **p. 203,** © Film Study Center, Harvard University—Gardens of War Plate #92; **p. 208,** Everett Collection; **p. 211,** © AP/Wide World Photos   **Chapter 10 p. 214,** © Keith Dannemiller/Corbis Saba; **p. 216,** © Reuters NewMedia, Inc./Corbis; **p. 218,** © Michael Newman/PhotoEdit; **p. 221,** © Megan Biesele/Anthro-Photo; **p. 222,** © Irven DeVore/Anthro-Photo; **p. 223,** © Robert Caputo/Aurora; **p. 225,** © Peter Essick/Aurora **p. 229,** © Peter Turnley/Corbis; **p. 232,** © Wendy Stone/Corbis; **p. 234,** © Film Study Center, Harvard University—Gardens of War Plate #145   **Chapter 11 p. 238,** © Reuters/Corbis; **p. 242,** © Ray Ellis/Photo Researchers, Inc.; **p. 244,** © Irven DeVore/Anthro-Photo; **p. 245,** © A. Ramey/PhotoEdit; **p. 247T,** © Jack Fields/Photo Researchers, Inc.; **p. 247B,** © A. Ramey/PhotoEdit; **p. 251,** © David Alan Harvey/Woodfin Camp & Associates; **p. 255,** © Irven DeVore/Anthro-Photo; **p. 257,** Courtesy Don A. Lenkeit; **p. 259,** Ryan McVay/Getty Images; **p. 262,** © Kal Muller/Woodfin Camp & Associates; **p. 263,** Courtesy National Anthropological Archives. Smithsonian Institution. (Neg. #36-NAA)   **Chapter 12 p. 266,** © Kevin Schafer/Peter Arnold, Inc.; **p. 268L,** © Susan Kuklin/Photo Researchers, Inc.; **p. 268R,** © Robert Frerck/Woodfin Camp & Associates; **p. 270T, © AP/Wide World Photos;** p. 270B, © Scala/Art Resource, NY; **p. 271,** © Giraudon/Art Resource, NY; **p. 273,** © Naturhistorisches Museum, Wien. Photo: Alice Schumacher; **p. 278T,** Courtesy of the Phoebe Hearst Museum of Anthropology and the Regents of the University of California. 15-4846 #2; **p. 278B,** Courtesy of the Phoebe Hearst Museum of Anthropology and the Regents of the University of California. 15-4840 & 15-4848; **p. 279,** Courtesy of the Phoebe Hearst Museum of Anthropology and the Regents of the University of California. #2062; **p. 280, 282,** Courtesy Roberta Lenkeit; **p. 283,** © AP/Wide World Photos

PART THREE p. 288, © Mike Yamashita/Woodfin Camp and Associates, Inc. **Chapter 13 p. 290,** © Attar Maher/Corbis Sygma; **p. 298,** © Rick Wilking/Reuters/Corbis; **p. 301,** © Amit Dave/Reuters/Corbis; **p. 303,** © Dilip Mehta/Contact Press Images; **p. 306, 307,** © AP/Wide World Photos; **p. 312,** © Steve Starr/Index Stock Imagery/PictureQuest   **Chapter 14 p. 316,** © Pedro Meyer/Black Star/PictureQuest; **p. 319,** © Mark Richards/PhotoEdit; **p. 324,** Photo by Pradeep Gidwani. Courtesy Dr. Elisa Sobo; **p. 327,** © Bob Krist/Corbis; **p. 328,** Courtesy Operation Green Leaves

APPENDIX   All photos Courtesy Roberta Lenkeit

REFERENCES

Adams, Kathleen M. 2005. Generating Theory, Tourism, and World Heritage in Indonesia: Ethical Quandries for Anthropologists in an Era of Tourist Mania. In *Tourism and Applied Anthropology*, ed. Tim Wallace. *NAPA Bulletin* 2 3: 45–59.

Ahmed, Akbar S., and Cris N. Shore. 1995. *The Future of Anthropology*. London: Athlone Press.

Anderson, Robert. 1996. *Magic, Science, and Health: The Aims and Achievements of Medical Anthropology*. Fort Worth, Tex.: Harcourt Brace.

Angrosino, Michael V. 2000. The Culture Concept and Applied Anthropology. In *The Unity of Theory and Practice in Anthropology: Rebuilding a Fractured Synthesis*, eds. Carole E. Hill and Marietta L. Baba. *Napa Bulletin* 18: 67–78.

Apodaca, Anacleto. 1952. Corn and Custom: The Introduction of Hybrid Corn to Spanish American Farmers in New Mexico. In *Human Problems in Technological Change*, ed. Edward H. Spicer, pp. 35–39. New York: John Wiley and Sons.

Archer, Dane. 1980. *How to Expand Your Social Intelligence Quotient*. New York: M. Evans.

Babb, Florence E. 2004. Recycled Sandalistas: From Revolution to Resorts in the New Nicaragua. *American Anthropologist* 106 (3): 541–55.

Balikci, Asen. 1970. *The Netsilik Eskimo*. Prospect Heights, Ill.: Waveland Press.

Barfield, Thomas, ed. 1997. *The Dictionary of Anthropology*. Malden, Mass.: Blackwell.

Bates, Daniel G. 1998. *Human Adaptive Strategies: Ecology, Culture, and Politics*. Boston: Allyn and Bacon.

Bates, Daniel G., and Fred Plog. 1990. *Cultural Anthropology*, 3rd ed. New York: McGraw-Hill.

Beattie, John. 1960. *Bunyoro: An African Kingdom*. New York: Holt, Rinehart and Winston.

Bell, Kirsten. 2005. Genital Cutting and Western Discourse on Sexuality. *Medical Anthropology Quarterly* 19(2): 125–48.

Benedict, Ruth. 1929. *Patterns of Culture*. Boston: Houghton Mifflin.

Betzig, Laura, and Robert Knox Detan, Bruce M. Knauft, and Keith F. Otterbein. 1988. Discussion and Criticism on Reconsidering Violence in Simple Societies. *Current Anthropology*: 29 (4): 624–36.

Bicchieri, M. G., ed. 1988. *Hunters and Gatherers Today*. Prospect Heights, Ill.: Waveland Press (originally published 1972).

Boas, Franz. 1938. *The Mind of Primitive Man*. New York: Macmillan.

———. 1964. *The Central Eskimo*. Lincoln: University of Nebraska Press (originally published 1888 as *The Sixth Annual Report of the Bureau of Ethnology*).

Bodley, John H. 1996. *Anthropology and Contemporary Human Problems*, 3rd ed. Mountain View, Calif.: Mayfield.

———. 1999. *Victims of Progress*, 4th ed. Mountain View, Calif.: Mayfield.

Bogin, Barry. 1978. Seasonal Patterns in the Rate of Growth in Height of Children Living in Guatemala. *American Journal of Physical Anthropology* 49: 205–10.

———. 1988. *Patterns of Human Growth*. Cambridge, England: Cambridge University Press.

———. 1998. The Tall and Short of It. *Discover*, February, 40–44.

Bohannan, Paul, and Mark Glazer, eds. 1988. *High Points in Anthropology*, 2nd ed. New York: Alfred A. Knopf.

Bohannan, Paul, and John Middleton, eds. 1968. *Marriage, Family, and Residence*. Garden City, N.Y.: Natural History Press.

Bonvillain, Nancy. 2000. *Language, Culture, and Communication*, 3rd ed. Upper Saddle River, N.J.: Prentice-Hall.

Bower, B. 1988. Murder in Good Company. *Science News* 133: 90.

———. 1999. Chinese Dig Sound from Ancient Flute. *Science News* 156: 197.

Brace, C. Loring. 1995. *The Stages of Human Evolution*, 5th ed. Englewood Cliffs, N.J.: Prentice-Hall.

———. 2000a. *Evolution in an Anthropological View*. New York: Altamira Press.

———. 2000b. A Four Letter Word Called "Race." In *Evolution in an Anthropological View*, ed. C. Loring Brace, pp. 283–321. New York: Altamira Press.

———. 2002. The Concept of Race in Physical Anthropology. In *Physical Anthropology: Original Readings in Method and Practice*, eds. Peter N. Peregrine, C. R. Ember, and M. Ember, pp. 239–53. Upper Saddle River, N.J.: Prentice-Hall.

———. 2005. *"Race" Is a Four-Letter Word: The Genesis of the Concept*. New York: Oxford University Press.

Brace, C. Loring, Henneberg, M., and Relethford, J. H. 1999. Skin Color as an Index of Timing of Human Evolution. *American Journal of Physical Anthropology* 28 suppl.: 95–96.

Braun, D. P., and S. Plog. 1984. Evolution of "Tribal" Social Networks: Theory and Prehistoric North American Evidence. *American Antiquity* 47 (3): 504–25.

Brettell, Caroline B., and Carolyn F. Sargent, eds. 1997. *Gender in Cross-Cultural Perspective*, 2nd ed. Upper Saddle River, N.J.: Prentice-Hall.

Brown, Michael Forbes. 1989. Dark Side of the Shaman. *Natural History*, November, 8–10.

Brown, Robert. 1963. *Explanation in Social Science*. Chicago: Aldine.

Brues, A. M. 1977. *People and Races*. New York: Macmillan.

Brumann, Christoph. 1999. Writing for Culture. *Current Anthropology* 40 suppl.: S1–S27.

Burton, Richard. 1991. *The Kasidah of Haji Abdu El-Yezdi*. London: Octagon (originally published private printing 1880).

Campbell, Bernard. 1983. *Human Ecology*. New York: Aldine.

Chagnon, Napoleon. 1997. *Yanomamo*, 5th ed. Fort Worth, Tex.: Harcourt Brace.

Chestnut, V. K. 1974. *Plants Used by the Indians of Mendocino County, California*. Mendocino, Calif.: Mendocino County Historical Society (originally published 1902 as *Contributions from United States National Herbarium* 7, Department of Agriculture, Division of Botany).

Chomsky, N. 1988. *Language and Problems of Knowledge: The Managua Lectures*. Cambridge, Mass.: The Massachusetts Institute of Technology Press.

Chun, Allen. 1996. The Lineage-Village Complex in Southeastern China. *Current Anthropology* 37 (3): 429–50.

Cohen, Yehudi. 1968. *Man in Adaptation: The Biosocial Background*. Chicago: Aldine.

Collier, John. 1967. *Visual Anthropology: Photography as a Research Method*. New York: Holt, Rinehart and Winston.

Comrie, Bernard. 1997. Historical Linguistics. In *The Dictionary of Anthropology*, ed. Thomas Barfield, pp. 235–37. Malden, Mass.: Blackwell.

Conkey, Margaret W. 1981. A Century of Paleolithic Cave Art. *Archaeology* 34 (4): 20–28.

Conkey, Margaret W., Olga Soffer, Deborah Stratmann, and Nina Jablonski, eds. 1997. *Beyond Art: Pleistocene Image and Symbol*. Memoirs of the California Academy of Sciences, number 23. San Francisco: California Academy of Sciences.

Copi, Irving, and Carl Cohen. 1994. *Introduction to Logic*. New York: Macmillan.

Cowan, Wesley C., and Patty Jo Watson. 1992. *The Origins of Agriculture: An International Perspective*. Washington, D.C.: Smithsonian Institution Press.

Davidson, Iain. 1997. The Power of Pictures. In *Beyond Art: Pleistocene Image and Symbol*, eds. Margaret W. Conkey, Olga Soffer, Deborah Stratmann, and Nina Jablonski, pp. 125–59. Memoirs of the California Academy of Sciences, number 23. San Francisco: California Academy of Sciences.

D'Azevedo, Warren L., eds. 1986. *Washo*. Vol. 11 of *Handbook of North American Indians*. Washington, D.C.: Smithsonian Institution Press.

Deetz, James. 1967. *Invitation to Archaeology*. New York: Natural History Press.

Dettwyler, Katherine. 1994. *Dancing Skeletons: Life and Death in West Africa*. Prospect Heights, Ill.: Waveland Press.

———. 1995. A Time to Wean: The Hominid Blueprint for the Natural Age of Weaning in Modern Human Populations. In *Breastfeeding: Biocultural Perspectives*, eds. P. Stuart-Macadam and K. Dettwyler, pp. 39–73. New York: Aldine DeGruyter.

DeVita, Philip R., and James D. Armstrong. 1998. *Distant Mirrors: America as a Foreign Culture*, 2nd ed. Belmont, Calif.: Wadsworth.

Diamond, Jared. 1987. The Worst Mistake of the Human Race. *Discover*, May, 64–66.

Dilly, Barbara J. 2005. Culture and Agriculture. *Anthropology News* 46 (5): 49–50.

Dissanayake, Ellen. 1988. *What Is Art For?* Seattle: University of Washington Press.

Douglass, William A., and Julie Lacy. 2005. Anthropological Angst and the Tourist Encounter. *NAPA Bulletin* 23: 119–34.

Downs, James F. 1966. *The Two Worlds of the Washo: An Indian Tribe of California and Nevada*. New York: Holt, Rinehart and Winston.

Dozier, Edward. 1966. *Hano: A Tewa Indian Community in Arizona*. New York: Holt, Rinehart and Winston.

DuBois, Cora. 1944. *The People of Alor: A Social-Psychological Study of an East Indian Island*. Cambridge, Mass.: Harvard University Press.

Duranti, Alessandro, ed. 2001. *Linguistic Anthropology*. Malden, Mass.: Blackwell.

Durkheim, Emil. 1961. *The Elementary Forms of the Religious Life*. New York: Collier (originally published 1912).

Elliston, Deborah A. 1999. Negotiating Transitional Sexual Economics: Female Mahu and Same-Sex Sexuality in Tahiti and Her Islands. In *Female Desires: Same-Sex Relations and Transgender Practices across Cultures*, eds. Evelyn Blackwood and Saskia E. Wieringa, pp. 230–52. New York: Columbia University Press.

Ember, Carol R., and Melvin Ember. 1999. *Anthropology*, 6th ed. Englewood Cliffs, N.J.: Prentice-Hall.

Ersen, Mustafa Türker. 2002. Parallel Brides. *Natural History*, May, 72–79.

Ervin, Alexander M. 2000. *Applied Anthropology: Tools and Perspectives for Contemporary Practice*. Boston: Allyn and Bacon.

Evans-Pritchard, E. E. 1940. *The Nuer*. Oxford, England: Clarendon Press.

Fagan, Brian. 1998. *People of the Earth*, 9th ed. New York: Longman.

Feder, Kenneth L. 1996. *The Past in Perspective*. Mountain View, Calif.: Mayfield.

Feder, Kenneth L., and Michael Allen Park. 1997. *Human Antiquity*, 3rd ed. Mountain View, Calif.: Mayfield.

Federal Bureau of Investigation. Uniform Crime Reports. Accessed at http://www.fbi.gov/ucr.htm#cius on July 12, 2005.

Fenton, Steve. 1999. *Ethnicity: Racism, Class and Culture*. New York: Rowman and Littlefield.

Ferguson, R. Brian. 1995. *Yanomani Warfare*. Santa Fe, N.M.: School of American Research Press.

Ferraro, Gary P. 1994. *The Cultural Dimension of International Business*, 2nd ed. Englewood Cliffs, N.J.: Prentice-Hall.

———. 1998a. *Applying Cultural Anthropology Readings*. Belmont, Calif.: Wadsworth.

———. 1998b. *Cultural Anthropology: An Applied Perspective*, 3rd ed. Belmont, Calif.: Wadsworth.

Fischer, Michael M. J. 1997. Postmodern, Postmodernism. In *The Dictionary of Anthropology*, ed. Thomas Barfield, pp. 368–72. Malden, Mass.: Blackwell.

Foley, William A. 1997. *Anthropological Linguistics: An Introduction*. Malden, Mass.: Blackwell.

Ford, Clellan S., and Frank A. Beach. 1951. *Patterns of Sexual Behavior*. New York: Ace Books.

Foster, George. 1962. *Traditional Cultures and the Impact of Technological Change*. New York: Harper and Row.

Fox, Richard G. 1977. *Urban Anthropology: Cities in Their Cultural Settings*. Englewood Cliffs, N.J.: Prentice-Hall.

Fox, Robin. 1983. *Kinship and Marriage: An Anthropological Perspective*. Cambridge, England: Cambridge University Press (originally published 1967).

Frazer, James. 1959. *The Golden Bough*. New York: Criterion Press (originally published 1911).

Frick, Thomas E. 1998. Home Work. *Anthropology Newsletter* 39 (7): 1–5.

Fried, Morton. 1967. *The Evolution of Political Anthropology: An Essay in Political Anthropology*. New York: Random House.

Friedl, Ernestine. 1978. Society and Sex Roles. *Human Nature* 1 (4).

Frobenius, Leo, and Douglas C. Fox. 1937. *Prehistoric Rock Art Pictures in Europe and Africa*. New York: Museum of Modern Art.

Gadsby, Patricia. 2004. The Inuit Paradox. *Discover*: 25 (10): 48–55.

Galanti, Geri-Ann. 1991. *Caring for Patients from Different Cultures: Case Studies from American Hospitals*. Philadelphia: University of Pennsylvania Press.

Garn, Stanley M. 1960. *Readings on Race*. Springfield, Ill.: Charles C. Thomas.

Geertz, Clifford. 1973. *The Interpretation of Cultures: Selected Essays by Clifford Geertz.* New York: Basic Books.

Gmelch, George, and Walter P. Zenner. 1996. *Urban Life: Readings in Urban Anthropology,* 3rd ed. Prospect Heights, Ill.: Waveland Press.

Goldstein, Melvyn C. 1987. When Brothers Take a Wife. *Natural History* 96 (3): 38–49.

Goodale, Jane C., and Joan D. Koss. 1966. The Cultural Context of Creativity among Tiwi. In *Anthropology and Art,* ed. C. M. Otten. New York: Natural History Press.

Goode, William. 1982. *The Family.* Englewood Cliffs, N.J.: Prentice-Hall.

Goodenough, Ward H. 1963. *Cooperation in Change.* New York: Russell Sage Foundation.

———. 1981. *Culture, Language, and Society,* 2nd ed. Menlo Park, Calif.: Benjamin Cummings.

Gordon, Claire C., ed. 1993. Race, Ethnicity, and Applied Anthropology. *NAPA Bulletin* 13.

Graburn, Nelson H. H. 1976. *Ethnic and Tourist Arts: Cultural Expressions from the Fourth World.* Berkeley: University of California Press.

Gray, J. Patrick, and Linda D. Wolfe. 2002. What Accounts for Population Variation in Height? In *Physical Anthropology: Original Readings in Method and Practice,* eds. Peter N. Peregrine, C. R. Ember, and M. Ember, pp. 204–18. Upper Saddle River, N.J.: Prentice-Hall.

Greenberg, David F. 1988. *The Construction of Homosexuality.* Chicago: University of Chicago Press.

Gregor, Thomas. 1985. *Anxious Pleasures: The Sexual Lives of an Amazonian People.* Chicago: University of Chicago Press.

Hadingham, Evan. 1979. *Secrets of the Ice Age.* New York: Walker and Company.

Hall, Edward T. 1959. *The Silent Language.* New York: Doubleday.

Hameda, Tamoko. 2000. Anthropological Praxis: Theory of Business Organization. In *The Unity of Theory and Practice in Anthropology: Rebuilding a Fractured Synthesis,* eds. Carole E. Hill and Marietta L. Baba. *NAPA Bulletin* 18.

Hannerz, Ulf. 1989. Notes on the Global Ecumene. *Public Culture* 1 (2): 66–75. Duke University Press. Reprinted in *The Anthropology of Globalization,* ed. J. X. Inda and R. Rosaldo. Malden, Mass.: Blackwell: 37–45.

Harris, Marvin. 1966. The Cultural Ecology of India's Sacred Cattle. *Current Anthropology* 7: 51–66.

———. 1968. *The Rise of Anthropological Theory.* New York: Thomas Y. Crowell.

———. 1989. *Our Kind.* New York: Harper-Collins.

———. 1998. *Good to Eat: Riddles of Food and Culture.* Prospect Heights, Ill.: Waveland Press.

Harris, Philip R., and Robert T. Moran. 1996. *Managing Cultural Differences,* 4th ed. Houston, Tex.: Gulf Publishing.

Haviland, William A. 1999. *Cultural Anthropology,* 9th ed. Fort Worth, Tex.: Harcourt College Publishers.

Haviland, William A., and Robert J. Gordon, eds. 1996. *Talking About People: Readings in Contemporary Cultural Anthropology.* Mountain View, Calif.: Mayfield.

Heider, Karl G. 1970. *The Dugum Dani.* Chicago: Aldine.

———. 1997. *Grand Valley Dani: Peaceful Warriors,* 3rd ed. Fort Worth, Tex.: Holt, Rhinehart and Winston.

Herdt, Gilbert. 1981. *Guardians of the Flutes: Idioms of Masculinity.* New York: McGraw-Hill.

———. 1987. *The Sambia: Ritual and Gender in New Guinea.* Fort Worth, Tex.: Harcourt Brace Jovanovich.

Hickerson, Nancy Parrott. 1980. *Linguistic Anthropology.* New York: Holt, Rinehart and Winston.

Hoke, Franklin. 1997. Mother's Milk: Nutrition and Nurture for Infants—and the Best Defense Against Disease. *News and Periodicals,* July 31. University of Pennsylvania Health System. Retrieved Oct. 23, 2002, from http://www.uphs.upenn.edu/news/News_Releases/july97/milk.html

Hole, Frank, and Robert F. Heizer. 1977. *Prehistoric Archaeology.* New York: Holt, Rinehart and Winston.

Holmberg, A. R. 1946. The Siriono. Ph.D. diss., Yale University.

Holtzman, Jon D. 2000. *Nuer Journeys, Nuer Lives: Sudanese Refugees in Minnesota.* Boston: Allyn and Bacon.

Hong Kong Department of Health. 2002. DH Fully Supports Breastfeeding. [News bulletin, August 3, 2002.] Accessed at http://www.info.gov.hk/dh/new/bulletin/02-08-03.htm on October 2, 2002.

Hunter, Christopher D. 2000. From Cultural Hegemony to the Culture of Code. Presented at the International Institute of Communications Annual Conference, St. Pete Beach, Florida. September 25–28, 2000. Accessed at http://www.asc.upenn.edu/usr/chunter/iic.html on July 22, 2005.

Hutchinson, Sharon E. 1996. *Nuer Dilemmas: Coping with Money, War, and the State.* Berkeley: University of California Press.

Hutter, Mark. 1981. *The Changing Family: Com parative Perspectives.* New York: John Wiley and Sons.

Inda, Jonathan Xavier, and Renato Rosaldo. eds. 2002. *The Anthropology of Globalization—A Reader.* Malden, Mass.: Blackwell.

Ingles, Palma. 2005. More Than Nature: Anthropologists as Interpreters of Culture for Nature-Based Tours. *NAPA Bulletin* 23: 219–33.

Jablonski, Nina G., and G. Chaplin. 1999. The Evolution of Human Skin Pigmentation. *American Journal of Physical Anthropology* 28 suppl.: 159.

Jacknis, Ira. 1995. *Carving Traditions of Northwest California.* Berkeley, Calif.: Phoebe Hearst Museum of Anthropology.

Jayne, Caroline Furness. 1962. *String Figures and How to Make Them.* New York: Dover Publications (originally published 1906 as *String Figures*).

Jones, Del. 1999. Hot Asset: Anthropology Degree. *USA Today*, February 18.

Jordon, Ann T. 1994a. Organizational Culture: The Anthropological Approach. In *Practicing Anthropology in Corporate America: Consulting on Organizational Culture*, ed. Ann T. Jordon. *NAPA Bulletin* 14: 3–16.

Jordon, Ann T., ed. 1994b. *Practicing Anthropology in Corporate America: Consulting on Organizational Culture. NAPA Bulletin* 14.

Keefe, Susan Emley. 1996. The Myth of the Declining Family. In *Urban Life*, eds. George Gmelch and Walter P. Zenner. Prospect Heights, Ill.: Waveland Press.

Keesing, Roger M. 1983. `Elota's Story: The Life and Times of a Solomon Island Big Man.* New York: Holt, Rinehart and Winston.

Keesing, Roger M., and Andrew J. Strathern. 1998. *Cultural Anthropology*, 3rd ed. Fort Worth, Tex.: Harcourt Brace College Publishers.

Kehoe, Alice. 1989. *The Ghost Dance: Ethnohistory and Revitalization.* New York: Holt, Rinehart and Winston.
———. 2000. *Shamans and Religion: An Anthropological Exploration in Critical Thinking.* Prospect Heights, Ill.: Waveland Press.

Keiser, R. Lincoln. 1979. *The Vice Lords: Warriors of the Streets*, fieldwork edition. New York: Holt, Rinehart and Winston.

Kelly, Robert L. 1995. *The Foraging Spectrum: Diversity in Hunter-Gatherer Lifeways.* Washington, D.C.: Smithsonian Institution Press.

Kent, Susan. 1996. *Cultural Diversity Among Twentieth-Century Foragers: An African Perspective.* Cambridge, England: Cambridge University Press.

Klass, Morton. 1995. *Ordered Universes: Approaches to the Anthropology of Religion.* Boulder, Colo.: Westview Press.

Kluckhohn, Clyde. 1951. *The Navajo.* Cambridge: Harvard University Press.

Kluckhohn, Clyde, and W. H. Kelly. 1945. The Concept of Culture. In *The Science of Man in the World Crisis*, ed. Ralph Linton, pp. 78–105. New York: Columbia University Press.

Knauft, Bruce M. 1987. Reconsidering Violence in Simple Human Societies: Homicide Among the Gebusi of Papua New Guinea. *Current Anthropology* 28 (4): 457–500.
———. 2005. *The Gebusi: Lives Transformed in a Rainforest World.* New York: McGraw-Hill.

Kohler-Rollefson, Ilse. 1995. Camels in the Land of Kings. *Natural History*, March.

Kottak, Conrad P. 1994. *Anthropology*, 6th ed. New York: McGraw-Hill.
———. 1996. *Mirror for Humanity: A Concise Introduction to Cultural Anthropology.* New York: McGraw-Hill.
———. 2002. *Cultural Anthropology*, 9th ed. New York: McGraw-Hill.

Krader, Lawrence. 1968. *Formation of the State.* Englewood Cliffs, N.J.: Prentice-Hall.

Kroeber, A. L. 1934. Yurok and Neighboring Kin Term Systems. *University of California Publications in American Archaeology and Ethnology* 35 (2): 15–22.
———. 1953. *Handbook of the Indians of California.* Berkeley: California Book Company (originally published in 1925 as Handbook of the Indians of California. *Bureau of American Ethnology Bulletin* 78).

Kroeber, A. L., and C. Kluckhohn. 1952. *Culture: A Critical Review of Concepts and Definitions.* New York: Vintage Books (originally published as *Papers of the Peabody Museum of American Archaeology and Ethnology* 47 [1]).

Kroeber, Theodora. 1959. *The Inland Whale.* Bloomington: Indiana University Press.

Kuper, Adam. 1999. *Culture: The Anthropologists' Account.* Cambridge: Harvard University Press.

Kutsche, Paul. 1998. *Field Ethnography: A Manual for Doing Cultural Anthropology.* Upper Saddle River, N.J.: Prentice-Hall.

Kuznar, Lawrence. 1997. *Reclaiming a Scientific Anthropology.* Walnut Creek, Calif.: Altamira Press.

Layton, Robert. 1981. *The Anthropology of Art.* New York: Columbia University Press.

Leach, E. R. 1965. *Political Systems of Highland Burma.* Boston: Beacon Press.

Lee, Richard B. 1993. *The Dobe Ju/'hoansi*, 2nd ed. Fort Worth, Tex.: Harcourt Brace College Publishers (first edition published in 1984 as *The Dobe !Kung*).

———. 2002. *The Dobe Ju/'hoansi*, 3rd ed. Belmont, Calif.: Wadsworth.

———. 2003. *The Dobe Ju/'hoansi*. 3rd ed. Belmont, Calif. Wadsworth.

Lee, Richard, and Ida Susser. 2003. AIDS and the San: How Badly Are They Affected? Appendix 1 to San of Southern Africa: A Status Report 2003. Accessed at http://www.aaanet.org/committees/cfhr/san.htm on July 20, 2005.

Lehmann, Arthur C., and James E. Myers. 1997. *Magic, Witchcraft, and Religion*, 4th ed. Mountain View, Calif.: Mayfield.

Lehmann, Arthur C., James E. Myers, and Pamela A. Moro. 2005. *Magic, Witchcraft, and Religion*, 6th ed. New York: McGraw-Hill.

Leroi-Gourhan, Andre. 1967. *Treasures of Prehistoric Art*. New York: Harry N. Abrams.

———. 1982. *The Dawn of European Art: An Introduction to Paleolithic Cave Painting*. Cambridge, England: Cambridge University Press.

Levine, Nancy E., and Joan B. Silk. 1977. Why Polyandry Fails. *Current Anthropology* 38 (3): 375–98.

Levinson, David, and Melvin Ember. 1996. *Encyclopedia of Cultural Anthropology*. New York: Henry Holt.

Linton, Ralph. 1936. *The Study of Man*. New York: Appleton Century Crofts.

———. 1937. One Hundred Percent American. *American Mercury* 40: 427–29.

Little, Michael A. 2002. Growth and Development of Turkana Pastoralists. In *Physical Anthropology: Original Readings in Method and Practice*, eds. Peter N. Peregrine, C. R. Ember, and M. Ember, pp. 219–38. Upper Saddle River, N.J.: Prentice-Hall.

Loustaunau, Martha O., and Elisa J. Sobo. 1997. *The Cultural Context of Health, Illness, and Medicine*. Westport, Conn.: Bergin and Garvey. Greenwood Publishing Group.

Magstadt, Thomas M., and Peter M. Schatten. 1999. *Understanding Politics*, 5th ed. New York: Worth Publishing.

Malinowski, Bronislaw. 1922. *Argonauts of the Western Pacific*. New York: E. P. Dutton.

———. 1964. *A Scientific Theory of Culture and Other Essays*. New York: Oxford University Press (originally published 1944).

———. 1987. *The Sexual Life of Savages in North-Western Melanesia*. Boston: Beacon Press (originally published 1929).

Marcus, George, and Michael Fischer. 1986. *Anthropology as Cultural Critique: An Experimental Moment in the Human Sciences*. Chicago: University of Chicago Press.

Marschack, Alexander. 1997. Image Making and Symboling in Europe and the Middle East: A Comparative Review. In *Beyond Art: Pleistocene Magic and Symbol*, eds. Margaret W. Conkey, Olga Soffer, Deborah Stratmann, and Nina Jablonski. Memoirs of the California Academy of Sciences, number 23: 53–91. San Francisco: California Academy of Sciences.

Mascia-Lees, Frances E., and Nancy Johnson Black. 2000. *Gender and Anthropology*. Prospect Heights, Ill.: Waveland Press.

Maybury-Lewis, David. 1997. *Indigenous Peoples, Ethnic Groups, and the State*. Boston: Allyn and Bacon.

McCurdy, David W. 2000. Using Anthropology. In *Conformity and Conflict*, 10th ed., ed. James Spradley and David W. McCurdy, pp. 386–98. Boston: Allyn and Bacon.

Mead, Margaret. 1937. *Cooperation and Competition Among Primitive Peoples*. New York: McGraw-Hill.

———. 1963. *Sex and Temperament in Three Primitive Societies*. New York: Dell (originally published 1935).

———. 1969. *Male and Female*. New York: Dell (originally published 1949).

Metcalf, Peter. 1978. Death Be Not Strange. *Natural History* 87 (6): 6–12.

Michaels, Eric. 1990. A Model of Teleported Texts. *Continuum: The Australian Journal of Media & Culture*: 3 (2). Accessed at http://www.mcc.murdoch.edu.au/ReadingRoom/3.2/teleport.html on July 22, 2005.

———. 2002. Hollywood Iconography: A Warlpiri Reading. In *The Anthropology of Globalization*, ed. Jonathan Xavier Inda and Renato Rosaldo, pp. 311–24. Malden, Mass.: Blackwell.

Michener, James A. 1968. *Iberia*. New York: Fawcett Crest.

Molnar, Stephen. 2002. *Human Variation: Races, Types, and Ethnic Groups*, 5th ed. Upper Saddle River, N.J.: Prentice-Hall.

Montague, Ashley, ed. 1964. *The Concept of Race*. London: Collier Books.

Morales, Manuel R. 1997. When Beasts Go Marching Out! The End of Pleistocene Art in Cantabrian

Spain. In *Beyond Art: Pleistocene Magic and Symbol*, eds. Margaret W. Conkey, Olga Soffer, Deborah Stratmann, and Nina Jablonski. Memoirs of the California Academy of Sciences, number 23: 189–99. San Francisco: California Academy of Sciences.

Morey, Nancy C., and Robert V. Morey. 1994. Organizational Culture: The Management Approach. In *Practicing Anthropology in Corporate America: Consulting on Organizational Culture*, ed. Ann T. Jordon. *NAPA Bulletin* 14: 17–26.

Morgan, Lewis Henry. 1963. *Ancient Society*. Cleveland: Meredian Books (originally published 1877).

Morgan, Marcyliena. 2001. The African-American Speech Community: Reality and Sociolinguistics. In *Linguistic Anthropology*, ed. Allessandro Duranti, pp. 74–94. Malden, Mass.: Blackwell.

Morris, Bernard. 1938. *Drums, Tomtoms, and Rattles*. New York: A. S. Barnes.

Mullins, Leith, ed. 1987. *Cities of the United States: Studies in Urban Anthropology*. New York: Columbia University Press.

Murdock, George P. 1949. *Social Structure*. New York: Macmillan.

———. 1950. Family Stability in Non-European Cultures. *Annals of the American Academy of Political and Social Sciences* 272: 195–201.

———. 1967. The Ethnographic Atlas: A Summary. *Ethnology* 6 (2): 109–236.

Murray, Gerald. 1987. The Domestication of Wood in Haiti: A Case Study in Applied Evolution. In *Anthropological Praxis: Translating Knowledge into Action*, eds. Robert M. Wulff and Shirley J. Frisk. Boulder, Colo.: Westview Press.

Nanda, Serena. 1999. *Neither Man nor Woman*, 2nd ed. Belmont, Calif.: Wadsworth.

———. 2000. *Gender Diversity: Cross-Cultural Variations*. Prospect Heights, Ill.: Waveland Press.

Nash, Dennison. 1996. *Anthropology of Tourism*. New York: Elsevier Science.

———. 1999. *A Little Anthropology*, 3rd ed. Upper Saddle River, N.J.: Prentice-Hall.

Natadecha-Sponsel, Poranee. 1998. The Young, the Rich, and the Famous: Individualism as an American Cultural Value. In *Distant Mirrors: America as a Foreign Culture*, eds. Philip R. Devita and James D. Armstrong, pp. 68–73. Belmont, Calif.: Wadsworth.

Niehoff, Arthur H., ed. 1966. *A Casebook of Social Change*. Chicago: Aldine.

Norbeck, Edward. 1961. *Religion in Primitive Society*. New York: Harper and Brothers.

Nordstrom, Carolyn, and Antonius C. G. M. Robben. 1995. *Fieldwork Under Fire*. Berkeley: University of California Press.

Oboler, Regina Smith. 1980. Is the Female Husband a Man? Woman/Woman Marriage Among the Nandi of Kenya. *Ethnology* 19 (1): 69–88.

Oliver, Douglas L. 1955. *A Solomon Island Society*. Cambridge: Harvard University Press.

———. 1989. *Native Cultures of the Pacific Islands*. Honolulu: University of Hawaii Press.

O'Neale, Lila. 1932. Yurok-Karok Basket Weavers. *University of California Publications in American Archaeology and Ethnology* 32 (1): 1–182.

Orion, Loretta. 1995. *Never Again the Burning Times: Paganism Revived*. Prospect Heights, Ill.: Waveland Press.

Otten, Charlotte M., ed. 1971. *Anthropology and Art: Readings in Cross-Cultural Aesthetics*. Garden City, N.Y.: Natural History Press.

Pasternak, Burton, Carol R. Ember, and Melvin Ember. 1997. *Sex, Gender, and Kinship: A Cross-Cultural Perspective*. Upper Saddle River, N.J.: Prentice-Hall.

Peregrine, Peter N., C. R. Ember, and M. Ember. 2002. *Physical Anthropology: Original Readings in Method and Practice*. Upper Saddle River, N.J.: Prentice-Hall.

Peters-Golden, Holly. 2002. *Culture Sketches: Case Studies in Anthropology*, 3rd ed. New York: McGraw-Hill.

Pfeiffer, John E. 1982. *The Creative Explosion: An Inquiry into the Origins of Art and Religion*. New York: Harper and Row.

Podolefsky, Aaron, and Peter J. Brown. 1997. *Applying Cultural Anthropology*, 3rd ed. Mountain View, Calif.: Mayfield.

Powell, Mary F. 1988. *Status and Health in Prehistory: A Case Study of the Moundville Chiefdom*. Washington, D.C.: Smithsonian Institution Press.

Puntenney, Pamela J., ed. 1995. Global Ecosystems: Creating Options through Anthropological Perspectives. *NAPA Bulletin* 15.

Rappaport, Roy A. 1968. *Pigs for the Ancestors*. New Haven, Conn.: Yale University Press.

Rathje, William L., and Cullen Murphy. 2001. *Rubbish! The Archaeology of Garbage*. Tucson: University of Arizona Press.

Rice, Patricia, and Ann Peterson. 1985. Cave Art and Bones: Exploring the Interrelationships. *American Anthropologist* 87 (1): 94–99.

Ricks, D. A. 1983. *Big Business Blunders: Mistakes in Multinational Marketing*. Homewood, Ill.: Dow Jones-Irwin.

Robbins, Richard H. 2005. *Global Problems and the Culture of Capitalism*. Boston: Pearson Education.

Rossbach, E. 1973. *Baskets as Textile Art*. New York: Van Nostrand Reinhold.

Sahlins, Marshall D. 1958. *Social Stratification in Polynesia*. Seattle: University of Washington Press.

———. 1968. *Tribesmen*. Englewood Cliffs, N.J.: Prentice-Hall.

———. 1972. *Stone Age Economics*. Chicago: University of Chicago Press.

Sahlins, Marshall, and Elman Service eds., 1960. *Evolution and Culture*. Ann Arbor: University of Michigan Press.

Salvador, Mari Lyn. 1976. The Clothing Arts of the Cuna of San Blas, Panama. In *Ethnic and Tourist Arts*, ed. N. H. Graburn, pp. 165–82. Berkeley: University of California Press.

Sapir, Edward. 1921. *Language: An Introduction to the Study of Speech*. New York: Harcourt, Brace.

———. 1949. *Culture, Language, and Personality*. Berkeley: University of California Press.

Saul, Mahir. 2004. Money in Colonial Transition: Cowries and Fancs in West Africa. *American Anthropologist* 106 (1): 71–84.

Schick, Kathy D., and Nicholas Toth. 1993. *Making Silent Stone Speak*. New York: Simon and Schuster.

Schneider, David, and Kathleen Gough, eds. 1962. *Matrilineal Kinship*. Berkeley: University of California Press.

Schneider, David, and G. Homans. 1955. Kinship Terminology and the American Kinship System. *American Anthropologist* 57: 1194–1208.

Schusky, Ernest L. 1972. *Manual for Kinship Analysis*, 2nd ed. New York: Holt, Rinehart and Winston.

———. 1974. *Variation in Kinship*. New York: Holt, Rinehart and Winston.

Schwimmer, Brian. 2003. Kinship Tutorial: University of Manitoba. Accessed at http://www.umanitoba.ca/faculties/arts/anthropology/tutor/kinmenu.html on July 20, 2005.

Scott, Eugenie C. 1996. Science in Anthropology. *Anthropology Newsletter* 37 (3): 52.

Scupin, Raymond D., ed. 2000. *Religion and Culture: An Anthropological Focus*. Upper Saddle River, N.J.: Prentice-Hall.

Service, Elman. 1962. *Primitive Social Organization: An Evolutionary Perspective*. New York: Random House.

———. 1978. *Profiles in Ethnology*, 3rd ed. New York: Harper and Row.

———. 1979. *The Hunters*, 2nd ed. Englewood Cliffs, N.J.: Prentice-Hall.

Sharff, Jagna Wojcicka. 1987. The Underground Economy of a Poor Neighborhood. In *Cities of the United States*, ed. Leith Mullings. New York: Columbia University Press.

Shipman, Pat. 1984. Scavenger Hunt. *Natural History* 93 (4): 20–27.

Shostak, Marjorie. 1981. *Nisa: The Life and Words of a !Kung Woman*. Cambridge: Harvard University Press.

Slow Food http://www.slowfood.com. Accessed on July 23, 2005.

Slow Food Foundation for Biodiversity. http://www.slowfoodfoundation.com. Accessed on July 23, 2005.

Smith, Bruce. 1992. *Rivers of Change: Essays on Early Agriculture in Eastern North America*. Washington, D.C.: Smithsonian Institution Press.

Smith, Raymond T. 1987. Kinship and Class in Chicago. In *Cities of the United States*, ed. Leith Mullings. New York: Columbia University Press.

Spicer, Edward H., ed. 1952. *Human Problems in Technological Change: A Casebook*. New York: John Wiley and Sons.

Spiro, Melford E. 1966. Religion: Problems of Definition and Explanation. In *Anthropological Approaches to the Study of Religion*, ed. Michael Banton. London: Tavistock.

Sponsel, Leslie E. 1998. Yanomami: An Arena of Conflict and Aggression in the Amazon. *Aggressive Behavior* 24: 97–122.

Spradley, James P. 1980. *Participant Observation*. New York: Holt, Rinehart and Winston.

Spradley, James, and David W. McCurdy, eds. 2000. *Conformity and Conflict*, 10th ed. Boston: Allyn and Bacon.

Stephens, William N. 1963. *The Family in Cross-Cultural Perspective*. New York: Holt, Rinehart and Winston.

Steward, Julian. 1968. Cultural Ecology. In *International Encyclopedia of the Social Sciences* 4, ed. D. Sills, pp. 337–44. New York: Macmillan.

Stuart-Macadam, Patricia, and Katherine Dettwyler, eds. 1995. *Breastfeeding: Biocultural Perspectives.* New York: Aldine DeGruyter.

Sutherland, Anne. 1994. Gypsies and Health Care. In *Conformity and Conflict: Readings in Cultural Anthropology*, 8th ed., ed. James Spradley and David McCurdy. New York: HarperCollins.

Tannen, Deborah. 1990. *You Just Don't Understand: Men and Women in Conversation.* New York: William Morrow.

———. 1994. Why Don't You Say What You Mean? *The New York Times Magazine*, August 28, 1994, 46–49 (adapted from *Talking 9 to 5: How Women's and Men's Conversational Styles Affect Who Gets Heard, Who Gets Credit, and What Gets Done at Work.* 1994. New York: William Morrow).

Textor, Robert B. 1967. *A Cross-Cultural Summary.* New Haven, Conn.: HRAF Press.

Thompson, David S. 1975. *Human Behavior: Language.* New York: Time-Life Books.

Trotter, Robert T., II. 1987. A Case of Lead Poisoning from Folk Remedies in Mexican American Communities. In *Anthropological Praxis: Translating Knowledge into Action*, ed. Robert M. Wulff and Shirley J. Frisk, pp. 139–50. Boulder, Colo.: Westview Press.

Trudgill, P. 1974. *The Social Differentiation of English in Norwich.* Cambridge, England: Cambridge University Press.

Turnbull, Colin M. 1983. *The Mbuti Pygmies: Change and Adaptation.* New York: Holt, Rinehart and Winston.

———. 1987. *The Forest People.* New York: Simon and Schuster (originally published 1961).

Tylor, E. B. 1958. *Primitive Culture.* New York: Harper and Row (originally published 1871).

Ucko, Peter, and Andree Rosenfeld. 1967. *Paleolithic Cave Art.* New York: McGraw-Hill.

———. 1971. Critical Analysis of Interpretations and Conclusions and Problems from Paleolithic Cave Art. In *Anthropology and Art*, ed. C. M. Otten. New York: Natural History Press.

Upjohn, Everard, Paul S. Wingert, and Jane Gaston Mahler. 1958. *History of World Art*, 2nd ed. New York: Oxford University Press.

U.S. Department of Health and Human Services. 2000. *Healthy People 2010*, 2nd ed. 2 vols. Washington, D.C.: U.S. Government Printing Office.

Van Gennep, Arnold. 1960. *The Rites of Passage.* Chicago: University of Chicago Press.

Wallace, Tim. 2005. Tourism, Tourists, and Anthropologists at Work. In *Tourism and Applied Anthropologists*, ed. T. H. Wallace. *NAPA Bulletin 23* (1): 1–26.

———. 2005. ed. Tourism and Applied Anthropologists: Linking Theory and Practice. *NAPA Bulletin 23.*

Ward, Martha C. 1996. *A World Full of Women.* Boston: Allyn and Bacon.

Waterman, T. T., and A. L. Kroeber. 1934. Yurok Marriages. *University of California Publications in American Archaeology and Ethnology* 35 (1): 1–14. Berkeley: University of California Press.

Weiner, Annette B. 1988. *The Trobriand Islanders of Papua New Guinea.* New York: Holt, Rinehart and Winston.

Weinreich, Uriel, W. Labov, and M. Herzog. 1968. Empirical Foundations for a Theory of Language Change. In *Directions for Historical Linguistics*, ed. W. P. Lehmann and M. Yakov, pp. 95–188. Austin: University of Texas Press.

Wheeler, Mortimer. 1956. *Archaeology from the Earth.* Baltimore: Pelican.

White, Leslie. 1959a. The Concept of Culture. *American Anthropologist* 61: 227–51.

———. 1959b. *The Evolution of Culture.* New York: McGraw-Hill.

White, Leslie, and Beth Dillingham. 1973. *The Concept of Culture.* Minneapolis, Minn.: Burgess Publishing.

Whiting, John W. M. 1993. The Effect of Polygyny on Sex Ratio at Birth. *American Anthropologist* 95: 435–42.

Williams, Jonathan, ed. 1997. *Money: A History.* New York: St. Martin's Press.

Williams, Thomas Rhys. 1967. *Field Methods in the Study of Culture.* New York: Holt, Rinehart and Winston.

Winterhalder, Bruce, and Eric Alden Smith. 1981. *Hunter-Gatherer Foraging Strategies: Ethnographic and Archaeological Analysis.* Chicago: University of Chicago Press.

Wolf, Eric. 1966. *Peasants.* Englewood Cliffs, N.J.: Prentice-Hall.

Womack, Mari. 2001. Emics, Etics, "Ethics" and Shamans. *Anthropology News* 42 (3): 7.

Wulff, Robert M., and Shirley J. Frisk, eds. 1987. *Anthropological Praxis: Translating Knowledge into Action*. Boulder, Colo.: Westview Press.

Yiridoe, Emmanuel. 1995. Economic and Sociocultural Aspects of Cowrie Currency of the Dagaaba of Northwestern Ghana. *Nordic Journal of African Studies* 4 (2): 17–32.

Zhang, Juzhong, Garman Harbottle, Chang-sui Wang, and Zhaochen Kong. 1999. Oldest Playable Musical Instrument Found at Jiahu Early Neolithic Site in China. *Nature* 401: 366–68.

Zihlman, Adrienne, Debra Bolter, and Christopher Boesch. 2004. Wild Chimpanzee Dentition and its Implications for Addressing Life History in Immature Hominin Fossils. *Proceedings of the National Academy of Sciences* 101 (29): 10541–43.

INDEX

Note: Locators beginning with A (A1–5) indicate pages appearing in the appendices after page 333. Locators beginning with G (G13) indicates pages appearing in the glossary after the appendices.

culture change, 131
diet, 130
family, 160
kinship system, 180
language, 77, 78, 79
location of, 106
nomadic lifestyle, 128
political systems, 223, 224
population size, 129, 130
technology, 128
nutrition. *See* diet

O

objectivity, 62–63
Oboler, Regina Smith, 202
Ojibwa, 61
Oldowan tools, 98, G6
Omaha, 187
O'Nell, Carl, 325
Onge, 208
On the Origin of Species
    (Darwin), 96
optimal-foraging model, 100, G6
organizational culture, 320
Otten, Charlotte M., 276
ownership. *See*
    property/ownership

P

paleoanthropology, 11, G6
pan-tribal sodalities, 223–224, G6
parallel-cousins, 152–153,
    181–183, 186, G7
parietal art, 269, G7
participant observation, 62–63,
    320, G7
Pasternak, Burton, 149, 160, 207
pastoral societies, 127–131
    culture change, 130–131,
        302–304
    current societies, 130–131
    defined, 127, G7
    diet, 129–130
    division of labor, 130
    energy budget, 130
    kinship systems, 130, 178–179
    and marriage, 149
    nomadic lifestyle, 128, G6
    political systems, 223
    population size, 129

property/ownership, 129
resource distribution, 130
technology, 128
patrilineages, 174, 201, G7
patrilocal bands, 111–112, G7
patrilocal (virilocal) residence,
    111–112, 161, 201, G7, G9
Peacock, Nadine R., 15
The People of Alor (Dubois), 308
Peters-Golden, Holly, 131
Petrini, Carlo, 137
Pfeiffer, John E., 275
Philippines, 86
phonemes, 75–76, G7
phonology, 10, 74–76, G7
photography, 67–68
phratries, 179, G7
physical anthropology. *See*
    biological (physical)
    anthropology
plant domestication, 120–121,
    125. *See also* horticultural
    societies
plasticity, 39, 42, G7
Plog, Fred, 32
Plog, S., 224
political systems, 215–229
    agricultural societies, 133–134
    band societies, 219–220
    and belief systems, 225,
        257–258
    chiefdom societies, 133–134,
        136, 225–226, G2
    definitions, 216–217, G2
    dimensions of, 217–219
    and power/authority, 217, 218
    and social stratification,
        227–229
    state societies, 226–227,
        228–229, G8
    tribal societies, 220–224, G9
polyandry, 21, 150–151, G7
polygamy, 21, 148–152, 225, G7
polygyny, 149–150, 225, G7
Polynesia
    belief systems, 239, 250–251
    gender, 191, 197
    kinship terms, 187
    marriage, 143–144
    resource distribution, 136

social stratification, 228
work ethics, 119
polytheistic belief systems,
    246, G7
Pomo, 30
Poor Richard's Almanac (Franklin),
    119
population size, 111–112,
    122–123, 129
postmodernism, 21–22, 52, 63, G7
power
    defined, 217, G7
    and political systems, 217, 218
    and postmodernism, 22
prehistoric archaeology, 7–8, G7
priests, 256–258, G7
primates
    defined, G7
    and language, 83–84
    plasticity, 42
    sexual dimorphism, 195
    study of, 11–12, 16, G7
primatology, 11–12, 16, G7
Primitive Culture (Tylor), 239, 293
property/ownership
    agricultural societies, 134
    foraging societies, 112
    and gender, 201–202
    horticultural societies, 124
    and kinship systems, 173, 174,
        175
    and marriage, 147, 154–155,
        164–165
    pastoral societies, 129
prophets, 261, G7
proxemics, 87–88, G7
psychological anthropology,
    192, G7

Q

quadrupeds, 11, G7

R

race, 3, 38–43
    and clines, 39, 40–42
    defined, 38, G7
    and endogamy, 144
    and holistic approach, 38
    and plasticity, 39, 42
    as social construct, 43